MOONLIGHT CRUSADERS

DEDICATION

For Eva and Wilfie

In memory of Sarah Smiddy (1979–2025)

MOONLIGHT CRUSADERS

SPECIAL DUTIES PILOTS OVER OCCUPIED EUROPE

PAUL SMIDDY

OSPREY PUBLISHING
Bloomsbury Publishing Plc
Kemp House, Chawley Park, Cumnor Hill, Oxford OX2 9PH, UK
Bloomsbury Publishing Ireland Limited,
29 Earlsfort Terrace, Dublin 2, D02 AY28, Ireland
Bloomsbury Publishing Inc.
1359 Broadway, 12th Floor, New York, NY 10018, USA
E-mail: info@ospreypublishing.com
www.ospreypublishing.com

OSPREY is a trademark of Osprey Publishing Ltd

First published in Great Britain in 2026

© Paul Smiddy, 2026

Paul Smiddy has asserted his right under the Copyright,
Designs and Patents Act, 1988, to be identified as Author of this work.

For legal purposes the Acknowledgements on pp.7–8 constitute an extension of this copyright page.

All rights reserved. No part of this publication may be: i) reproduced or transmitted in any form, electronic or mechanical, including photocopying, recording or by means of any information storage or retrieval system without prior permission in writing from the publishers; or ii) used or reproduced in any way for the training, development or operation of artificial intelligence (AI) technologies, including generative AI technologies. The rights holders expressly reserve this publication from the text and data mining exception as per Article 4(3) of the Digital Single Market Directive (EU) 2019/790

A catalogue record for this book is available from the British Library.

ISBN: HB 9781472873477; PB 9781472873460; eBook 9781472873484; ePDF 9781472873507;
XML 9781472873491; Audio 9781472873453

26 27 28 29 30   10 9 8 7 6 5 4 3 2 1

Quotes from *A Pacifist At War* by Ray Jenkins published by Hutchinson. Copyright © Ray Jenkins, 2009.
Reprinted by permission of The Random House Group Limited.

Maps and diagrams by www.bounford.com
Index by Mark Swift
Lysander divider © Osprey Publishing

Typeset by Lumina Datamatics Ltd
Printed and bound in Great Britain by Clays Ltd, Elcograf S.p.A.

Osprey Publishing supports the Woodland Trust, the UK's leading woodland conservation charity.

To find out more about our authors and books visit www.ospreypublishing.com. Here you will find extracts, author interviews, details of forthcoming events and the option to sign up for our newsletter.

For product safety related questions contact productsafety@bloomsbury.com

Contents

Acknowledgements   7
List of Illustrations, Maps and Figures   9

Introduction   12
1 The Gestation of the Lysander   15
2 The Customers: The Special Operations Executive and the Secret Intelligence Service   25
3 The Lysander Goes to War: Bloodied and Bowed   33
4 Finding Their Feet   45
5 Racing Ahead: Newmarket Takes on Military Garb   57
6 Scaling Up: The Formation of No. 138 Squadron   71
7 1942: The Formation of No. 161 Squadron   87
8 A Home is Found: Tempsford   103
9 The 1942 Pause and Knowles Lurches to His Maker   117
10 The Dream Team Forms   131
11 1943   149
12 Tangmere Life   169
13 Treachery   189
14 A Mission   215
15 Tangmere Death   227
16 1944 and the Déricourt Dénouement   247

17 The Boxer Era	267
18 Last Flights	285
Conclusions	301
Epilogue	311
Appendices	327
Glossary	340
Bibliography	343
Notes	348
Index	376

Acknowledgements

My first thanks go to Dick Nesbitt-Dufort – it was conversations with Dick that first sowed the seeds of this book in my mind. Thank you to Simon Rymills, another son of a Special (Duties) pilot, who also has been hospitable, welcoming and very helpful. I much enjoyed my chats with James Vaughan-Fowler, son of Peter.

The staff of The National Archives is a team of (largely) unsung facilitators of the foundations on which this and most other British historical tomes are built. I am also grateful to the teams at the archives of the Royal Air Force Museum at Hendon, and the Imperial War Museum in Kennington – again, fabulous national resources. Thanks also to Dr Michael Fopp for guidance and encouragement; David and John Rosier for access to some of their father's papers; Kate Jackson, archivist at Framlingham College, for assorted information on Pickard; Tony Martin, alumnus of said College, for further information; Suzanne Foster, archivist at Winchester College, for background on Wykehamists mentioned in passing; and Anne Alexandre, for a story about her father Pierre Hentic. Keith Dennison and Dave Hadfield, foremost proponents of flying Lysanders in the modern era in the UK and North America, respectively, have been very helpful in sharing their knowledge. Thank you too to Gus Corujo for some very high-quality images. The archivists at Leonardo (now owners of Westland) have also kindly allowed me to use some of their material.

Thank you to Brianne Bellio, Margaret Haynes and the team at Osprey for bringing this book into the public gaze.

I would also not have written this (or indeed any other of my books) without the help and labours of Penrose Troughton who inculcated in me a love for, and a little knowledge of, English language and literature.

But the biggest thanks go naturally to my wife Tina: during the protracted course of writing this book, it has caused me to be absent, even when I was present. As well as succour, she has also proved a great proof-reader.

We have tried to find the owners of the copyright of all material used, but if you feel some acknowledgements have been omitted please contact us to ensure future editions are corrected. I should be very interested to hear from descendants of any of those mentioned in this narrative.

List of Illustrations, Maps and Figures

ILLUSTRATIONS

Westland's Lysander production line at the Yeovil factory. (Leonardo)
The Mk III SCW Lysander as modified for the Special Duties squadrons. (Leonardo)
The Lysander preparing to take off. (Gus & Clara - Gusair)
The Lysander cockpit. (Author's collection)
161 Squadron Hudson departs from Tempsford. (IWM HU 60553)
161's crew room at Tangmere Cottage. (IWM HU 60563)
Edward 'Mouse' Fielden helps the Prince of Wales don his flying suit. (TQFA)
Lewis 'Bob' Hodges. (Photo by George W. Hales/Fox Photos/Hulton Archive/Getty Images)
Frank 'Bunny' Rymills. (The National Archives HS9/1295/7)
Guy Lockhart. (The National Archives HS9/932/8)
John Tonkin, leader of the SAS's *Bulbasket* raid. (John Tonkin Collection)
The 161 'Dream Team' outside the Cottage. From left to right, James 'Mac' McCairns, Hugh Verity, Percy 'Pick' Pickard, Peter Vaughan-Fowler and Bunny Rymills. Old English sheepdog Ming and cocker spaniel Henry are in front of them. (piemags/ww2archive/Alamy)
161 Lysander pilots at Tangmere. From left to right, Robin Hooper, Mac McCairns, Peter Vaughan-Fowler, Hugh Verity, Bunny Rymills and Stephen Hankey. (Simon Rymills)
John Nesbitt-Dufort's Lysander after his crash in France. (The National Archives AIR40/2659)

N.H. Attenborrow collects a wounded American officer in Friuli, Italy. (piemags/ww2archive/Alamy)
The graves of James Bathgate and his passenger, agent Emile Cossoneau, at La Ville-Aux-Bois cemetery, France. (Author's collection)
Leslie Whitaker's grave at Guillerval cemetery, France. (Author's collection)

MAPS

Map 1: 161 Squadron bases and landing sites	11
Map 2: 148 Squadron bases in the Mediterranean	278

FIGURES

Figure 1: Causes of Lysander accidents, 1937–45	330
Figure 2: Layout of Lysander landing strip for pick-up operations	339

LIST OF ILLUSTRATIONS, MAPS AND FIGURES

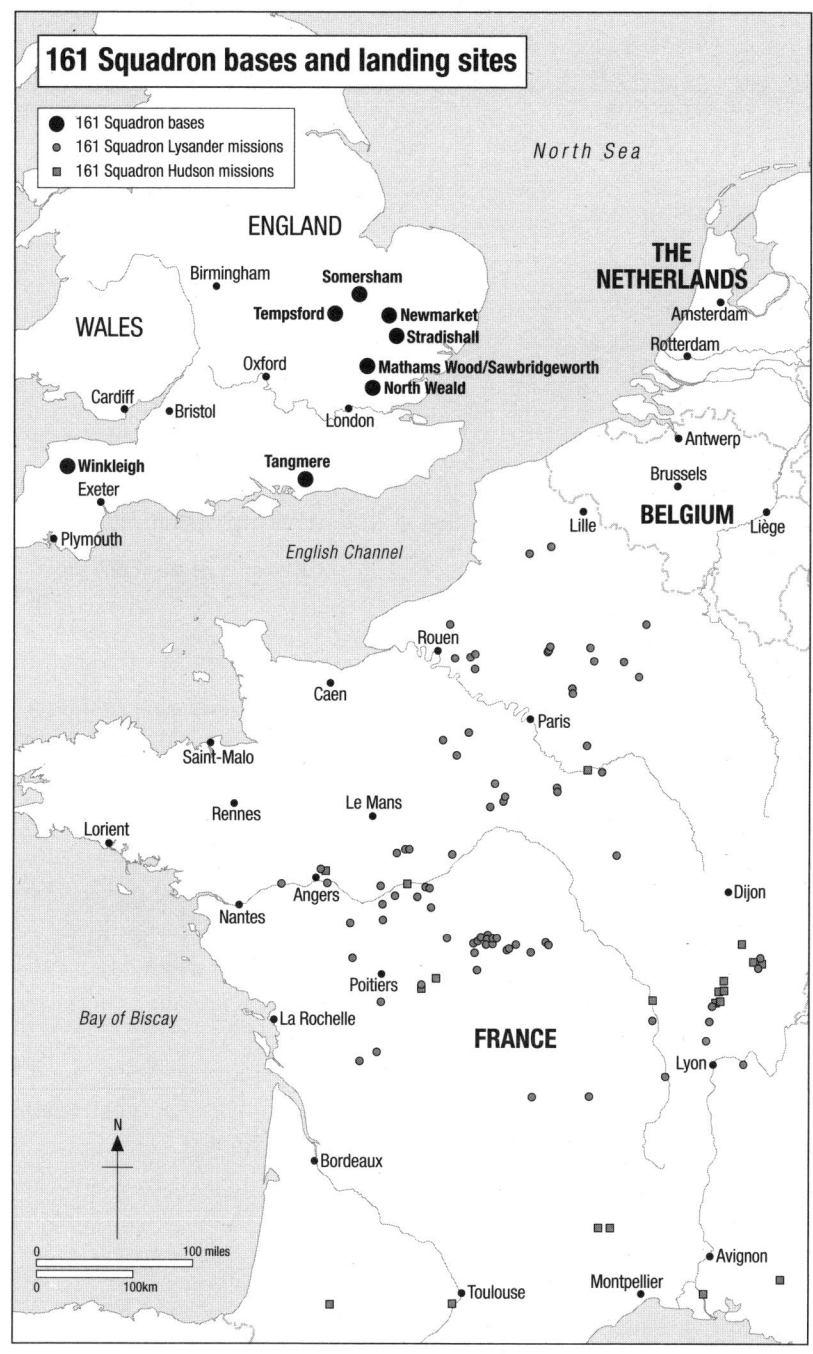

Introduction

What you have to do is to remember, because it is a duty one has to the people who did great things, to one's comrades, to all the good and brave people.

Odette Sansom/Hallowes[1]

The most beautiful burial place for the dead is in the memory of the living.

André Malraux

Having been obsessed with aeroplanes from a very young age, it was perhaps not surprising that I picked up a book called *Black Lysander* from the shelves of a book shop in my mid-teens. I read John Nesbitt-Dufort's autobiographical account of flying Lysanders on clandestine missions with fascination and delight. It evoked something of the thrills of military aviation that W.E. Johns' *Biggles* novels had stirred in me a few years earlier, whilst opening a window into a certainly more obscure, and occasionally darker, side of military flying.

Only a year or two later I was fortunate to be taught to fly by the RAF, and a couple of decades later still, embarked on a flying sport where a fellow British competitor was Nesbitt-Dufort's son, Dick, nearing the end of his competitive flying career. It was a happy coincidence to meet him: his zest for life and wry sense of humour paralleled that of his father. The Lysander Special Duties pilots were once again front of mind.

This sport has taken me to competitions in France many times. After completing one such weekend, I was heading home on a Sunday afternoon from somewhere in central France. A vicious west–east weather front spread laterally across my homeward path. 'Get Homeitis' is an affliction that can affect pilots, and is known to be particularly prevalent on Sunday afternoons. Confronted by a wall of black cumulo-nimbus clouds, I should have done a U-turn and landed at a small-town aerodrome – which are plentiful in France – to savour that evening another *plat du jour* and a glass or two of red. But I had the disease and pressed on; with plenty of luck, but also many aids, I slept in my own bed that night. The following day, I reflected on the help I had had to hand: before take-off I had access to up-to-date weather forecasts for the journey that I was flying in daylight; with modern satellite navigation, I knew where I was all the time; I was in radio contact with a delightful lady, probably on the fringe of Paris, who had access to a radar, and could tell me, if necessary, where the worst storm cells were.

John Nesbitt-Dufort had a parallel experience (described in Chapter 7), but he was flying at night when the worst (and least worst) of the storm was invisible to him; he had no helpful voice on the radio; he was flying by map, compass and stopwatch, trying to thread his way through thunderous canyons; and he was under continual threat of being coned by a German searchlight, to be shot at by a keen flak battery or night-fighter pilot. Moreover, if he had to land in a sodden field, he would have faced being chased like a lame hare by a pack of coursing Wehrmacht greyhounds. My esteem for Nesbitt-Dufort and his successors in 161 Squadron rose even higher.

These pilots delivered supplies and agents to Western Europe, predominantly France, and brought back fatigued agents, political and Resistance leaders, or those under threat of imminent arrest, together with vital messages and other intelligence matériel. Large-scale deliveries of agents and stores were dropped by parachute from two- and four-engined bombers (the Whitley, and later Stirlings and Halifaxes). But only the Lysander (and later the twin-engined Hudson) could land in a French field and retrieve these agents for debriefing, rest and re-briefing in London. For older politicians and staff officers, it was the only practical means (other than a protracted boat journey) to travel between the two nations.

The focus of this book is then on the pick-up operations carried out by these smaller aircraft that dropped into French meadows and gave the tangible message that Britain was at their side to those elements of French society that had not succumbed to the Nazi oppression.

Maurice Buckmaster, as head of F Section at Special Operations Executive (SOE), was one of the main clients for these pilots. In 1974, he penned this appreciation:

> I would strongly wish to be associated in a tribute to the men of the RAF who, with tremendous courage and pertinacity, made possible the sending of liaison officers from the UK to the French Resistance, which, according to the highest authority, had the effect of shortening the war by several months. No praise is too much for their gallantry, devotion and technical skill. All staff were and are unanimous in their deep appreciation and gratitude to [them]. The essential need for security in a very perilous game made it impossible to know names but our admiration and respect were unbounded.[2]

In the following pages, I try to describe these pilots, with their special skills and courage that enabled them to carry out some of the most difficult flying of World War II.

I

The Gestation of the Lysander

Perched high in the nose, with the engine at my feet, and a vast amount of window all around, I felt at first as though I was projected into space.

Harald Penrose[1]

Harald Penrose fell into his job; Teddy Petter was parachuted into his. Together, they made the Lysander. Teddy put in the flaws, and Harald did his best to eradicate them.

When Harald Penrose landed after his first flight in the Lysander, there was a very big 'but' at the end of his comments to his boss. Like many a successful pilot, Harald Penrose had contracted the aviation bug at an early age. In his case, it was at the age of five in 1909 when his father showed him newspaper coverage of Blériot's crossing of the Channel. Unlike many early aviators, Penrose persevered with tertiary education, pursuing a four-year course in aeronautical engineering at Northampton. On graduation, he joined Westland Aircraft in 1925, secured flying training in the Royal Air Force (RAF) Reserves, and acquired a commercial licence by 1928. Three years later, Louis Paget, Westland's chief test pilot, spun into the ground in a Westland Widgeon; Penrose had returned from a tour of South America demonstrating the Wapiti only that day, and so, at the tender age of 27, was appointed to replace the dead Paget. Unlike many engineers, he could write exquisite prose – not that that skill was what attracted Petter's attention.

William Edward Willoughby ('Teddy') Petter was the young son of Westland's Chairman, Sir Ernest Petter. His intellect was not in doubt. After

Marlborough, Teddy had studied mechanical science at Caius College, Cambridge, gaining a First in the Tripos and sharing the John Bernard Seely prize in aeronautics. Wearing heavy horn-rimmed spectacles, this shy intellectual had no great love of the practice of aviation, preferring walks in the countryside and reading philosophers such as Nietzsche and Kant. Nonetheless, his father bequeathed him the role of Technical Director at the Yeovil-based factory. Young Petter came up with some revolutionary experimental aircraft such as the tail-less Pterodactyl and, although not a draughtsman, took an intense interest in the work of his staff in the drawing office. As Denis Edkins, his subsequent personal assistant, noted, 'He was a creative designer both in the overall sense and in detail, so that there were many good ideas embodied in the Lysander.'[2] Petter's wife, Claude, of French and Swiss descent, became close to Penrose's wife, Norn. The two couples lived only half a mile apart in the Somerset countryside; they both drove little Austin 7s.

In April 1935, when the state of the British armed forces was beginning to raise eyebrows, the Air Ministry issued specification A.39/34 for a two-seat aircraft to replace the antiquated Hawker Audax in the Army Co-operation role (ferrying senior officers around battlefield rear areas, observing the artillery's fall of shot, short-range photo-reconaissance, and so on). This was a derivative of the Hawker Hart biplane, which had only been in service for a couple of years. Amongst others, Roy Fedden of the Bristol Engine Co. lobbied the Air Ministry's Director of Technical Development and the Director of Operational Requirements for Petter's supposed technical skills to be more fully utilized. They succeeded – Westland was invited to tender for this project.[3] Petter and his team then wisely took counsel from current Army Co-operation pilots on what characteristics were desired. This team went to the School of Army Co-operation at the curvaceous Wiltshire airfield of Old Sarum, which sits in the lee of an Iron Age hill fort.[4] Good low-speed handling, good visibility downwards and forwards, and short take-off and landing (STOL) characteristics were the key attributes universally desired, although Penrose found a variety of other aspirations.

By June that year, Westland was awarded a contract for two prototype aircraft. But the atmosphere at the Yeovil factory under Petter's hand had been, and remained, strained, and the 'rubicund, persuasive' Victor Gaunt (the Experimental Superintendent) resigned, having lost all faith in Teddy, due to his (wilful) lack of understanding of engineering issues.[5]

Westland's answer to A.39/34 was initially known as the P8. In the view of Penrose, its appearance betokened Petter's 'devotion to France, the machine had a French appearance'.[6] Its look – dainty from some angles, pudgy from others – drew from the experience of Arthur Davenport, the chief designer, in strut-braced high-wing monoplanes. It approached the objective of benign low-speed handling – vital for an Army Co-operation machine – in a novel way: leading edge slats that operated automatically, the inner portion connected to the trailing edge flaps. As the aircraft slowed (and therefore neared the stall), the outer slats popped out first, then the inner together with the flaps, all designed to bond the airflow to the wings in a slow-speed regime. The pilot did not have to worry about them. In theory.

With its rust-red primer-doped fabric, and an absence of fairings over the undercarriage, the prototype looked both strange and ungainly. Nonetheless, on 10 June 1936, it was ready for taxiing trials with Penrose at the controls. In lieu of the two-position metal prop envisaged by the design team, it had a fixed-pitch wooden propeller on the end of its Bristol Mercury engine. These trials were successful; Petter, adorned with his trilby, looked relieved. The prototype was given a silver paint finish, its wings temporarily removed, and the ensemble was transported to the grass airfield at Boscombe Down, where more extensive tests could be made.

Five days later, all was set for the first flight: as soon as Penrose opened the throttle the tip slats were fully out, within a few yards the slats nearer the wing root extended, and the interconnected flaps came down a little. It leapt into the air in less than 150 yards. These vaunted slats worked as planned, although unsurprisingly were in need of some adjustment. 'The view was magnificent', although Penrose found the controls 'a little heavy', particularly the ailerons (to control roll), but nothing that could not be sorted out by the addition of servo tabs. After climbing to 5,000 feet over the Wiltshire countryside, he essayed some stalls. No drama. However, as he came to return to land at Boscombe, an issue surfaced which was to haunt the machine for the rest of its life – Penrose ran out of elevator (longitudinal) control when he was still ten feet above the runway. His skills enabled him to use a touch of throttle to arrest the rate of descent, and 'she settled gently'.[7] The tests in Westland's wind tunnel had failed to predict this change in controllability in the landing configuration.

Penrose let Petter know of this defect immediately, to the latter's chagrin. 'Are you sure?' he said, 'Your landing seemed perfect.' Petter was adamant that the machine should make its public debut only two weeks hence at the Society of British Aircraft Constructors' (SBAC) annual air show, ironically, and unusually, to be held at the Hatfield base of Westland's rival manufacturer, de Havilland.

The pressure was on: every configuration tried by Penrose showed that the combination of full flap and open slats, the two being mechanically linked, resulted in a much greater nose-down dip than the design team had predicted. Increasing the tailplane area mitigated the instability but meant that proper three-point landings still could not be achieved. So a tailplane trimmer was installed, which altered the whole incidence of the tailplane relative to the airflow. Despite this trimming gear being re-designed several times, the team could not avoid an excessive negative angle for the tailplane in the landing phase. The problem was that if a pilot opened the throttle fully to abandon a landing, the nose would rear up so strongly that the pilot would be very hard pressed to correct it with forward stick. This was bound to cause fatal accidents. Penrose refused to accept it.[8] He and Petter had as yet no idea of how their creature would find its fame: 'None of us dreamed as we pushed her inside that within a few years the Lysander's destiny was to be hundreds of night landings in enemy-occupied territory.'[9]

Sir Ernest came to watch the trials, but Teddy's contorted relationship with his father led him to forbid Penrose and his colleagues to share their doubts with their ultimate boss. So, unaware of the underlying flaws, Ernest hosted a lavish dinner party for his son and Penrose with their wives at a suitably upmarket hotel on the Somerset coast.

Westland's new baby was first seen in public in the New Type Park at the RAF Hendon air display on 27 June 1936. It went to Hatfield for the SBAC Show two days later where its ability to take off and land on an area the size of a football pitch was noted. Foreign observers included Captain José Cabral, Chief of the Portuguese Air Force, General Lindquist, his Finnish counterpart, and, most notably, General Erhard Milch, the 44-year-old head of the Luftwaffe under Göring.

Penrose still believed that some hard re-design work was necessary to resolve this tailplane issue, but Petter pushed on, confident of knowing better. So three weeks later, the prototype, by now given the serial K6167, a three-bladed two-speed propeller, and proper fairings for its imposing undercarriage and wheels, was despatched to the Aircraft and Armament Experimental Establishment (A&AEE) at Martlesham Heath, hard by the Deben estuary in Suffolk.

Here it was scrutinized by not only the cream of the Air Ministry's pilots, but also on 8 July by King Edward VIII and his brother, the Duke of York. The pair had arrived in the royal de Havilland Rapide piloted by Flight Lieutenant (Flt Lt) Edward Fielden, who was to feature large in the

Lysander's wartime service. The royal duo had first inspected Fury and Gauntlet fighters at RAF Northolt and 11 Flying Training School (FTS) at Wittering, then proceeded to Mildenhall to inspect Heyford and Hind bombers – a busy day. They were both in RAF uniforms adorned with mourning bands after the death of their father, King George V. Lysander K6167 was lined up at Martlesham, along with other new monoplanes such as the Spitfire and Hurricane, procured in the era of the RAF's rapid expansion in the mid-1930s, in front of the hangars of No. 15 Squadron. The Spitfire did a flypast at 'well over' 300mph. The new king used a ladder to inspect the silver Lysander's cockpit – piloting the machine was a young man's game, requiring five or six climbing steps onto the wheel spat and up the fuselage before sliding into the pilot's seat. Soon after this visit, Fielden was officially appointed Captain of the King's Flight.

Such was the urgency to recover from years of complacency and banking unwarranted peace dividends, that the Air Ministry awarded the Yeovil company a production contract for 169 examples of the Mk I Lysander in October 1936. Yet the Martlesham team only began flying the first prototype in earnest from the following month; it was joined by the second, K6128, in March 1937. The pilots' reports were thorough: the ailerons were praised, the rudder considered slightly too light at higher speeds, with some trimming facility suggested. But they soon latched on to Penrose's fear:

> At the stall and when landing the elevator control is heavy. Response is slow and not very effective… a rocking of the control column fore and aft in tight turns… There does not seem to be enough fore and aft movement in the control column. When landing the control column is always in the fully back position before touching down when the aircraft is trimmed fully aft… The elevator control is not sufficiently powerful to keep the nose down if the engine is opened up fully with the aircraft trimmed for landing.

They were not impressed by the tail trimming gear: this 'is rather stiff and takes a long time (around 13 seconds) to get full movement'. So flying into a foreign field – at night – might prove problematic.

> Should a pilot for any reason take-off with the tail set for landing, he will be unable to prevent the nose rising even with the control column fully forward. Under these conditions the aircraft climbs at a steep angle, but will not stall or roll over one way or another. The pilot will be able

to regain full control by winding the tail adjusting wheel forward whilst holding the control column fully forward. This is facilitated by easing the throttle back slightly first, as the tail heaviness is increased with the throttle fully open.

Thirteen seconds of terror then. The official Pilot's Notes were later to laconically note:

> The aeroplane has been made to stall in the following way, but this should not be attempted. The aeroplane was trimmed to glide at about 80 mph Indicated Air Speed, and the throttle was then opened fully. No attempt was made to move the control column. The aeroplane assumed an excessively steep attitude, and then did a gentle flick half-roll to the right on to its back, before starting a right hand spin.[10]

However, one other attribute of an Army Co-operation aircraft (and useful for its later work on Special Operations) came in for praise: its stability and controllability at very low speeds around the stall was excellent. 'The aircraft can be held in a stalled glide at any landing down to about 40 mph.'[11] And its ratio of top to slowest speed was an excellent 4:1.

The tested prototype was sprightlier in take-off than the design specification, taking only 310 yards to clear a 50-foot obstacle, but took a slightly longer landing run – 275 yards against the desired 150 yards.

The factory increased the area of the tailplane, eliminating the instability near touchdown, but still a full landing flare was impossible. The designers set to with some speed, and made the tailplane incidence manually adjustable by the pilot, but for this to work, the change in incidence had to be great, and this exacerbated the climbing-away issue noted by the Martlesham team. Under full throttle, the tailplane received all the propeller wash, and with the trimmer set fully aft for landing, the nose would rear up, possibly leading to a stall, whilst the pilot struggled to wind forward the incidence control. Even at half power, it required all the pilot's strength to push the control column fully forward until he could wind the elevator trimmer forward. Penrose could see the risk of fatalities, and insisted on a modification. Fashioning a silk purse from a sow's ear, an automatic re-trimming device was suggested, but John Fearn (known as 'Daddy') vetoed it. The 53-year-old Midlander was Westland's Works Supervisor, and, like Petter, knew little of flying. To its shame, the Martlesham team acquiesced, and as Penrose later succinctly noted, 'fatal accidents ensued'.

THE GESTATION OF THE LYSANDER

Modern-era Lysander pilots concur with Penrose's concern that 'the tailplane trimming system can be lethal'.[12]

Penrose took Petter up to demonstrate the trim changes during an aborted landing. Teddy was so terrified, it is said he never flew in one of his own designs again; he retreated to confer with Fearn, his confidant in such matters. Like Petter, Fearn was not noted for his understanding of pilots' difficulties and readily agreed that no change to the production programme could be entertained, saying, 'A note in the cockpit should be sufficient.'[13] This conversation, this decision, as we will see, contributed to the death of several British pilots in English and French meadows.

The Air Ministry went along with the Petter bulldozer, keen to push the type into service for its intended role as an Army Co-operation aircraft. By now, the A.39/34 had been christened the Lysander, as a mythical match to the Hawker Hector (fellow heroes in the famous British marching tune, *The British Grenadiers*), which Westland was manufacturing under sub-contract, and which the Lysander had been procured to replace. It had beaten the Bristol 148, and responses from Avro and Hawker that had never left the drawing board. Bristol's response failed because its low-wing configuration was felt to render the wings susceptible to damage in rough field operations, and also reduce downward visibility. So the Lysander had not had to face any high-winged competition.

In February 1938, the second prototype Lysander was sent to Old Sarum's School of Army Co-operation to check the type was suitable for its intended role. It was the first such machine to be adorned with a machine gun in a wheel spat. The boss of No. 59 Squadron, Squadron Leader (Sqn Ldr) John Fyfe, and Flt Lt Peter Donkin, a flight commander from No. 16 Squadron, flew it and gave it their seal of approval. The School's commandant, Group Captain (Gp Capt) Arthur Capel, wrote to the Air Ministry in March; Air Vice Marshal (AVM) Bertine Sutton, Air Officer Commanding (AOC) 22 Group, concurred with him and concluded that 'this type of aircraft is suitable for Army Co-operation duties generally and during the short time that this aircraft was available, few disadvantages for this type of work were discovered'. But there were two very important provisos: its cruising speed of 170mph was considered 'slow in comparison with that of other modern aircraft... it is considered that the Army co-operation pilot working alone in wartime would require a considerably greater turn of speed'. And further they questioned whether a single 0.303 machine gun was sufficient defensive armament.[14] They failed to notice the potentially fatal slow-speed characteristics. As Clive Richards concluded much later, the Lysander was 'in effect a state of the art RE8, just as vulnerable to anti-aircraft fire as the RE8 had been and it was even less able to cope with enemy fighters than its predecessor'.[15] The RE8 was the World War I reconnaissance aircraft that bumbled over enemy lines in many a *Biggles* novel.

Although Petter had swept aside concerns about the landing characteristics, he had confidence in the strength of the undercarriage – this was another of his innovations. With the help of the 'bustling' Colonel (Col) Wallace Devereux, a director of High Duty Alloys, this was a single duralumin extrusion, bent into a hairpin shape, with internally sprung wheels at each end.[16] In wartime use, this was to prove not quite as strong as Petter assumed. Moreover, in the rougher French fields it was to encounter, the wheel springs bottomed out.

Final inspection by the RAF of the first production aircraft was held at Yeovil at 0900hrs on 5 April 1938, with deliveries to squadrons starting a month later. The production lines at the Westland factory reached desired efficiency and the type entered operational service with 16 Squadron in June. By this time, Sir Ernest Petter was actively pursuing export markets for the Lysander. A test pilot from the Turkish Air Force had arrived at Yeovil, and had watched Penrose start his 150-yard take-off run aiming just off a cottage on the far airfield boundary. The 18-stone Turk decided to start his take-off run from the same spot, but with the cottage clearly in his sights. The factory's ambulance started its engine. The occupants of the cottage were probably not amused by the heavy Lysander sliding just over their roof. But the Turks placed an order for 36 machines.[17]

The French were also a target customer, and their test pilot had been impressed by the factory pilot demonstrating a 'fully slotted descent' (i.e. very slow and steep). When he tried to replicate this feat, he hit the serious slope at one end of the field, and snapped one undercarriage leg off. Instead of giving up gracefully, he opened the throttle to go round for another attempt. With only one leg and wheel, he inevitably nosed over on landing.[18] The French did not place an order. A single Mk I machine was, however, delivered to the French Air Force in June 1939. Transported by road from Yeovil to Les Invalides in the centre of Paris for a brief exhibition, it was then towed by road to the aerodrome at Persan-Beaumont. The Lysander undercarriage was not designed for such maltreatment. The journey had to be interrupted several times to pour water on the overheating axles. A rather pointless escapade as the French never flew the machine.[19]

By mid-July, Sir Ernest had sold his controlling interest in Westland to the Clydeside shipping firm of John Brown. The toxic atmosphere in the upper echelons of Westland continued: Teddy had high hopes for the Whirlwind, a twin-engine fighter that was ahead of its time. But to improve the efficiency of the wing, Petter had routed the exhaust pipes through fuel tanks in the wings. When Penrose 'emphatically' disagreed with this philosophy and pointed out the attendant risks for a fighter, Petter retorted, 'You pilots have to accept a few risks you know.' By early 1939, the senior management of the firm was dysfunctional: the schisms between design, testing and production were deep. The glazed interior walls of the offices rattled with arguments. By Easter 1940, Petter was ruling Westland like a dictator.

Penrose could appreciate Petter's organizational skills, but Teddy struggled to comprehend other people and their motives. Like many a son of a successful and aggressive entrepreneur, Teddy wanted to better his father and stamp his own imprint on the firm.[20] Penrose was a man of great sensitivity, as evidenced by his later lyrical writings about his flying, and would have felt bruised by Petter's attitude.

Even before the outbreak of war, however, Petter's obduracy had started killing Lysander pilots. Some had been lulled by the type's supposedly infallible low-speed handling. On 28 April 1939, a II Squadron pilot, Flying Officer (F/O) Ronald Petrie, was doing a demonstration to a visiting group of soldiers at his home base of Hawkinge in Kent. He did a low and slow flypast at the end of which he turned through 180 degrees, but stalled and crashed, and the Lysander burst into flames. The same day, a No. 13 Squadron pilot, returning from Denham to Odiham on a navigational exercise (possibly trying to impress bystanders), made too steep a climb on take-off and stalled in a turn.[21] The 1939 Royal Aeronautical Society (RAeS) Garden Party on 14 May enjoyed better weather than a year before – when only the Vickers Wellesley had managed to crawl through the murk – until the flying display was due to start. Nonetheless it went ahead, and Westland's new assistant pilot, Flt Lt George Snarey, demonstrated the Lysander without issue.[22] However, only six days later, Pilot Officer (P/O) H.G. Malcolm stalled and crashed when displaying a No. 26 Squadron Lysander (L4784) at the Empire Air Day at Manchester's Ringway aerodrome. Malcolm was a relatively inexperienced pilot with only 314 flying hours, yet was doing a slow flying demonstration, and was turning at only 250–300 feet when he stalled. The brief accident report said, 'Raised nose and full engine, known characteristics.' He had disobeyed orders not to fly below 60mph.[23]

So, despite its known and potentially fatal characteristics, the Lysander was pressed into service. Pretty and ugly at the same time, or *jolie laide*, as French Resistance fighters might have termed it, the aircraft resembled a tadpole in profile, yet from above its wings looked like those of a dragonfly, or perhaps a pterodactyl, if one wanted to attribute more threatening qualities to it. For pilots used to being cocooned in the bosom of a Spitfire or Hurricane, sitting in a Lysander cockpit they felt unusually exposed, surrounded by so much glazing 'and nakedly accommodated in a bucket seat with two wings sprouting from my ears'.[24]

The British Army was trying to explore how all aircraft could be used to their best advantage. So the Lysander was pressed into service for other tasks. In 1939, several were sent to a trials flight at the government's chemical warfare establishment at Porton Down, to be fitted with equipment designed to provide a smokescreen for troops on manoeuvres, and also to spread toxic gases over enemy troops. These trials had a tragic result in October 1943 when the smoke generation equipment fell off the airframe, killing seven men and injuring eight.[25] More mainstream tasks awaited the machine, and in the meantime, the UK government was beginning to consider how to conduct clandestine warfare.

2

The Customers: The Special Operations Executive and the Secret Intelligence Service

Churchill stood head and shoulders above his political contemporaries in grasping the importance of intelligence and harnessing it to his cause.

David Stafford[1]

The Prime Minister witnessed how 'conventional military forces could be vulnerable to the calculated stratagems of the weak and occupied'.[2] In March 1938, the Foreign Office created a branch named EH (after its headquarters (HQ) in Electra House), its role being to examine ways of influencing German public opinion. At the same time, Section D was founded 'to investigate every possibility of attacking potential enemies by means other than the operations of military forces'. It too was under the auspices of the Foreign Office. The third body created was GS (R) – the research section of the War Office's General Staff, which, despite its embryonic resources, was tasked with creating a guerrilla warfare strategy. Early in 1939, it was renamed MI (R) (Military Intelligence (Research)).[3]

The Battle of France (10 May–25 June 1940) created urgency in Whitehall not only to buttress French fortitude, but to establish the base for civil resistance against the Germans. Lord Maurice Hankey was, on 25 May 1940, 'in the midst of organising with different English agencies and in particular the Intelligence Service the resistance of the civilian population against the eventual invasion of England; this organisation is being carried out on a vast scale. Lord Hankey has drawn my attention to the extreme importance that the similar organisation in France should be put in direct contact with its English counterpart to share experience and co-operate completely.' The anonymous writer encouraged the addressee (M. Paul Baudoin, the Under Secretary of State to French Prime Minister Paul Reynaud in Paris) to 'form at the earliest opportunity centres of sabotage in France and Belgium'.[4]

MI (R), the department which was to merge with Section D in July 1940 to give birth to the Special Operations Executive (SOE), realized that it would be easier to put structures and matériel in place before the Germans overcame the bulk of France. It fired off memos with increasing urgency.

Douglas Dodds-Parker was to become intimately involved in the development of intelligence networks. Suitably imposing for a Grenadier Guards captain at 6 feet 5 inches, he was initially educated at Winchester, then at Magdalen College, Oxford, after which he joined the University Air Squadron (UAS) where he gained some insight into the ways of the Air Force. After the Guards, he soon eased sideways into intelligence: 'On 25 May 1940, I flew out with 3 SIS friends to Cairo, including Arthur (brother of T.E.) Lawrence for the Jewish Agency.' His remit was to improve communications with the Poles and the Czechs through the Balkans.[5] His UAS experience was to stand him in good stead since his first major wartime role was as head of transport for SOE, overseeing arrangements for both air and sea. Dodds-Parker noted after the war, 'earlier staff talks and preparations might have mitigated the coming disaster even if too late to prevent it. A year later I was concerned with putting into Europe, by air and sea, many brave men and women, sent to set up organisations and communications in circumstances rendered the harder and more dangerous by the lack of prevision.'[6]

At the outbreak of war, Secret Intelligence Service (SIS), the arm of Government tasked with overseas espionage, had its Section IV as the Air Section, headed by Wing Commander (W/Cdr) Frederick Winterbotham, who had been in post since 1936. An energetic character, he had used all means at his disposal to monitor the build-up in the Luftwaffe's strength, and was well versed in the benefits of photo-reconnaissance.

Whilst SIS had existed pre-war, and was supposed to have a network of agents in place in what was soon to become Occupied Europe, it soon found that its networks could do with considerable enhancement. In 1935, its head, Admiral Hugh Sinclair (known as 'C'), lamented that his annual budget equated to the running costs of just one naval destroyer. It was under similar pressure to that on GS (R). Most of its agents and networks in Western Europe had now been overcome by the speed of the Nazis' advance, leaving it operating just from the capitals of those countries that were now (more or less) neutral. The indefatigable Polish intelligence network, exiled in London, was running an 'embryonic' network in the south of France.[7]

Winston Churchill had become Prime Minister on 10 May 1940 at the age of 65 – 'his energy was undiminished and the flame of his eloquence was undimmed'.[8] His fondness for unconventional warfare had been formed by two influences – his experience of the Afrikaans' guerrilla tactics in the Boer War, and the inter-war exploits of T.E. Lawrence in the Middle East.

With several horses thus bolted, Churchill acted. The War Cabinet met on 19 July 1940 with Neville Chamberlain in the chair as Lord President of the Council. Philip Cunliffe-Lister, Lord Swinton, was given control of the Home Defence (Security) Executive, together with MI5 (the arm of the security services charged with maintaining domestic security) and SIS's activities in the UK.

> The Prime Minister has further decided after consultation with Ministers concerned, that a new organisation should be established forthwith to co-ordinate all action, by way of subversion and sabotage, against the enemy overseas. This is to be known as the Special Operations Executive.

This was to be under the direction of Hugh Dalton with the assistance of Sir Robert Vansittart. Dalton was also to have the co-operation of the Directors of Intelligence of the three Service Departments, and of SIS (MI6) for the purposes entrusted to him.

That 'co-operation' was to prove difficult to achieve; it is notable that the War Cabinet did not discuss transport resources that day. Chamberlain's minutes concluded, 'The Prime Minister has requested that Lord Swinton and Mr Dalton should regard me as the member of the War Cabinet whom they should consult and to whom any inter-Departmental differences, should they arise, would be referred.'[9] They were to arise – and strongly – but this meeting was to be one of Chamberlain's last before he succumbed to bowel cancer.

Hugh Dalton took the role as he was already Minister of Economic Warfare – and he had grabbed that ministerial role because he wanted it.[10] He did not fit easily into the milieu into which he had inserted himself, described by a junior colleague as a 'doctrinaire economist, tall, with a big bald head, a loud voice and a thrusting manner'.[11] His fan club had few members; he was blessed with 'almost limitless energy', and cursed with 'a virtual inability to conceive that in any circumstances he could be wrong... also formidably hideous, his appearance described by another colleague like "that of a Chinese executioner"'.[12]

But as John Beevor, who was to join SOE at a senior level in 1943, later noted, 'We had special problems with the Prime Minister as long as Dalton was our Minister, as the PM disliked the socialist intellectual', and seldom summoned him to discuss SOE matters.[13] Churchill loathed Dalton – 'Keep that man away from me, I can't stand his booming voice and shifty eyes' – but the PM had had to offer a bone to Labour in his coalition government after having given the Foreign Office to a Tory.[14] Moreover, Dalton kept his two departments in very different pigeonholes – the Ministry of Economic Warfare (MEW) was in the public domain; SOE was hidden from view. In previous days, the Machiavellian Brendan Bracken had lobbied Churchill that no minister should be responsible for SOE, believing that Lord Swinton should take the role.[15]

Lord Halifax (the 'Holy Fox') handed over control of Section D, which had hitherto been under his own control, to Dalton, in a short memo dated 18 August 1940. Dalton had long believed that an organization such as SOE should stand apart from the War Office: 'Its purpose was to co-ordinate all action by way of subversion and sabotage against the enemy overseas... I accepted the Prime Minister's invitation with great eagerness and satisfaction. "And now", he exhorted me, "set Europe ablaze."'[16] Dalton was impressed with Ireland's Sinn Fein as a guerrilla role model; and in his vision, to emphasize its different *modus operandi*, the new organization should 'be entirely independent of the War Office machine'.[17] For senior roles, he asked Halifax for Gladwyn Jebb, then Private Secretary to Alec Cadogan, the Foreign Office Permanent Under Secretary, to be his chief executive officer (CEO). From the business world, he pulled Charles Hambro, director of the family bank and the Bank of England – 'He kept more balls in the air than any man I know.' The embryonic SOE was set up in Berkeley Square.

All Whitehall agencies looking at how to defend Great Britain, and how to take the battle to the enemy, faced an immediate problem – after its defeat, France had become an even more fractured and fractious society than it had been in peacetime. This was reflected in its politics. The fissures were everywhere: from hard left to hard right, from collaborationist to resister, the divisions were deep.[18]

Across the Channel, after France's ignominious capitulation at Compiègne, a new puppet government was installed under Marshal Pétain, centred in Vichy in the Unoccupied Zone (ZNO). Even within this Vichy government there were shades ranging from the arch-Pétainiste to those who were closet (at least potential) resisters. As Tony Brooks, who was to became a very successful SOE agent in south-west France, noted in the 1980s, 'Well, in 1941, when I was working as a sort of local recruiter for an escape organisation, I would have said probably 1% [of the French] were prepared to even contemplate doing anything. Helping escaped prisoners they felt was less dangerous, I think probably very erroneously, but they felt they could justify it, that they were being sort of humanitarian.'[19]

The British security services were to find that only a handful of European populations – particularly the Poles and the Cretans, who had been used to oppression and wars – were intrinsically ready to rebel and resist an invader. Colin Gubbins, SOE's military head, had had direct experience of the Poles, and was perhaps a little disappointed with the initial response by the French nation (not to mention their armed forces). France did not seem an obviously fertile ground for creating resistance movements.

With a Military Cross (MC) from World War I, and a Distinguished Service Order (DSO) from the 1940 Norwegian campaign, always immaculately dressed and principled, Colin McVean Gubbins was recruited as a colonel, but was soon promoted to brigadier, as some sort of rank parity was needed with those with whom he would be dealing in other services. 'A born leader of men', in Dalton's view, his knowledge of the benefits of guerrilla warfare had also been shaped by his dealings with the Irish Republican Army (IRA) in the inter-war years. Peter Wilkinson, who was to become his military assistant, was equally enthusiastic, calling Gubbins 'a wonderful leader of the young, whom he inspired'. There is no doubt that he was widely liked and inspired fierce loyalty and confidence in his staff.[20] However, Gubbins 'was highly disliked by people in the War Cabinet and Foreign Office. They could not stick his guts.'[21] Jebb said, 'I have seldom met a man more vigorous and a more inspiring soldier, or incidentally possessing more political sense. There is no doubt he is the lynchpin of the existing machine.'[22]

The Phoney War period was largely spent by Whitehall agencies probing to see precisely whom they could trust (in most cases overseas), and to whom it was worth sending men and matériel. The agencies were like a man entering a darkened house, expecting to find some modest ambient light in the first room, and finding none; walking forward, arms outstretched in the dark, searching for any possible friends. As fingertips met a huddled figure, cautious words were whispered about where other possible friends might be, and the agencies shuffled on.

One of the critical self-inflicted problems was that by now Britain had five security agencies trying to carry out joint intelligence operations with the French. SIS had as its country head for France the magnificently named Commander 'Biffy' Dunderdale. His real Christian name was Wilfred, so the Poles naturally called him 'Wilski'. He was said to have been endowed with 'Biffy' on account of his boxing prowess during his naval days. His highly cosmopolitan upbringing had left him multilingual and with contacts across Europe from the Levant westwards. Derring-do in Russia at the tender age of 17 (he had carried out sea trials of submarines for the Imperial Navy, during which he sank four German ships) left observers in no doubt of his military credentials. Joining SIS soon after World War I, he had headed up their mission in Paris since 1926, when he was only 27. Here he was a frequent visitor to the best restaurants, nightclubs and possibly *maisons closes*.[23]

Biffy was hampered by the fact that most of his French contacts went over to the Vichy regime. Stewart Menzies (appointed 'C' in 1939) instructed him to maintain contact with such types, but to focus on General Charles de Gaulle's Free French teams. Added into the mix was Commander Kenneth Cohen (widely known as 'KC') who had been in Paris as part of the clandestine spy network Z Organisation run by Claude Dansey, Menzies' subordinate but rival, also trying to keep in touch with the Vichy teams for SIS. Biffy commanded A4 Section (reporting to Menzies), whilst Cohen headed A5. (Cohen's snooty résumé of his colleague and supposed friend Dunderdale, who was almost the same age but had much more experience of France, was 'a genial expense account salesman'.)

MI5 had a country section for France under the charge of Kenneth Younger. Finally, SOE itself understandably split its efforts in France into its own F Section, which ran SOE's own teams, and RF Section, which liaised with de Gaulle's team. This latter team was commanded by its head of intelligence, Colonel André Dewavrin (known as Agent *Passy*, in a spate of agents being named after Paris Metro stations). Balding at the age of 41, the pasty-faced and right-wing *Passy*/Dewavrin came from a 'solid industrial family in Northern France' and enjoyed a privileged education culminating in the École Polytéchnique; he had served with an élite regiment (the

Chasseurs Alpins) in the ill-fated Norwegian campaign before arriving in England on 18 June 1940.[24] *Passy* was one of de Gaulle's first recruits in London, and in KC's view was 'brave, able, but distinctly unsaintly', yet even *Passy* was unnerved by his interview with de Gaulle: 'the encounter was glacial and the only contact I felt with the General was his grey, piercing gaze'.[25] Even the urbane John Beevor found the young general a 'giant but forbidding presence'.[26] Back in his homeland, many of the population still did not know quite what to make of him.[27] By January 1942, *Passy*'s strengthened outfit was christened Bureau Central de Renseignements et d'Action (BCRA) – a bold title to live up to.

SOE's coverage of Western Europe was divided into country sections, of which F Section was the largest. It was headed by the beaky snob Maurice Buckmaster, formerly manager of the Ford Motor Company's plant at Asnières, outside Paris. He had good knowledge of French ways and topography, but his life thus far had not prepared him to assess the trustworthiness of potential secret agents, whether male or female. Buckmaster had arrived at SOE from the Intelligence Corps, and was first a staff officer in F Section, then head of the Belgian Section, and finally, from December 1941, head of F Section. His work ethic was unparalleled.

F Section had been formed because 'De Gaulle could not be trusted to enact British orders'.[28] Moreover, the Resistance was much larger in scale than de Gaulle's band of followers, and it was incumbent upon SOE to provide succour to this larger, and more catholic, grouping. Finally, Dalton and Jebb presciently decided at the outset that RF Section's policy of centralizing command and control would lead to security issues. The health of British agents in F Section would be better preserved by a cell-like structure.

It was entirely unsurprising that the relationship between SIS and SOE was at best uneasy. An illuminating example of this friction was given by Philip Johns, who, quite rarely, ended up working for both organizations, starting with SIS. 'I was indoctrinated into the belief that SOE was rash and untrustworthy, lacking in security. I was briefed that in "setting Europe ablaze" our own agents might well be compromised and endangered so that caution was the watchword in all forms of collaboration with the Baker Street [SOE HQ] irregulars… SOE was considered to be untrustworthy, unreliable, and at worst a serious threat to security.'[29] Johns did not stint in his criticism of SIS: its country heads were to show 'complete failure to appreciate local conditions and problems… the whole atmosphere at HQ at this time was most distasteful'.[30]

THE NEED FOR AIR TRANSPORT

The 'easy' way to deliver agents into Europe was by parachute. The RAF had practised dropping airborne troops during the inter-war period, developing a habit of using only obsolescent bombers for this task – a habit which was to prove hard to break.

But parachuting was an unsuitable means of transport for anyone beyond early middle age – and was therefore inappropriate for the multitude of French politicians who would need to be returned to their homeland in due course. Moreover, it carried its own dangers. There were six fatal parachuting casualties in F Section during the war (estimated to be one in 900 jumps). Older people, if they did use a silken descent, were more at risk from bone fractures that would take too long to heal.[31] And, most pertinently, parachuting was a one-way enterprise – the Chiefs of Staff needed to source a service that would enable agents, saboteurs and political leaders to be brought back to Britain. The RAF offered the prospect of the speediest means of so doing.

Perhaps obvious in retrospect, it was soon realized that it would be foolish for senior members of either SOE or SIS in the UK to visit France (by whatever means), as they could potentially release too much information under torture if arrested. It would be more sensible to bring back and return circuit organizers as necessary.[32] But how?

3

The Lysander Goes to War: Bloodied and Bowed

THE LOST HISTORY OF THE RFC'S SPY TRANSPORT IN WORLD WAR I

The British armed forces had learned how to insert and retrieve agents from behind enemy lines in World War I. It was just that by 1939 the War Office had forgotten the need for this capability and the techniques involved.

Jules Védrines was a vastly experienced aviator, and had made his name winning many international air races before World War I (including Paris to Madrid, which took him 15 hours over three days). His experience in navigating over unfamiliar countryside and flying by moonlight stood him in good stead for his duties in the war. Védrines became the main French pilot to carry out clandestine missions behind the German lines. He used a Blériot XXXVIbis monoplane, which he christened *La Vache* (*The Cow*), thought to be the only such named machine in the Aviation Militaire. A carbine by his right leg was his only defence against any interference from German troops.

Britain's Royal Flying Corps (RFC) carried out similar flights, albeit on an ad hoc basis. Captain Thomas Mulcahy Morgan, originally of the Royal Irish Fusiliers, flew over to France with No. 4 Squadron in 1914. On 13 September 1915, in his BE2c, he was the first RFC pilot to land an agent behind the lines. The idea was to find a field with a nearby wood for the agent's escape. Unfortunately, the field was rather small, he hit a tree, and both he and the agent were severely injured. Escaping back to Britain by April 1917, he was awarded an MC for these exploits.[1] From 1915,

No. 70 Squadron under Captain G.L. Cruickshank began to fly agents for SIS across the lines.[2] No. 3 Squadron was also involved in spy transport.

By comparison with their successors 30 or so years later, putative clandestine mission pilots in World War I were hampered by the mechanical reliability of their machines. Claude Alward Ridley was a pilot with No. 60 Squadron in France in 1916. On 3 August in his Morane monoplane, he took the spy Victor Marié of the Réseau Victor to a field near Douai in Picardy. Unfortunately, after his landing, the engine stopped and could not be restarted. Marié procured papers and some civilian clothes for him, and by November, Ridley had managed to evade into Holland, from where he made his way back to Great Britain. He was awarded the DSO for this mission, and received an audience with King George V.[3] The RFC also carried out behind-the-lines missions in Mesopotamia.[4]

Tony Brooks, who was to become a celebrated SOE agent in France in World War II, related his father's experiences in the RFC in the Great War:

> Oh well, he didn't have any problems at all, after all he'd got self-starters on the aircraft – he landed near Metz in an RE8 in a stubble field in later 1917 to pick up a British agent and he didn't turn up for an hour and a half, and when he did he was so sawn-off, he couldn't swing the prop. So the agent climbed in, and to use my father's expression, 'I wedged the throttle with my flying gloves, "sucked in" (or whatever the revolting term is) with the propeller, gave her a twirl and she started like a bird. I dived under the wing, and just managed to get my feet on to the edge of the wing, and get into the cockpit, otherwise he'd have flown home on his own.'[5]

If such exploits were to be repeated in World War II, the only suitable machine in the RAF inventory was the Westland Lysander. However, its introduction to battle in its primary role was to be bloody and Petter's design flaws were to magnify that bloodshed.

THE LYSANDER'S USE BY THE BRITISH ARMY AS WORLD WAR II STARTS

The School of Army Co-operation Flying remained the nursery for Lysander pilots. The bulk of its recruits came straight from Advanced Flying Training Schools with between 100 and 200 flying hours under their stable belts. Its picturesque location on the convex turf of Old Sarum in Wiltshire was very handy for pilots learning to work with the Army, as it was only minutes from the main training areas on Salisbury Plain to the north. 'We studied detailed map-reading, aerial photography, air-to-ground Morse, artillery shoots and long-distance reconnaissance,' noted Richard Hillary, who was to gain fame as a fighter pilot (he was posted from Old Sarum in the middle of the Battle of Britain) and as a fine author (of *The Last Enemy*). 'The Lysander proved to be a ponderous old gentleman's plane, heavy on the controls but easy to handle. It seemed almost impossible to stall it.'[6] However, it was not so ponderous as to prevent young Hillary essaying some aerobatics (strictly against the rules), to his observer's great discomfort.

Hillary and his chums had not looked on the course at Old Sarum with much enthusiasm: whilst the Lysanders looked as if they could cope with the rough and tumble of Army flying, they thought its armament somewhat pathetic.[7] The course was tough, the working day being from 0900hrs to 1900hrs, with a day of ground school followed by a day of flying instruction on the Lysander or the Hector. There were 20 young pilots on Hillary's six-week course. At its close, such was the attrition to fighter squadrons caused by the Battle of France, three-quarters were posted not to Lysanders but to Spitfires, via an operational training unit (OTU) in Gloucestershire.

It did not take long for Petter's design flaws to find their first wartime victim. On 6 November 1939, 20-year-old P/O Michael Smith took off for some night-flying practice. He climbed steeply to 400 feet and turned sharply before his nose dropped, and the Lysander dived into the ground. Almost certainly, Smith had mis-set his trim wheel and lost his orientation to the horizon.

Andrew James Wray Geddes was an unusual type: born in Belgaum in India to a major in the Anglo-Indian Army, who died when he was aged only eight, young Geddes had already been bitten by the flying bug. A school friend had a father, Commander Edward Masterman, who was at the forefront of aviation – the captain of a naval airship, the *Parseval*. When Masterman told his son he could bring a chum with him on a flight, Andrew was the chosen one, and indeed was tasked by Commander Masterman with winding the handle to release ballast after take-off.[8] His prep school's location on the Kent coast also gave him a good vantage point to watch the Navy in action in World War I, as well as RFC pilots flying across to France.

Andrew was then sent to Wellington College, which looked after Army sons, including those who had lost their father. After leaving Wellington, he spent much time hanging around aerodromes, and determined that he wanted to join the newly created RAF. Sadly, he encountered a frequent hurdle – parental approval. His mother considered flying aeroplanes far too hazardous a career for her only son. She coerced him into applying for the Royal Military Academy (RMA) Woolwich as the precursor to a career in the Royal Artillery (RA); he graduated in 1928, joining 18 Medium Battery RA. But now aged 22, he was legally an adult and exercised his autonomy by taking advantage of a new scheme for Army officers to have four-year secondments to the RAF. The aim was to provide a balance of expertise amongst the Army Co-operation squadrons. He switched services in October, and was taught to fly in the Avro 504 at 5 FTS at Sealand, the bleak Cheshire airfield. Geddes' instructor was the magnificently named Flt Lt Aleth Thomas Septimus Léguen de Lacroix. He graduated to the Siskin and the Avro Lynx, after which he was classed 'Exceptional', with the proviso 'This pilot must not be allowed to get overconfident'.[9] The students wore mess kit from their original unit, so when, at the graduation ball, young Geddes was introduced to a notoriously snobbish young woman who saw his dark blue outfit with red stripes down his trousers, she commented, 'How peculiar to be dancing with you. I never realised that the RAF invited the Fire Brigade to these dances.'[10]

However, earlier that year, Lacroix had gone beyond the normal remit of an RAF flying instructor and introduced Geddes to a more charming woman, Anstice Leach. By the time of the ball, they had decided to wed – but he was still seven years too young to qualify for the RAF's Marriage Allowance. After the ball, he was posted to IV Squadron at Farnborough on the none-too-modern Bristol Fighter, to learn the nuts and bolts of Army Co-operation flying. He also qualified on the Armstrong Whitworth Atlas, and used this vehicle for numerous forays (which he called 'courting sorties') back to Cranwell to see his beloved.[11] They married in October 1929.

His flying was typically with a gunner/observer from the RAF ranks in the back seat. Their attitude towards being conducted through the air by an Army officer was expectedly cynical: Geddes overheard one such crewman mutter, 'If God had wanted the Army to fly he would have painted the sky green.'¹²

By now known as 'Gunner Geddes', his training progressed with a ten-week course at the School of Army Co-operation at Old Sarum in January 1930. But just as his expertise was becoming operationally useful, in June 1930 he was pushed back to the Artillery. Moreover, he, with Anstice and a four-month-old daughter in tow, was despatched by sea to India. Once there, he supplemented his meagre income with breaking in horses, racing them at meetings, and later, performing at civilian air displays with the Madras Flying Club. He participated in set piece 'attacks' by four aircraft on a Pathan fort. Each aircraft carried a female passenger who secreted four home-made bombs (with sticks of dynamite and a shotgun cartridge as a fuse!) under her skirt and dropped them over the side. He survived this but contracted pneumonia at Mhow; pleurisy and dysentery soon added to his woes. Whilst in hospital feeling very sorry for himself, he drew his sheet over his head to keep the flies away. Dozing, he heard two soldiers chatting away – they were measuring him for a coffin, thinking he had crossed the Styx. During this period, he narrowly avoided being shot dead by a gunner, who was later determined to be insane.

So it was with no great reluctance that he returned to the UK in October 1935 with his unit (14th Field Brigade RA). He might as well have had one trouser leg of his dress uniform in Russian blue and the other in khaki, for his career was to have no fewer than three transfers between the Army and Air Force. Now, after a brief refresher course at 1 FTS, he went to II (AC) Squadron RAF, the Army Co-operation unit.

By January 1938, there were some 37 Army officers serving in the RAF's Army Co-operation squadrons. This was not without predictable friction. By February 1940, the War Office's ambition was to ensure that Army pilots would comprise half of these squadrons' manpower.

In 1935, Geddes was made a flight commander in II Squadron. He was becoming known as a firm but fair leader – not without a sense of humour, as evidenced when a new pilot officer arrived at the Hawkinge officers' mess as a party was in full swing. Warmly welcomed by Gunner Geddes, as ever with a pipe glued to his mouth, young P/O Walford was disconcerted half an hour later when his new boss remonstrated with him for parking his Austin 7 in the entrance hall. Its move had, of course, been orchestrated by Geddes.

For reasons lost in the mists of time, II Squadron was known as 'Shiny Two'; with typical Air Force reticence, the squadron also liked to be known as 'Second to None'. In summer 1938, the squadron replaced its Hawker Hectors with the first Lysanders. Geddes picked up the squadron's second Lysander from the Yeovil factory, and before he landed at Hawkinge decided to do some aerobatics over the field, for which the aircraft was not, of course, cleared. As he carried out a roll off the top (of a loop), there was a bang and he discovered that one of the leading edge slat brackets had broken.[13] Geddes was sent back to the Royal Artillery for a brief spell but returned to II Squadron as commanding officer (CO) on 29 April 1939.

After war was declared, the RAF was ordered to support the attempt by the British Expeditionary Force (BEF) to save France, and on 6 October he took the squadron over the Channel to be based at Abbeville. Here, all of Geddes' resourcefulness was required to try to improve the facilities on a Spartan aerodrome during what was shaping up to be a very hard winter. In total, five Army Co-operation squadrons of Lysanders were sent to France (Nos 2, 4, 13, 16 and 26). They were tasked with tactical reconnaissance (their main missions to ascertain the forward line of the advancing German troops), light bombing, and resupply. Snow arrived at Abbeville just after Christmas, and working conditions became even more difficult.

A month after P/O Smith's death, Flt Lt Malcolm Skinner of 13 Squadron took off in L4673 from his base at Mons-en-Chaussées, hard by the World War I Somme battlefields; with little horizon, the weather was northern European winter grim. He recovered too slowly from a stall, and was attempting to turn at low altitude to avoid trees when his wing hit the ground. He had full fuel and so was near maximum weight; further, he had hampered his chances of a stall recovery by locking the flap mechanism. He had earned his wings three years earlier, and so was fairly experienced by Army Co-operation operational standards, yet the Lysander still killed him.[14]

The British and French were soon on the back foot. Geddes was relocated with his squadron to the desolate airfield of Wevelgem in Belgium, and his men were tasked with rather pointless bombing sorties: the 12 little 20lb Cooper bombs on the Lysander's two stub wings attached to the undercarriage offered little more than nuisance value for the Panzer tank columns they were ordered to attack.

The Lysanders' daily operational cycle now focused on finding out how far the Germans had advanced since the last intelligence assessment. When the BEF was forced to retreat from a line along the River Dyle in Belgium to the Scheldt, on 19 May, II Squadron was given the job of finding out which bridges were still usable and not in German hands. Because of the dangers that this unescorted mission posed, W/Cdr Geddes took on the operation himself. Nearing the bridges, he could not fail to notice two groups of Stuka dive-bombers (ten in each) circling the bridges at 5,000 feet, eyeing their target.

Geddes' gunner, Leading Aircraftman (LAC) Clarke, was as gung-ho as himself. Clarke, reading his pilot's mind, thought that they 'should teach the buggers a lesson'.[15] The German formation leader had seemingly mistaken the RAF aircraft for its German counterpart (a Henschel HS 126) and so was not initially perturbed when Geddes attached himself to the rear of the second group of Stukas.

Any dive-bomber is at its most vulnerable when it pulls up after dropping its bomb load; as the last Stuka did so, Geddes followed suit and Clarke let rip with his Vickers machine gun. The Ju 87 shed debris, and its rear gunner appeared to have been hit. The German formation dissolved in panic, but soon re-grouped and pursued Geddes, who chose the only viable option – to descend to tree-top level and use his slow-speed ability to make very tight turns. The most able of the Stuka pilots fired a salvo, which passed between the starboard side of Geddes' canopy and the wing strut. But after clearing a stoppage, Clarke gave a long burst that caused his Stuka adversary to smoke and then crash. Geddes shook off their other pursuers by following the road back to his base at almost ground level: 'the undercarriage brushed through the trees from time to time, but luckily the propeller was undamaged even though I hit the top of a poplar tree'. Remarkably, Geddes' victory, which was confirmed later that day, was not the only Stuka kill recorded to the squadron in that period.[16]

II Squadron retreated to the World War I airfield of Béthune, with resupply missions becoming more critical. On 27 May, 12 Lysanders were ordered to drop water supplies to beleaguered British troops in Calais, and later in the morning 17 dropped ammunition supplies to troops in the city's Citadel. These were fruitless missions, since the Germans had already taken the city the previous evening – the enemy was presumably grateful for the gift of 224 gallons of water, 22,000 cartridges and 864 grenades. Four days later, Flt Lt G.R. Shepley of 16 Squadron survived being shot down by home team fighters.

The Battle of France created a woeful dent in Britain's military assets. Only 15 per cent of the 452 Hurricanes sent across the Channel returned to the UK at the battle's close, thus vindicating the refusal of Air Marshal Sir Hugh Dowding (Commander-in-Chief Fighter Command) to accede to Churchill's demands to send more to aid the French.[17] The 23-year-old

P/O Christopher Foxley-Norris[18] flew Lysanders with 13 Squadron in the Battle of France until the squadron retreated to the UK in some disarray by June 1940. Those pilots whose Lysanders had ceased to function joined the rag-tag snake towards Dunkirk. Foxley-Norris switched immediately to Hurricanes to participate in the Battle of Britain. He was coruscating about the suitability of his Lysanders: 'Their performance was inadequate and the tasks they were set were impossible.'[19]

The scorecard made for depressing reading: across the five squadrons, 174 Lysanders had been sent into the Battle of France; 88 had been shot down in combat, and another 30 destroyed on the ground. That left only 32 per cent of the force flyable back to the UK, and most of those aircraft were in a very ragged state. One hundred and twenty aircrew had died, whilst IV Squadron had lost 60 per cent of its ground crew.[20]

Notwithstanding its failure in its primary role, the Westland factory at Yeovil continued churning out new machines, by now upgraded to the Mk III, benefiting from a Bristol Mercury XX engine that produced a maximum of 870hp.

Gunner Geddes, who now more than usual sought solace in his pipe, brought his exhausted squadron out of Béthune on 20 May; they landed in dribs and olive drabs at Lympne in Kent, and were ordered first to Bekesbourne and then to Hatfield.

Around this time, one of Geddes' pilots approached him in a state of anxiety. A Channel Islander, he had left his wife and daughter on the Islands in the custody of his mother, and was now keen to retrieve them before the jaws of the Nazi war machine snapped shut on the territory. Geddes was approached to sanction the first ever Lysander pick-up operation. Quite rightly he said he could not authorize it, but if the pilot wished to carry out a long-range air test, appropriately fuelled, Geddes would authorize that. Indeed, he helped the pilot with his pre-flight planning to ensure no mistakes. The pilot circled the area of his wife's house at low level, landed and dashed to the house. She refused to join him, because of that 'silly old man in Germany', but handed over the baby, and the flight back to Bekesbourne was uneventful. The air test was concluded to be 'quite successful'.[21]

As Hatfield was the headquarters of de Havilland's manufacturing operation, it made no sense to imperil the factory by siting a semi-active squadron there, and indeed de Havilland management were extremely uncooperative. So Geddes had to find alternative accommodation. He scouted various landing grounds to the north and north-east of Hatfield, and after some aerial reconnaissance latched upon Mathams Wood. This site had some World War I history, but Geddes determined it needed some enlargement for Lysander use. This was easily achieved with judicious compulsory purchases of land and tree felling. The squadron opened for business on 15 June, with the establishment of a flight office at the adjacent Blounts Farm.[22] Later, in July, a hard runway made of coir matting overlaid with Somerfield track extending to some 950 yards was constructed.

Meanwhile, SIS had been trying both to retrieve its staff from France and to preserve its links with the government's intelligence arm, the Deuxième Bureau. By the middle of June, the need for extraction of key personnel from France was thought urgent, none more key than de Gaulle himself. 'General, you are all alone,' said Churchill. 'Well alone, I stand with you.'[23] The most junior general in the French Army, de Gaulle had been just a colonel mere weeks earlier. The RAF flew him from Bordeaux (via a lunch and refuelling stop in Jersey) in a de Havilland Dragon Rapide on 17 June. Once in flight, he was given a cup of coffee, took one sip and pronounced, 'I don't drink tea.'[24]

He landed at Heston and saw Churchill the following day. De Gaulle's wife Yvonne and their 12-year-old daughter Anne (who had Down's Syndrome) were the next priority. Major Hope of Section D tried to mount an operation to pick them up on 18 June, the day of de Gaulle's famous address to his fellow countrymen on BBC radio. His family had been waiting in the Brittany town of Carentec; the RAF sent Flt Lt Bell in a staid and ungainly Walrus amphibian over the Channel. He became lost in poor visibility. Attempting to land in a field that proved to have been 20 miles from his intended destination, he hit an unseen embankment, the Walrus burst into flames, and all on board perished.[25] Yvonne and Anne drove to Brest, leaving for England in the last boat before the Germans took the port.

The single-minded French general's position as leader of the Free French was anointed by Churchill, who gave him a headquarters in 4 Carlton Gardens, conveniently close to Whitehall. De Gaulle ordered that only the French language be spoken there (despite *Passy*/Dewavrin speaking excellent English and being an able interpreter).[26] During World War I, Churchill had become friends with Edward Spears. With later irony, Spears had been born in Passy in Paris and had had an unusual upbringing around Europe, and as such spoke excellent French. In World War I, he was a liaison officer with the French general staff, and continued in this role during the inter-war years. During the Battle of France, he was deputed to be

Churchill's representative with the French Prime Minister, Paul Reynaud. After the 1940 Armistice, the Prime Minister gave him possibly the most challenging job for a major-general – the liaison role with de Gaulle. In one spat with Spears, the French leader ranted, 'I do not think I will ever get on with les Anglais. You are all the same, exclusively concentrated upon your own interests and business, quite insensitive to the requirements of others... Do you think I am interested in England winning the war? I am not. I am only interested in France's victory.'[27]

John Hunter Coghlan entered the world on 7 September 1914 in Shanghai, with rather more fanfare than that with which he slipped out of the world too few years later. He came back with his family on the *Empress of Britain* to Southampton in September 1932 to live in Southsea, and was enrolled at the Imperial Service College at Windsor. This committed public servant sat an examination for the Indian Police Service in 1934, but joined the RAF only two years later. He served initially with Nos 1 and 72 Squadrons, but, by the time war was declared, he was flying Hurricanes for No. 56 Squadron. This was one of a handful of fighter squadrons that were not deployed to France, but nonetheless operated over the Channel from their English bases. Short, square-jawed and broad-shouldered, serious and with a proper RAF moustache, by the time of the Battle of Britain in 1940, Coghlan had been promoted to lead 'A' Flight, gaining the Distinguished Flying Cross (DFC) after six victories.

Whilst the Battle of Britain still raged, at short notice on 7 August 1940 he was posted to the somewhat secretive Parachute Training Unit (PTU) at Manchester Ringway. With only half an hour's flying time on the Lysander, which he would have found very cumbersome after having had a Hurricane strapped to his backside, he was given an unenviable mission – to become the first pilot to attempt to deliver a secret agent from the UK into Occupied Europe in World War II.

On 17 August, Coghlan flew down to RAF North Weald, Essex, in Lysander R2625. The Parachute Training Unit (or Parachute Training Centre in some accounts) had, as its title suggests, no operational function. It is quite possible that Coghlan had been appointed as first pilot, and therefore commanding officer (at the time being an acting flight lieutenant) of 419 Flight – the first dedicated special operations unit, as the aircraft is recorded as having been allocated to 419 on 10 August. The Lysander had been cursorily prepared for night operations and agent transport by having its rear machine gun removed.

The following night, he collected the SIS agent Henri Leenaerts. This Belgian had squeezed a fair amount into his 37 years: he had carried out his compulsory military service in the Belgian Air Force in his younger days before developing a career as an insurance salesman. After the invasion of Belgium, he had managed to escape to Great Britain and been snapped up by SIS. Having been trained as a wireless operator, his orders were to take a set to Momignies, south of Mons, hard by the French border, and make contact with an embryonic network set up by another Belgian *émigré*, Anatole Gobeaux.

The pair landed at RAF Manston in Kent to top up the Lysander's tanks. It is not known whether any reception committee had been set up in Belgium to greet Coghlan and Leenaerts. In any event, Coghlan, who had had precious little experience in night flying, failed to find the intended landing ground, and set course back for Britain with his passenger. Possibly he was shot down by a flak battery on the Belgian coast; perhaps he had an engine failure or ran out of fuel over the sea (he would have had little idea of how to extract maximum economy from the Lysander's engine). Coghlan's body washed up more than a month later on the beach at the pretty seaside resort of Wimereux, south of Calais. Leenaerts' body was never found. So, the first Lysander Special Duties operation of the war ended in failure and death.[28]

With the benefit of a few months' more experience of Special Duties operations, it was obvious that it was militarily insane to send Coghlan on such a mission with such little experience of flying the Lysander, and with none at all of night-time operations. Although he was later described by Hugh Trevor-Roper as 'an utter shit, corrupt, incompetent, but with a certain low cunning',[29] Claude Dansey (head of SIS's Z Organisation) noted frankly two years later, 'We were inexperienced, we were groping in the dark, and the first essay was a failure.'[30]

The Battle of France had demonstrated that the Lysander could only be safely flown in theatres where the Allies had air supremacy – or at night. Coghlan's fate had underlined that Special Duties operations required experienced pilots with extensive and specialist training.

4

Finding Their Feet

The winter of 1939/40 was harsh – many days even seagulls thought twice before taking to the air, but the needs of war meant that the tempo of both operational and training sorties had to increase. At this stage, the standards of the RAF's flying training left something to be desired, and the failings would not be remedied until a few months later when Keith Park wrought some much-needed changes after he had retired from managing Fighter Command in the Battle of Britain. Young Lysander pilots in training, and in their first operational tour, continued to be caught out by the weather, and the resulting forced landings usually caused serious damage – to the airframe, if not the pilot. However, in some cases, the Lysander was proving quite robust: if the aircraft overturned (greasy grass or ploughed earth in the chosen forced landing field being typical causes), the pilot usually escaped with little injury.

But another feature of Petter's design now proved to be a weak point – the tailwheel assembly. For the role of an Army Co-operation aircraft, all elements of the undercarriage needed to be robust in order to cope with the day-to-day task of landing in unprepared fields to visit troops. The main undercarriage was indeed quite strong, but showed itself to be susceptible to breaking if a swing developed on landing, perhaps as a result of a tyre burst. The tailwheel, or its suspension oleo, broke depressingly often; ground crews became very adept at replacing them.[1]

Further, the Lysander was relatively short coupled – its tail feathers were quite close to the wings; this was one of several factors making it not the easiest aircraft to handle. On 9 March 1940, P/O Adamson was flying out of Lille-Rouchin for IV Squadron; on his return, he carried on side-slipping too close to the ground – with fatal results. A month later, his colleague F/O Clarke, who should not have been on operations with only 108 flying hours to his name, had been posted to the squadron's base at Mons-en-Chaussée. On his return, he levelled off too high (at 30 feet) and stalled. The 25-year-old was barely injured, and soon returned to operations. However, on 14 May, he took off from Monchy-Lagache on a reconnaissance mission over Belgium; an hour later, he was caught by a Messerschmitt Bf 109 between Brussels and Liège. He and his gunner, LAC Rodulson, fell to earth.[2]

Back at Mathams Wood, now re-christened RAF Sawbridgeworth, Geddes' II Squadron had its share of accidents. In July, Flt Lt Ayres arrived in dramatic fashion after a training flight: the accident report noted that his aircraft 'dropped suddenly in an air pocket near [Mathams] wood'. He had a heavy landing on the tail. Geddes considered it 'poor airmanship', but ordered that an appropriate gap be cut in the wood to avoid a repetition. With 650 flying hours, Ayres would have been expected to cope with the odd air pocket. Several accidents at Sawbridgeworth make reference to the airfield's poor surface, but the worst Lysander field in this respect was clearly Hooton Park on the Wirral. A succession of Lysander tailwheels was claimed by this rough field – before it gained hard runways. The most serial offender was P/O Jack True, who broke two tailwheels in August, and capped his summer with a crash in a forced landing at Bangor, which was attributed to his own errors.

Netherthorpe near Sheffield was the home of No. 613 Squadron and its Lysanders. The problem with this Yorkshire aerodrome was its small size – in July, P/O Tudge was lucky to escape with his life after overshooting and hitting the roof of a bungalow. Only two months later he was judged culpable in creating an engine failure which led to a forced landing near Scampton, which he also mishandled.[3]

It had fallen to Geddes to create an aviation ecosystem for Britain's Special Operations. Though it was sparsely documented (failing to make it into II Squadron's Operations Record Book (ORB)), he probably carried out the second Special Duties Lysander mission of the war. On 3 September, he left Sawbridgeworth for RAF Newmarket, and that evening took an agent to a field near Tours. His logbook merely notes the 3.5-hour flight as a 'Long range air test, nothing of interest to report', fibbing 'Passenger – none', so the agent's name remains a mystery. Given its notorious secrecy, the flight is likely to have been on behalf of SIS.[4] Geddes had become the main advocate for the Lysander as being the tool of choice for agent deliveries and pick-ups.

FINDING THEIR FEET

419 FLIGHT AND THE WHITLEY

After Coghlan's operation in the shadows, the first dedicated Special Duties unit, 419 Flight, was formed at North Weald on 21 August 1940 under 11 Group of Bomber Command; its commanding officer was Flt Lt Walter Farley. Known as Wally, he had joined the Air Force at the end of 1930, aged 21, on a short service commission. On finishing his flying training, he entered the world of Army Co-operation flying. After some instructing, he went onto the reserve list in late 1938 but was recalled to arms the day war was declared.

North Weald proved an unsuitable location: this was essentially a fighter station and hence frequently attracted the attention of Luftwaffe bombers during the Battle of Britain. After two attacks within a week, 419 was relocated to Stapleford Tawney, a few miles to the west. Here the small number of aircrew and ground crew lived in bell tents. Another Whitley was procured. But living under canvas did nothing for morale when, in its turn, Stapleford received attention from Heinkel 111s. The RAF men relocated to farm buildings nearby.[5] 419's initial equipment was a brand new Armstrong Whitworth Whitley bomber (P5029) and a couple of Lysanders. A Rolls Royce staff car, manned by a Women's Auxiliary Air Force (WAAF) staff driver, was procured.

From the outset, the Special Duties units were set up to provide a full package to their customers – both the delivery and collection of agents. Clearly, the Lysander was inappropriate for dropping humans by parachute (it could only deliver a small amount of stores from its stub wings in that way), and could deliver a maximum of three agents by landing in a field.[6] For parachute delivery, the RAF chose the Whitley. Being dropped from this was 'like sitting blindfold on top of a sixty foot well, and pushing yourself through the hole'.[7] The Whitley crews christened their victims 'Joes', after the service slang 'Joe Soap' – someone who was lumbered with a rotten task; this came to be the standard term for agents delivered by parachute or Lysander.

This twin-engined aircraft needed a five-man crew, and was of the same vintage as the Westland product, its first flight being in 1936. It was, however, only used for bombing missions for the first year of the war; after its shortcomings were recognized, it was relegated to dropping leaflets, agents, and other secondary duties.[8]

In his Lysander, Farley with Philip Schneidau (a Franco-British citizen who had served in the RAF, and now a putative agent) carried out a number of trial pick-ups at North Weald and Stapleford aerodromes both by day and by night, and finally carried out some half dozen 'off the record' trials in fields in the Newmarket area. On one occasion, at night, on returning to North Weald, the aircraft was compelled to circle for nearly an hour owing to the enemy bombing the aerodrome.[9]

Farley hired the very experienced Flt Lt Jack Oettle, 'a wonderful character', who always flew in his greatcoat. He did a handful of missions to Holland in the Whitley in the first few weeks. Keen not to miss out on the thrills of the embers of the Battle of Britain, during leave periods Farley could not resist joining a fighter squadron (No. 46 Squadron) to fly its Hurricanes. But whilst Farley enjoyed his co-location with fighter units, 419 Flight was operating bombers and under the control of Bomber Command's 11 Group, so it needed a permanent home on a base operated by that Command.

This marked the start of an unhappy relationship: Arthur Harris, Deputy Chief of the Air Staff (DCAS), treated 419 and its descendants as unwanted offspring. He did not like the 'distraction' of 419 lodging at a main bombing station, and proved very reluctant to furnish it with resources, be it men or matériel. Robin Brook, a banker, was one of Dalton's early recruits to SOE with 'a lively intelligence, a clear mind and a calm humour'.[10] He later noted, 'Harris would hold on to his aircraft at all costs, including ignoring instructions from Churchill. He looked on us as an intrusive nuisance. Competition between SOE and SIS was nothing in comparison with competition with the RAF.'[11] Even RAF official historians noted the flaws in Harris' character – he 'made a habit of only seeing one side of a question and then exaggerating it. He had a tendency to confuse advice with interference, criticism with sabotage and evidence with propaganda... he was seldom open to persuasion.'[12]

After Farley's choice of Bassingbourn was discarded, 419 was despatched to Stradishall in north-west Suffolk, and received its third Whitley on 9 October.[13] Farley had by now recruited a third pilot, Flt Lt Francis Keast, who had flown with No. 24 Communications Squadron at Hendon during the Battle of France. This was the only RAF unit whose pilots were allowed to fly in any weather, at any time. Its pilots therefore developed a degree of self-sufficiency that prepared them well for Special Duties operations – the unit was to prove a useful source of talent for more recruits. Having been with civil airlines before the war, Keast was vastly experienced with more than 3,500 hours; he was destined to fly only Whitleys, not Lysanders.

In September 1940, 419 was tasked with delivering an SIS agent to northern France. Oettle was to captain the Whitley, with Farley acting as second pilot. The duo made several attempts in the September moon period (a moon period was generally the six days either side of the full moon), but were thwarted by the weather at every turn. They tried again on the first date in the October moon period, the 9th, and again had to return to RAF Tangmere in Sussex after a frustrating seven-hour flight. The following day, they finally succeeded, although the agent, Philip Schneidau, had a fairly bumpy landing with his early model unsteerable parachute.[14]

The short, square-jawed Schneidau was born in France to wealthy British parents; he was educated at a British public school, but opted to play hockey for France before the war. He chose British nationality at the age of 21, and married Simone, a French woman, and they soon had a son, Peter. Trained as an accountant, earlier in 1940 Philip started acting as interpreter and driver for the AOC British Air Forces in France, Air Marshal 'Ugly' Barratt, having been given the rank of sergeant. There he also met Sidney Cotton, the civilian pilot who had pioneered spy missions in a Lockheed Electra over Germany before the war.

Schneidau was recruited for SIS by the academic J.C. Masterman on the hockey pitch,[15] and made pilot officer in the RAF. Originally, he was due to be flown back to France by Ugly Barratt's personal pilot in a de Havilland 89B. This was vetoed by the RAF, so after four failed attempts he was finally dropped from a Whitley.

After gathering up his parachute, he trudged to the nearby house of Simone's father, Paul Schiffmacher, who was christened Agent *Napoléon*, or *Félix*, and was to provide financial assistance in establishing his resistance network.[16] This trip was planned to be a short visit to France, at the end of which he would be picked up by Lysander.

Before Schneidau's outward journey, Farley and Schneidau had dined together at Oddenino's Restaurant ('Ye Olde Cambrinus Brasserie') next to the Café Royal in London's Regent Street. They had debated the thorny problem of how to guide Farley for Schneidau's pick-up and return into the right part of the chosen field, and indeed how to select an into-wind landing run. On the tablecloth, they sketched out an L-shape comprising three torches, held aloft by the agent's Resistance colleagues, with the pilot landing in the direction of the base of the letter (Lamp 'B'). The plan was to taxi round Lamp 'C' at the base and back to the top of the 'L' (Lamp 'A') positioned for a take-off (see Appendix F), before loading the passenger(s).[17] Such details for the return had to be agreed in advance, for at this stage of the war there was no radio communication with agents once in the field. Farley and Schneidau tested their procedures by both day and night at North Weald and Stapleford aerodromes.

When 419 relocated from Stapleford to Stradishall, its ownership switched to 3 Group of Bomber Command. 'The question of its operational control was the subject of much discussion.'[18] The physical relocation of three Lysanders and two Whitleys proved eventful. On 11 October, Farley took one Whitley (P5025) to Abingdon for some maintenance, with a P/O Greenhill as a second pilot. Towards the end of that sunny day he returned to Stapleford, where he handed over control of the Whitley to Greenhill to take it to the new base at Stradishall. With Sergeants (Sgts) Bernard and Davies aboard, Greenhill flew down the approach in the manner of a Lysander, and overshot, stalling the aircraft, with the tail striking the ground. In the resulting 'spectacular' crash on the edge of the airfield, smacking into a tree, Bernard in the rear turret, which snapped off, was injured (carrying a scar on his face for the rest of his life). Davies had a lucky escape; but both he and Bernard were sent on operations the following night. It turned out that Greenhill was a Lysander pilot, and not qualified to fly the Whitley. A black mark for Farley, and it was little surprise that Greenhill was posted off 419 within a few days.[19]

Meanwhile, an extraordinary secret mission was being mounted. In May 1940, nine ungainly Fokker T VIII floatplanes of the Dutch Naval Air Service had been spirited to the UK ahead of the advancing Wehrmacht, and formed the new No. 320 Squadron at Pembroke Dock in Wales. In October, one Fokker was flown down to Felixstowe on the Suffolk coast, and on 15 October it was despatched to pick up four Dutch secret agents from the Tjoukemeer in Friesland. However, the pilot, Lt Heije Schaper, was thwarted by fog at his destination. The crew repeated the attempt the following night, but the agents had been betrayed and a horde of Germans was waiting for the Fokker – as it taxied to the shore it was met by a boat. Once it was coned by a searchlight, a heavy machine gun opened up at it. Schaper turned tail and took off, with his rear gunner doing his best to return fire. On returning to East Anglia, the hapless crew was then fired upon by the Home Guard. Despite this, they made a safe landing and the three airmen received Dutch gallantry awards.[20]

If one discounts Coghlan's overlooked mission, and Geddes' very clandestine trip, the first official pick-up operation for 419 Flight was to collect Schneidau, and was carried out by Flt Lt Farley on 19 October. Since at this time SIS had neither wireless sets nor operators on the ground,

Schneidau had had to take a basket of pigeons to France as his only means of communicating with his masters at SIS in London. Surprisingly, the birds behaved and flew back to their home at the appropriately named Wing House, opposite St James's church in Piccadilly. SIS HQ received Schneidau's request for a pick-up a little more than 12 hours after he had released the birds.

Farley flew down to RAF Tangmere, its position on the Sussex coast shortening the flight-time. Thwarted initially by heavy rain, Farley in the end pressured the station commander into letting him go. He landed at around 0115hrs in a field at Montigny-sur-Loing, near Fontainebleau, and only 41 miles south-south-east of the Arc de Triomphe. The rear canopy on Farley's Lysander had been removed, and a short ladder fitted by the Fairfield Aviation Company to ease Schneidau's entry. The disadvantage of this arrangement was that Farley's radio set, located behind his own seat, became thoroughly soaked, and therefore useless. The landing was without drama, and the L torch layout worked perfectly (this technique was to remain in use by the Special Duties units for the rest of the war). However, after take-off, a German rifle bullet passed between Farley's legs and destroyed his P6 compass – possibly a lucky shot from the sentry outside the residence of the CO of the nearby German garrison. For the first half hour or so, he could map-read by moonlight, but the weather worsened, and Farley was forced to climb through cloud, levelling out at 16,000 feet. A sodden Schneidau was bitterly cold in the open rear cockpit. The heavy rain had been brought in by south-westerly gales, and Farley was worried he might drift towards Belgium and even Germany; he could not call Tangmere for a radio fix to locate his position. His fuel gauges had been reading empty for half an hour when Schneidau finally sighted some cliffs at 0650hrs. They could have been Ireland or possibly Scandinavia; Farley thought it might be north Germany. Schneidau disabused him of this notion, since he had read Erskine Childers' classic *Riddle of the Sands*, and knew that all German coasts were sandy! Farley had no option but to glide into the nearest field. Late on the approach, he spotted anti-invasion stakes and shouted to Schneidau to lie down to avoid decapitation if the aircraft hit one. That did not happen, and they slithered to a halt.

Farley, bizarrely, told his passenger to take off his civil disguise as they might be in enemy territory, so Schneidau stuffed all his clothes into a backpack (together with two bottles of brandy) and leaped out of the shattered Lysander, very concerned it was about to catch fire. Farley knew better: 'If there's one thing this won't do, it's catch fire. There's no fucking petrol!' He left the shivering near-naked Frenchman by the wrecked Lysander to find help – or ascertain the disposition of the enemy.

Farley returned ten minutes later in front of two burly local rifle-carrying policemen. Communication was strained as Farley, not to mention Schneidau, struggled with the coppers' thick accents – from which they deduced they were in Scotland. The Home Guard showed up too. It turned out they had landed near Oban on Scotland's west coast. The exhausted pair was escorted under arrest to the nearby RAF station. Here their clandestine mission training caused more than a little difficulty: Farley revealed no more than his rank and number, whilst the SIS man would not even give his name. This was too much, or rather too little, for their interlocutor. Only once Farley's overdue Lysander's serial number had been matched with that of the crash at Oban were they released. They eventually returned to Stradishall a day later.[21]

In the three-week period to early November, three Lysander pilots were killed in separate accidents – in each case they had set the elevator trim incorrectly for take-off, sending them into an ever-slowing climb from which there was no recovery. Word had yet to spread sufficiently well of Petter's trap.[22]

Having left Keast in charge of 419, on 8 November Wally Farley was visiting North Weald when an air raid developed. In a reflex action, he jumped into a Hurricane and gave chase to the Luftwaffe. Within minutes, his Hurricane was engaged in combat by a Messerschmitt Bf 109, and he had to bail out. Sadly for his day job, he broke a leg on landing; he was in plaster and off flying for many weeks. 419 now urgently needed a replacement pilot.[23]

In the last week of November, F/O Ron Hockey was posted to 419, again from 24 Squadron at Hendon, but was immediately sent to the sick bay suffering from exhaustion.[24] He noted that all the unit's five pilots (including himself) were 'very experienced for that era. Most had done much flying pre-war: 1,500 hours was the minimum requirement'.[25] On his arrival, Farley had briefed him that after doing a few Whitley trips he would 'probably get the opportunity of a few Lysander trips as a rest!'[26] In Farley's view 'SOE had not developed as a major client', SIS was the major user and overall the tempo of pick-up operations would be modest. But Hockey would not emerge from hospital until the following March.

Geddes at II Squadron had been told to find a small group of above average pilots, who were then instructed to practise take-offs and landings from confined spaces, without ever being told why. He selected F/Os Robinson and Gordon Scotter, and Flt Lts Chapman and A.E. Housman. (Presumably Housman was a relative of the noted poet since he shared the same initials.) Robinson was not an obvious choice, having had his moments with II Squadron – on 4 July, he had got lost during night training, and overshot into a hedge in the ensuing forced landing.[27] Geddes started training this brood on 8 January, introducing them to the 'L' shaped torch-lit flarepath, and making them land in progressively shorter distances.

Francis Keast, by now a squadron leader, flew his first Whitley mission as captain to France on 13 February. The following night, he transported three Polish agents to their home turf – a gruelling 11-hour trip facilitated only by the fitment of extra fuel tanks. It provided a great morale boost to Polish forces, and quietened Whitehall naysayers. 419 Flight was very short staffed so Keast was called to the flight line for the third successive night to drop an SIS agent into Belgium. Having performed that task, he was unlucky to lose an engine to flak whilst still over Belgium. The other engine failed under the extra load, and the six-man crew glided into the hands of the Germans.

This left 419 in dire straits: the CO was a prisoner of war, Farley was in plaster and Hockey was in hospital. The saviour was the rather eccentric, gifted and ultimately doomed Sqn Ldr Edward 'Teddy' Knowles, who took over command at the end of February. Not, and never to become, a Lysander pilot, he was joined by John Nesbitt-Dufort, who was. Knowles had been to see Gunner Geddes the day before New Year's Eve, to pick his ample brains about agent delivery flights. By February, he told Geddes he needed some trained pilots and F/O Scotter had proved himself the pick of the quartet.

Whilst enduring his basic training at RAF Uxbridge, the 18-year-old P/O John Nesbitt-Dufort had cast covetous glances at a Brough Superior motor bike owned (and 'ridden expertly') by a serious-faced fair-haired leading aircraftman, who was to go on a few months later to ferry Nesbitt-Dufort to his beautiful Southampton flying boat in the Solent. It was of course LAC T.E. Shaw, better known as Lawrence of Arabia.[28]

Like most that flew the Hawker Fury, after 116 hours in the less sprightly Siskin, Nesbitt-Dufort revelled in the former's performance, not to mention its aesthetic lines. It was during an air combat exercise with the Harts of No. 33 Squadron that he nearly met his maker. He and a colleague converged on the same target, and his chum's undercarriage came close to removing Nesbitt-Dufort's helmeted head. In his haste to remove himself from the scene, he caused the whole squadron attack to disperse. At the rather one-sided debriefing, his CO, Sqn Ldr Walter Bryant, barked, 'And where the bloody hell did you think you were anyway? Whipsnade Zoo?' He was immediately christened 'Whippy' – the nickname stuck.

On another occasion, young Whippy did receive a whiplash injury – after an engine failure taking off in his Fury at Hawkinge he crashed into a tree, the accident giving him substantial neck pain for a while. His mechanics turned part of the damaged aircraft into a cribbage board for him.[29]

Nesbitt-Dufort had already done a tour in Fighter Command before war was declared, which found him instructing on the Harvard in various Flying Training Schools including Brize Norton, before being sent to Gwelo in Rhodesia. Like many in such a backwater, he was itching to move to an operational role.

In early 1941, he was transferred to No. 23(F) Squadron at Ford in Sussex, operating the underwhelming Blenheim NF1 in the night-fighter role. By mid-summer, he was promoted to command the squadron at the time it was being re-equipped with Douglas Havocs. He had a major altercation with his ultimate boss – the AOC of 11 Group, AVM Trafford Leigh-Mallory – regarding the deployment of the new machines.[30] The Havocs had had extra equipment fitted for the night-fighting role and the compasses had not been properly re-calibrated afterwards. In consequence, the poor pilots were getting lost 'all over the place'.[31] Although backed up by his men, Nesbitt-Dufort was relieved of command peremptorily by Leigh-Mallory: 'If you don't like this sort of stuff, I will find you something more dangerous.'[32] Whippy was understandably upset – and at a very loose end.

As was to become the pattern for the Lysander Boys, Nesbitt-Dufort was soon head-hunted to join this very select gang. Wally Farley had known Nesbitt-Dufort from his time at II (AC) Squadron at Manston (when the latter had been piloting Hurricanes at nearby Hawkinge). Farley summoned him by phone to a meeting at the Air Ministry without divulging what he had in mind.

Still hobbling about in plaster with the aid of a stick after his careless parachute descent, Farley started his grilling. Having ascertained that Whippy had flown the Lysander and had plenty of night-flying hours without getting unduly lost over northern France, and had signed the Official Secrets Act, Whippy progressively revealed the role in the Special Duties unit. Farley was probably unaware that Whippy had the added advantage for this role of speaking fluent French due to his father (who had joined the French Army in 1914, and died soon after). Whippy's mother had also died during World War I, so he was brought up by his grandparents, aunts and uncles, who had all nurtured his French heritage.

Still smarting at his treatment at the hands of Leigh-Mallory, once appraised of the dangers, Whippy jumped at the chance – 'When do I start?'[33] The answer was early May. Gunner Geddes flew from Martlesham in a Tiger Moth to pick up Nesbitt-Dufort and take him to his new home. He was welcomed to the Flight at Stradishall by a rather taciturn Teddy Knowles, who at the time had only one Lysander to entrust to Whippy. So rather than risk his sole prized operational asset (apart from his three Whitleys), he sent Whippy across to Sawbridgeworth to perfect his handling on the II Squadron machines, under the supervision of Geddes. Nesbitt-Dufort careened around Essex until he (along with Geddes) was satisfied that he had mastered the type's STOL characteristics, claiming to become airborne 'in under 36 yards in anything but a dead calm'.[34] Geddes considered him 'an exceptional pilot' – Nesbitt-Dufort was now fit to fly to his ancestral lands with clandestine cargo.

5

Racing Ahead: Newmarket Takes on Military Garb

I cannot divert aircraft from a certainty to a gamble.
Air Chief Marshal Sir Charles Portal[1]

The War Cabinet, which naturally included Air Chief Marshal Sir Charles Portal as Chief of the Air Staff (CAS), met on 3 February 1941. The second item on their agenda that morning was Operation *Savannah* (also referred to as *Savanna*). 'The point was raised whether the RAF should be used to transport men in civilian clothes, who were destined to carry out operations which were not covered by the rules of warfare. The Committee affirmed the general principle that the services could not be formally associated with highly irregular forms of warfare unless the men concerned were dressed in uniform. Whenever cases of this nature arose the Service Departments would refer them to their respective Chief of Staff.'[2] With the usually urgent requirements of irregular warfare, this was effectively stymying at source any aerial support to SOE.

Gladwyn Jebb, as CEO of SOE, had already broached this project to Portal, whose response was both immediate and withering: 'I think the dropping of men dressed in civilian clothes for the purposes of attempting to kill members of the opposing forces is not an operation with which the Royal Air Force should be associated. I think you will agree that there is a vast difference in ethics between the time-honoured operation of dropping a spy from the air and this entirely new scheme for dropping what one can only call assassins.'[3] As remembered by Harry Sporborg after the war, Portal went on to make the claim, 'My bombing offensive is not a gamble.

Its dividend is certain; it is a gilt-edged investment. I cannot divert aircraft from a certainty to a gamble which may prove a gold-mine or may be completely worthless.'[4]

Savanna(h) was a project to drop five Free French parachutists into Brittany to ambush the Luftwaffe aircrews of Kampfgeschwader 100 on their way to work at Meucon airfield. It never happened. But the RAF's desire to spurn transporting irregulars did not, as they say, survive first contact with the enemy. To ease the sensitivities of the senior echelons of the RAF (there is no evidence that pilots and ground crew had such scruples), the Air Intelligence Directorate set up a new unit called AI2(c), which handled requests for Special Duties missions.[5]

Dalton was justly not prepared to be bulldozed by Portal or the combined Chiefs of Staff. He had a conversation with Churchill at the beginning of March, and on the 6th sent the Prime Minister a letter underlining his stance. Churchill knew Portal quite well, not least because they were fellow members of Churchill's beloved The Other Club. By contrast, Churchill's active dislike of Dalton possibly caused the Prime Minister to take a less close interest in SOE than he might otherwise have done. Yet Menzies, as head of SIS, was a much more frequent visitor to No. 10.[6] Portal's attitude was to prove contagious. John Beevor, assistant to Sir Charles Hambro at SOE, 1942–43, later recalled, 'Our most serious opponent was the Chief of the Air Staff, Sir Charles Portal. The Air Marshal naturally opposed attempts by any other service or organisation to put forward competing requirements for bombers. His attitude was naturally reflected in all senior officers with whom we had to deal.'[7]

After Jebb's prodding, Harris, as Commander-in-Chief Bomber Command, was softening just a touch, and Jebb thought there would now be a modest increase in resources for his 'Special Flight'.[8] To the existing establishment of three Whitleys, one Glenn Martin, and three Lysanders was to be added a pair of Harrow bombers (for the exclusive use of SOE). Dalton and Jebb appear not to have realized that SOE was only being offered these because, as antediluvian beasts, Bomber Command had no further use for them.[9] SIS was still to have first call on this very limited number of Lysanders.

Charles Medhurst was the RAF's Director of Plans, and hence at the sharp end of assessing how to resource SOE's and SIS's needs. In a memo to his boss, Air Chief Marshal (ACM) Sir Wilfrid Freeman (Vice Chief of the Air Staff, or VCAS), he recognized that whilst its aims were laudable and potentially war-influencing, the still-nascent SOE was trying to do too much with too little. He advocated more resource, but his focus was on dropping men and stores from Whitleys, and not on pick-up operations.[10]

But a few months later, Dalton was to feel badly let down by SOE's progenitor; during the debate about the place of SOE in British strategy, he had received 'not a word, either orally or in writing, from the Prime Minister'.[11] Churchill was innately empathetic to the RAF, three years later describing it as 'the cavalry of modern war'.[12] However, he had an implicit faith in what was to become the keystone of Portal's and Harris' strategy, in July 1940 assessing that Hitler could only be brought down by 'an absolutely devastating, exterminating attack by very heavy bombers from this country on the Nazi homeland'.[13]

THE GENESIS OF NO. 138 SQUADRON

Teddy Knowles' arrival at the newly formed 138 Squadron in February 1941 to replace the lame Farley was a straight swap: Knowles had been assisting Gp Capt John Bradbury DFC in AI2(c), which had operational control of 419 Flight. (Bradbury held the role of Deputy Director of Intelligence (2), or DDI 2.) Farley limped to Whitehall in Knowles' stead on 1 April. Philip Schneidau had been training with Farley in the selection of landing grounds and flarepath layouts; Farley's departure meant this role was now taken by a F/O Baker, a Kiwi who had been recruited from No. 1 Squadron. However, he was soon shot down over northern Europe when sent on a Whitley mission to improve his navigational skills.[14]

One of Knowles' first moves was to hire F/O Stanley 'Granny' Baker (another Baker), but before he could join from No. 66 Squadron, he was lost over Europe in his Spitfire on 11 February. Flt Lt Gordon Scotter was Knowles' second choice, and came from that natural recruiting ground for special operations Lysander pilots – Geddes' II Squadron, which he had joined in January 1939. Scotter, a 21-one year-old Cumbrian, had endured the Battle of France with the squadron, and in May 1940 had been chased by 15 Messerschmitt Bf 109s whilst doing a tactical reconnaissance mission near Boulogne. Diving to sea level, he managed to flee back across the Channel, his salvation being that the Germans were reluctant to fly more than four miles out to sea that day. On landing at Hawkinge, his Lysander was found to have been comprehensively riddled with bullet holes.

Scotter was to become one of the longer-standing members of 419 and its successor Special Duties units. At the same time, F/O Jackson and F/O A.E. Housman arrived. During his period of tutelage under Geddes, the strapping Housman had crashed a Lysander at Sawbridgeworth on 21 February, when he had hit the ground before rounding out.[15]

419 was re-christened 1419 Flight at the beginning of March. The reason for this new name was that the burgeoning Royal Canadian Air Force was being given squadron numbers starting with 400, and 3 Group did not want to risk confusion. 1419 Flight was destined to last for less than six months.

At SOE, Gubbins was by now in no doubt that he was the poor relation in terms of securing the services of 1419. He drafted a minute lamenting the state of affairs: 'C' had sequestered at short notice a Whitley which had been earmarked for an SOE mission to Czechoslovakia (Operation *Benjamin*).[16] The crew failed to return from this SIS trip, which was doubly unfortunate as this was the only Whitley modified for team jumping. 1419 had another Whitley stranded in the Orkneys, awaiting a new tail; whilst one long-range Whitley was available at Stradishall, it lacked a crew to man it. Knowles could see that existing resources would not be adequate for the 16 missions scheduled for the next moon period.

This prompted Jebb to visit Major General Hastings 'Pug' Ismay the following day 'in some distress', and to set down his worries in a letter. He was saddened by the sloth of the Vice Chiefs of Staff to devote more resources to SOE, which they had lumped into 'intelligence requirements'.[17] Pug was military secretary to the War Cabinet, and chief staff officer to the Minister of Defence, and sat on the Chiefs of Staff Committee – he was therefore a keystone in many politico-military bridges. He was a soothing balm on some of Churchill's occasionally fractious relationships with his leaders. In his own words, Churchill 'needs someone to use as a whipping boy on whom to blow off steam', and admitted that was his own chief function.[18] A perspicacious military mind, he had noted 'the quality and morale of the French army to be lower than was generally supposed well before their capitulation in 1940'.[19]

Jebb pointed out that SOE was increasingly in a position to conduct subversive and aggressive activity, leaving intelligence gathering to SIS. Piecemeal allocation of resources would diminish SOE's ability to achieve Churchill's objectives: 'It is rather as if SOE were in the position of a young man whose father will not give him a definite allowance but insists on feeding him with occasional £5 notes. It is surely far better to make provision for the young man and to set him up, if only in a modest way, on his own.' He considered that current resources would only be sufficient to carry out a paltry three of the 16 sorties planned for the next month. He

RACING AHEAD: NEWMARKET TAKES ON MILITARY GARB

sought an upgrade to squadron status immediately. Ismay sympathized with Jebb's thinking, if not with the verbiage of his letter, and prodded Portal to respond. The hot potato was passed to the ever-sensible VCAS Freeman who ordered Air Commodore Lionel Payne, a 49-year-old veteran of World War I (who was about to start a new role as Director of Intelligence (Operations)), to visit 1419 at its Stradishall base, and then to discuss solutions with Jebb.

Meanwhile, Sawbridgeworth's W/Cdr Geddes was summoned to London to be invested with his OBE at Buckingham Palace on 15 March, awarded in the New Year's Honours list. Citations for awards to Special Duties pilots were destined to gloss over the meat of their (secret) achievements, but this was particularly cryptic – 'For services to aviation'. The pilots of II Squadron took advantage of the boss's absence to celebrate his 'gong' (medal) by going on a shoot. Whilst the odd rabbit and pigeon might have found its way to the officers' mess afterwards, this was at some cost – Flt Lt George Kenning, a flight commander, managed to shoot himself in the foot.[20]

Scotter's experience meant he did not need a prolonged training period before he could fly 1419's Lysanders on operations. He and his fellow trainees had by now been told the exact purpose of the unit, and who their clients would be. However, everyone else in II Squadron, including the ground crew, was kept in the dark. On 11 April, he was sent from Tangmere in Lysander V9287, which now had an underslung long-range fuel tank fitted, and a primitive ladder for the rear cockpit. He had to pick up a Lt Cartwright (clearly a *nom de guerre* of an SIS agent) from a field north of Châteauroux. He evaded German night-fighters on the outward journey, became temporarily lost when he mistook the shadows of clouds for woods, and landed on the very rough field without further incident. He loaded Cartwright as quickly as possible, and when climbing away, he noticed his take-off had been timely, as a car's headlights were nearing the field. Scotter's return across the Channel was uneventful, but on his arrival overhead Tangmere, he found the place in darkness due to an air raid alert. He stooged around until boredom took the better of him, and he landed uneventfully in comparative gloom.[21]

The weather in London on the morning of 10 May was 'spectacularly fine', but Douglas Dodds-Parker noted 'the spectacle of devastation, after eight months of bombing which was to culminate that night, was surpassed by the spirit of resistance'.[22] That night, Scotter contributed to keeping the spirit of French resistance alive – he flew to a field near Châteauroux to bring Philip Schneidau back to England.

Scotter's trailblazing sorties were recognized with the award of a DFC on 21 May. This was presented at a special dinner in the splendid if haunted surroundings of the Tudor-era Great Hyde Hall, which served as Sawbridgeworth's station headquarters and officers' mess.[23] Field Marshal Sir Alan Brooke (later Lord Alanbrooke) was guest of honour. The Chief of the Imperial General Staff had come to visit the station to learn more about how Special Duties pilots were being trained.[24]

Meanwhile, the success of these missions using a locally modified machine encouraged the Air Ministry to place an order with Westland for modifying a few Mk III Lysanders with a 150-gallon long-range tank and a ladder for the rear cockpit. The former extended the range from about 600 miles to more than 1,000, its endurance rising to a bladder-bursting eight hours. This necessitated an increase in the size of the oil tank. Other changes included a smaller radio, and extensive alterations to the rear cockpit providing a two-man rearward facing bench seat with a locker underneath, and a shelf at the back that could be used as an additional seat if required. Most importantly from the pilot's viewpoint, the variable pitch propeller was replaced by a constant speed one – which would reduce the workload in the hectic landing phase – and the Mercury engine was beefed up to 890hp with the Mk XII version. Some 40 Lysanders were eventually thus converted to so-called Mk III SCW ('Special Contract Westland'). The initial colour scheme was matt black overall, but after some experience the pilots changed this to dull camouflage.

On 22 May Knowles led his Lysanders, Whitleys and men to 1419's new residence at Newmarket, the home of British horse-racing. The vast green expanse of the blasted heath racecourse (in fact two racecourses – the Rowley Mile and the July) invited wartime use as an airfield. Temporary use had started in November 1917, but No. 190 Squadron, a night-training unit, was the first squadron to be based there in March 1918, soon joined by No. 192 Squadron. Two decades later, its endless acres of flat grassland were ideally suited for overloaded Whitleys with questionable performance.

As war had looked increasingly likely in 1939, the War Office was primed to retake control of a large tract of land there under the aegis of RAF Mildenhall up the road. Wellingtons of No. 99 Squadron arrived the day before war was declared. The RAF had forgotten to warn the Jockey Club – the owners of this historic real estate – that they were coming. The Clerk of the Course walked over waving his stick in anger at the new arrivals.

RACING AHEAD: NEWMARKET TAKES ON MILITARY GARB

This was indeed a strange place for the young 1419 to put down roots. Conditions for the unlucky RAF men left something to be desired. Beds were set up for airmen in the grandstand (albeit covered), and the Long Bar. Washing facilities were a single cold-water tap. Being a canny bunch, the non-commissioned officers (NCOs) had sequestered for themselves the Royal Retiring Rooms (the only part of the grandstands that benefited from a hot water supply), and also the Jockey Club itself. In due course, the officers were billeted in the stable lads' quarters above the stables at Sefton Lodge. Ron Hockey slept in one such hayloft. It took several months for proper sleeping quarters to be erected for the airmen. At least Knowles was on home turf: he had been brought up in Warboys, only 22 miles to the north-west. His parents and his wife still lived in that damp Fens town.

Flt Lt Dr Roland Winfield was an early aviation medicine specialist with an inclination to root out flying-induced health problems from the sharp end. He was given a project to review parachuting injuries. So, as an empirical researcher, he endured (and survived) a spell at the centre for parachute training at Ringway, after which he was sent to Newmarket. Having just spent a few nights in the grandstand at RAF Gatwick (also a pre-war racecourse), he was none too impressed to see the same sleeping arrangements in this corner of Suffolk. His orders were to present himself to the CO of 1419 Flight. On arrival one Saturday morning, he went past a sign that said 'Jockeys Only' and faced a door with a sign – 'Mister Edward Knowles, Mus Bach'. Within was a man in tweeds and flannels, surrounded by untidy piles of music manuscript paper, creating a score whilst humming a tune from an obscure Czech opera. This should not have been a surprise since another sign on the door had said 'Composing' (its obverse said 'Decomposing'). Winfield was a little disorientated, but said he was looking for the officer commanding the Whitley Flight. After some ribbing, the musician showed a little more energy and said, 'Come along. I'll take you to the man you are looking for.' Once through the door behind him, it was evident this was the Operations Room. A large map of Europe graced one wall, with ribbons denoting recent raids.

In an instant, the tweedy gent turned into Sqn Ldr Knowles, and briefed the stunned Winfield (whom Knowles had been expecting) on the activities of the unit. Just as his Ops Room was well concealed from most of the station's visitors, so were the Lysanders and Whitleys, which were parked more than a mile away at the most northerly part of the Heath. The ground crew were based in Nissen huts hidden in the edge of nearby copses. The energetic Knowles immediately recruited Winfield for co-pilot duties, but directed him to find ways in which the well-being of the agents being transported in the Whitleys to the middle of Europe could be improved.[25]

The CO did indeed have a Bachelor of Music qualification, and was also an Associate of the Royal College of Music. At the outbreak of war, he had been commanding No. 56 Squadron flying Hurricanes, which he led through the battles of France and Britain. Whilst contemporaries called him Teddy, his young pilots called him 'Führer' – indicating some firmness of control. His gung-ho approach was already evident in poaching staff from 10 OTU in order to man his unit.

Like many doctors, Winfield was an astute judge of character. He noted Knowles' total focus on trying to win the war in the shortest time possible: the squadron leader had concluded that the best way to use his own talents to that end was to deliver as many highly trained agents into enemy territory as possible. In Winfield's view, Knowles had great intelligence – with an imagination to match – though he would no doubt have disapproved of his habitual cigarette, smoking away at the end of its long holder. Teddy carried out many Whitley missions, but, although he had command of two Lysanders, never did any missions in the single-engined aeroplane.

On 11 June, Whippy picked up his personal Lysander (T1770) from Harald Penrose at Westland's Yeovil aerodrome, who gave him 'some invaluable tips on its handling'.[26] Whippy was to become very fond of its strengths, and adept at avoiding the effects of its weaknesses. Even in non-moon periods, he continued to practise night flying; after a month or two 'he could make the aircraft dance'.[27] By war's end, this above average pilot had accumulated 168 hours in the type, and concluded it was 'a truly magnificent machine'.[28]

The other units operating the Lysander continued to suffer a steady stream of accidents, largely down to the low level of experience of the pilots, compounded with Petter's inbuilt design flaws. Fatalities were now running at around one per month, with May being particularly bad: both P/O David Watts and the Canadian F/O Peter Lochnan flew into hillsides in bad weather.

F/O Alan 'Sticky' Murphy was another Knowles recruit, arriving at 1419 in March. Also a Cumbrian, he had spent much of his childhood in South Africa, but the family had returned to Great Britain due to his father's ill health. After schooling at Canford in Dorset, he entered the RAF College at Cranwell in 1936 – to the disappointment of his father, who wanted his son to go to sea, like many of his forebears. Murphy was a very gifted athlete, specializing in the high jump and long jump, at which he trounced service rivals from Sandhurst and Woolwich with record-breaking leaps.

One of his close friends amidst his Cranwell cohort was Brian Kingcome, who was to go on to star in the Battle of Britain. Kingcome noted Sticky's 'zest and enthusiasm for life', and that he was 'so memorable a companion'.[29] The six-footer was described by colleagues as having a 'wispy moustache' and speaking in a 'limpid drawl' – these were not necessarily normal attributes for someone who was going to develop into a star pilot. His twinkly blue eyes betrayed a sparkling underlying personality. After Cranwell, he had a tour on the doomed Fairey Battle, then instructed on the same machine at an OTU.[30] He attended a specialist navigation course at St Athan in south Wales, and spent 83 hours as navigator in Ansons, pottering around the UK. His next posting was as station navigation officer at Lossiemouth in Scotland, which was a Bomber Command OTU. But, feeling he was missing out on hurting the enemy, he managed to procure an operational mission on his way up to Scotland, acting as second pilot in a Wellington bombing northern France.[31] Once at Lossiemouth, the 23-year-old met a diminutive young WAAF officer, Jean Leggat, the daughter of a Scottish GP, with whom he fell madly in love and the couple soon became engaged.

Murphy managed to fly a couple of anti-shipping patrols in Blenheims. A trip in a Magister trainer with a colleague to Yeadon in Yorkshire was thwarted by bad weather, and he force landed on the North York Moors in poor visibility next to the only building he could see; Sticky was pleased it turned out to be a pub, but he was chafing for some proper operational action.[32]

His experience was below the minimum requirements for Special Duties flying that would be set a few months later: Murphy had a total of 857 flying hours, of which 140 were at night, but his navigational skills ensured he was accepted into the fold. He was lucky to be able to join the unit during what was to be the quiet before the storm, and was able to spend the summer of 1941 becoming better acquainted with the Lysander and its foibles. His first few missions were as second pilot in Whitleys skippered by Knowles (whom he found 'a real tough nut').

He went on to fly some Whitley missions in the autumn as captain. Sticky soon became well loved by his colleagues – his zest for life (honed at Canford), love of a good party (and bad singing), an underlying good nature and ability to get on with everyone unknowingly set the role model for his successors in the Special Duties units. He became particular friends with Nesbitt-Dufort and Ron Hockey.[33]

The quiet was due to three linked factors. Firstly, as Dodds-Parker had realized, 'the operational state in May 1941 was hardly encouraging, either in Baker Street or in the field. Most of Europe lay stunned under Nazi/Fascist/Communist oppression.'[34] Secondly, there were wide-ranging discussions in Whitehall on how to advance special operations, and thirdly, debate raged in the higher echelons of the RAF as to how best to execute the government's bidding.

AVM Arthur Harris had been appointed AOC, 5 Group, on 11 September 1939, but his power base increased markedly on 25 November 1940 when he was also made Deputy Chief of the Air Staff (DCAS). He took a forceful view in husbanding the RAF's bombers. When the need for aircraft to drop agents into Occupied Europe had first arisen, as we have seen, he had tried to foist the obsolete Harrow onto 419 Flight. This lumbering monoplane with a fixed undercarriage had failed in its primary role of heavy bombing, and was withdrawn from use in that role by the end of 1939. It is thought that two Harrows were sent for modification for Special Duties operations at an aerodrome near Nottingham. If so, they were allowed to collect dust in the corner of some hangar, rather than imperil the lives of crews over Europe. 1419 had received the Whitley, which was an improvement. But only just. It was generally viewed as 'an awful machine for the job', and parachuting from it was 'not for the faint-hearted'.[35]

Harris' standpoint was that Bomber Command operated 365 days of the year (weather permitting). The Special Duties units only operated for less than half the month – the so-called moon period. In his view, it was a blatant under-use of resources. In reality, Bomber Command's ability to achieve any useful level of bombing accuracy at night outside of the moon period was very limited until the advent of electronic navigation aids in March 1942. This weakness was later to be brought into sharp focus by the debriefs of Bomber Command's operations on the night of 7/8 November 1941, when Command lost 37 aircraft of 392 sent on three separate missions, with no damage inflicted on the enemy at all.[36]

At the end of May, Harris left the role of DCAS (to be sent to the US to talk its government into supplying aircraft to the UK). His replacement was a Yorkshireman, AVM Norman Bottomley, who thankfully was more open-minded.

Gp Capt Bradbury, as DDI 2, had been supervising 1419's operations since October 1940. On 18 June 1941, he wrote to AVM Charles Medhurst, Assistant Chief of the Air Staff (ACAS) (I), with a progress report on what had been achieved.[37] Training and procedures for agent delivery had been refined, but with only three operational crews, 'I feel it is a great pity that the establishment is at present so small that we can hold no trained reserve crews.' Going on to the Lysander operations, he noted that 'three agents have been successfully picked up by night'. He was therefore ignoring, or was ignorant of, Geddes' operation. Again training methods had been refined to his satisfaction, including that of agents in selection and organization of landing grounds. This agent training had been carried out at Christchurch, Dorset (which would have been handy for the SOE finishing school at Beaulieu). Bradbury was optimistic that the pick-up methodology worked well, and urged that greater use be made of the skills gained. His final suggestion carried less import: 'I would suggest that the Lysander could easily operate from the deck of an aircraft carrier if necessity arose in the Mediterranean.'[38] Several later cohorts of Lysander pilots would give silent thanks that this idea was not enacted. In his covering note, Bradbury requested Medhurst to upgrade his operations to a 'squadron basis'.

Medhurst had another Special Duties worry land in his in-tray that week. The Czechs and Poles had been badgering the RAF for some months to create squadrons of their own exiled aircrew in order to fly supplies and agents into their home countries. The Polish lobbying had been led by General Sikorski, who had approached the Secretary of State for Air. Sikorski badly needed a flow of agents to and fro in order to communicate with his resistance leaders on the ground. The Polish leader, having been charged with defending miles of Scottish coastline, had established a headquarters at Perth, and had forged a relatively close relationship with key UK players. Dalton, Jebb and Gubbins had flown up to meet him in his Scottish lair at Christmas 1940, and Dalton inspired the Polish men with a stirring talk.[39]

Bottomley, as DCAS, had some sympathy, and in a memo to Medhurst dated 23 June, reckoned it 'may be necessary to build up to a full squadron, say of Whitleys, for these special missions. If technical considerations permit, the squadron could then operate on favourable nights in this way, carrying out normal bombing tasks at other times.' He added at the end, in manuscript, 'I know the views of my predecessor.'⁴⁰ Harris would have been completely opposed to the idea. Moreover, Bottomley would have had a better than average understanding of the sociological currents in Europe, at least in France, since, very unusually for the era, he had had his university education in France, at Rennes in Brittany.

By 30 June, Medhurst had told Jebb that some idea of the volume of flights for the coming autumn and winter needed to be notified to DDI 2 in good time, and had concluded that 1419 Flight was unlikely to be a sufficiently large unit to cope. Within days, Menzies had told Bradbury that SIS alone would anticipate up to 12 long-distance trips per month, and recommended that four to six Handley Page Halifaxes (with superior performance and range to the Whitley) should be procured 'to start with' – a recommendation rather above his station.

Medhurst's staff consolidated the numbers. The forecast demand from both SOE and SIS was for 20 men and 30 containers a month to Poland, rising from September to 56 and to 154 by March 1941. The Low Countries (including France) together with Norway and Denmark had a combined requirement of 32 and 38 for each month over that forecast period. Northern Italy, Czechoslovakia and the Iberian Peninsula were considered to have a much lower requirement.

So far 1419's assets of three Whitleys (plus one for training), and one Lysander together with one Maryland (an American twin-engined light bomber that had had insignificant use) 'have been sufficient to carry out on average 12 operations per month'. But as SOE's agent networks were still embryonic, these had required few container drops; so Medhurst concluded that the fleet and staffing needed material enlargement.⁴¹

By the end of July, Sikorski, through his emissary the Polish Air Attaché Colonel Bogdan Kwiecliski, thought it was better to have a mole within the Special Duties unit, even if a dedicated squadron had yet to be sanctioned, so he asked Gubbins for two of his (RAF) officers to be seconded to 1419 in the interim. Gubbins had already scheduled some supply- and agent-dropping flights to Poland for September. Sikorski was pushing for two Polish (Whitley) crews to be set up; Bradbury thought this was impractical given the small scale of 1419.

The Poles had, however, started flying the Lysander in the Army Co-operation Flights from autumn 1940, and had had more accidents than average. Sgt Andrzejewski had been killed at Lyneham on Guy Fawkes Night. The accident report noted he had climbed too steeply after take-off, with the trim set incorrectly. It cited 'language difficulties', and concluded tartly that Andrzejewski 'was practically useless for ferry work' (his allotted task). The Poles also had their own squadron for Army Co-operation (No. 309, formed on 8 October at Abbotsinch in Scotland). They encountered the normal problems of the Lysander punishing any poor landing technique, but some also had difficulties in navigating over an unfamiliar country. By the middle of August, Bottomley had kicked the Polish can a few hundred yards down the road: he sanctioned two Polish crews being sent to a Whitley OTU for training on 'our type of work'. When they passed out from that, they would be allowed to be attached to 1419 for operations.

But it was not just the Poles who were fighting for aviation resources. The hunger of SOE was entering a decisive phase.

6

Scaling Up: The Formation of No. 138 Squadron

> *SOE was a fledgling organisation; it was unconventional and improvisational, since there were no precedents, no previous experience or strategy to help and guide its leaders.*
>
> Noreen Riols[1]

Gladwyn Jebb (Minister of Economic Warfare) had been lobbying Pug Ismay for more air resources for SOE since the spring. In August, key decisions were taken. On the 14th, the Chiefs of Staff Committee discussed the future of SOE at length, having received a report from Jebb. The Chiefs decided that it was as well to over-budget for arms drops due to the chances of a significant proportion of drops not being collected by their intended targets. The outlook for this in 1942 'did not look very promising'. They agreed that 'subversive activities should be given every encouragement'. They 'took note that the Air Ministry would try to expand as soon as possible the special flight, which was set aside for the use of SO2 [the Operations branch of SOE] and SIS'. But they also 'agreed that in view of the paramount importance of good intelligence, the provision of sorties for SO2 should not be allowed to interfere with the requirements of SIS'.[2]

The Joint Planning Staff put a slightly different spin when reporting to the War Cabinet on 15 August 1941: 'It would be unsound to sacrifice the effectiveness of our bombing effort to these activities. Nor at present is it possible to judge how far in fact the sorties required will prove to be necessary or practicable…' However, they also agreed that the provision of sorties for SOE should not interfere with SIS's needs.[3] The 'effectiveness' of the RAF's bombing activities at that time was of course not quite as great as the Chief of the Air Staff was promoting.

By 24 August, Medhurst had to let Gubbins know that 'it is improbable [that 1419 Flight] will be able to fulfil all the requirements of both "C" and SOE for the forthcoming moon period'. He had instructed that a further two Whitleys be added (making six plus a sole Lysander).

So this was the background for expanding 1419 Flight – a squadron was needed. But the bad news for Gubbins was that SOE remained the poor relation. Whilst much of the top-level discussions had centred on the Whitley operations, Gp Capt Bradbury considered that the possibilities of Lysander operations 'may not have been fully appreciated' by either SIS and SOE. In a memo to Medhurst clearly designed for onward distribution, he claimed that techniques had been refined such that time on the ground (in enemy territory) had reduced to 60 seconds. (This was an exaggeration, since the later 161 Squadron standard was three minutes.) Moreover, he wrote, 'I am now confident that the operation may be regarded as no more hazardous than a bombing trip to a well defended area; it is probably less so, because, although the aircraft is defenceless in the rear, it lends itself excellently to evasive tactics at night', which was true. 'In good weather the chances of success are now 95%.' He went on to claim an operational range of 1,200 miles, bringing western Germany, as well as the whole of France, within reach, and that, via a stop at Gibraltar, operations could be considered in the Mediterranean. Trials of 'food extracts' and Benzedrine derivatives had been successful so that a pilot could be kept 'fresh and fit' for flights of six hours or more. This was giving the lily a lavish coating of gilt.

But the most significant suggestion came at the end of Bradbury's sales brochure. He lobbied for the appointment in each enemy-occupied country of an agent with previous flying experience (this call to arms is given in full as Appendix C). After a special course with 1419, the agent would be able to:

1. select in his country as many sites as possible which would be ideal from every point of view, to survey them, and to communicate their fullest details to this country. We will arrange for air photographs and agree to his selections.
2. be present, when required, at the site of a proposed pick-up and to supervise the flare path layout and embarkation procedure.[4]

Once this was in place, he pointed out that the return passengers need not be agents – they could be 'political refugees, or even kidnapped senior

SCALING UP: THE FORMATION OF NO. 138 SQUADRON

members of the enemy'. This was critical – whilst Whitleys (or later the Halifax) could drop agents in small groups to their destination (or close by), only the Lysander could deposit VIPs of a certain age, and of possibly dubious health, who could not make the jump; similarly, only the single-engined aeroplane (and subsequently the Hudson) could pick up agents and VIPs, of whatever health and age, and return them to England. Now with highly skilled crews and well-honed techniques, the Lysander had proven to be a unique asset, and now was the time to exploit it.

Bradbury's suggestion that a landing ground supremo for each country in Occupied Europe be appointed was to have far-reaching implications for SOE's operations in France – and not all for the better.

The Chiefs of Staff somewhat reluctantly agreed to an upgrade to squadron status; Ismay (whose tail had been tweaked again by Jebb) told Churchill, and on 25 August 1941, 1419 Flight was reformed as 138 Squadron. This was under the command of Teddy Knowles: the Whitleys of 'A' Flight were commanded by Sqn Ldr A.D. Jackson, and 'B' Flight's two Lysanders were under Nesbitt-Dufort. The War Cabinet regarded one squadron as enough to make an efficient beginning both in subversive activities and in the organization of secret armies. For the latter, northern France was to be given the highest priority.

Knowles had encouraged his Lysander men to act as co-pilot/navigator on Whitley operations over France, in order to gain expertise in night navigation on the other side of the Channel. Whippy did so many trips that he ended the war with more operations on Whitleys than any other type of aircraft.[5] One of Sticky Murphy's first missions for 138 was to drop 300,000 cigarettes from his Whitley over the Netherlands to celebrate their Queen's birthday. This was not enough for a man whose personal motto was 'Right lads – after the bastards!', so he released a few bombs over Amsterdam's Schipol aerodrome for good measure. Three weeks later, he married Jean at St Georges Church in Newbury, having spent his stag night the previous evening in London's Piccadilly. A short honeymoon (also including his birthday) at the Lygon Arms in Broadway was interrupted several times by tiresome phone calls from his colleagues.

On 4 September, the Lysander Flight restarted operations. Nesbitt-Dufort flew his machine from Newmarket down to Tangmere on the Sussex coast on Operation *Levée/Facade*, and picked up agent Gerard (Gerry) Henri Morel. He had been an insurance broker, was fluent in three languages – English, French and Portuguese – and had returned to the UK from South America earlier in the year, via Lisbon, before offering his services to the War Office. He was left for dead on the beaches of Dunkirk, but having recovered he made his way to London via South America and Portugal and signed up to SOE. Now with the rank of major, on this mission he was charged with recruiting agents and forming circuits in south-west France.

His health precluded a parachute drop so he ended up in Dufort's Lysander. They took off just before 2100hrs, and with a tailwind crossed the French coast little more than half an hour later at 9,000 feet. At the destination field some eight miles north-east of Châteauroux, it took a quarter of an hour of circling down at 300 feet before the reception committee's torchlights appeared, but the correct recognition signals were exchanged, so he committed to land. On final approach, he noticed it was an exceedingly small field, but as he touched down it was apparent that 'the surface of the field was the roughest I had ever come across and it pulled me up very quickly.'[6]

Morel leaped out, with Whippy losing no time in telling his return passenger, the 'jovial giant' 34-year-old Jacques de Guélis, what he thought of his choice of field. He held the Lysander on the brakes as he took the Mercury engine up to its fullest power (including the boost over-ride), but when he released the brakes, the acceleration was agonizingly slow over the bone-shaking surface. Cursing the generous weight of his passenger, Whippy's vision was first engulfed by the trees at the field's edge, and then by a blinding flash as his propeller cut through high tension cables he had not noticed. Progress was also impeded by some telephone wires that had appeared out of the gloom.

An hour and a half later, just when his heart rate had settled down, he was disconcerted to notice two green lights nearing him to his left, which could only belong to German night-fighters. Fortunately, they slipped above him only 300 feet away, not having noticed the black-painted Lysander. Whippy had used all his wiles to manoeuvre his aircraft so that they would not see the flames from his exhaust. Two further problems arose: on trying for a homing steer from Tangmere, he found that his involuntary connection to the French grid had fried his radio. In spite of the silence, he arrived back at Tangmere only to find it covered in fog. However, the lead-in lights were on poles sufficiently high to poke above the fog layer. Whippy let the Lysander mush down as slowly as possible where he believed the runway threshold to be, and landed safely. Once at a standstill, the tired Nesbitt-Dufort needed the arrival of a jeep to guide him back to his parking spot. On clambering out, he found his undercarriage adorned with several French telephone wires.

Over a restorative drink, he could now chat with de Guélis, and the reason for the state of the field emerged. The agent, whose family still had roots in the Loire valley, had been finishing his dinner at a hotel near the landing ground when the *gendarmes* arrived to conduct a check of all the diners' papers. This delay caused him understandable anxiety. Although he pedalled out of town as fast as possible, he was still rather late for the rendezvous. When he saw Whippy's machine circling, he simply diverted into the nearest field and started flashing his torch. He had brought a couple of bottles of champagne and one of perfume as a gift for his aeronautical saviour, but such was his agitation that he left them on the field. Fortunately, Morel spotted them and made good use of the bounty.[7]

Jacques Theodore Paul Marie Vaillant de Guélis had already packed much into his war: a French father and an English mother made him bilingual. After going up to Oxford (where he befriended Douglas Dodds-Parker), he was working in advertising in both London and Paris when the Germans invaded his homeland. He was co-opted into the British Army in 1940 as a translator for Lord Gort and General Alan Brooke and was caught alongside André Simon (of the wine merchant family), but both escaped over the Pyrenees to England where Brooke had commended de Guélis' skills to Gubbins. De Gaulle was not interested in him as he had worked for his arch-rival André Giraud. But de Guélis did obtain an audience with Churchill.[8]

Despite political views 'well to the right of Louis XIV', he was soon working as a briefing officer for F Section in London but, rather unusually for a staff officer, was sent on this reconnaissance trip to France, hoping his abundant moustache would offer some sort of disguise. The most useful results of this mission were his recruitment of several key agents, some of whom (e.g. Philippe Liewer, a journalist before the war) were to become Lysander passengers in due course. So both of Whippy's two passengers that night were of great importance.

Only three days later, Whippy accompanied Ron Hockey on a Whitley sortie to the Pyrenees (Operation *Fengler*), which was uneventful. But on 9 September, the duo did another that was very nearly their undoing. They successfully made their parachute drop after several hours of flight, and were only 30 or so miles south of the Belgian coast when cloud cover disappeared. Their worries about their nakedness were soon proved vindicated when they were coned by searchlights. Despite violent evasive action by Hockey, they received a flak burst under the tail which upended the aircraft. It required the strength of both pilots to pull the weary Whitley out of the ensuing vertical dive; their four feet planted on the bottom of the instrument panel, and a last heave arrested the dive at only 400 feet above the ground. Ron Hockey was unperturbed, Whippy a little less calm. They crossed the North Sea at a more comfortable 4,000 feet, but then suffered the indignity of being fired at by three destroyers, which turned out to be British, a few miles off the Essex coast. Their home base at Newmarket, together with the rest of East Anglia, was fogged in, so they trekked further and further north, not finding a fog-free airfield until Leuchars in Scotland. The exhausting seven-hour mission for the crew barely left them energy to eat their combat breakfast of bacon and eggs.[9]

By this stage, both SIS and SOE had realized that they required accommodation for their agents near to the aerodrome used by 1419/138. The peripatetic history of 1419 to date had made it difficult to put down such roots. Meanwhile, Portal, the tall, slim and reticent Chief of the Air Staff, was continuing to receive pressure from General Sikorski as to when supply drops to Poland could start. Bottomley and senior officers below him, having agreed in principle to the creation of a Polish crewed flight within 138 Squadron, concluded that the only practical way that such drops could be achieved by Whitleys was for the flights to continue to Russia (due to range considerations), and then to return to the UK 'in due course'. The spurious excuse for not providing a Liberator (the four-engined US bomber, just coming into service, which was what the Poles desired) was that 'their armament is at present inadequate to permit them flying over enemy territory'.[10]

Polish (and Czech) supply issues continued to dominate development of 138 Squadron strategy and resources through the summer and autumn of 1941, to the detriment of growing Lysander operations in France and elsewhere. But as the plans for these long-range Whitley sorties gathered pace, one important consideration was inserted – the Whitleys would carry a few bombs to be dropped on the return journey on strictly military targets so as to disguise the true nature of their missions. By October, it had also been agreed for 138 to be given three Halifaxes – a four-engined bomber with superior payload, range and performance to the Whitley – specifically for long-range missions (primarily to Poland, but also to other European countries).[11] The aircraft had to be dedicated to 138 as it was not economic to remove its specially installed long-range tanks so it could participate in normal bombing missions. Portal had also agreed for a single Polish crew to be trained in preparation for a supply drop in their own country, and one or two Czech crews for similar reasons. It is difficult to overstate the amount of time that Portal and other senior colleagues had to spend in placating Sikorski that autumn. Nonetheless, the Poles' stance did help nudge a gentle shift in attitude by the (British) Chiefs of Staff, who agreed at their 287th meeting 'that subversive activities should be given every encouragement'.

Having kept his hand in with Whitley drops, in the following moon period Nesbitt-Dufort did his next pick-up on 2 October. He flew down to RAF Ford in Sussex, and departed without any outbound passenger on this SIS mission. He landed at the fallow aerodrome of Estrées-Saint-Denis, just to the west of Compiègne, at 2234hrs, the field being controlled by Lt Roger Mitchell (Agent *Brick*), a French artillery officer with a Scottish grandparent, who had been sent back to France by de Gaulle. W/Cdr Roman Garby-Czerniawski had brought two of his fellow SIS agents to act as torch bearers in the reception committee.[12] Roman hopped in quickly and they were airborne again in just three minutes. He had been a fighter pilot and then staff officer in the Polish Air Force but escaped to France to fly with the Armée de l'Air, and was injured in a flying accident. Remaining in France after the German invasion, he chose for his new agent identity that of his mistress's late husband – Armand Borni. Having been involved in the foundation of the Polish fiercely anti-communist resistance group POWN, he was now hired by SIS as Agent *Valentin/Walenty*, and tasked with setting up the INTERALLIÉ circuit in autumn 1940. Unfortunately, one of his first recruits was Mathilde Carré (*La Chatte*), who later became a traitor after taking a German lover.[13]

Philip Schneidau, Wally Farley's first passenger a few weeks before, had transmuted into Flt Lt Philipson of the Inter-Services Liaison Department (as SIS was sometimes disguised), and had become SIS's liaison man for clandestine air and sea operations, and a conducting officer. In that capacity, he had come to Tangmere to welcome Garby-Czerniawski. It emerged that the Pole had been betrayed by Carré and arrested by the Germans, but allowed a token 'escape' on the understanding that after his return to London, he became a double agent. He was given radio crystals and transmission instructions. On arrival in London he was interrogated by his own intelligence service, which had some suspicions about his story; after a month he confessed, and began to work as a double agent for the British under the fabled XX Scheme and was christened Agent *Brutus*.[14]

Ford was only ten minutes' drive from the Nesbitt-Dufort home, 'Seagulls' in Middleton-on-Sea in Sussex, so Whippy took his charge there for some sleep in what remained of the night. He had neglected to explain his current duties to his wife Beryl, who was therefore somewhat taken aback by the state of Roman/*Armand*, particularly his bleeding feet after he removed his shoes and socks. A stiff drink was produced.[15]

Agents were brought to and from the UK airfields by escorting officers, who were typically middle-ranking staff officers within SIS or SOE, as appropriate. Gubbins, head of SOE, had realized back in 1940 when he had to expand his organization rapidly, that suitable recruits would most easily come from the old boys' network, or rather youngish ex-public-school types. The Director of Military Intelligence, the beaky Brigadier Frederick Beaumont-Nesbitt, had the aristocratic public school background that Gubbins (who had left school at 16) lacked, and became his de facto recruiting officer.[16] The tall, good-looking Guards officer hired in his own image. In his initial haul were: Geoffrey Household (Clifton and Magdalen, Oxford); the Etonian Peter Fleming (who also went up to Oxford); Bickham Sweet-Escott (Winchester and Balliol); and another Wykehamist, Douglas Dodds-Parker, also a Dark Blue graduate. The privations of an English public school were rightly thought to have provided the ideal toughening up experience for SOE work.

It was Capt Dodds-Parker, the 22-year-old, 6-foot 2-inch Guards officer, who had arrived at Whippy's house to take a cleaned-up *Armand* back to London, unaware that he was (at least in theory) a German double agent. Dodds-Parker had had a colourful time before the war, including seeing Hitler speak in Berlin's Sportpalast in April 1933, and in 1936, had spent a couple of days at a Nazi rally in Nuremberg. That year also caused a moment of great regret for the Guards officer: he had been invited to a performance of Wagner's *Lohengrin* at Bayreuth, and sat near the main box, where Hitler was the guest of honour. 'Had I brought my pistol…'[17] After a rare breakfast at home, Whippy took off for Newmarket.

With a few Lysander operations under his belt, Whippy had become frustrated with mistakes being made in embarkation and disembarkation on the French fields, the most irritating being leaving sacks of outbound

SCALING UP: THE FORMATION OF NO. 138 SQUADRON

courier (i.e. mail) on board, which therefore returned to the UK. He wrote, 'Slight mishaps on embarkation operations have shown that concentrated and prolonged training is necessary.' At least a week's training for agents was mandated. Up to this point, when ad hoc training was carried out, agents had stayed overnight in hotels in Cambridge or Newmarket – with attendant security risks. But now a house at Godmanchester was requisitioned: Farm Hall was to offer a more secure environment. It was a very pleasant 18th-century house with about 14 bedrooms exclusive of staff accommodation. Behind it was a discreet garden where lectures could be given in summer.[18]

The mood of the squadron darkened on 30 October: the previous night, only a day after arriving on the squadron, Flt Lt Jackie Oettle had taken off in his Whitley with two crew for his first training flight, and stalled on his approach back into Newmarket. All three crew members perished.

On 6 November, Nesbitt-Dufort attempted to take Garby-Czerniawski out to the same part of France as his last flight, this time to an old aerodrome nearer Soissons, but had to return – the lambent rain had prevented him sighting the torches of the reception committee. The following night he was more successful. The field organizer had taken the risk of hooking up an old car headlight to a battery to produce more light. Whippy picked up Lt Mitchell and Claude Lamirault (Agent *Fitzroy*), who headed up Biffy's JADE-FITZROY network. They had travelled to nearby Compiègne from Paris by train, and had been at the field for ten nights in bitter weather. Morale was at a low ebb when Whippy finally bounced to a landing around midnight. Mitchell had inspected 16 different fields before alighting on these two. Lamirault was a fervent anti-communist who was later described by John Cordeaux (at that time Deputy Director of SIS (Naval)) as 'as tough as a Chicago gangster, and a rather ugly customer'. Lamirault's redeeming features were an overweening hatred of the Nazis, and the ability to form an intelligence network with a broad spread of recruits ranging from government officials to prostitutes.[19] His Resistance colleagues meanwhile found him reliable, brave and fired with a passion for justice and liberty, albeit with a tendency to dress like a dandy. Pierre Hentic, his younger colleague who assisted at the field when Whippy landed, was transfixed by the Lysander, as an emblem of a country on which rested the world's liberty, and which, faced with the Nazi monster, had not capitulated. As Whippy's machine burbled over the horizon, tears came to Pierre's eyes.[20]

A few days later, the musical commanding officer of 138, Teddy Knowles, left Newmarket to take command of No. 296 Squadron and RAF Jurby on the Isle of Man; Wally Farley, freshly promoted to wing commander, was given charge of 138.

In the autumn, 138 had acquired quite an exotic recruit.[21] The 29-year-old Antoine Jean Emile Laurent had escaped the grip of the Germans after an interesting career in the French military. After entering the French Naval Academy at the age of 20, he had served in the Far East for two years before being sent for flying training at Versailles in 1936. With exquisite timing, he qualified as a fighter pilot on 15 April 1940, but was on operations mainly in Africa. Laid off after the Armistice, he mouthed pro-British views, so his commanding officer suggested that, for his own safety, he should become a commercial pilot with Air France in Morocco; this he did, and was earning a very good salary. Nonetheless, he fled Morocco in a four-seater light aircraft, a Caudron Simoun, to Gibraltar on 16 June 1941, simply diverting from his instructed destination of Meknes. Laurent immediately signed up for the Free French forces (thereby being condemned to death for treason by the Vichy government).

He was brought to Great Britain on board the *Cameronia*, and after brief refresher training joined 1 Squadron RAF, with whom he flew 42 operations on Hurricanes. Laurent was then (possibly with the influence of de Gaulle) posted to 138 Squadron on 1 November.[22]

Before he could fly a Lysander back to his homeland on operations, he obviously had to carry out some intensive training on the type. Three weeks after his arrival on the squadron, he took the prototype long-range Special Duties Lysander, T1771, on a navigational exercise up to Turnhouse, the airfield outside Edinburgh. LAC John 'Ox' Harkness, one of the original Lysander fitters from 419 Flight days, accompanied him in the back seat. The weather forecasts for the return trip were very poor, but Laurent decided to take off from Turnhouse anyway, even without authorization.

The Frenchman made it as far as Surrey. Lost in fog, he struck trees on the side of a hill at Long Bottom just north of Farnham. The aircraft caught fire and both perished. His flight commander, Nesbitt-Dufort, was livid, not so much at the loss of Laurent, who was not yet ready for operations,

SCALING UP: THE FORMATION OF NO. 138 SQUADRON

but for the loss of Ox, one of his most able fitters. In the accident report, Farley judged that the control officer at Turnhouse should have prevented the impetuous Frenchman from taking off: 'In view of the conditions which were to be expected, [this] indicates a measure of over-confidence on his [Laurent's] part'.[23]

The burden of operations on Whippy had become too great, and Laurent was to have become his first Lysander colleague. So 138's Lysander recruitment programme now had a large hole. Sticky Murphy and Guy Lockhart volunteered to step into the breach.

There had been a month's pause before the next 138 Squadron operation: 8 December saw Sticky Murphy's operational début as a Lysander jockey (by now he had made seven Whitley sorties as captain). Whippy had been due to take the mission but was suffering from a cold which had affected his sinuses. Sticky was the natural substitute.[24] He was ordered to retrieve Captain Jean Cassart of the Belgian Army. Cassart had been taught field selection and management techniques by Nesbitt-Dufort, who had also taken the opportunity to induct him into the art of golf whilst he was in England. Having developed a strong affection for Whippy, the Belgian had parachuted back into the Ardennes in his homeland with his radio operator, Sgt Henri Verhagen, on 26 August. Cassart had kept quiet about breaking three vertebrae and having ankle issues before the war, otherwise he would have not been accepted onto the parachuting course at Ringway. Now his safety had been compromised by encountering a Luxembourg double agent named Richir (and possibly his own loquaciousness).[25]

Taking off from Stradishall at 2210hrs, Murphy was over the French coast 50 minutes later; he found the field rather easily – an old Luftwaffe landing ground at Neufchâteau in Belgium. It was covered in snow, the night quite misty. Cassart and his wireless operator Henri gathered a couple of cases of documents he wished to return to London and left their car. They trembled in a mixture of cold and apprehension. As they were setting out their landing torches they heard some voices, and with the rising moon saw some shadows. A German soldier shouted out 'Halt, who goes there?' Cassart shouted 'Run!', but was wounded in his left arm. He narrowly managed to escape the search party of ten Wehrmacht, but with them still in the vicinity, he was not going to flash the agreed letter 'L' on his torch in order to confirm to the circling pilot (who he thought was Nesbitt-Dufort) that it was safe to land.[26] He ran a further three or four miles before collapsing in a fever.[27]

Murphy had believed the agent's torch was continuing to flash and so, concluding that Cassart 'was being chased', decided to land. On his approach and only 20 yards short of the first light, Murphy turned on his landing light and noticed to his dismay that the ground seemed to 'dip very sharply', so he opened up his engine and went round. It was a far from ideal choice of field – in a bowl, surrounded by woodland. For his second attempt, he decided to land on the eastern side of the old aerodrome and, sensing that something might be amiss, unholstered his revolver before the Lysander came to rest. A few minutes later, there was an explosion, which he took to be his revolver going off 'but this was not the case, and it was due to enemy approaching and being belligerent'. He took off post haste (obviously without picking up Cassart* and Henri); once in the climb, he realized he was bleeding profusely and used his lucky charm – one of his wife's silk stockings – to staunch the wound, and landed back at Tangmere at 0300hrs. Murphy had taken a rifle round through his neck from one of the 20 or so Jagdkommandos under Capt Schnepp that had closed to only 30 yards away. All of the Lysander's fuel tanks had been hit, which meant he arrived back at Tangmere with enough for only a few minutes' more flying.[28] Cassart had been the operator of this field that night: what had happened was that he had driven his car over it the previous evening to check if the layer of snow was thick enough to prevent the Lysander's landing safely. The Germans had spotted the car tracks the following day and laid an ambush. Victor was caught, and, with a gun in his back, ordered to flash the right light to Murphy's Lysander. 'He flashed the wrong one. During the landing he spun round, stabbed the German and fled into the night.'[29]

---

*Cassart's injuries were tended to by locals but his location was again betrayed by the same traitor in his network who had betrayed the date and location of the pick-up to the Germans. The traitor was executed by the Belgians after the war. Cassart was taken to Berlin and tortured for weeks. Unbelievably, he escaped from his Berlin prison, made it back to Brussels, and was brought back to England before parachuting back into the Ardennes in the late summer of 1944. Some war!

SCALING UP: THE FORMATION OF NO. 138 SQUADRON

Cassart had been due to be escorted back to London by Philip Rea, a personal staff officer to Gubbins. Meanwhile, Nesbitt-Dufort was so worried by the mission he had bequeathed to the novice Murphy that he raised himself from his sick bed and went to the Tangmere control tower to await his substitute's return. Murphy being well overdue, Whippy and Rea were even more concerned when they heard his feeble voice over the airwaves. Recognizing Murphy's declining state, Whippy gave him as much verbal encouragement over the radio as he could, largely comprising a torrent of 'blue limericks'. Despite his debilitated condition, Murphy made a decent landing, but as he stumbled out of the cockpit, his ashen complexion and blood all down his left arm startled his comrades. 'Whoopee John, I've been wounded!' he exclaimed to Nesbitt-Dufort, before walking unaided to the ambulance.

The following morning, the mechanics counted 30 bullet holes in the stricken Lysander (the Germans reckoned they had fired a hundred rounds). As for its pilot, Murphy spent five days in hospital, where he was worried that the blood transfusion 'had upset the delicate balance of alcohol in his bloodstream', and was rewarded with 14 days' leave and a DFC.[30] Whilst he returned to service, his Lysander did not.

On 16 December, in the moonless period, the squadron formally moved from Newmarket to Stradishall, all of 11 miles to the south-east. SOE's lobbying had paid off, and the squadron by now had received the three Halifax four-engined bombers for long-range parachute-dropping operations. One was put to use in the defining special operation of the first half of the war. The squadron's commander, Ron Hockey, took off from Tangmere at 2200hrs on 28 December in Halifax L9613. He crossed the French coast at Le Crotoy, a now favourite coasting-in point for the squadron because its position at the wide mouth of the Somme estuary was easy to spot and provided a good fix. Heading across Germany, they met a night-fighter near Darmstadt, but it failed to attack them. On the crew went, a snow-covered landscape making navigation difficult. They found their first target fix, Pilsen, and at 0224hrs dropped the first two of the six agents on board – Jan Kubis, a Czech, and Jozef Gabcik, a Slovak – near the village of Lidice. The duo's mission, Operation *Anthropoid*, was to assassinate the loathed Reinhard Heydrich, Reichsprotektor of Bohemia and Moravia; a man who would as soon murder your aunt as take tea with her. They achieved their objective, albeit at great cost in terms of Nazi retributions and their own lives. The success of this mission – which had meant a more than ten-hour flight – provided strong evidence for Gubbins to prove that SOE could facilitate impressive military feats deep in the occupied territories. It thus gave succour to the Lysander operations as well.

Meanwhile, agents Maurice Duclos (BCRA) and Roger Mitchell (SIS) had been in hiding, expecting a Lysander to bring them back to the UK. They sent a 'plaintive' message to SIS in London: 'We have just spent Christmas holidays in the woods. Bitter cold. No food. Weather was fine for days. What has happened?' Duclos, one of Dewavrin's first recruits, liked his comforts: a good meal, a good bed, and a bad woman. All seemed to be lacking at this moment. They could not comprehend that their putative British saviours might be hampered by bad weather in England.[31]

As the calendar flipped into 1942, Gubbins had been hard at work setting out his vision of how the air support to SOE should develop. Instead of sending his wish list up the chimney for Father Christmas, he appended it to his memo to DDI 2 (Gp Capt James Easton):

[A] full station with all the facilities which that implies set aside for our work. The station would be required to accommodate:

a) The Operational Squadron
b) Possibly a Special Flight for the use of 'C' [i.e. SIS]. This would avoid the difficult question of priority which so frequently arises at present.
c) A Lysander Training Flight.
d) An experimental Flight.

With some foresight (and presumably after discussion with Farley and colleagues), he also suggested that the station might have its own meteorological staff. He concluded with a list of his extensive accommodation requirements.[32]

Sir Alan Brooke had just taken over as Chief of the Imperial General Staff, and was more sympathetic to SOE than his predecessor, Field Marshal Sir John Dill. On 6 January, he lunched with Hugh Dalton, and expressed the view that supplying resistance movements could be given higher priority. Roundell Palmer, the newish Lord Selborne, replaced Dalton as Minister of Economic Warfare in a Cabinet reshuffle in February 1942; the royalist and orthodox Tory was better placed than Dalton to resist meddling in SOE affairs by other ministers. Dalton, 'a brilliant but temperamental left-wing intellectual' in the view of one

SCALING UP: THE FORMATION OF NO. 138 SQUADRON

of his acolytes, was somewhat reluctantly shuffled to run the Board of Trade, and noted waspishly that Selborne 'had been out of politics for many years and had never held any office higher than Assistant Postmaster-General. But he was said to be "very close to the Prime Minister".'[33] Stung by SIS's sniping, and their quest to take control of SOE, one of the methodical Selborne's first acts was to commission from W.E. Playfair (a senior Treasury man) an independent report into the management and efficiency of SOE. This correctly identified the poison coming from SIS.

By mid-January, Farley was becoming frustrated at his embryonic squadron's lack of progress. Over the previous month, his unit had completed only nine of its allotted 26 operations (Whitley, Halifax and Lysander). He listed several reasons for this, unhelpful weather being the most important. He was disappointed in receiving just the 'sweepings' of Whitley and Halifax crews from 4 Group, their poor quality leading to six accidents; only one pilot showed enough promise to carry out an operation. The quantity and quality of maintenance personnel was similarly lacking. Hockey also lacked an intelligence officer and assistant, which had meant he had had to process the targets handed down from AI2(c) by himself.

But Farley was most vexed by his dealings with SOE:

[While taskings fed down from SIS] with the utmost smoothness and ease… the staff work of ISRB [Inter-Service Research Bureau, a cover name for SOE] is found to be confusing and distracting. Targets have been changed two or three times per day, priorities are changed from day to day… Consistently distracting pressure is exerted to have operations attempted in the face of better judgement regarding weather by introducing pressure from higher authority and generally the most unhelpful attitude is adopted by the visiting officers. It is quite evident that they have no conception whatever of the inconvenience and work that one operation involves and they take no pains to hide their critical attitude. The Poles, are of course, by far the worst offenders and despite my most urgent protests in several quarters I have had staying at this Unit a Polish Engineer Officer who each day telephones London and gives them details of my maintenance organisation and serviceability state.

This was tangible evidence that SOE was struggling to emerge from its toddler phase, whilst the long-standing SIS was clearly in well-functioning, if arrogant, adulthood.

Aside from the strange complaint that mounting an operation causes 'inconvenience', these are strong representations for an officer of Farley's rank. He ended with:

> I request that steps be taken with higher authority to:
> i) Prevent country section officers from visiting the Station.
> ii) Educate ISRB liaison officers in Air Force etiquette and Air Force procedure.
>
> This analysis of reasons for failure to carry out the programme is forwarded not as a series of excuses but as an attempt to place these points before proper authorities so that steps may be taken to bring the Squadron on to a proper footing.[34]

The new year of 1942 was to see special operations scaled up, and some of Farley's wishes come to fruition.

7

1942: The Formation of No. 161 Squadron

There was a hiatus in operations until 28 January 1942, caused largely by bad weather. But that evening was eventful: the squadron despatched on operations seven Whitleys together with Nesbitt-Dufort in Lysander T1508.

By now promoted to squadron leader, Whippy was ordered by SIS to take out one agent, and to bring back Maurice Duclos (the 'genial giant, gourmand and womanizer'[1]) and Roger Mitchell from a field in open countryside outside Issoudun, Indre, in the centre of France. This was Operation *Beryl*, so named by Whippy after his own wife. He took off from Tangmere at 1915hrs, and did a cruise climb over the Channel, experiencing some icing as he negotiated thin layers of cloud. These prevented him seeing his coasting-in point – the popular seaside resort of Trouville in Normandy – but a few minutes later he spotted some bends in the Seine which told him he was well left of track. He found his destination just after 2200hrs, and landed without difficulty.

Mitchell, a French agent recruited by Dewavrin, was bringing important *courier* to London; Duclos had been Dewavrin's first recruit, and had been fleeing from the Gestapo since the previous August after his network in Paris had been betrayed. Choosing a slightly more northerly track towards Fécamp on the coast for his return, Whippy chatted away to Duclos and Mitchell for a few minutes before the intercom and then the radio failed – no doubt due to the heavy rain he was encountering. Whippy was forced into hedge-hopping by solid cloud that extended down to only 700 feet. 'Extremely bumpy conditions' added to the agents' discomfort. It was 'the most wicked looking and well defined active cold front I had ever seen'. The night sky was continually illuminated by shafts of lightning. As ever, the side glazing of the Lysander's canopy was loose and draughty; standing at the wheel of a windjammer rounding the Horn in a force 10 would have been less uncomfortable. But at least Dufort's knees and backside were warm – a coolant pipe ran down each side of the Lysander cockpit, providing natural heating. After weeks of evading the Gestapo, Duclos' nerves were well stretched; nonetheless, as Whippy later recalled, the Frenchman 'displayed a hardness that would have made high tensile tungsten steel appear like putty'.[2]

When a thin coat of ice formed on the windscreen and leading edge of the Lysander's wings, Whippy was too low to take the normal avoiding action of descending into warmer air. His only option was to turn back towards Issoudun and climb into the slightly less malign weather, but being unable to see the ground he could not obtain any fixes, so became somewhat uncertain of his position. At 8,000 feet, severe icing started accumulating on his airframe. An aircraft's carburettor has a great gift for turning moisture in the air into ice, which tends to prevent the engine providing the correct mixture of fuel and air, and therefore normal levels of power – the Lysander's Mercury engine was more susceptible than most to this evil. That night, the air was very moist – Whippy's engine began to falter. His air speed indicator had also stopped working due to ice. By now, three or four inches of clear ice had accumulated on the leading edges of the wings, enough to pluck most aircraft out of the sky. Whippy pulled the boost over-ride on the engine to extract every last horsepower, but could not climb out of the weather – the aircraft was 'practically unmanageable' and still sinking.

Estimating he was somewhere between the Seine and the French coast, he shouted to his two agents to bail out, but they could not hear him in the din. He had no option but to dive to attempt to evade the icing layer, and broke cloud at 1,000 feet, flying first 40 miles west then 70 miles east to try to find a gap in this vicious cold front. Five and a half hours' flying at full throttle had left him with only 50 gallons of fuel remaining, so he decided the best course of action for the safety of his passengers was to fly back to the Unoccupied Zone whence they had come, and where the agents might contact their own Resistance network. He found a likely looking field, and a precautionary circuit indicated it was reasonably flat, so he put it down. With his air speed indicator still failing to tell him his speed, he did what any pilot would have done, and erred on the side of caution by approaching slightly fast. At the end of the landing run, T1508 tipped onto its nose – he had tripped over an unseen banked ditch. The two agents were unhurt, and Whippy suffered only a cricked neck.[3] The

1942: THE FORMATION OF NO. 161 SQUADRON

agents were perplexed there was no car at hand to whisk them away to London – they had been blissfully unaware that they had landed near their point of departure!

The self-destruct mechanism in the secret IFF equipment* had done its job, triggered by the collision with the bank. His duty now was to destroy the rest of his aircraft. The axe was wedged into place and could not be extracted. Could Whippy set his Lysander alight? Only with difficulty, since he was reduced to using his penknife to try to puncture the tanks and there was precious little aviation spirit left to fuel the fire. He eventually started it only with the aid of his Very pistol. But by the time they had all legged it across two fields the fire had extinguished itself. The Vichy authorities later found Whippy's maps and other useful documents in the wreck.[4]

It was only after leaving his beloved machine that Whippy realized how much the seven-hour fight with the elements had drained him. Lysander pilots had to keep their feet on the rudder pedals at all times – this made the machine more fatiguing than most types in bumpy weather. But his navigation had been superb, and 15 miles' walking brought them near Issoudun; he was too exhausted to go further, and, together with Roger, tried to sleep in a crude shepherd's hut 100 yards from the road. What with heavy rain still falling, the cold front's strong winds, and not having a raincoat, Whippy was chilled to the bone. He was wearing his normal blue uniform with only a blue mechanic's cotton overall on top. The RAF uniform had the normal crude compass concealed in one button, and he had a small survival kit in a hip pocket. This should have comprised some Benzedrine tablets, matches, a water-purifying kit using Halazone tablets, some chocolate, Horlicks tablets and, most importantly in Nesbitt-Dufort's opinion, a map of France and some francs. Despite frozen fingers, he managed to open it, but was disgusted to find a load of reichsmarks, accompanied by a map of Germany!

Maurice Duclos walked into Issoudun, and procured a car and driver, returning to the hut at 1400hrs the following afternoon. He tossed to Roger and Whippy some French farm workers' smocks, a beret and a tatty peaked cap. And, even more welcome, a thermos flask of ersatz coffee with a good shot of cognac. They managed to have a much-needed late lunch at the

---

*Identification Friend or Foe – an electronic box of tricks which helped RAF or Fleet Air Arm aircraft avoid shooting down their own. Its concept is still used by commercial and military aircraft today.

railway station in Issoudun, and were given shelter by the station master, M. Combeau, and his family. There was no doubting this patriarch's courage – he had won the Médaille Militaire in World War I, and his willingness to help was cemented by Duclos' masonic handshake. For 30 days, they had to hole up in a small brick building at the side of the railway track – Whippy was acutely aware of the dangers to which the Combeau family were now exposed. The father achieved what Whippy had failed to do: he organized his local Resistance friends to haul the Lysander (at the Germans' behest) across the nearby Paris–Nice railway line, and its tailwheel conveniently stuck in the tracks just before the next passing train neatly destroyed it.[5]

After a few days, some light appeared in the gloom: it transpired that the local *curé* (priest) at Saint-Florent (the village nearest to where they had landed) had been arrested by the Milice* and handed over to the Gestapo for interrogation. He had only arrived in his parish the previous day, and so was unknown to the locals – he had been mistaken for the missing *pilote Anglais*. Even the Gestapo soon realized their mistake, and he was released, unharmed in body if not mind.

On the night of Nesbitt-Dufort's failed mission, Bomber Command had lost 36 aircraft due to the unforecast dreadful weather. On 1 February, the postman delivered to Beryl Nesbitt-Dufort at 'Seagulls' in Middleton-on-Sea the Air Ministry telegram that any RAF wife dreaded: 'Madam, I am commanded by the Air Council to express to you their great regret on learning that your husband, Squadron Leader John Nesbitt-Dufort, DSO, Royal Air Force, is missing as a result of air operations on the night of 28/29th January 1942…' The Air Force decided against including his name in the daily communiqué of the missing and dead – the fate of this Special Duties pilot on his clandestine operation had to remain secret.[6]

Although Roger and Maurice already had adequate forged identity papers, Whippy clearly did not, and it took some days for these to be created – which meant that he remained incarcerated in the cold trackside hut until they appeared. Meanwhile, word was discreetly sent back to Beryl that her husband was in fact still alive – somewhere.

Whilst Whippy was enduring this enforced rest, his squadron was undergoing a long discussed change. 161 Squadron was formed on 14 February

---

*The Milice was a paramilitary force created in Vichy France to assist the Germans; much recruitment was from the French underclass. Members worked closely with the feared Gestapo (more formerly the *Geheime Staatspolizei*), Germany's secret police.

1942: THE FORMATION OF NO. 161 SQUADRON

at Newmarket, and as the font of Lysander special operations knowledge, Sqn Ldr Murphy was transferred across. 161 was now to carry out most of the Lysander work together with a handful of the bombers, whilst 138 was to focus on Whitley and Halifax parachute-dropping missions. Moreover, 161 was to be allied with SOE, and 138 was charged with SIS, although in practice both squadrons served both masters. The following day, Singapore fell to the Japanese. A few weeks earlier, Dalton had dined with Sir Alan Brooke, the new Chief of Staff, who had said, 'I don't feel we are doing anything like enough' (for SOE); Admiral Mountbatten, new Chief of Combined Operations, concurred. The Head of Naval Intelligence also thought that RAF chiefs were dragging their feet with SOE.[7] Resources were beginning to be unblocked.

161's crest featured an opened red shackle; its motto was simply 'Liberate'. But its most notable feature on its formation was the choice of commanding officer – W/Cdr Edward Hedley Fielden, MVO, AFC, known as Ned by his family, but better known as 'Mouse' by everyone else. His Member of the Victorian Order (MVO) gave a clue to his background – he had previously commanded the King's Flight. This had effectively been disbanded, and its assets – including its CO – handed over to 161. The ORB proudly noted, 'Our Commanding Officer is HM The King's personal pilot'.

Fielden was born in 1903 to a well-off middle-class family in Bracknell. His father, also Edward, was a GP and acted for a couple of Berkshire schools, including the prep school Heatherdown, to which the young Mouse was sent, before going on to Malvern. With his Latin too poor to join the Navy, he joined the RAF aged 21 for a short service commission. After training he flew fighters with Nos 25 and 23 Squadrons. In September 1926, in recognition of his piloting talent, he was posted to Duxford's Meteorological Flight. Although awarded the Air Force Cross (AFC), Fielden retired from the service at the end of his commission because opportunities for advancement were limited at that pause before the RAF's expansion era.

On moving to the RAF Reserve, with his reputation now secured as 'a brilliant pilot', he became personal pilot to the aquiline politician and polo player Freddie Guest, and also taught him to fly. By 1929, the very air-minded Prince of Wales had acquired a de Havilland Gipsy Moth, and required a professional pilot to fly it. The Prince had been up in an aircraft three times in World War I, whilst his brother, Prince Albert, had taken a flight in a Handley Page 0/400 bomber during that conflict. The Gipsy Moth enabled the Prince of Wales simply to don an Irvine suit over his formal attire, and be flown to meetings around the country. Mouse was hired because of his reputation as both a competent and safe pilot; his first act as royal pilot was to move the aircraft from its base at Northolt (to the west of London) to RAF Hendon at the bottom of the A1. He then traded up from the Gipsy Moth to a Puss Moth, which was a cabin monoplane, therefore affording the Prince (and Mouse) greater creature comforts. These aircraft were all liveried in scarlet, reflecting the Prince's allegiance to the Guards over the Air Force!

Mouse's first contact with Petter and Penrose was in 1930 when he oversaw the modification of a Westland Wapiti for use on the Prince's tours. Mouse also flew the Prince's Comper Swift to second place in the 1932 King's Cup air race. And when the Prince succeeded to the throne, Mouse flew him from Sandringham down to London in a recently acquired de Havilland Dragon Rapide to attend the Proclamation. This was therefore the first aircraft to carry a reigning British monarch. The King's Flight was formed at Hendon on 21 July 1936, with Mouse in charge – by this time promoted to wing commander, and anointed Equerry in Waiting.[8]

Mouse was perfectly suited to the role: 'strong, silent, devoted, good-looking in the spruce, close-cropped manner that reminds you of a well-groomed Airedale [terrier] (the same gingerbread coloured eyes and moustache). When he speaks it is in the clipped authoritative voice of a thoroughly disciplined, self-effacing soldier.'[9] Although his good looks had become a little weather worn with too much flying in open cockpit biplanes, and his poor teeth much in evidence, he was invariably very smartly dressed. Whilst not a book lover, he excelled at ballroom dancing.

Fielden remained on very good terms with the new King throughout his life, such that in due course the King became godfather to Mouse's son, Mark. Mouse had married Angela Ramsden-Jodrell in October 1940, and received a silver cigarette box from the King. By the standards of 161, Fielden was abstemious, and even rationed himself to only a few of his favourite Virginian cigarettes. His management style was a mark of the man – plenty of praise preceded any rebuke; but as younger pilots came into his orbit at 161, he was regarded by them as an old-school RAF type.

Mouse Fielden and Gp Capt James Easton (Deputy Director of Intelligence, who was the Air Ministry man responsible for Special Operations) went to visit Graveley and an embryonic station, Tempsford, in the middle of January with a view to their being used as bases for 138 and the soon-to-be-formed 161. The former was viewed as having north/south runways that were too short for Halifaxes, whilst the latter was simply a 'poor aerodrome'. Dalton was so cross with the lack of progress that he was intent on going to Churchill to speed up matters.[10] Jack Baldwin (then Acting Commander-in-Chief Bomber Command) disagreed about Tempsford's demerits, and decided it would become the parent aerodrome for special operations, with Graveley and Gransden Lodge as its satellites.[11] On 22 January, Mouse Fielden was told by Easton about what had been agreed, and was instructed to tell King George VI that the Royal Flight's Lockheed Hudson was going to be appropriated by the new squadron.[12] The regal imprimatur followed swiftly.

By the end of February 1942, the squadron had moved into Graveley, the dregs of Bomber Command's real estate. On 26 February, Fielden and Murphy flew down to Tangmere, so that on the following day Sticky could carry out the new squadron's first operational Lysander mission – *Baccarat* – a short trip to a field outside Saint-Saëns, north of Rouen. Leaving shortly before 2200hrs, he was in solid cloud at 8,000 feet over the Channel, and so failed to find his coasting-in point. Against standing instructions (which ordered radio silence after leaving the English coast), he radioed Tangmere for a direction finding fix, and was then able to correct his course to Abbeville. It is possible that Murphy had taken such a circuitous route to his destination because that night Mountbatten's Combined Operations were mounting the infamous Bruneval Raid to capture a Wurzburg radar near the coast north of Dieppe. It was sensible for Murphy's health to avoid such activity.[13]

Despite cloud down to 700 feet and bad visibility, he found his intended field at Saint-Saëns and landed at midnight. Laughing at being back in his homeland, his outbound passenger *Anatole* disembarked and vanished into the night. A BCRA agent Pierre Julitte (known as *Julie*), and the filmmaker Gilbert Renault-Roulier (*Rémy*), founder of the Free French Catholic intelligence network called CONFRÉRIE NOTRE DAME (CND) and an ardent Gaullist, leapt into the back of the Lysander, arriving back at Tangmere by 0120hrs. Julitte was a special envoy of Dewavrin, who had been tasked with improving CND's radio communications with London. The two agents had suitcases of material that London was desperate to see – detailed plans of the Germans' U-Boat bases in north-west France, and the fruits of those parts of the Paris INTERALLIÉ network that had not been destroyed by the traitor *La Chatte*. Their retrieval had originally been planned for late January but bad weather had intervened.

The two agents had had to spend days sharing a single bed in a café awaiting the next moon period.¹⁴ Renault-Roulier was debriefed over dinner at London's Waldorf by Dewavrin, who was most impressed with the amount of intelligence material he had brought back.

William Guy Lockhart, a 'striking looking slim young man with good rather thin features and wavy brown hair',¹⁵ was the other transfer over from 138 Squadron apart from Murphy, and had already had a very eventful war. Born in Mortlake in 1916, he had had seven years of schooling in China, before going to Sevenoaks School in Kent. A six-month spell at school in Canada had improved his French. Lockhart joined the RAF in 1935 and flew Furies and Gladiators. However, he was court martialled only three years later for unauthorized low flying when participating in the Empire Air Day flying display at Stoke-on-Trent. When war broke out, he was working as a civilian flying instructor at the West Suffolk Flying Club, but was called back to arms as a sergeant pilot.

He was flying Spitfires with No. 74 Squadron when, on 7 July 1941, he took off from RAF Biggin Hill, Kent. An hour later over northern France, he was blown out of the sky – a German shell found the magazine in his port wing. Its detonation took off two-thirds of the wing and Lockhart bailed out at 16,000 feet. He landed unconscious in a tree at Ergny, whilst his aircraft crashed a few miles away at Avesnes. When he came to, he found a farmer who was 'unhelpful', and a few moments later a boy told him that the farmer was going to telephone the Germans to collect his reward of 80,000 francs for turning him in. Some friendlier folk took him a few miles east to Renty, where he rested for three weeks whilst his arm, ribs and leg healed. He was not best equipped for this evasion lark: at Biggin he had not been issued with francs, compass or any of the normal gear. However, he was escorted to Lille and met up with another evader, F/O D.N. Forde, a Spitfire pilot from Tangmere who was similarly ill-equipped. Together, they made for the Unoccupied Zone – they crossed the demarcation line at Chalon-sur-Saône on 9 August. Lockhart was, however, arrested by the Germans – he pretended to be a Frenchman, but an English letter in his pocket was difficult to explain.

Taking him to the train station, the Germans instructed him to go to Paris (unescorted, to his surprise). After dark, Lockhart hopped on a goods train going south instead, and met up again with Forde in Marseille. Together they made their way to Perpignan to join the COMÈTE escape line, one of three created by MI9 to assist Allied evaders over the Pyrenees. Once across the border, he was incarcerated by the Spanish, but released to get to Gibraltar on 10 October. An RAF flying boat brought him back to Devon 11 days later.[16]

At the end of November whilst on leave at his Colchester home, Guy received a letter from Major Lewis Gielgud at the War Office (elder brother of the actor John): 'Your name has been passed to me with the suggestion that you possess qualifications, which might be of value in connection with a phase of the War Effort, regarding which I should be glad to have a personal conversation with you...'[17]

By 4 December, he was being interviewed in London by SOE; the interviewing officer 'indicated to Lockhart that if we asked him to return to France it would be for organisation purposes with a view to sabotage. His comment was: "That should be easy. I spoke to a number of Frenchmen whilst I was there about sabotage, and they know the tricks, all they want is financial support and direction from England. The point is that they will not take direction from other Frenchmen because they distrust each other so profoundly".' Guy was confident he could pass himself off as a native Frenchman, as he had met a 'British Intelligence Officer' in France who 'speaks French with a cockney accent which is unmistakeable'.[18] He was also keen to return to the Lille area and link up with his former helpers.

The SOE team decided that, whilst Lockhart's French was not quite as good as he thought it was (it had a hint of Canadian, for a start), a two- or three-week course would sort it out. However, the Air Ministry had the last word – they refused to let this (well) qualified pilot disappear to become an agent. His skills were needed in the skies, and he was posted to 138 Squadron, and thence to 161, where he 'was considered eccentric by some' and 'rather intense' by others.[19] He had acquired a reputation as a successful poker player in the clubs of London. With wavy brown hair, F/O Lockhart had high sartorial standards, and wore French wings on the right breast pocket of his RAF tunic, in addition to his normal wings on the left.

By now, Baker Street had received the signal from the Resistance that Whippy was safe, and it was therefore imperative to retrieve him – if taken by the Germans, the Gestapo would soon extract much detail of the operations of Lysander operations and SOE. Best placed to retrieve him were his colleagues; however, because it was not just Whippy, but his two agents and another person to be collected, a Lysander was impractical. Fielden ideally wanted to take the Lockheed Hudson he had flown for the King, but this was away being overhauled and given a more military interior (all its velvet-covered seats were being ripped out). So he borrowed from the Bomber Command OTU at Abingdon an Avro Anson – a twin-engined workhorse, by this stage of the war only used for navigational and gunnery training, and the occasional coastal patrol. Unsuitably yellow, it was quickly slathered with matt black paint.

SIS records indicate that Nesbitt-Dufort was not the main focus of the mission: 'the Air Ministry had refused to lay on a special operation to pick him up.' The key passenger was Wincenty Zarembski, 'Head of an important Polish Reseau'; Zarembski had been the Polish Deuxième Bureau's representative in Paris, operating from the embassy there under the cover of Commercial Attaché. He had done a sterling job in helping Polish evaders in the southern half of France escape over the Pyrenees to Spain. Radio contact had been made with the Polish Directorate in London, and SIS had then given him the codename *Tudor*.[20]

P/O Harry 'Titch' Cossar, a wireless operator/air gunner, had been approached a few days earlier in Newmarket's officers' mess by Murphy, who told him that he had been tasked with retrieving Johnny Nesbitt-Dufort: 'Will you come and help me; I can't give you any details except that it will be an Anson and we'll be landing in France.'[21] 'Alright Sticky, when do we go?' Titch was given the task of supervising the fitting of a long-range fuel tank and an additional radio. After testing short landing techniques at Newmarket, they flew down to Tangmere to await an improvement in the weather.

On 1 March it came, and Baker Street told BBC radio to transmit the message that Whippy in France had been waiting for in the 1800hrs *messages personnels* – '*Philippe va bien et attend ses amis*' ('Philippe is fine and waiting for his friends'). He only heard the first three words, but that was enough. Whippy, Duclos and Mitchell retrieved their personal weapons from their cache in Mme Corbeau's piano, and he donned his uniform, with M Corbeau's donated 'threadbare' overcoat on top. The trio had a last supper (which they hoped would not be their last supper) of cabbage soup, and to their surprise were then joined by this General Zarembski, together with his wife Edwidge, both now also on the run from the Germans. What with a large suitcase (largely containing intelligence material), the pilot in Nesbitt-Dufort was already worrying about the weight of the aircraft's payload. After an emotional farewell with the Combeau family, the group set off for the airfield south east of Issoudun at 2000hrs, to be out of town before the curfew started. They took it in turns to carry the heavy case, but Whippy felt rather unfit after his month of confinement. The party made it over the icy landscape to reach the field by 2130hrs, and laid out the flare-path with torches on stakes. But there had been a potentially serious flaw in communications: Whippy had no idea of what sort of aircraft would be sent to collect them, therefore no idea of the precise landing and take-off run it would require. All he could do was assume that the landing field – which was after all a pre-war airfield – would suffice. A barking dog added to his anxiety. The torches were switched on twice at the sound of incoming burbling aircraft – which turned out to be RAF Whitleys on bombing raids.

Sticky and Titch were bumbling over a snow-covered French landscape at a mere 100 knots, and at midnight the by now well-chilled agents were getting anxious. Whippy encouraged them to be patient and 15 minutes later he heard the unmistakeable drone of an Anson's two Cheetah engines. In Nesbitt-Dufort's judgement, Murphy 'made a beautiful landing' by the well-laid-out flarepath, and drew back his cockpit window to launch some cheery swear words at his squadron chum, who Murphy claimed 'smelled like the Paris Metro'! After they had boarded, the somewhat heavy Anson was taxied to edge of the field: its take-off run over the soggy ground proceeded at no more than a 'steady trot' in Whippy's words, before gaining just enough speed at the far end to lumber into the air. The remainder of the trip was 'uneventful, if slow'.[22] The relieved group landed back at Tangmere at 0240hrs on the 2nd. The Anson was flown back to its home base on the 3rd, its crew hopping into the accompanying Lysander before anyone at Abingdon could query why their plodding treasure had become a sooty black.

When the operation was written up, a very grateful Nesbitt-Dufort could not help having a dig at his rescuers: 'The skill of the pilot and navigator proved in this case to be exceptional, as we were only lost the majority of the time on the way home, which only goes to prove!' In his side of the story, Murphy pointed out the journey down was carried out in conditions of 10/10ths cloud, heavy rain and visibility of no more than 1,000 yards. On the return, he had found his turning points on the Loire and the Seine rivers, as also his coasting out point at Dieppe. Murphy reported:

The above laconic report marks the completion of a very stout effort by the pilot and navigator and the Cooks Tour passenger, but the writer must point out that, although the story appears to end at 0240 [the landing time], at 0241 hours a party commenced over which a veil has been drawn both by the participants, a select three, and those members of the squadron who were so glad to see our DSO able to use the return half of his ticket.

A score draw between pilot and passenger then.

Murphy's rescue mission was not the only operation for 161 that night. Fielden had taken a Whitley for a parachute drop only a few miles away. And the intense Guy Lockhart was busy too on his first Lysander operation – *Crème*. He lifted off from Tangmere at 2025hrs in V9428. Initially hampered by low cloud in finding his landing field – a few miles south of Vatan in the squadron's sweet spot between the Loire and Châteauroux – this was only nine miles north-west from where Nesbitt-Dufort and his fellow passengers were liberated. The area was chosen because it was just south-east of the demarcation line in the Unoccupied Zone, and the latter town was chosen because the several straight Roman roads leading into it made it easier to identify. He landed after a surprisingly long four-hour flight.

This was an SIS mission to bring back Stanislas Mangin (Agent *Mojon*) and Louis Andlauer; the latter was a Free French pilot, who had already been imprisoned and escaped twice, and was keen to join the French forces in London. Mangin was the son of General Charles Mangin, and had been captured by the Germans in the Battle of France in 1940. Escaping to the Unoccupied Zone, he had formed a resistance group, ALI-TIR, and was returning to London for orders. The turnaround must have been very efficient for Lockhart was only on French soil for 'approximately 110 seconds'.

He found the return flight rather trying due to a lot of cloud, but finally landed back at Tangmere just after 0400hrs. This was the first time that incoming SIS agents were taken from Tangmere to Bignor Manor, a delightful Elizabethan manorial farmhouse on the South Downs rented from a local farmer by Major Anthony and Mrs Barbara Bertram. Of Prussian-Jewish descent and with a Jesuit education, Tony Bertram, now a pipe-smoking countryman, was commissioned at the outset of war into the Yorkshire and Lancaster Regiment (in which he had fought in World War I), and had languished in that regiment for some months until a short shift with the Durham Light Infantry. There he was approached in a typically oblique way and recruited into SIS with a promotion to captain. It was the brother-in law of Kenneth Cohen (who was by now ascending the ranks of SIS) who had talent spotted him. Within a few days, he was asked if he knew of a house in Sussex suitable for the reception of French agents. He volunteered his own as it was so close to Tangmere, which was only seven miles to the south-west.

1942: THE FORMATION OF NO. 161 SQUADRON

For a manor, it was remarkably cosy, and when Barbara was asked to sleep up to 18 French (mostly men), it was rather cramped. It was not only beds that were in short supply, but plates and cutlery too. In order to free up space, the Bertrams' two sons, Tim and Nicky, were sent away to become weekly boarders at their school. Because they could not understand this strange language used by the young adults who had invaded their house, the children termed them 'Hullaballoos' – this term stuck, in the family at least.

For this first use of the manor, one of the Frenchmen, atypically grateful for British wartime cuisine, noted, 'A car takes us to a very British meal… the next morning a delicious breakfast, egg, toast and tea'.[23] Whilst the French visitors to Bignor might have found the cuisine unusual, they were impressed by the quantity of food available – the Bertrams kept 12 hens, ducks, rabbits, two bee hives, and Caroline (a goat); the family also tended a large vegetable patch, and British rations were more generous than those in Occupied France. Moreover, the French treasured the availability of real coffee, as only liquid made from acorns was available in their homeland. Indeed, French agents were known to steal into the Bignor kitchen at night and pop a coffee bean into their mouths.[24]

It was not just foodstuffs that were hoarded at Bignor: the Bertrams held a store of nefarious and innocent equipment with which to equip the outgoing agents. Their arsenal comprised revolvers (with ammunition), bludgeons, tear-gas fountain pens, daggers and knives. In the more benign category were compasses, magnifying glasses, field indicators, French branded chocolate, cigarettes and matches, watches, and also anodyne, unbranded soap, razor blades, toothbrushes and toothpaste, and torches with batteries.[25] Similar provisioning at Tempsford was carried out by one 'Pink Gin Percy', more formally known as Courtley Naismith Shaw.[26]

Since Nesbitt-Dufort now knew too much about Resistance activity and escape lines, he was withdrawn from duties at 161 and sent to the Central Landing School at Ringway. There he was subject to dangers of a different kind: he was told to investigate the Lysander's use as a glider tug – at night. (These are described by Whippy himself in Appendix D.)

As mentioned, at the beginning of 1942, Gubbins had circulated his *SOE Transport Requirements*.[27] Clearly, Gubbins felt frustrated that his needs were being trampled by SIS on a regular basis. The paper gained the needed endorsement of Medhurst, whose superior, Norman Bottomley (DCAS), was also broadly in favour, but rightly worried that a demarcation of facilities between SIS and SOE would lead to an inefficient use of scarce assets. SIS must have got wind of this bid by SOE for more resources, for on 17 January, Anthony Eden wrote to Sir Archibald Sinclair (the Liberal leader who had been appointed Secretary of State for Air) enclosing a paper, *Shortage of Aircraft for Political Purposes*. This did make reference to SOE's needs, but bizarrely focused on 'the breakdown of air transport to West Africa'.[28] Sinclair had an Army heritage and knew little about aviation before taking the post, but understood the military machine.

The Air Ministry and its senior officers down to Fielden continued to be exercised by the run of pleas from Polish generals in London to establish a dedicated Polish flight of Halifaxes within 138 Squadron. The RAF held firm for two reasons: the problems of mixing Polish and native English speakers within maintenance teams; and the likely inefficient use of aircraft and crews that would result. By the end of March, ACM Wilfred Freeman (VCAS) had to fire a shot across the bows of Harris, again in charge of Bomber Command: 'Your Command still does not seem to realise the great importance [of special operations]. I understand that there is a certain reluctance to complete the establishment of flying crews and to see that priority is given to the task of maintaining these units in a really high state of serviceability.' Thankfully, the Lysander force was less affected.[29]

Fielden was critically short of pilots and requested an additional five Lysander pilots and one more Whitley captain. 138 continued to feed across pilots who had experience of Whitley and Halifax operations to 161. 138 itself acquired an exotic recruit – Sqn Ldr Boris Romanoff, aged 27 (a Czech who was a cousin of the murdered Tsar); he had earlier unofficially accompanied Ron Hockey on some Whitley operations. Boris had been liberated from the rather tedious task of dropping trainee parachutists (and agents) at Ringway's Parachute Training School. Stalin had asked Churchill as a favour if he could arrange for two German communist agents to be parachuted into Germany. Gubbins and Dodds-Parker were summoned to No. 10 to be given the good news – it was at the extreme end of the Whitley's range. Aided by the London branch of the NKVD (the Soviet Union's interior ministry and secret police), the two agents were equipped for the drop with all the correct German passes. Romanoff was given the mission. Soon after taking off from Stradishall on this, his first Whitley operation for 138, the heavily laden aircraft stalled and crashed, with all bar the tail gunner and one agent perishing. Perhaps Romanoff was unaccustomed to the handling of a Whitley with a full operational payload.[30]

In March, Lord Selborne, 'a small stooping figure with a deceptively mild appearance',[31] was charged by Churchill with investigating SOE. At the end of the month he wrote to Anthony Eden, the Foreign Secretary, and expressed his worries about the 'friction' between SOE and SIS. At its heart was the mutual antipathy between Eden and Selborne's predecessor, Hugh Dalton. Despite being a Wykehamist, Lord Selborne had only taken a third in history at Oxford; but, with chancellors and prime ministers in his immediate ancestry, a high office of state was not a surprise. While Dalton did not make friends easily, the more clubbable Selborne was a friend of Churchill. Despite being an Etonian, Eden developed slightly better relations with Selborne than he had enjoyed with his predecessor.

Sir Frank Nelson and Jebb's contemporary statements 'reveal a deplorable state of affairs'. SOE 'is a mushroom organisation which has sprung up during the war and has been pushed with the greatest energy by those who are responsible for its gigantic task'. They now had around 300 trained agents in the field. 'A great deal of information is sent back by these agents, all of which is transmitted through SIS. For some territories more information is received from SOE than SIS agents, because they happen to be more numerous in that country. There is an inevitable overlap, which means the two services must work in harmony.' So, weekly meetings between the heads of the two organizations were mandated.[32]

Jebb penned a memo to Selborne: 'We have now formally requested "C" to also agree to a complete separation of communications in respect of secret signals sent to agents in Western Europe... With regard to the paragraph on transport, technically we still share a Special Squadron with C but, in practice, this is now being divided up into aeroplanes always at C's disposal and others always at ours... Finally, we show the SIS our Progress Reports, though they give us nothing in return.'[33] Jebb emerges from this period as very level headed, and keen for the greater good of Great Britain:

> Another fruitful source of difficulties between the two organisations is SOE's policy with Allied Governments which, for reasons it is hardly necessary to state in detail (we use so many of their nationals both here and overseas), is as close as we can possibly make it. The attitude however of SIS is to use Allied Governments as much as possible, whilst telling them as little as possible and helping them not at all unless forced to do so; and in no circumstances having any kind of partnership with them. This makes endless trouble for SOE because it is extremely difficult for foreigners to understand that SOE and SIS are absolutely separate organisations, and we are constantly having our relations with Allied Governments impaired as a result.[34]

Free French agents whom SOE had trained wrote 'not less' than six important despatches of which SOE HQ was not aware until the agents returned to Britain. The despatches had been handed over in Barcelona by the Consul General to one of C's representatives. When SOE found out and challenged SIS, they denied the receipt of the messages.

C wrote a lengthy retort and was 'confident that if the control of SOE reverted to the Foreign Office, many difficulties would automatically disappear, and if it is not improper to take a German analogy, the subversive organisation would be under the Head of the Secret Service.'[35]

At the time of Selborne's report submitted to the War Cabinet in April 1942, SOE had:

> Some 1600 men trained in the arts of sabotage and subversion, over 200 agents in enemy occupied countries, some 900 serving with Allied armies, and 350 waiting transport aboard... SOE has reached a stage where it is capable of very important expansion. The principal bottleneck is the provision of transport. Until December transport facilities were very inadequate, but since then the Air Ministry has placed at the disposal of SOE five Halifaxes and eight Whitleys, while 3 Lysanders are shared with C... Very fine results have been accomplished by the personnel of SOE.[36]

It was perhaps strange to ask a man recently placed in charge of an operation to audit it; nonetheless, Selborne's report would have given Churchill confidence that his baby, after some stumbles, was learning to walk. Selborne had, however, had to cede control of SOE activities in neutral countries to the Foreign Office.

The reports continued: 'The Admiralty have given what help they can in fast motor boats for coastal landings. If these facilities could be doubled full use would be made of them.'[37] Selborne concluded by saying that the malicious rumours (about supposed inefficiency and extravagance within SOE) 'have got to cease... If SOE is to function, it must receive fair play as well as give it.' There was little doubt he was pointing the finger at SIS.

So 138 and 161's masters were still at loggerheads. The pilots of the two squadrons had demonstrated that they could achieve what was asked of them – if they only had adequate resources.

8

A Home is Found: Tempsford

138 and 161 Squadrons finally moved to Tempsford (the 'poor aerodrome') on 14 March 1942. Completed by John Laing and Sons only six months previously on what some termed a 'reclaimed bog', it was sited nine miles east of Bedford. Bizarrely, for what was to be the centre of the RAF's most secret operations, it was adjacent to LNER's London–Edinburgh main railway line, and the A1 trunk road. Furthermore, to the east was a ridge which precluded crawling in to the westerly runway when the cloud base threatened to kiss the ground. Fielden's team's first impressions were not positive.[1]

War had come to Tempsford before, but centuries ago: in 917, it was a fortified Danish settlement, built as a forward operating base for attacks on territory held by the indigenous Angles. The English leader King Edward the Elder took umbrage and stormed the settlement, killed a Danish king and many of his followers, and blunted the Nordic threat.

In 1942, the 'Hobson's choice' of Tempsford reflected Harris' stance that Special Duties operations required less than special priority. 138 mounted its first operation from its new base on 23 March. Wilfrid Freeman (VCAS) wrote to Harris that day:

> Lately we have been subject to very strong political pressure to increase our subversive and other activities in Allied territory occupied by the enemy… In spite of the emphasis which has been laid on these special operations in the past, your Command still does not seem to realise their great importance. I understand that there is a certain reluctance to complete the establishment of flying crews and to see that priority

is given to the task of maintaining those units in a really high state of serviceability... I must ask you to impress on all concerned the claims of these special operations.'[2]

Bottomley (ACAS) wrote to Harris in similar vein. The bomber chief's response was obdurate: 'I am writing an official letter to propose that the Squadrons as such should be abandoned and that the specialised work be undertaken by ordinary bomber squadrons as part of their normal duties. Such an arrangement would be very much more economical than the present one, and any special equipment or specially trained personnel would be held in addition to the normal establishment.'[3]

On 28 March, Harris wrote a 'Secret & Personal' letter to Portal about 'Charles Medhurst's cloak and dagger Squadrons', arguing that they should be re-incorporated into Bomber Command to avoid wasteful use of scarce resources. He thought the formation of 161 simply increased the waste. 'We had thirty-one tons of nickels [propaganda leaflets] sent to us to drop all over France purely for the purpose of explaining why we had bombed the RENAULT factories. This is a typical example of how these sidelines and comic departments get entirely out of control and perspective.'[4] Perhaps his duodenal ulcer was playing up that day.

Harris' plan would have diluted the skill levels in Special Duties of the Whitley and Halifax crews and would have weakened the security of the whole organization; and, of course, he was entirely overlooking the unique position of the Lysander element. If the Whitley and Halifax crews (of 138 and 161) were to carry out normal bombing duties in between special operations missions, the loss rate of Bomber Command crews in 1942 overall was such that these specially trained crews would become needless casualties quite quickly. Harris' stance was greatly to his discredit; it was the good fortune of thousands of Resistance members around Europe that Harris' superiors overruled him.[5] One should note that Harris continued to have the ear of Churchill and was a regular visitor to Chequers. It is illuminating that Henry Probert, the definitive biographer of Harris, never mentions 138 or 161 Squadrons, and the main mention of Lord Selborne and MEW is regarding the latter's supposed meddling in Bomber Command's target selection. Harris' parsimony regarding Special Duties squadron assets merits just one paragraph.[6]

At least Portal's deputy, Norman Bottomley, had a sense of proportion. On 31 March, he noted in a letter to the Chief of the Air Staff, 'I am sure that if the C-in-C [Commander-in-Chief] Bomber Command realised the

A HOME IS FOUND: TEMPSFORD

importance of the work which is being done by the [Special Duties] squadrons he would take a more sympathetic interest in their work. Their work is not opposed to but complementary to the bombing effort of Bomber Command. When we send the directive to him it would be well for him to see a copy of Lord Selborne's latest paper as to the achievements and aims of SOE.'[7]

The Lysander crews decamped from Tempsford to Tangmere as was now their habit for the end-March moon period, and Guy Lockhart had the honour of carrying out the first mission. Gilbert Renault (alias Agent *Rémy*) was ushered into the Cottage (see page 172) that afternoon, but Guy was too busy preparing his charts to entertain him. Guy's emotional state was strained – when he walked out for transport to 161's apron, he was clutching a pair of small white children's shoes – a memento of his young son who had just died.[8] The dynamic Renault had had a varied past with jobs including banking and insurance, but at the outbreak of war he was in Spain directing a film on Christopher Columbus.

At 2125hrs on 26 March, Guy set off from the Sussex airfield with Renault on board, who was returning after his one-month rest and debriefing in England. Heavy cloud over the Channel meant Lockhart had to fly on instruments; when Renault tried to make small talk over the intercom, he was abruptly cut off. Letting down to 1,000 feet nearer their destination, he found the Loire and crawled along eastwards at that height until he found the town of Saumur – unmistakeable from its castle, island and two bridges. His objective for *Baccarat II* was a field surrounded by dense woodland ten miles to the south. Unfortunately, at shortly before midnight, Lockhart landed long, and did not stop until he was 30 yards past Lamp 'A', and became stuck in heavy plough. Gunning the engine made no difference, so the operator Georges Geay summoned his helpers, and the seven men, with another two lifting the tail, managed to swing the Lysander onto firmer ground, albeit only after doing some damage to the wheel spats.

By the time Lockhart's two return passengers could embark, he had been on French soil for a sweaty 17 minutes. They were Christian Pineau and François Faure (Agent *Paco*); the latter, having recognized Renault, paused for a brief chat before mounting the black bird. Pineau was another from an elite background (educated at Sciences Po followed by the Paris Law Faculty), and had become a trade union leader in 1934. Mobilized into the infantry in 1939, he was appropriated by his stepfather, the noted novelist and playwright Jean Giraudoux, to join his Ministry of Information. Pineau had been encouraged by his colleague Pierre Brosselette to go to London to meet de Gaulle to brief the general on the state of the Resistance and persuade him firstly to use what powers he had to urge the young communists to stop engaging in counter-productive poorly organized action, and secondly to unite the warring factions of the Resistance. To that end, in the preceding days, Pineau had canvassed the views of the likes of Henri Frénay and de la Vigerie.[9]

By the time *Paco* and Pineau boarded Lockhart's machine, they were well refreshed, not to say handicapped by the remnants of a good hangover. They had arrived by train from Paris at their pre-departure rendezvous (a farm a mile or so from the appointed field) early that morning and breakfasted on bread, rillettes and saucisson – with some excellent Loire wine produced by René, the farm's owner. The atmosphere was relaxed: René assured them that there were no Boches nearer than Saumur. They started with his current vintage, 'If that harms you, you can hang me from my feet. Anyway, it's not you flying the aeroplane!' The party progressed to a 1934 Saumur. *Paco* and Pineau had to recline in some willow chairs for the rest of the morning. René's vines stretched across to a cloudless sky; the first tinge of spring warmth was in the air. Pineau could scarcely believe that in 16 or 17 hours' time 161's magic carpet would transport him to England.

Lunch was meat and chicken, goats' cheese and chocolate pudding, with a bottle or two of a 1921 Champigny red. Life in Lyon under rationing seemed distant. After a much-needed afternoon nap, *Paco* and Pineau woke at 1700hrs with slightly sore heads. But René now proffered a glass or two of his 1904 vintage. As this was the year of his birth (*Paco* was seven years older), Pineau found it hard to refuse. Obviously, a supper with more wine was required to toast their onward journey. Afterwards the party gathered round the family radio for the *messages personelles*. Theirs was one of the last – the operation was confirmed. It was little surprise then that after the stroll to the field near Douvy, Pineau wandered over to the hedgerow and simply fell asleep on the grass. As Lockhart arrived overhead, *Paco* had to shake him awake. Once the Lysander came to a halt, Gilbert Rémy climbed out. Lockhart smiled at Pineau and said, 'You're my first passenger who's been asleep on the landing ground!'[10]

There were so many parcels of *courier* slung into the Lysander that *Paco* and Pineau were wedged in like champagne corks. On the return, the Lysander's leaky canopy glazing ensured that any sleepiness evaporated; all on board noticed the Loire sliding below, but soon Lockhart again entered cloud at 6,000 feet, spoiling their view of rural France bathed in the light of a lambent moon. He climbed to 8,000 feet still in solid cloud. As soon as he thought he was beyond the French coast, which had been marked by the dull thuds of flak bursts, he radioed for a homing fix from *Médoc*, the codename of Tangmere's secret radio aid for 161's missions. The clouds dissipated 15 miles from the coast and he landed uneventfully at 0145hrs. If they did not already know, whisky and Barbara Bertram's welcome dinner announced that they were truly back in England.[11]

After a few hours' sleep at the Bertrams', they were taken to London by a conducting officer, and reached the capital shortly after 1100hrs. When Pineau went on to meet Dewavrin at his Duke Street lair, the latter's first question to Pineau was, 'Does the French Resistance recognise the authority of de Gaulle?' To which Pineau replied, 'Yes, without hesitation.'[12] Pineau then dined with de Gaulle at the Connaught Hotel, his London residence; he was the first senior Resistance figure from France to meet de Gaulle in London. 'Now talk to me of France.' The main topic of discussion was his radio broadcast, 'Declaration to the Resistance Movements'. Pineau later noted, 'I realise that like Passy, he knows almost nothing about the Resistance.'[13] He made the telling observation, 'We look at the problem from the perspective of Liberty; he conceives it from the point of view of History.'[14]

Passy/Dewavrin's reputation in British quarters was to plummet around this time. Maurice Dufour, a member of CARTE, reached London via Gibraltar and volunteered for SOE, but while waiting for his acceptance he was invited to BCRA's headquarters in Duke Street. There he was tortured until 0300hrs, and kept in a low-ceilinged basement cell with beatings every night for ten days. His crime? *Passy* and his gang were upset he had volunteered for SOE first.[15] Yet on one level, *Passy* enjoyed reasonably cordial relations with F Section: the building in which he lived was connected to the mews where Buckmaster lived. If the two had difficulties, they were ironed out whilst walking together up and down the mews.[16]

Sticky Murphy, who had been promoted to acting squadron leader four weeks earlier, and given an 'Exceptional' rating by Mouse, ventured forth for his next op on All Fools' Day, or rather night, just before Easter. It was another SIS trip, on which he took out a BCRA agent to a field east of Les Andelys on the Seine. Blessed with good weather and a full moon, he could see the French coast from 20 miles away; he also noted the 'commendable fireworks display' from the ground defences at Le Havre. But then he encountered solid cloud over the land, and carried on before letting down with dead reckoning when he thought he was near Les Andelys. To his horror, he soon realized the river he was following was not the Seine. 'I came to the conclusion there was no future in wandering round France like a lost lamb', so he retraced his steps to Le Havre at midnight, and flew back down the Seine at 500 feet. Once at his target field he had difficulty noting the torches through thin cloud, but found the field after a circuit or two. After landing, his passenger 'smartly decanted himself', and he embarked Claude Lamirault (Agent *Fitzroy*), and a female SIS agent (*Micheline*). He set off northwards and nearing the French coast at Le Tréport encountered a thunder cloud 'of monstrous proportions', which bounced the Lysander severely. 'At 0105 the female passenger was violently sick, but as she was unable to speak English I could not find out whether it was the bumps or my blind flying which had caused this regrettable effect.' The shaken and stirred trio landed at Tangmere at 0225hrs.[17]

The last part of this moon period saw a strange reappearance of Flt Lt Gordon Scotter in the logs. He carried out an anonymous SIS operation under the aegis of 161 Squadron on 11 April to retrieve his old friend Philip Schneidau from a field outside Nemours, south of Paris. He had to evade 'considerable activity' by German night-fighters on the way down, who approached as close as 1,000 yards but did not open fire. He dived and corkscrewed his Lysander with aileron turns. Heavy rain and the relative lack of moon hampered his quest to find the landing field. So he was quite surprised when, slightly opportunistically 'bursting' his engine (the agreed recognition signal), Schneidau's torch flashed up almost beneath him. After a rough landing (crossing three small ditches), once Schneidau had collected his torches he climbed up to the front cockpit for a chat – Scotter reported, 'I did not recognise him and pulled out my revolver, he said "Put that bloody thing away!", so I refrained from shooting him.' After his five-hour mission, the pair made it back to Tangmere well before dawn.[18]

Flight Sergeant (Flt Sgt) Arnold John Mott arrived at 161 in March – and soon had his first Lysander crash. On 23 March, he was taking off from a field at Bishops Waltham in Hampshire when his engine failed: he hit the far hedge, tore off most of the tail, and the aircraft overturned. Notwithstanding this escapade, he received his commission at the beginning of April. Almost 26 by now, he had enlisted in 1938; it is said he developed the urge to fly at a young age having seen a German Zeppelin drone overhead when a schoolboy at Christ's Hospital (the Blue Coat School) in Sussex.

After training, he was posted to Dishforth in Yorkshire to fly Whitleys. On 28 December 1940, whilst on a 78 Squadron mission to bomb the German U-boat pens at Lorient in Brittany, his aircraft was shot down over Brittany; Mott bailed out and managed to avoid arrest. He was cared for by the Delavignes in Nantes, and for a while helped the local Resistance with communications with London. He managed to pick up excellent French in a matter of weeks from his hostess Mme Tantine Delavigne. But on learning in September 1941 that another UK airman – who knew Mott's whereabouts – was being interrogated by the Gestapo, the Delavignes did all in their power to ensure his successful escape. A Hungarian resister known as 'Rips' took him south into the Unoccupied Zone; together they took the train to Bordeaux, from where he made Toulouse by 4 October. Many of those who had helped him in France were captured by the Gestapo, tortured, and some sent to concentration camps. Eight days later, Mott trekked over the Pyrenees and followed the by now traditional route from a British Consulate to the British Embassy in Madrid. He hitched a ride back from Gibraltar in the usual way for an airman – a Sunderland flying boat.[19]

On 24 April, Guy Lockhart considered the weather forecast was 'about as bad as it could be' for a planned combined SOE and SIS operation; it was a long trip of over 600 miles; moreover he had already flown four hours that day. Nonetheless, he was ordered to go ahead. After take-off, he was thwarted firstly by engine problems and then the filthy weather.[20] Two nights later, he had more success, taking Pierre Beech (a radio operator under the name of Agent *Gazelle*) to a field ten miles north-north-east of Châteauroux. Lockhart recounted:

> Unfortunately the landing ground was on a hill and as I descended Mother Earth came up to meet me, the result being a dull thud. The engine commenced to burn with considerable ill-feeling so I switched off and searched for a fire extinguisher, but could only find an incendiary bomb. Meanwhile Gazelle disembarked with luggage and faded into the gloom, leaving me to go up with the aircraft like a good Captain. After six or seven minutes I was about to burst into tears as a last resort but this was unnecessary as the flames died out unaided. I therefore started up and taxied back to light A where the two passengers embarked like men possessed.[21]

The operation had been put on because a young Resistance leader, Edgard Tupet-Thomé, had sent a message demanding a Lysander urgently. Gaston Tavian and Capitaine de Vaisseau Mariotti were the returning cargo. The choice of a hill as a landing ground had been Tavian's (his codename was *Collin* and '*colline*' in French translates as 'hill'!), and his poor selection led to 161 refusing to use further landing grounds unless they had already trained the agent concerned in field selection and organization. Tavian had this remedial instruction after his return to Tangmere.[22]

Lockhart's entertaining write-up of his mission was clearly an attempt to match Murphy's badinage in the ORB, but this was the main communication to go up the chain of command, and senior officers were unimpressed. Mouse Fielden was told that Murphy's reports 'rather savour of the mess fireside', and that Lockhart's were not suitable for passing up the line to Sir Charles Portal. Fielden ordered Lockhart to re-draft his report of this mission.[23]

The following night, Murphy (in Operation *Bridge*) was to return the Pineau and Faure duo to their homeland after seven weeks in London, Pineau carrying a message from de Gaulle. The pair had dined at the Bertrams before being ferried to the aerodrome, but found their appetite wanting. The whisky, however, went down well. At the Cottage, one of the pilots handed Pineau an envelope in de Gaulle's handwriting – it contained a late re-draft of the leader's message. Sticky said to his passengers, 'Are you ready, gentlemen? The trip will be quick, I have to put you down in Normandy.' After take-off at 2330hrs, he tested the engine's magnetos before crossing the Sussex coast. 'I viewed this with considerable gloom, a gloom which deepened when the engine cut a minute later for no apparent reason at all', so he returned to Tangmere. The spare aircraft had a punctured tailwheel from Lockhart's operation two nights earlier; the ground crew worked 'like blazes' to replace it, and Sticky managed to take off again in a sound aircraft well after midnight.[24]

After landing in France, the operator Robert Delattre greeted the two arrivals, 'Quickly, hurry up; get the courier out, a company of German soldiers entered the town at the end of the evening. It was too late to warn you. They are only 1500 metres away.' Pineau and Faure leaped out quickly, to be replaced by two figures in the gloom.

Once airborne again, Murphy reported, 'I immediately became conscious of the powerful smell of perfume, and I assumed I had a female on board, and it was with pleasurable anticipation that I flew back.' Alas his passengers were the rather chunky BCRA agent Jacques Robert (known in England as 'Popeye') and Pierre Brosselette (known as 'Pierre Le Gris' because of a distinctive lock of grey hair, which he had dyed black) of SIS. He still had a distinctive visage with a cleft chin, swarthy eyebrows and deep penetrating eyes; a journalist and radio broadcaster before the war, with two teenage children, Brosselette had distinguished himself as an infantry captain. His strident views on Hitler's rise to power meant that Vichy had forbidden him from teaching after the Armistice, so he had bought a bookshop and stationers' in Paris. The basement of his Rue de la Pompe store became something of an intelligence hub, and most of his efforts went into producing *Résistance*, one of the foremost secret newspapers, and acting as a propagandist for Gilbert Renault's CND network. De Gaulle was now keen to tap his knowledge of Resistance networks in northern France. Pierre was to become the main channel of communications between de Gaulle and Jean Moulin, the charismatic *préfet* of the Eure-et-Loir department and later Resistance leader.

Murphy's misplaced reverie must have been caused by a leaking scent bottle, brought by these two hulks as a gift for their friends in London. The pair stayed at Bignor Manor for a few days whilst British ID cards were procured. Barbara Bertram ended up having to drive them up to London; as they did not speak any English, their presence in the UK was best kept a secret. Barbara was not pleased when they demanded a stop at a pub for a call of nature – 'Please I must stop'; this was prolonged to allow more liquids to be imbibed. This delay meant they were running late, and Barbara put her foot down. Speeding into London down Roehampton Lane, she was stopped by a police officer, and was terrified her charges would start speaking in their native tongue. They made it.[25] After his debriefing, Robert, 'a fine man' in Barbara's view, was sent up to Ringway for parachute training, and was heard dangling from an extra-large parachute singing 'I'm Popeye the sailor man…'[26]

The 'sharp, lively and witty' Brosselette meanwhile was debriefed by Dewavrin in London, and impressed him greatly – Pierre's 'mind ground and assimilated ideas at such a rate that few people were able to keep up with his stunning pace. Behind stinging comments he hid a great sensitivity, giving the impression of understanding and foreseeing everything.' Dewavrin considered him 'the most intelligent man I have met in my life'.[27]

Nesbitt-Dufort, who had returned to the squadron for a brief time after his European adventures, was posted to the books of HQ Fighter

Command.²⁸ The sole agent who had survived the Romanoff crash had serious burns and required plastic surgery. Once healed, the agent was keen to have another go. Pressure from Stalin and Churchill to fulfil the original mission was intense, so Wally Farley, 138's CO, volunteered to carry it out himself in the role of second pilot and despatcher. Dodds-Parker had put himself forward for this role, but was overruled by Farley. On 21 April, Halifax V9976, captained by Flt Lt Voellnagel, set off to deliver the two NKVD agents into Austria, on this mission that had already failed several times. In thick fog, Farley flew into a Bavarian hill near the Tegensee, just before the Austrian border, with the loss of all eight crew and the Russian agents. Farley was buried in Durnbach War Cemetery. Ron Hockey was promoted to lead 138 in his stead.²⁹

In the next moon period, two operations were mounted on 28 May – it was not a good night. Lockhart returned from an unsuccessful Operation *Gean* without having seen any reception signals – because the agent André Simon was already in prison. The same night, Mott was sent forth on his first Lysander operation. He was to deliver Alex Nitelet, a former Belgian fighter pilot who had lost an eye in combat over France. He had been recruited by MI9 to be a badly needed wireless operator for Pat O'Leary and his PAT escape line, operating across the Pyrenees. Visibility was very poor at the destination airfield (Issoudun Fay/Ségry). Mott's approach was poor; Nitelet later reported 'that undoubtedly Mott touched down from too high, that contact [i.e. touchdown] was at Light B, and that Mott seemed unable to throttle back'.³⁰ There was some later debate that the lights had been laid out incorrectly; the Frenchmen on the ground thought his approach had been unusually fast, and he bounced heavily. Mott's Lysander came to rest beyond the designated strip and became bogged in newly tilled soil – he could not free it. Jumping down, he greeted the team, 'Good night, gentlemen!' But their combined efforts could not get the Lysander to move the six feet to firmer ground.

The operator (who would arrange pick-ups in their homelands) was Claude Lamirault, 'to the right of French politics' (who coincidentally had been involved in organizing Mott's previous escape); one of his team ran over to say that he thought the airfield's generating plant had been turned on to allow the lighting to be switched on, so Lamirault told everyone to disperse. Lamirault's assistant, Pierre Hentic (much more left wing than his superior), selflessly gave his identity papers (in the name of Henri Trellu) to Mott to aid his escape, but when Pierre was stopped by a French roadblock he was arrested, and ended up in the same cell as André Simon (who had been waiting for a Lysander to take him back to England). They had had the misfortune to arrange an operation in an area through which Pétain was travelling, and the security services were out in force.

Nitelet fled into the night, to go on to carry out his allotted tasks in Marseille. Mott tried to set the stricken Lysander on fire, but encountered the same problems as Nesbitt-Dufort months earlier. The Vichy authorities (for Ussel was just beyond the demarcation line in the Unoccupied Zone) arranged for the Lysander to be towed away for inspection.[31]

As Mott and Lamirault ran from the field, they noticed 'a considerable number of men' spreading out across the aerodrome, but the pair got away and Lamirault was later able to give Mott civilian clothes, ration cards and a bicycle. The 161 Squadron pilot made it to La Chartre, a strongly pro-Vichy town 25 miles to the south, where he was arrested by the French police. After enduring several prisons in France, he was sent to Gavi Campo No. 5 in Italy. Following the Italian armistice, Mott was despatched by train towards Austria. He and others cut through the floor of their truck and dropped onto the tracks to make their escape. Joining up with some partisans, his band was taken to Yugoslavia, where he paired with an RAF flight lieutenant. By February 1944, the two British airmen were being hosted by a Contessa Cancellucia. After stays in Bologna and Formo, they made the Italian coast and with difficulty obtained a small sailing boat (which they named *Pitch and Toss*). They reached the Allied lines at an RAF radar station on the coast at Ponte della Penna near Monte Cassino in March 1944. The first British officer he saw was his younger brother, whom he had not seen since 1937! Mott was later awarded the MBE 'for his great fortitude and determination to return to active duty'. His exploits deserved more.

However, Mott's disappearance on operation put greater pressure on 161's remaining Lysander pilots. Sticky Murphy did his final Lysander operation on 29 May 1942: he took Tavian/*Collin*, now with field selection training under his belt, back to Vatan on 29 May. Tavian, who had orders to set up a Gaullist network in Corsica, was SOE, but Sticky also took an SIS agent. Sticky left the squadron with a freshly minted DSO, the citation, as always with 138 and 161, glossing over the exact nature of his exploits: 'On five recent occasions at night this officer has carried out operations requiring the highest standards of skill and organisation. Squadron

Leader Murphy has personally organised his Flight and trained his pilots. He has displayed inspiring leadership.'[32] De Gaulle had even awarded him a Croix de Guerre with Bronze Palm a month earlier, its citation being a little more explicit about his working with the Resistance movement. Lockhart was given the DFC on the same day as Murphy's DSO – he 'surmounted many difficulties with great skill and initiative'. Murphy's citation could have added, 'Always one for a drink and a party, Sticky's discordant rendering of *Rip My Knickers Away* heralded the real singing sessions', but did not.[33]

With 1,350 hours in his logbook, Sticky was due a rest from operational flying, so he became a controller at the headquarters of 3 Group, Bomber Command, and then moved to the Navigation Branch of the Air Ministry. He found this stultifying: 'There I stayed for ten dreary months.'[34] Back at 161, Lockhart was promoted to acting squadron leader – a meteoric rise since he had been a P/O only three months earlier – and took over command of the Lysander flight.

Harris had bequeathed 161 a very rough and ready airfield: the Tempsford officers' mess was just another Nissen hut. Fortunately, the officers' sleeping quarters were at Gaynes Hall near St Neots (more formally known as 'Station 61'), a classically fronted Georgian mansion, in which they could live in a modicum of style. The Hall was also used as a training centre for SOE agents, run by a young Scots major; the agents were invariably impressed by its scale and ambience. Its outbuildings also housed the packing facility for the containers dropped by the Whitleys and Halifaxes. In front of the Hall was a large lawn, at the end of which was a long L-shaped canal cum lake; a canoe languished in the boathouse at the far end, and was a popular form of relaxation.

Many of the support staff at Tempsford were members of the First Aid Nursing Yeomanry, known as FANYs. Female agents in SOE also became FANYs in a fruitless attempt to give them the gossamer-thin protection of being a uniformed officer. The presence of these women at Tempsford together with the station's 'particularly attractive WAAFs... in a secluded WAAFery in a good defensive position on the top of the hill above Everton village' near Gaynes Hall was irresistible to the Polish aircrew – whose nightly forays up the hill to the Hall were a major disciplinary headache for Fielden and Hockey. These young women were probably the most fragrant in the British armed forces – 161's Lysander pilots gave them so much scent (that they had received from French operators) that they used the surplus as lighter fuel![35]

Later in the year, Gubbins sent the Norwegian saboteurs under Joachim Rønneberg to Gaynes Hall as part of their work-up for the planned destruction of the Norsk Hydro plant* (Operation *Grouse*).³⁶ With Knaut Haukelid as ring-leader, they spent much of their down-time ahead of the mission entertaining a group of FANYs in the hostelries of Cambridge, and back at Gaynes Hall. The women did not find the company of these blonde Nordic soon-to-be heroes much hardship, and late-night sessions around the piano were popular until Rønneburg decided his Romeos were becoming too soft. One of the SOE officers, Major Mackenzie, offered him use of his house at Crispie in the Highlands. The trysts were concluded.

In May, the War Office had also requisitioned Hassells (or sometimes Hazells) Hall, built at the turn of the 18th century, from Frederick Pym, the father of Francis Pym, later a Tory Minister. On the road to Sandy from Tempsford, it was used for staff and agent accommodation. By now it had been realized that a more structured training programme had to be arranged for French agents destined to be operators. Hitherto this had been done by Farley and Dodds-Parker on an ad hoc basis at Sawbridgeworth.³⁷ Now the training focused on two issues – field selection and procedures on the night. Fielden proposed establishing the training field at Barton Bendish in Norfolk. As SIS noted in disapproval, 'This would have involved a car journey of 114 miles for every exercise!'³⁸

More sensibly, some fields at Somersham 15 miles away in Cambridgeshire were appropriated. These had previously been used as a 'Q' site – where dummy flarepaths were laid out to distract German bombers from their real targets (in this case the nearby RAF Wyton). It received SIS approval: 'It was an ordinary field as agents might have found in France. It was far enough from all roads and houses – the farm adjoining the road was unoccupied – to allow of reasonable security being assured. As its dimensions were only just regulation, and adjacent obstacles and slopes were most varied in character, it offered great scope for problems in laying flare paths.'³⁹

The 161 Squadron pilots, when back at Tempsford for the non-moon period, would fly over to Somersham in the afternoons, looking for the adjacent wind pump as a landmark, to meet six or so agents (in the hands of Major Tony Bertram if they were of the SIS variety), and instruct them

---

*The mission was lauded by the CIA whose declassified report on their work stated it was 'the most important series of sabotage raids in history'.

in laying out a flarepath in the correct fashion using yellow flags instead of torches. After nightfall, the flags would be replaced by torches and they would fly circuits with the agents practising embarkation and disembarkation procedures. These sessions gave the pilots time to bond with the agents, and impress upon them the characteristics needed for a safe and successful landing ground.

But again the choice of airfield for such clandestine activities was strange – Somersham was adjacent to the St Ives–March railway line, where passengers travelling might have been surprised to see three torches pointing skywards in the middle of rural Cambridgeshire!

After Lord Selborne's review of SOE's activities and organization, Sir Frank Nelson was squeezed out, to be replaced by Sir Charles Hambro (one of his many roles at the time), with Brigadier Colin Gubbins as his deputy. Jaundice at SIS continued; Menzies remarked to Robert Bruce-Lockhart (a distinguished and experienced SIS agent) that SOE 'are bogus through and through. Never achieving anything, compromising my agents, and are amateurs in political matters.'[40]

On 19 May 1942, General Brooke recorded in his diaries that at that day's Chiefs of Staff meeting, he and Portal had 'heated arguments'. The RAF head then went on to have another 'heated argument', this time with Admiral Dudley Pound, the First Sea Lord. The subject was of course Army and Navy air requirements. The strategic direction under which 161's pilots operated remained turbulent. If 138 and 161 were (non-identical) twins, how could these adolescents ever reach adulthood with parents like Portal and Harris?

9

The 1942 Pause and Knowles Lurches to His Maker

There were no pick-up operations by 161 in June or July – this was due to the aftermath of Selborne's report into SOE, and also the chaos at Baker Street and in France. Gubbins and Buckmaster were aghast at the way in which networks in France were floundering. AUTOGIRO, a large *réseau* (network), had disintegrated, leaving F Section without any organized circuits in the Occupied Zone.[1]

The reason was simple – INTERALLIÉ agent Mathilde Carré (*La Chatte*, but also known as Agent *Victoire*) had been arrested in November 1941, had been turned by the Germans, and soon started an affair with Hugo Bleicher, the talented Abwehr sergeant charged with countering French resistance movements. Betrayals flooded from her lips.

Yet the engineers of 161 had no rest: on 7 July, Warrant Officer (WO) Kingham, a relatively newly recruited pilot, had an accident when the front tailplane attachment bolt failed. To the consternation of the mechanics, newly arrived Peter Vaughan-Fowler suffered a similar accident two weeks later. It fell to the engineers back at Westland's Yeovil factory to find a solution.

On 10 July, General Alan Brooke lunched with de Gaulle at Claridge's, but recorded later, 'I fail to see how we are ever going to make any use of him.'[2] Four days later (Bastille Day), the French leader changed the name of the Free French to the Fighting French (La France Combattante) thereby positioning himself as the leader of those both within and without France who resisted the invaders.[3]

Sunday 23 August 1942 was a momentous day. The previous night, Teddy Knowles, the former CO of 138, had been in fine form at the piano in the officers' mess at RAF Andreas, where he was still station commander – as with any party in which he was involved, it went with a swing.

On the Sunday morning, he invited a few friends to join him for lunch in the Mess. These included Major Geoffrey Wait MC, who was in charge of the local anti-aircraft guns. Such relaxed weekends were clearly a tonic for Knowles after the stresses of flying bombers over Germany and France. Moreover, his wife Thelma had come over to the Isle of Man and was living with him in the station commander's house in Ramsey. She joined him for lunch at the Mess and wine was taken. For Teddy, opportunities for flying were now few; he was therefore very intrigued when, after a 'convivial luncheon', an NCO came to his table in the ante-room and informed him that a Whitley was diverting to RAF Andreas, Isle of Man.

The Mk V Whitley, BD417, was being flown over to Nutts Corner in Northern Ireland by P/O Thomas Tennyson of No. 296 Squadron, a Whitley unit engaged in glider training; if a more boring task existed for a bomber pilot, it had yet to be found. Tennyson had indeed been towing a glider across the Irish Sea when the tow rope broke. As the glider and its crew floated down to the waves, Tennyson radioed for help, intending to circle overhead until it arrived. After an hour and a half, fuel was running low so he diverted to the Isle of Man. When he landed at Ronaldsway, he found there was no suitable fuel, so Tennyson hopped a few miles to RAF Andreas, where there was.

No. 296 Squadron's motto was 'Prepared for Anything', but Tennyson was not prepared for Knowles. By now late afternoon, he just wanted to be making haste to his home base of Ringway to enjoy what was left of the weekend. Unfortunately, Knowles came over and informed him that he was taking up his Whitley for a short flight. Tennyson and the station's duty pilot, P/O Andrew Paton, both remonstrated, but were overruled by Knowles, who summoned Major Wait and Thelma to the aircraft. He also ordered the unhappy Paton, together with a corporal and three airmen of the station's crash section, to join them on the joyride as ballast. But Paton had to take a phone call in the Mess – it was his WAAF girlfriend asking why he had not showed up for their date. By the time she had finished remonstrating with him, Paton had missed the transport to the Whitley, and decided to stay on the ground.

Settling into the once familiar confines of a Whitley cockpit just after 1730hrs, Knowles started the engines and taxied round to the beginning of the 1,100 yards of runway 06. He opened up the throttles and the never-sprightly Whitley trundled to the north-east. After it had lifted off, the nose of the aircraft reared up, the aircraft stalled and it crashed at West Kimmeragh Farm only a mile from the end of the runway. Knowles, whose last actions in the Mess had been to sign for another two bottles of port, had mis-set the elevator trim, making a stall almost inevitable.

The aircraft broke in two. Those in the cockpit died instantly of multiple injuries; the NCO and airmen stumbled from the rear section in a state of shock. The station's crash team, hampered by some of their number being in the aircraft, arrived on the scene, and took the airmen to the station's medical centre. But LAC (Acting Corporal) Alfred Henderson of the Station Police was seriously injured and had to be transferred to the military hospital nearby, where he died that night. For Corporal Butler, Aircraftman First Class (AC1) Williams and AC1 Salt, it was a salutary lesson in the dangers of flying – particularly when intoxicated. Paton's illicit girlfriend had saved his life.

In the manner of his death, Knowles had not only destroyed a Whitley and killed three other people, but set in chain a process which was to tie up many mid-ranking officers over the coming weeks. After securing the crash site and taking the wounded to hospital, the first job of the military authorities in the case of a fatal accident is to notify the next of kin. When Knowles' father received this news, he phoned up RAF Andreas with the alarming information that his son's wife was alive and well, residing only a mile or so from him at Warboys in Cambridgeshire. Mrs Thelma 'Knowles' was not Knowles' wife at all; she was Mrs Thelma Oliver, although she had been living with Knowles as his wife for two to three years, and was known to all at Andreas as Mrs Knowles. His real wife Gladys was living back at the Manor House, Warboys, near Newmarket, with their nine-year-old daughter. She eventually found out about the fate of her estranged husband via a letter from the Air Ministry dated 8 September.[4]

The accident created waves of bureaucratic anguish with RAF Andreas its epicentre. An inspired choice was now made for Knowles' urgent replacement as station commander – W/Cdr Stephen Beaumont, who had been a lawyer with his family firm in Wakefield, Yorkshire. He had learned to fly at his own expense at the West Yorkshire Flying Club at Yeadon before joining the RAF Volunteer Reserve (RAFVR) in 1937, and gained his wings that August.[5] Meanwhile, W/Cdr Roger Burges was in charge of P4 – the RAF's Casualty Branch. Fortuitously, the two knew each other from 1939 when Beaumont was with No. 609 Squadron at Yeadon at the beginning of the Battle of Britain, and Burges was in charge of converting what had been Yeadon Airport into RAF Yeadon. 'They were good days.' Beaumont, in a letter to his friend a week after the crash, noted it was 'one hell of a mess', and was trying to keep the true facts to as narrow a group of people on the island as possible.[6] Even Beaumont, who had known Knowles for a year, had had no idea Thelma was anything other than his real wife. But her true husband, Llewellyn Oliver of Cirencester, was divorcing Thelma, citing Knowles as correspondent, and had obtained a decree nisi in June. Beaumont had had to tell the local vicar the true state of affairs so that Knowles/Oliver could be buried in her real name. He had succeeded in keeping the press out of the loop, and ensured that no station staff attended the funerals – very unusual since most aircrew would have wanted to send their station commander on his way. However, Knowles' father was able to attend, and there he met Thelma's brother, W/Cdr Kersley, who was also in the RAF as station medical officer at RAF Cardington.

Llewellyn Oliver wrote to the Air Ministry that week and reminded them that he had written to them in November 1940 'with ref to Sqn Ldr Knowles abducting my wife'. He was now exercised to learn of his wife's death in such odd circumstances a few days earlier, and that she had been buried 'in a common grave' on the Isle of Man. Having been swept aside by those at Andreas, he now wanted to know more about the circumstances of Thelma's death. Not obtaining much immediate satisfaction, Oliver than dashed off a letter to Sir Archibald Sinclair, Secretary of State for Air, complaining that no notice of the deaths in the incident had appeared in the papers, and demanding a Court of Enquiry.

Burges drily noted that Llewelyn Oliver 'seems to profess a solicitude out of keeping with his reported divorce proceedings'. The unstoppable Oliver penned another letter to the Air Ministry on 2 October asking how Thelma had been allowed to fly in an RAF aircraft, 'and in what capacity she had been acting? ... Surely the RAF are entirely responsible for this tragedy?' Burges and Beaumont were by now beginning to understand why Mrs Oliver had preferred life as Mrs Knowles.

Burges for the Directorate of Personal Services responded masterfully: 'The proceedings of service Courts of Enquiry and Investigations are confidential... It is contrary to the instructions of the Royal Air Force that unauthorised passengers should be given flights in service aircraft. Wing Commander Knowles was the pilot of the aircraft and was also the officer responsible for the flight, and as he was killed in the accident it is not known in what circumstances Mrs Oliver was flying.'[7]

On the night of Knowles' death, a new recruit at 161, John Bridger, 'a quiet little man', was sent off to bomb a railway marshalling yard at Mézidon in Normandy, and returned to the same area the following night. That week, two other new 161 Squadron pilots – Warrant Officer Kingham and Flt Lt Huntley – were also sent across the Channel in Lysanders on such tasks. Bomber Harris had decided that he wanted his pound of flesh from the Special Duties units. If the Lysanders were not being used to transport agents, they could jolly well participate in the bomber offensive. Two 100lb or 250lb bombs seem a scant reward for the risks the Lysander pilots were facing on such missions.

At 29, John Cameron Bridger was older than his new colleagues, and vastly experienced, with 4,000 flying hours already in his logbook. Short of stature, his broken nose gave him a rather tough appearance, which a neat moustache failed to soften. He was a man of few words, who quietly went about his work with his own proven and deliberate methods. Despite his experience, Bridger had severely damaged a Lysander during his work-up period.[8]

On the night of 23 August, Guy Lockhart had set out to warm up the squadron's pick-up skills with an SIS flight. His destination was the pre-war aerodrome of Thalamy-Ussel on a hill-top in the Corrèze, 340 nautical miles from Tangmere, to help Marie-Madeleine (Méric) Fourcade (*Hérisson*, 'Hedgehog'), the highly regarded 41-year-old chief of the ALLIANCE network. 'She had the memory of an elephant, the caution of a snake, the cunning of a weasel, the perseverance of a mole, and she could be as dangerous as a panther.'[9] His passenger for the return flight was Léon Faye, a violently anti-communist commandant in the French Air Force, who had been summoned to London for discussions with SIS, in place of Fourcade. She wanted to remain in the field a little while longer despite having been under immense operational strain for several months.[10] Lockhart was very impressed with this field, despite the flare-path having been laid downwind (which caused him some issues), and it was to become a field of choice for 161 in south-east France.

Lockhart had by now carried out considerably more Lysander operations than anyone else; he had ominously briefed James McCairns ('Mac'),

'No man has ever done more than five.'[11] On his sixth at the end of August, his luck ran out: he was sent on another SIS mission down to Burgundy to pick up Christian Pineau and Jean Cavaillès. The latter was a brilliant mathematician and philosopher, with eyes that shone with hope and optimism. Notwithstanding his career, he was fired with a pugnacious spirit of resistance: at the outbreak of war, he had been lecturing in arts at Strasbourg, but joined the Army's deciphering department, moving to a lecturing job at the Sorbonne after the Armistice. Here he became involved with Pineau's LIBÉ-NORD network. After manoeuvring with de Gaulle, Cavaillès was given command of the COHORS intelligence network in the Occupied Zone. This extended from Belgium to Brittany, and he recruited mostly teachers and former students of the École du Louvre.[12]

Pineau decided he needed to return to London to discuss with the BCRA his disappointment at the slow progress the PHALANX network was making. But the operator for this pick-up was Jean-Louis Tangre (known to SIS as *Tarn*, but to Pineau as *Lot*), who was responsible for the disappointing performance of the PHALANX network, and therefore less than keen for Pineau to report back to London. As he marched to the field with Tangre and two other helpers, Pineau's worries mounted. He took solace from the clear sky and rural calm.[13]

The weather in Burgundy was fine; for Lockhart, finding the landing field was little problem, as it was very near the River Saône, which was a couple of hundred yards wide there – a shining ribbon pointing him to his meadow. The unusual twin towers of the 11th-century church at Tournus told him he was nearing his target. His would-be England-bound passengers had almost given up hope of his arrival. After a normal landing, as Lockhart taxied around Lamp 'C', one wheel fell into a ditch, and the undercarriage was wrecked. Pineau and team heard a rending sound and ran over.

The cause was simple – Agent *Tarn* had turned up both drunk and late, and had laid the flarepath over the ditch instead of many yards away. 'Quick,' said Lockhart in his rusty French, 'take the courier, and I'll join you on the track.'

The field, in Lockhart's later report, was 'large enough for three landings', but *Tarn* 'had laid out his flarepath in the worst manner possible'. Guy was understandably furious; he waited for all but one of the reception committee to leave for their emergency rendezvous 15 miles away, and gave them an hour's start before setting his machine on fire. With enough fuel in the aircraft's tanks for his return flight, it created an explosion and then burned well.[14] During this wait, he heard another Lysander burbling across the night sky – it was the novice McIndoe attempting an SOE pick-up nearby. Such a potential saviour was not to be scorned, so he signalled his name in Morse to his colleague, but gained no reply and with his companion set off to join Pineau and his crew. McIndoe later reported he had seen distress lights but had thought they might be a ruse to lure him to the wrong field.[15]

The party, now including Lockhart, had a moment of danger crossing the Saône at the bridge at Fleurville, then walked south along the railway track 'ten good kilometres' to Mâcon. Pineau too was livid, and with his pistol in hand gave serious consideration to executing *Tarn* there and then, but lost his nerve. He had a clever solution – a day later he wrote to another agent in his *réseau* who happened to be a senior policeman in Lyon, and arranged for *Tarn* to be arrested and imprisoned on a trumped-up charge.

Pineau knew the flames would quickly attract the local *gendarmes*, so decided he needed to obtain some civilian clothing for Lockhart (whom he knew as 'Lieutenant-Colonel Henry') rather quickly. Whatever his emotions, Lockhart managed to look unperturbed, although he had gained a slight limp when his knee had hit the Lysander's dashboard on landing.

They all took a train from Mâcon to Lyon where Pineau arranged for Lockhart to be hosted at a friend's house for two days. It was decided that Lockhart would escape on a submarine from the coast in Provence. Pineau sent a message to London to assure them of Guy's safety, and then accompanied him by train to Narbonne. He had to order Lockhart to stop using his badly accented French to the others in the railway carriage, as he was drawing attention to himself. 'Why? Everyone says I don't have much of an accent. I said I was Canadian'![16]

Guy made it to the Provencal beach of Narbonne Plage in the company of the two agents, Pineau and Cavaillès (who had come down separately from Paris); the duo intended also to take the sea route back to Britain. By this time, Lockhart had acquired the contents of two other escape kits apart from his own. The group had a picnic dinner amongst the sand dunes. The party of would-be escapers on the beach was by now quite large; but the dinghy arrived from the felucca (substituted for the submarine) at 0100hrs with space for only five passengers. The organizing officer did not allow Lockhart onto the first ferry trip. Whilst he was waiting there to start his homeward journey, some Vichy police arrived, a battle ensued and Lockhart escaped after kicking a *gendarme* in the stomach and waded out to the dinghy, by now returned near to the shore. Pineau and the other agents were, however, later arrested fleeing the scene.[17]

The end of August saw an unusual mission from Tempsford, named by some wag in 3 Group as Operation *Gasper*. Three Whitleys of 161 distributed one ton of cigarettes over a wide area of the Netherlands 'to commemorate Queen Wilhelmina's birthday'. Let us hope it was wide areas of land rather than inland sea (two of the target areas were either side of the Zuider Zee). Prince Bernhard had made a special request for this mercy delivery in order to raise Dutch spirits, depressed by the increasing privations of the Nazi occupation.

Back at Tempsford, morale in the Mess was also low once it was realized that Guy was missing. So there was considerable surprise when he walked in 13 days later – tanned, relaxed and still in summer uniform shorts. At Gibraltar, he had unburdened himself of a large amount of French francs (some which a guilty Pineau had gifted him, some of which he had liberated from the escape kits), and secured a good rate of exchange with the MI9 station chief who badly needed them to fund his escape lines. Lockhart used his ill-gotten gains to purchase sherry and cigarettes – which increased the warmth of his reception at Tempsford. Lockhart had flown back from Gibraltar in a 138 Squadron machine. At the end of the month he was awarded a DSO.

F/O Huntley had joined the squadron in April and had completed some training, being promoted to acting flight lieutenant in June. On 4 September, he returned from his first pick-up operation after only ten minutes with engine trouble (his mechanics later found that the plug leads were burning through). On 23 September, he returned from Operation *Vesta* shortly before reaching his destination, claiming he had encountered heavy anti-aircraft fire and solid cloud at 600 feet over the Loire, together with confusing lights on the ground. Huntley was not sent on operations again, and was soon posted elsewhere.

In the spring, one of Fourcade's key leaders, Jean Boutron, had been arrested – thankfully by the Vichy police (amongst whom there were many Resistance sympathizers), rather than the Gestapo. He had previously been appointed by Vichy as Deputy Naval Attaché in Madrid; despite having been shelled by the Royal Navy at Mers el-Kébir in 1940, he was very pro-British, and had been recruited by Georges Loustaunau-Lacau (the head of ALLIANCE before Fourcade) into his intelligence-gathering network. He had only recently been liberated from prison by his Resistance colleagues; in late summer, a French doctor had injected him with a substance that gave him the symptoms of a urinary tract infection, and under that pretext the doctor transferred him from a fortress prison in the Alps to a hospital in

Grenoble. Fourcade's ALLIANCE managed to liberate him from there, and she wanted him sent to England for safety. Bridger was despatched to rescue him from the field near Mâcon on 11 September; he was taking out Major Léon Faye (otherwise known as Agent *Eagle*) with much-needed cash; he was not only Fourcade's number two in the ALLIANCE network, but also her lover. (He was later to father a child with her.) The 26-year-old agent Pierre Dallas called at Fourcade's Marseille villa to tell her he had received a signal that Bridger had taken off from Tangmere despite poor weather in southern England. The target field was at the limits of the Lysander's range – there is no doubt it was a stern test for a novice 161 Lysander pilot. The wind and rain in Provence increased Fourcade's anxiety. The mission was a failure – Bridger had to return to Exeter, thwarted by the very poor weather, as Fourcade learned two days later. The operation was rescheduled for 25 September.

Lockhart's year did not end well: having unusually been allowed back on operations, he was now on a double with Vaughan-Fowler on 18 November (*Squid* and *Skate*). They flew in formation to the Loire, and then lost sight of each other. Lockhart orbited the supposed field several times without seeing any lights, so set course back to Cabourg, where the cloud was down to the deck. Whilst over Saint-Malo, his concentration was disturbed by heavy flak and searchlights probing for him. When he climbed above the cloud bank, by now over Jersey, he 'was jumped by seven plus FW 190s in bright moonlight. Two made a head-on attack whilst another fired by rear starboard quarter.' Lockhart pulled back the throttle and dived for the safety of the clouds once more. But the Germans had the measure of him in cloud, so he dived towards the waves. As he was narrowly avoiding a barrage balloon, his passenger warned him that an Fw 190 was coming in for second helpings, so he retreated into the cloud, and unsurprisingly soon became unsure of his position. When he called the RAF's homing stations on the south coast, they informed him he was over the English coast at Selsey Bill – at just the time he noticed he was over Alderney! By the time he was mid-Channel, he had become very worried about his low fuel state, so gave the order to his passenger to prepare to bail out. After further argument with the ground stations, and with his passenger's agreement, Guy changed his mind. He landed at the first available field – Warmwell in Dorset, indicating how much he had drifted westwards, and later discovered he only had five gallons of fuel remaining.

His next operation, on 17 December, was equally memorable. Lockhart damaged the tail of his machine landing on Operation *Starfish*. Only two nights later, his tailwheel struck an obstruction on landing in France, and snapped back into the fuselage, causing damage to the fuselage of V9283, and leaving the elevator and rudder controls stuck. Leaping out, he managed to free the rudder with some brute force, and decided to attempt to take off with only the elevator trim tab for longitudinal control. This was arguably a very rash decision, which proved vindicated when he made it home in a surging flight path by skilful use of the throttle.

P/O James Atterby McCairns, known to one and all as Mac, arrived at 161 on 8 August from a brief respite at HQ Fighter Command. He had already done a tour at Tangmere flying Spitfires for No. 616 Squadron, part of the renowned Bader Wing. Its role now was fighter sweeps over northern France: on one such mission on 6 July 1941, Mac was raked hard by a Messerschmitt Bf 109, but made it back to Tangmere. His Spitfire was a write-off, and when, after landing, he removed a flying boot to find out why his foot was hurting, out tumbled a loose armour-piercing round.

Still just a sergeant pilot with 616, he was told by his CO he was being put forward for a commission – this provoked mixed emotions as, although he had long aspired to be an officer, the received wisdom in the ranks was that such promotion for members of Fighter and Bomber Commands seemed to result in death within days. McCairns was pleased to receive a shiny new Spitfire, but less happy after he took it for an air test and found its controls unnaturally stiff. At the time, he was dating a nurse, and on that flight took the opportunity to beat up the cottage where she was spending the weekend. On landing, he had a strong premonition that the fighter sweep over northern France scheduled for later that day would be his last. He took off in his Spitfire from Westhampnett (Tangmere's satellite airfield) and, after his flight's prolonged skirmish with a group of Messerschmitts, was felled by cannon fire and wounded in the leg. He was over Gravelines on the French coast when the engine stopped completely. Rather than risk a ditching, he turned back to France and made a forced landing just inland from the coast, but found his canopy jammed, so was forced to wait for German soldiers to release him. They took him to their nearby flak battery, plied him with beer and tended his wounds, whilst repeating '*Pour vous la guerre est finie!*' ('For you the war is over!'). Mac was taken to hospital in Saint-Omer that evening.[18]

THE 1942 PAUSE AND KNOWLES LURCHES TO HIS MAKER

Mac eventually ended up at the prisoner of war (PoW) camp Stalag IXc. This was international in flavour, with strong French and Belgian contingents. From the former, he quizzed their leading escape artist on the German railway stations with the most stringent security checks; from the latter, he gleaned addresses of likely safe houses in their homeland. The following January he escaped, and soon mastered the German railway system. Mac had escaped with a Belgian chum, Lucien Charlier, but they became separated on the second day. That night he made it into Belgium at the frontier at Saint-Vith. He had dropped off a slow-moving train onto an embankment just as a severe blizzard started, which was to last three days. He trudged through the blinding snow along the tracks until he could find some sort of shelter under a bridge for a brief respite. Mac continued walking through the night until he started hallucinating, and eventually found paltry refuge in a tiny trackside tool hut. At length he walked into Waimes, which turned out only to be seven miles from his original intended border crossing destination of Malmédy. After some hesitation – he had only eaten two Horlicks tablets over the previous 48 hours – his hunger told him more walking was impossible, so he bought a ticket at the station and reached Malmédy itself. Fearing German border guards, he spent the afternoon in a snow hole in some allotments on the town's edge: the cramp, chill and misery were insufferable. At nightfall he continued his westward walk, guided only by the most primitive of compasses. By now almost dead on his feet he arrived at a village; he stumbled up to the church, and thanked every deity he knew that the notices were in French.[19]

The next, less demanding, walk was to the Hotel Moderne in Francorchamps, where his French PoW colleague had advised him to go, accompanied by a letter in French. The proprietor wanted nothing to do with him. After some prevarication by several Belgians, he was escorted to the nearby town of Spa, where he received great hospitality from M Delannion, a café proprietor. From here he walked to Verviers, thence by train to Brussels where he was embraced by the COMÈTE escape line which ushered him to Gibraltar, via Paris, Bayonne and Madrid. For making a rare 'home run' (becoming only the fourth RAF airman to do so), Mac was awarded a much deserved Military Medal (MM). He arrived at RAF Hendon on 30 April.[20]

After such tribulations, RAF pilots were usually rewarded with a safe ground tour in Britain. Mac spent a few weeks at HQ Fighter Command, touring bases giving lectures on escape and evasion techniques. But he had decided that the best way to repay the Resistance movement which had helped him so much was to apply to join 161 as a Lysander pilot. Mac had heard of 161's activities when in Brussels from a rather indiscreet Belgian agent, Captain Jean Sabier, who had done the operators' training course at Tempsford and Somersham, and told him of the scale of 161's activities. It was whilst he was waiting for his flight home from Gibraltar that he had another lucky encounter – this time with Lt Jimmy Langley who did his MI9 debriefing. When asked how he saw his flying career progressing, Mac revealed his idea was to start an 'air taxi service to Belgium'! Langley, who had lost an arm earlier in the war, and effected his own escape from France, replied, 'Splendid, you are just the man we are looking for.'[21] Mac received Langley's endorsement for a move to 161 – Langley was a good friend to the squadron and frequently visited the pilots at their Tangmere lair.

By now, Fielden had decided the criteria by which 161's Lysander pilots would be recruited: candidates needed to have more than 1,000 flying hours, of which 500 should be at night, and ideally they should have some French. Mac met none of those criteria, and indeed was only freshly commissioned. Undeterred, he flew over to Tempsford one morning in June for an interview with Mouse. All was quiet – there had been Whitley operations the previous night. Eventually, just before lunch, Mac was summoned into the CO's office; he was somewhat overawed, but Mouse's charm made an immediate impression, as did his red braces and red lined tunic – the former royal pilot maintained certain sartorial standards. He stressed to Mac that the pilot role at 161 was entirely voluntary, and Mac could withdraw at any time.

The next interview was with Lockhart, the Lysander flight commander. 'Sitting at ease behind one desk in the room was, I thought, the modern equivalent of Lucifer.' Mac 'respected him, admired him, and was fascinated by his personality, but all the time I was terrified by him'.[22] They did share some common ground, however – both had been shot from the French sky in their Spitfires within a day of each other, and had developed the same motivation for wanting to do Special Duties Lysander flying. Guy did his best to dissuade Mac, painting a picture of endless strains: planning for operations that were cancelled even at the very last minute when the pilot was keyed up in the cockpit 'trying by the light of the moon to map-read your way hundreds of miles into France, searching for some miserable plot of land which from the air looks no bigger than a pocket handkerchief'. Testing Mac's resolve further, he added, 'It is not a pleasant job, and I would not recommend anyone to try it. Do not be deceived by the glamour.'[23]

But even if he was over-awed by the faintly threatening Lockhart, the newly commissioned P/O was as keen as mustard, and was hired to become in due course one of 161's busiest and most successful pick-up artists. Mouse had recognized that behind Mac's cheeky demeanour was a steely resolve, and his successful escape from Germany was testimony to quantities of initiative and stamina that would prove most useful. There was perhaps one reservation for this diminutive warrior: he was no lover of night flying – Mac felt that only bats should fly at night.[24]

Mac had been born in Niagara City, US, but when he was 12, his British engineer father moved the family back to Retford in the UK. He had joined the RAFVR early in 1939. Now, after finishing his lecturing tour, he started his training at 161 under the tutelage of Lockhart a month after his interviews. He did not take to his new steed initially – 'after the delicate handling of a Spitfire, the Lizzie [as the Lysander was affectionately known] with its stiff controls reminded me more of a bomber'.[25]

At the beginning of October, Gp Capt MacDonald left Tempsford for the different climate of Air HQ India, and Fielden, newly promoted to group captain, took over as station commander. Whilst Mouse was a 'soul of tact and charm' with 'a spontaneous smile which endeared him to all',[26] other squadron pilots were to note that, whilst 'a lovely fellow', he was also 'a total autocrat'.[27]

Mouse's replacement as 161's squadron commander was W/Cdr 'Pick' Pickard, arguably the best-known pilot in the whole of Bomber Command. A more forceful era for 161 beckoned.

10

The Dream Team Forms

Nothing worthwhile was ever accomplished without risk and daring.
Dick Rutan

Peter Erskine Vaughan-Fowler had arrived at 161 in April 1942, at the same time as F/O Huntley. Whereas Huntley failed to make the grade, Vaughan-Fowler, the youngest and most inexperienced recruit to the Lysander unit yet (he was only 19), became one of the squadron's stars. Flying was in his blood – both his father, Guy, and his brother being pilots, the former with the Royal Naval Air Service from 1911. Indeed, Peter's first flight had been in an Avro 504 biplane piloted by his father.

When war broke out, he was a schoolboy at the Imperial Services College near Windsor, appropriately enough since he had been born in Lahore, India; but he signed up to the RAF as soon as possible in 1941. He must have made a deep and positive impression during flying training, as most unusually he was recommended for a posting to Special Duties work directly afterwards, despite having only 244 flying hours, and no night-time experience at all. When he saw a signal asking for volunteers with 250 night-flying hours, the 'night' had been omitted. His charm and flying skills carried him through the recruitment process – Mouse had spotted his talent.

Despite his youth compared to his well-worn colleagues, which might have contributed to the impetuosity they sometimes noticed in him, Vaughan-Fowler fitted in perfectly in the Tempsford and Tangmere messes, a chum later noting 'his height, his striking good looks, charming smile, debonair manner, and serene disposition'; a degree of shyness was unsurprising given his age. This very slim young man was also a jazz aficionado.[1]

Due to his relative inexperience, his Lysander training took slightly longer than average, and his first pick-up operation (*Catfish*) was not until 25 September, although he had been sent on a bombing sortie or two in that spate of summer madness. Now aiming for Mâcon, he was thwarted by bad weather and became lost; failing to spot the Saône valley, he turned for home but drifted westwards and had to land back at Exeter. He later claimed the winds were not as forecast – an unsettling debut.

John Bridger and Major Léon Faye (Agent *Eagle*) departed Tangmere on 25 September for postponed Operation *Vesta*. Faye was also an experienced pilot, but with no English. He could therefore not express his concern over the intercom to his chauffeur when Bridger chose to hedge-hop over central France in siling rain. The Frenchman had recognized the terrain and knew that radio masts and factory chimneys loomed nearby.[2] On approach to the destination field, Bridger noticed there was a line of tall trees between him and the landing spot; he had to fly level and as slowly as possible before entering a semi-controlled stall to flop onto the wet soil. After touchdown, taxiing back to the light, the port wheel of Bridger's machine sank into cloying mud; he climbed down and simply unscrewed the wheel spat, throwing it into the rear cockpit. With the help of agent Pierre Dallas and his three helpers, the wheel was dug out. The problem had been that the operator had set up the lights a third of a mile away from the agreed field.[3] The ALLIANCE agent Bridger was supposed to bring back to England, Boutron, was not at the field that evening. Having contracted flu from waiting in a cold damp field for too many nights, he was resting in a nearby tavern. Pierre Dallas had told him that, although they were going to the field for one last try, he thought there was little point in Boutron leaving his sick bed as the weather was too bad for the RAF![4]

Although he only had one sack of mail in the back, Bridger had 'considerable difficulty' in taking off from the mud – it was 'sticky and violent', but arrived back at Tangmere at dawn. Faye later sent a signal applauding Bridger's skills: 'My return journey [to France] was successful thanks to the exceptional virtuosity of the pilot.' On this return sector, they were blown westwards by the same wind that Vaughan-Fowler endured, and were weaving to avoid thunderstorms that hampered their path over northern France and across the Channel.[5] Bridger made it back to Tangmere with little fuel remaining, to conclude his first successful operation. He always appeared highly strung after an operation, never more so than after this debut.

Faye had much to tell his boss and lover: he had squeezed a lot into his month in London, which had included a short sojourn in Algiers. He could therefore brief her on the extraordinary convolutions of General Giraud, who was to be spirited from France by SIS (in a submarine) so as to lead the French contingent in the Allied invasion of North Africa. (In the event, he was to drive Eisenhower and Churchill to distraction by demanding to lead all Allied troops.)

The next moon period heralded a bout of bad autumnal weather in northern Europe. The novice F/O R.G. McIndoe headed off to the Lons le Saunier area, but cloud and rain there prevented him picking up the reception committee's recognition signals. The same problem arose for him on another operation four days later; he was removed from 161's operational payroll by the beginning of December.

Bridger had soon developed a reputation amongst his colleagues for extreme diligence in his flight planning, though he was happy to give any less experienced types some tutorials in his mysterious ways. On 26 October, he carried out Operation *Achilles*, taking out Mary Lindell and Ferdinand Rodriguez (Fourcade's Spanish–English deputy leader) for SIS to the Thalamy/Ussel aerodrome. The formidable Lindell was also important cargo: an auxiliary nurse in World War I, she was awarded the Croix de Guerre, and honoured by the tsarist Russians. Soon afterwards she married the Comte de Milleville; by the time World War II started, the couple and their two teenage children were living in Paris, but once northern France was overrun, Mary decided to set up an escape route over the demarcation line. Arrested in early 1941 by the Germans, the middle-aged Countess was released that November, and returned to her old ways, setting up the MARIE-CLAIRE escape line. With US assistance she made it back to the UK in July 1942, where this whirlwind received instruction from Airey Neave at MI9, before returning to France to restart her line.

Neave had escorted her to Tangmere on 20 October, wracked with worry that he was sending this woman into mortal danger; he introduced her to Bridger, who took her hands and with atypical emotion said, 'I just wanted to say thank you for going over there… All the boys have tremendous admiration for what you are doing.' 'Don't be silly, you're the heroes,' she replied.[6] Neave helped her into her parachute harness and lifejacket.

The operator of the field was again the experienced Pierre Dallas, but his experience did not prevent him falling asleep on the train, thereby missing Ussel station. In his stead, Arthur Louis Gachet had improvised a flarepath lit by solid paraffin fuel. After landing, Bridger encountered an unusual difficulty: as he rose from his seat in the back of the Lysander ladder, Rodriguez had accidentally pulled the rip cord of his parachute; the slipstream from the Lysander's Mercury inflated it, delaying his departure from the aircraft and the field. He and Mary left hurriedly without the help of the attendant Frenchmen, who they noticed were haplessly drunk.[7]

Bridger did not pick up any passengers for the return journey; Fourcade's brother Jacques was supposed to have taken the rear seat on that flight, but to his sister's dismay, he arrived too late, 'sprinting onto the field' just after Bridger had taken off.[8] So the back seats of the Lysander were empty. Or were they? Many years later, *The Times* of London suggested he had an important cargo.[9] *The Times* related that the exiled French Navy was based in the Isle of Wight, and their sailors were badly missing that staple of their native cuisine – garlic, not grown in Great Britain, and therefore unobtainable. Bill Spidy, the landlord of the matelots' favourite pub, the Painters Arms in Cowes, contacted SOE/161 Squadron at Tangmere with a request to bring back some bulbs on one of their trips to rural France. According to the *Times* piece, two sacks of this distinctive foodstuff were waiting for Bridger at Thalamy. Once they were delivered to the island successfully, the sailors were happy, and the unintended consequence was that the Isle of Wight developed into (and remains) the centre of garlic growing in Great Britain. This very sniffy story raises the question of how a pub landlord across the Solent came to realize exactly what the highly secretive black Lysanders were really doing in their moon period forays over the Channel…[10]

After Bridger landed back at Tangmere, his 'A' Flight colleagues were astonished that the quiet Bridger had pulled off his first two sorties, both of which were long range. A man of few words, Bridger simply muttered, 'a piece of cake'.

Two F Section agents needed to be extracted from the Lyon area – London was recalling Benjamin Cowburn (*Benoit* or *Valérien*), a calm, effective and bilingual Englishman, and Georges Dubourdin (*Alain*), a French SOE operative who had lived in London before the war. The latter had been upsetting most of his colleagues, and was distrusted by many of them. He was being recalled before creating more upsets.

The same night as Bridger's operation, the German wireless jamming teams were at full tilt. The Reich knew that the *messages personelles* of the BBC transmitted at 1930hrs (and repeated at 2115hrs) were coded messages to SIS and SOE teams across Western Europe. Jean-Marie Régnier, Cowburn, Joseph Marchand and Evelyn Le Chêne were dining at Le Chêne's Lyon flat straining to hear the radio at 1900hrs. 'Can't hear a damn thing!' exclaimed Le Chêne in frustration. They finished their meal not having heard their coded phrase indicating the pick-up was on, but with a nagging thought that it might have been. The intended field was 32 miles north of the city, on the left bank of the Saône; travel during curfew hours was fraught. The trio transferred to Marchand's flat shortly after 2000hrs, and waited for the 2115hrs messages. Interference was much less; the first message given was theirs. It was too late for the obvious means of transport – a train to Pontanevaux. They had to borrow a car from someone who had a permit for driving at night; but if young Vaughan-Fowler set off from Tangmere too early, they would miss him.

For Operation *Sadler/Electrician*, Peter was taking out Jean Paimblanc and Auguste Florias (a wireless operator). Paimblanc had been tasked with establishing contact between de Gaulle and the French Communist Party.[11]

Dubourdin was already at the farmhouse of Nicholas Gauge near this, one of 161's favourite fields in Burgundy, and was setting out the torches (despite having had no training from 161 in how to do so). Cowburn and colleagues decanted from their Citroën to the sound of a Bristol Mercury thrumming in the distance – but they still had to cross the Saône. They found three small rowing boats and put to the oars in a state of some panic. After a four-and-a-half-hour flight in cloud which parted just as he reached the Saône valley, Vaughan-Fowler had circled the field, and was now on final approach. They scrambled up the bank and ran the half-mile to the field. But as they approached, Gauge opened fire on them with his .22. In the gloaming, the farmer's aim was poor. '*Merde*,' shouted Le Chêne, '*C'est moi, Nicholas!*' – confusion ceased. Cowburn scrambled up the Lysander's ladder, but Dubourdin was shouting at Vaughan-Fowler, refusing to embark his aircraft without a parachute. At the same time, the obdurate agent was refusing to tell Le Chêne the location of the circuit's arms dumps (which he had bizarrely previously promised to do on his departure).

Le Chêne knew that every moment on the ground for a 161 Lysander added to the danger, and his frustration with Dubourdin's attitude boiled over. Kicking him up the backside he shouted, '*Rentres, espèce de con!*' ('Go back, you moron!'), and Dubourdin reluctantly climbed in; he then turned to Vaughan-Fowler, 'Off you go!' Cowburn pulled the rear canopy forward and shouted 'OK!' at the top of his voice. He was amazed by the speed with which the reception party's torches disappeared from view.

Meanwhile, bemused at the turn of events, Paimblanc and Florias were sheltering by some trees. Vaughan-Fowler had been on the ground for six minutes – twice as long as the target time – before setting off for Tangmere at 0040hrs.[12] Vaughan-Fowler had a flak-free return, and on his landing, two figures from Baker Street emerged from the brightening light to escort Cowburn and Dubourdin to the Cottage where they enjoyed a whisky and soda.[13]

Three days later, 25 November, saw an operation by Vaughan-Fowler which raised eyebrows at Tangmere, Tempsford and Whitehall. He took out an operator for Léon Faye and ALLIANCE and, after this operator had been disgorged at Ussel, three strange men bundled into Fowler's Lysander. They were police inspectors named Piani, Rutali and Reverbel, who were completely unknown to SIS. Once back at Tangmere, an explanation emerged: as sympathetic Vichy policemen, they had facilitated the escape from Castres jail of Marie-Madeleine Fourcade, who had promised them a safe passage to the UK as a reward. Had they stayed behind they would undoubtedly have been arrested, tortured and executed by the Gestapo.

That same night, McCairns made his operational debut. Before departure, Lockhart had told him his course to the target was unduly complex; McCairns disagreed – a bet of half a crown was made, with the added incentive that McCairns would be turfed off the Flight if he failed. The very bumpy landing in France was partly Mac's fault – in his haste to touch down he had forgotten to set the elevator trim properly; but the operation was a great success, taking two agents in either direction. Instead of the standard colour-coded message to Tangmere's tower to confirm success or not, Mac's first radio transmission once over the Channel on his way home was to let his flight commander know that he owed him half a crown. Lockhart now knew he had lost 2s/6d but acquired a character.

Three nights later, on 28 November 1942, Vaughan-Fowler was in the air again, for what was to be the squadron's first dual operation or 'double' for SIS – Operation *Perry*. Mac was to accompany him in another Lysander in order to pick up a group of SIS operatives. This double had

THE DREAM TEAM FORMS

been planned since May, and did not have universal endorsement within SIS; one senior figure drolly commenting, 'These proposed dual operations do not fill me with enthusiasm.' Air Ministry instructions were that either both pilots would land or neither – SIS did not want to spoil the landing field (near Morgny, to the east of Rouen) for half a load. Advice to the pilots at Tangmere before their departure was rather less clear cut.[14]

The trip should have been one of the shortest for 161's Lysander operations: Mac and Vaughan-Fowler flew in formation for the first half hour, but had to cross the Channel at only 500 feet due to low cloud. As they neared France, they had to extinguish their navigation lights, meaning that Mac at the rear had only the glimmer of two small blue lights on Vaughan-Fowler's aircraft to help him maintain formation. Unsurprisingly, they then lost touch with each other. Vaughan-Fowler became uncertain of his position in cloudier weather and asked Mac to circle for a while in order for him to catch up. When they failed to renew contact, the younger pilot told Mac to 'go ahead'. Mac did wait for a while at the agreed rendezvous point at Les Andelys (an easy-to-recognize town on the Seine), but then proceeded to Morgny and landed. Vaughan-Fowler never found the rendezvous.

Communication between the two pilots then became very confused: Mac heard Vaughan-Fowler say that he was 'just setting course for home', and assumed he had picked up his passengers. Although by now well past the agreed time, Mac flew north to the field, which was easy for him to pick up just to the east of the enormous Forêt de Lyon; the appropriate code letters were exchanged by light, and he landed. Such was his stress that it was a heavy landing (which was subsequently found to have damaged his tailwheel). His passengers embarked with the usual hurry – four in all. Just as well that it was not four adults – it was Max Petit (a CND operator), his wife and two young sons, who had been on the run for some time, having spent the last two nights hiding in a barn. The boys' first flight was an exciting one hour and four minutes – however the family was 'lavishly sick over one another'. Once back safely at Tangmere, the children were confused – their father had not told them his plans, and when Army and RAF officers approached the Lysander, they thought they were in Germany. The younger Petit stood open-mouthed on the tarmac, dressed in a filthy, vomit-covered fur-lined jacket that reached the ground. Mac on dismounting was 'in a suicidal state', and concluded 'there was no future in Doubles'. The grateful Mme Petit gave a somewhat strained, but invariably polite Mac a lipstick as a gift for his mother, and a small gold token for himself.¹⁵ After turning back, Vaughan-Fowler had arrived safely back at Tangmere.

W/Cdr Percy Charles Pickard, a giant of a character, had arrived at Tempsford on 1 October to command 161. Known universally as 'Pick' (he hated his first name), he was possibly the most famous bomber pilot amongst the British public, due to his starring role as Sqn Ldr Dickson in the film *Target for Tonight*, which had been released the previous July. Pickard had played the captain of a Wellington, *F for Freddie*, which was central to the plot. His piloting skills were exceptional, his acting skills less so. But at least the film enabled him to hold his head high in family gatherings since his older sister Helena (known in the family as 'Pixie') had become a film actress and married the director Cedric Hardwicke. Indeed Pickard was given the film role after being introduced by his sister to *Target for Tonight*'s director at a party in London.

Born at Handsworth outside Sheffield in 1915, he was despatched down to Suffolk to attend Framlingham College at the age of 13, where he found pleasure on the sports field (at Second XI level) rather than the classroom. He was a keen shot, and a good horse rider – both skills that betokened a successful future career as a military pilot. Indeed fresh air was what he craved, and on Sundays he was spotted more than once riding a cow in a neighbouring farmer's field. In his latter years at the school, as he rose in seniority, he developed a reputation as a bit of a thug – a prefect who delighted in beating juniors with more vehemence than was necessary.¹⁶

His poor academic record was probably due to his then-undiagnosed dyslexia. University was not therefore an option, so after Framlingham he went to Kenya in the company of a school friend whose father ran a farm there. Pick fell into the orbit of a World War I veteran RFC pilot, 'Timbertoes' Carlin MC, DFC, DCM, who had lost a leg in a flying accident. This had not slowed Carlin's progress on the polo field, and he imbued his young charge with a love of the sport.¹⁷ Pick also joined the 3rd African Rifle Reserve, but by 1936 he had heard the drums of war beating in Europe and considered it his duty to return home. With three of his young polo chums, he bought a car and started the journey back to England. It was little surprise that after several nights of camping under the African sky, he contracted malaria, but he pulled back from the brink after 11 days. They caught a boat to Marseille and motored along the less demanding roads of France.

With exquisite timing, their antiquated Ford expired just outside London. He walked to his parents' London flat; his mother was surprised to be woken at 0300hrs by her son, whom she presumed to be still in Kenya, looking like a tramp. Pick's first priority was to secure a commission in the Army. His poor academic record, supplemented by a struggle with written communication, led to his failure – they decided he was 'not bright enough for commissioned service'.[18] He turned to the RAF as the next best alternative. Thankfully for both sides, he was accepted, and started pilot training in the November of 1937. Drawing the short straw, he found himself at Airwork Services Reserve Training School at Perth in Scotland – there were better times of year to be flying around those latitudes in an open cockpit biplane. His title now became Pupil Pilot Percy Pickard, a title which caused him 'mild hysteria'.

His first solo flight, on 2 December 1936, was after 11 hours' instruction. Pick graduated from advanced flying training on the Hawker Hart and Hawker Audax at Wittering in May 1937 with an 'Average' rating. Despite his loathing of mathematics, he had found the navigation phase quite easy.[19]

Pick was a tall and imposing figure; when Dorothy Hodgkin was invited to a Mess Ball at the officers' mess at Wittering near her home, he made quite the impression. The resulting courtship struggled against waves of paternal disapproval, so she left home to seek employment in London. Her Svengali provided the answer – she became PA to his actress sister. Pick's height and physique made it doubly ironic that he was known by both his family and Dorothy as 'Boy'.

His first posting was to No. 214 Squadron to fly the obsolescent Harrow bomber (the type that Arthur Harris had tried to foist on 138 Squadron), where he qualified as captain on 5 April 1938, by now classed as 'Above Average' as a pilot. His logbook notes a few flights in a 'Majister' [Magister] – his dyslexia sometimes caused him to mis-spell the types of aircraft he was flying. Similarly, he had a few flights in the 'Wallis' – the Westland Wallace was the aircraft the RAF chose to try to (successfully) fly over the summit of Everest. By 1939, Pick had the prestigious job of being aide de camp (ADC) and personal pilot (in a Miles Mentor) to Air Marshal Sir John (Jackie) Baldwin, then commandant of the RAF College at Cranwell. This gave Pick plenty of time to represent the service at polo.[20] When war was declared, Pick had already amassed 734 flying hours. Hitler's bellicosity spurred Pick and Dorothy into marriage the following month.

Pickard was soon on operations with No. 7 Squadron flying the Hampden bomber (known as the 'Flying Pencil'). He swiftly moved onto the Wellington with No. 99 Squadron at Newmarket Heath where he coupled up with another Yorkshireman, Alan Broadley, then a sergeant, who was to remain his navigator for the rest of Pickard's career. It developed into a close symbiotic relationship.[21] Here his leadership qualities began to impress, with Norman Didwell, one of his ground crew, calling him, 'the most decent and straightforward of men'.[22] The squadron at this time had an onerous run of missions off the north German coast bombing enemy shipping.

On 19 June 1940, whilst on another mission to the Ruhr, his Wellington *'O' for Orange* was hit by flak, damaging the starboard engine which failed after they had dropped their load of eight 250lb bombs. During the slow haul homewards, the oil pressure in the port engine ebbed lower, until eventually Pickard had to ditch in the North Sea. Luckily, the dinghy had not been damaged by shrapnel and the five-man crew managed to crawl into it. Pick ripped the top button from his tunic, unscrewed the top, and handed the now-revealed small compass to Broadley: 'Right Alan, it's over to you now. Remember the Ancient Mariner? You are now the instant mariner!'

Some months before, Pick had bought an Old English sheepdog called Ming, who was to become a familiar sight to the crews of all the squadrons in which he served. In the early hours of the following morning, the dog went into Dorothy's bedroom in the married quarters at RAF Newmarket, and tugged at the blankets on her bed until she arose. Dorothy let the dog outside, thinking it needed to do what dogs do; instead the sheepdog just scanned the night sky from side to side, like some animal radar antenna. This alarmed Dorothy such that she phoned the Operations Room at the station, and was told that of the six aircraft that had taken off for the mission, Pick's aircraft was missing.

After dawn, the squadron's aircraft were sent off to search for the missing crew in the North Sea. Thirteen hours after their dunking they were found drifting through a minefield and eventually rescued by RAF Air Sea Rescue (ASR) Launch 112 based at Felixstowe. As they neared the Suffolk harbour, a naval destroyer pulled alongside and offered to take them aboard. The RAF ASR crew refused, content to look after its own. Pick returned to Newmarket a little over 24 hours after he had left.[23] A photo

THE DREAM TEAM FORMS

of Pick alongside Dorothy taken the following day shows him unscarred and rather relaxed after his ordeal.

To assuage his love of the outdoors, he bought two race horses – not a luxury as horse racing had ceased for the duration – and early each morning he would ride out on one, with Ming alongside, hunting for rabbits. By the end of August and now commanding No. 9 Squadron, he and Broadley had completed an amazing 64 operations, and he now showed all the signs of being addicted to taking the war to the Boche. A six-month ground tour was well overdue, but not much to his taste, so he was pleased to be given command of No. 51 Squadron for a special operation. This was the infamous Bruneval Raid, which had occasioned Murphy's dog leg route on his mission of 27 February 1942; Pickard's men dropped 120 parachutists together with their weapons and stores, and no aircraft were lost. A contemporary photo shows Pickard at this time somewhat burdened by the cares of command, bags under his eyes betraying long hours. As subsequent 161 member Hugh Verity was later to note, 'He was still in his twenties but seemed ten years older. One got the impression he was driving himself hard and burning himself up.'[24]

It was his success in planning and executing the air component of this raid that gained him a bar to his DSO (to add to his DFC), and brought him to the attention of SOE. So he was sent to 138 Squadron within weeks to experience their Whitleys. Whilst officially on leave on 29 August 1941, he acted as co-pilot for Ron Hockey on a mission.

On 13 July 1942, he returned to his alma mater, Framlingham College, to give a talk to its enraptured pupils. The headmaster gave the boys a day off 'in recognition of the remarkable achievements of this 26 year-old OF [Old Framlinghamian]'.[25] Naturally, he had flown to Framlingham, arriving at the nearby RAF Parham (officially known as Framlingham, USAAF Station No. 153).

Pickard's operation with Ron Hockey was merely the *hors d'oeuvre* for his command of 161. So by the time Pick arrived at Tempsford in October 1942, he had already had a storied war. Whereas many Bomber Command crews by this time merely wanted to survive their tour of 30 operations, Pick was addicted – his very being needed the oxygen of flying on operations.

His desire, and his pugnacious approach to warfare, was further stimulated by an episode during the filming of *Target for Tonight*. When he was required on the set, he would pop down to London from RAF Wittering, and stay in the family flat. On one such occasion, on arrival at their Duke

Street residence he and Dorothy found that an air raid the previous night had gutted the building. The dead included their friend, the singer Al Bowlly, who owned the adjacent apartment. Instead of retreating to the shelter, Bowlly had remained reading in bed; the blast from the parachute mine had killed him outright. Pick was very moved by the sight of all the body bags.[26]

Pickard also brought with him experience of using leading-edge bombing/navigation technology: the Bruneval Raid was one of the first occasions the Eureka and Rebecca navigation and communication systems were used in anger. Robert Hanbury Brown and John Pringle at Malvern's Telecommunications Research Establishment had invented the Eureka beacon for Bomber Command – primarily to improve its lamentable bombing accuracy.

SOE realized this would also ease the job of 161 and 138, so the Stirlings dropped sufficient numbers for the Resistance to create a grid of beacons providing coverage of all relevant areas. Eureka in particular had the potential to make the finding of landing and drop zones almost foolproof. But almost all were dumped into rivers or put at the back of barns – SOE's agents in the field 'took too little interest in such delicate and complicated toys.'[27]

When he arrived as CO at 161 on 1 October 1942, in his small, child-like handwriting Pickard noted his new base as 'Thamesford'. The intensity of his war had been such that he had now done more than 1,000 flying hours since hostilities had begun. Pick had of course brought across to 161 his navigator Broadley, now a newly commissioned P/O, in due course becoming the squadron's navigation officer. It was only nine days before Pick had his first Lysander flight – a gentle navigation exercise to Honington in Suffolk.

Pickard had to abandon his first Lysander operation (*Squid*) on 27 October because of weather in the target area. On his return, he suffered the ignominy of being fired at by the Royal Navy. Four days later, he made another failed attempt. That night, Mac had done a 'special reconnaissance' flight to the Saumur area, and was able to observe his chosen field from 100 feet, concluding it was safe to use as it had not been ploughed up. He had also noticed the flarepath of a German airfield some ten miles away, and reported it to Lockhart in his debriefing, who deflated him somewhat by telling him it was a 'gypsy internment camp'.[28] Mac's first successful operation for 161 was captaining a Whitley to drop four containers east of Blois on the Loire.

THE DREAM TEAM FORMS

On the first night of the November moon period, Pickard tried again, and took Mac in the back to show him the ropes. He crossed the French coast at Cabourg on schedule, and flew up the Loire valley from Blois as intended, but he circled the target field just before midnight for a full one and a half hours, waiting for the reception committee to arrive. Eventually, he told his two passengers he was happy to land anyway. They sensibly rejected his offer, which was lucky because it was not the right field. In his report on the operation Pick had to eat humble pie: 'No excuse can be made, other than the fact that I thought this job was easy and did not do sufficient training.' A lesson for the novice McCairns.

Lockhart's attempt to complete this mission the following night in a double (*Squid/Skate*) with Vaughan-Fowler was equally unsuccessful. The underlying problem was the same as Pickard had encountered: after the chosen pinpoint at Selles-sur-Cher for the run in to the target field, the intervening 20 miles were devoid of any landmarks – a different pinpoint should have been chosen.

That December Pick hopped into an Airspeed Oxford, a trainer and dogsbody of an aircraft, in the company of Lockhart, to become reacquainted with flying in smaller twin-engine machines.

'A' Flight, the Lysander boys, at this time comprised Lockhart, Bridger, McIndoe and Vaughan-Fowler. McIndoe was shortly to be posted out, presumably because he fell short of Pickard's high expectations of his men – Lockhart was beginning to suffer from battle fatigue – so Pickard needed some more Lysander pilots.

One presented itself from the natural poaching ground – 138 Squadron, across the aerodrome at Tempsford. On the night Pickard had returned from his first abortive Lysander mission, he sauntered across the perimeter track at Tempsford and was nearly run over by a 138 Squadron Halifax hurrying to its parking spot. P/O Rymills was at the helm. Over a drink in the crew room, Pickard recruited him with some haste, and Rymills carried out only one more mission with 138, joining 161 at the beginning of November. Pickard himself had a poor spell: he failed to complete three successive Lysander missions in October and November, the last through lack of a reception committee, the others thwarted by bad weather.

Frank Ernest Rymills was 22 when he arrived at 161. Known to one and all as Bunny, this was a nickname singularly inappropriate to his stature – he was an imposing 6 feet 4½ inches. The name had actually been inherited: his uncle Wilfred was given the nickname at school, in honour of a 1916 film cartoon character. When Frank went to the same school, he assumed the mantle. Family also influenced his putative career: his elder brother had trained to become an architect, so Bunny decided to follow the same route, graduating in due course from the Oxford School of Architecture. His lovely neat handwriting was testimony to his artistic skills and draughtsmanship; he rarely went anywhere without a pencil at hand, ready to do a quick drawing. An additional skill that was not to have much bearing on his later flying was that he was ambidextrous.

Bunny's father had fought in the Boer War, and instructed Army recruits in World War I. So it was unsurprising that Bunny enlisted in the RAFVR on 9 June 1939 as a sergeant pilot, and towered over his colleagues in flying training that summer in the Miles Magister. In spring 1940, he endured 6 Elementary Flight Training School (EFTS) at Sywell before spending four months at an advanced training squadron at Cranwell. His spell at an OTU at Abingdon was marked by his marriage on 7 December 1940 to Violet Florence Stanley. She had been visiting a nearby pub with some girlfriends; Bunny was playing bar skittles with his chums. Violet was impressed by the tall RAF pilot, and the courtship was short.[29]

His first operational squadron was No. 58, which operated Whitleys from Linton on Ouse in Yorkshire and his first operation was as co-pilot on New Year's Day 1941. Rymills was eased into the captain's role with a relatively simple operation on 16 May, bombing Boulogne.

His 21st birthday was on 11 August 1941; Bunny celebrated on his mission that night by going round for another run at his target, and arranging this time for his crew to drop a crateful of empty beer bottles at it, and afterwards the crate itself of course. (The bottles were found to produce a pleasing whistling sound as they fell to the ground.) This was not without financial penalty – the crew was forgoing the 15 shillings refundable deposit.[30] The bottles were courtesy of his crew, for Bunny himself was not a big beer drinker, smoking being his main vice – even when on operations. Having been given 'Average' ratings through his flying training, after a few operations he was being rated 'Above Average'. Whilst he had acquired certain poaching skills in his youth, the dog that was now usually to be found by his side (and sometimes in his aircraft) was Henry, a young cocker spaniel.

THE DREAM TEAM FORMS

After 59 Squadron, Bunny was posted to 19 OTU at Kinloss, a Whitley conversion school, presumably as an instructor. Its officer commanding (OC), W/Cdr Geoffrey Jarman, was allegedly less than impressed when one day Rymills taxied into another aircraft. In the subsequent hats on/no refreshments interview, Jarman said, 'One of us has to leave this station, and it's not going to be me. The next posting to come up is yours.' This turned out to be one for a crew with operational experience to take a Hudson to Singapore. With two airmen, Bunny was posted to Stradishall, where it turned out he was destined for 138 Squadron.[31] A tour dropping agents from Whitleys followed at 138, before his unusual recruitment into 161.

Bridger started the November moon period: the operator for this mission, M Fassin, had been alerted by a particularly bizarre BBC *message personnelle*: 'The white wool teddy bear is trotting at this hour around the world'.[32] Bridger carried some important passengers to and from a favourite field, the old aerodrome at Lons-le-Saunier. Outbound, he took Henri Frenay and the lantern-jawed Baron Emmanuel d'Astier de la Vigerie. Frenay had married a Swiss Protestant in 1935 who had given him a political education with a leftwards slant. A graduate from the Saint-Cyr military academy, he was a captain in 1940 when he was taken prisoner on the Maginot Line. He escaped and made his own way to Marseille by late July. By Christmas, he had been appointed to the Deuxième Bureau (the French equivalent of MI6) in an intelligence role at Vichy, where he thought he might be able to glean useful military secrets for the British. By January 1941, he realized he needed to take a more active role in the Resistance, and formed a group, mostly of extreme right-wingers, around the Resistance newspaper *Les Petites Ailes*. 'A young man, with bright blue eyes, a firm handshake, square chin, the physique usually but mistakenly associated with the man of action', he founded the COMBAT network, and became intensely ambitious.[33]

Baron Emmanuel d'Astier de la Vigerie was from an aristocratic clan which became very influential in Resistance circles. Emmanuel attended Naval School after World War I, but dropped out to be a writer – and developed an opium habit. When war was declared in 1939, he joined the French Navy in an intelligence role in Saint-Nazaire. Failing to secure a boat passage to Britain, he joined the Resistance, where his colleague Raymond Aubrac later described him as 'a spindly personage, like a Giacometti sculpture, nose like an eagle's beak and a questioning smile that had something aristocratic about it. At least he smoked a pipe.'[34]

Some of the potential resisters he had tried to attract had been deterred by his drug-taking. De la Vigerie with his haughty demeanour recognized that he had joined a member of a rather odd club, later noting, 'I think you could only have joined the Résistance if you were maladjusted.'[35] He had been sent over to the US in June by de Gaulle to win over the American administration. Later he certainly won the admiration of Churchill, who told Roosevelt, 'This is a remarkable man of the Scarlet Pimpernel type... He is a fine fellow, very fierce and bitter but one of the best Frenchmen I have struck [sic] in these bleak times.'[36]

There was both personal and political animosity in the back of Bridger's Lysander. De la Vigerie's LIBÉRATION was full of trade unionists and socialists – the other end of the political spectrum from Frenay's crowd, which they distrusted for being too militaristic. Frenay was uncertain he could trust de la Vigerie, and gave him only qualified approval: 'the man has talent, even class... His secret weapon is probably his smile and he smiles often and good naturedly.'[37] Moreover, the pair had plenty to talk about during their flight. Whilst in London, they had both been jostling for control of the Resistance movement. Frenay had tried to assume leadership of the Armée Secrète (de Gaulle's resistance army in the Unoccupied Zone), claiming he had 22,500 men under his command (against de la Vigerie's 12,000); de la Vigerie pushed back, so Frenay suggested General Charles Delestraint instead. De la Vigerie had reluctantly agreed to the creation of a 'Co-Ordination Committee'.

The duo carried a letter from de Gaulle to Jean Moulin, together with a lot of francs. Moulin was now on his way to becoming a central figure in the unification of the disparate Resistance movements, tasked with creating order out of this chaos. He founded the Service des Opérations Aériennes et Maritimes (SOAM, Department for Aerial and Marine Operations) to organize communications with the UK by air and sea for the northern part of France, and the Bureau for Air Operations (BOA, the RF Section umbrella organization in the Occupied Zone) for the southern half.

Emmanuel also carried a missive to his older brother François, an air ace in World War I who had commanded the French air assets in the Battle of France in 1940, inviting him to join him in England. The letter achieved its intended purpose, and General François hopped into the Lysander, together with Yves Morandat (a BCRA member, also on the steering committee of LIBÉRATION).[38] As Pierre de Crevoisier de Vomécourt had once said to Frenay, 'The British services are very efficient, much more so than the French – as you've probably noticed. And then, as we all know,

THE DREAM TEAM FORMS

the two of them show no mutual trust whatsoever. Anyway, if it's efficiency you're after, the English are the ones that can help you.'[39] He was well placed to judge: having been educated in an English public school, he had acted as a liaison officer for the 7th Cameronians in France in 1940, and arrived back in the UK that June, volunteering for SOE as soon as he discovered the relaxed attitude of the Free French in London.

As Pickard's first couple of Lysander missions had been unsuccessful, the CO felt more than normal pressure for the next one on 22 November (Operations *Squid* and *Skate*), to a favourite field south of Vatan, near Châteauroux. There were three SOE agents who needed retrieving, so Pickard decided that two Lysanders would be sent, piloted by Bridger and himself.

McCairns was not happy and requested that he be allowed to take one machine – Pick was firm, but told him he could accompany him as a passenger/navigator in his own aircraft.[40] It was an early take-off, so the crews had an early supper at Tangmere with their two outgoing agents. Mac's butterflies precluded enjoying his meal.

Once airborne, Mac understandably found map reading facing backwards somewhat difficult. The two Lysanders were greeted by a flak gun near the Normandy town of Falaise, and were in radio contact for the journey down, meeting at the agreed rendezvous of Blois on the Loire. But on his way to the landing field, Pick made a novice error – he decided to cut a corner of his intended course, and route direct, quickly becoming lost. Bridger had no such problems and landed. Once on the ground, he turned on his navigation lights, enabling Pick finally to spot the intended field. Thereafter the operation proceeded successfully. They had been helped by better visibility than during Pick's two previous efforts, and also by Bridger's meticulous mission planning.[41] The celebrations once back at the Tangmere Cottage went on 'long into the night'. The following lunchtime, Pick and Mac had to fly back to Tempsford, where that night the younger pilot was whisked off to a very successful dance by a Kiwi pilot chum.

The success of his double probably had a bearing on Pick's attitude to the mix-up during Mac and Vaughan-Fowler's double a week later (as mentioned above). In the debriefing at Tangmere, Lockhart as flight commander chose not to rule on this breach of orders. It fell to the CO, and Pick was less than charitable – of Vaughan-Fowler he said, 'No excuse for this failure, perhaps over-confidence', whilst McCairns' performance was a 'very bad show'. Both 'completely disregarded orders… completely ruined this double operation'.[42] Mac had also done a heavy landing in

France on the 25th, having forgotten to trim the Lysander properly beforehand (Petter's problem again). Pick suspended Mac from operations for an indefinite period – purgatory for this keen pilot.[43]

In his detailed summary of November operations for Gp Capt Easton at the Air Ministry, Pickard concluded, 'It is hoped in the future more operations will be organised as 7 pilots and aircraft are now available, also it would help considerably if they could be buttoned up sooner so that pilots can study their route.'[44]

The pilots of 161 Squadron were left in no doubt that their new CO would expect the highest standards. But, as Mac later noted: 'With the arrival of Pick a new wave of optimism and ambition swept through the squadron.'[45]

11

1943

France was made by God with SOE in mind.

Vera Atkins

The issues with the double carried out (or not) by Bridger and Vaughan-Fowler showed that the movement of more than two or three agents could create problems. And whilst the Mk III Lysander that the pilots of 161 were using had a useful range of just over 1,000 miles, this meant that operations to the very south of France were taking unacceptable risks. Moreover, as Resistance (and intelligence-gathering) activity was stepping up a notch, an ability to move agents and matériel in quantity was needed. SIS had in fact suborned a Coastal Command Hudson for a pick-up operation in May 1941, totally outside the organization of 138 and 161 Squadrons. It failed.

161's heavy fleet was shifting from Whitleys to the four-engined Handley Page Halifax. Unsurprisingly, the Halifax was a Bomber Command reject – Harris had found it 'utterly unsatisfactory', and had been telling Portal 'of the fearful maintenance problems largely caused by the unreliability of its engines'. Its other faults included poor performance, 'vicious handling habits', and poor exhaust flame damping (critical for clandestine missions).[1]

Mouse Fielden supervised the squadron's conversion to the Halifax, and was chatting to Douglas Dodds-Parker one day: 'I don't like double Lysanders.' Dodds-Parker replied, 'Neither do I, but this operation is urgent and there is no alternative.' 'I've got an aircraft,' confided Fielden, 'I've got the King's Hudson.' 'But you couldn't land a Hudson on a Lysander strip' – Dodds-Parker was half right there. 'I could, old boy,' averred Mouse. He brought across the King's Flight Lockheed Hudson.[2] Now with the military serial FH406, and its luxury interior having been stripped out, up to eight passengers could be carried, albeit sitting on their bags rather than in the monarch's comfortable velour chairs. Mouse took it on its operational debut on 25 November 1942. The destination, the airfield at Vinon-sur-Verdon beyond Avignon, had been too distant for the Lysanders. The station commander had a frustrating time, as there was no proper lighting visible at the field, so he returned home, landing seven hours after take-off.

Carte (André Girard) was the operator and had comprehensively fouled up the operation. This had been intended to take himself, Vautrin and five ancient French generals to England. *Carte* had selected the field, but on the evening of the operation, when Peter Churchill, a British SOE agent, asked to inspect it, *Carte* brushed him off saying there was no need whatsoever. He claimed that his team ('all of whom are distinguished aviators') were quite content that the field was 'in every way suitable for the reception of a bomber [in reality, the Hudson was much smaller than a bomber]'.[3]

Nonetheless, Churchill paced out the positions of the lights and found to his horror a five-foot-high bank running diagonally across the intended flarepath. *Carte* deflected criticism to a French Air Force pilot in the party, who claimed that any decent airman could land on his chosen field. But the pilot had only operated a light aircraft (a Potez 43), and had no concept of the needs of a Hudson. Churchill refused to allow identification light signals to be flashed to the circling Fielden. The party left the field with recriminations still at full flow.[4]

It was around this time that Harald Penrose asked Mouse – whom he had known for several years – if he could possibly accompany a 161 Lysander mission to France. Twirling his moustache, Fielden shook his head and affirmed, 'Too secret. Quite impossible.'[5]

The once very keen Lockhart was becoming burned out. After the Lysanders had been grounded by foggy nights at the beginning of the moon period, the flight commander took off on 17 December on *Starfish*. Guy found his field at Chavannes, south of Bourges. But on landing, his tail-wheel caught in a very rutted farm track which crossed the strip, punching it upwards through the tailplane. Lockhart decanted his two agents, but found that he had no fore and aft movement in the stick, and the rudder was jammed solid. Some Anglo-French brute force cured the latter problem, at the cost of breaking one of the rudder supports. But all attempts to free the elevator failed. Mindful of his tribulations the last time he was marooned in France, Guy apprised his returning agents of the dangers of trying to make it back to England; he was game, and so were they. After take-off, the Lysander climbed well enough, if too steeply, on full throttle, but the only way he could descend was by cutting the throttle, combined with some use of the tail trimmer. After a porpoising journey across France he made it back to Tangmere, where fire engines and ambulances were prepared for the worst. He made a safe landing at 0400hrs – it was to be Guy's last successful Lysander operation.[6] By now, his nerves were shot, and he badly needed to recover with a tour away from operational flying. Lockhart was sent to work in the SOE Operations Room in Baker Street, to be cosseted by its secretaries.[7]

In the days running up to Christmas 1942, 161 mounted five Lysander sorties. All were thwarted apart from Pickard's flight on the 22nd (Operations *Lobster/Cuttlefish*), when he managed to take two SOE agents in, and two out. Bridger's New Year celebrations were turbocharged by news of his award of a DFC. At the start of the January moon period, he was finally able to carry out *Ajax* to Ussel-Thalamy, which had failed twice the previous month, bringing back three SIS agents, including Léon Faye, Fourcade's number two.

Fourcade was grateful for Bridger's outgoing cargo of *courier* and stores, not least some proper coffee (albeit powdered), which made breakfast the following morning more palatable in the absence of her lover. Bridger was lucky to succeed in taking off with three in the back – the operator had chosen a field of heather between six and 20 inches high, and it was wet. Faye ('an extremely experienced pilot', at least in the eyes of SIS) was less than grateful after they had landed back at Tangmere, stating that 'there was no heather anywhere on the field, and that the pilot handled his aircraft badly on take-off. [Bridger] was in an extremely excitable and nervous condition on landing.' This was later denied by the squadron commander, but the SIS commentator considered that Bridger 'was always highly strung after an operation'.[8] Bridger had the support of his colleagues, one later describing him as a 'tough little fellow'.

The same night Vaughan-Fowler had a failed mission, but Sqn Ldr Hugh Verity carried out his first successful pick-up (Operation *Corinne*), of not one but three passengers, including Christian Pineau. The operation had been delayed for a while because of the snow that covered the favoured Saône landing grounds. Now Verity was harried to the Channel by German night-fighters. The field near Lyon had been set up by a radio operator known to Barbara Bertram as *Pierre le Paysan* (Peter the Peasant), and provided a good ground, but it was less than two miles from a German

Army garrison! Outbound over France, Verity put his head down 'to study the map, a few seconds too long. When I lifted it, I was heading straight towards a large radio pylon.' He then made a hard turn to starboard pulling 2 or 3 G. 'I was scared stiff. A flow of adrenaline left me all trembling.' He made the error 'due to my inquisitiveness about a brightly lit building with no blackout'.[9]

This was one of the longest Lysander operational flights – the return trip was delayed by strong headwinds. By the time he landed at Tangmere, Verity had been in the air for almost nine buttock-numbing hours – the Lysander pilot sat on his dinghy pack, and this was tailored for utility rather than comfort. Pineau had brought back two of his new recruits for training, who were rather relieved to be welcomed by Tony Bertram once back at Tangmere. Ever the gentleman, Verity concluded his report the following day with 'One of my passengers very kindly gave me a bottle of scent as a souvenir. This thoughtfulness is very much appreciated.' Pickard put a line through this recognition of the by now customary French generosity before the report was typed up for onward dissemination!

By this time, Pineau had developed a strong friendship with Guy Lockhart. Despite, or perhaps because of, his trade union background, the Frenchman enjoyed the good life, and found that the wine, women and song in London provided a welcome antidote to the necessarily parsimonious months in his homeland. Indeed, he had requested this trip back to England because the stresses of outfoxing the Gestapo for weeks on end, together with the gastronomic privations of Occupied France, had sapped his resolve and his health. Now he was dining with Lockhart and his wife, together with 30 other RAF pilots. With his roving eye, Pineau found it no hardship later to have to accompany Lockhart, plus wife and 'ravishingly blonde' sister-in-law to the Coconut night club.[10] Meanwhile, Pineau's wife was coping with a new-born child back home. His usual informal debriefing with *Passy* followed a few days later. Dining also with agents of SIS, he realized they were already pondering how de Gaulle would control France after its liberation.

On the night before Christmas Eve, Mac had a frustrating time on Operation *Ajax*; his outbound passenger Vladimir Bouryschkine, a French-speaking White Russian, was even more frustrated, as he had endured endless failed flights. Bouryschkine was yet more exotic cargo: a basketball player in the US (where he was known as Val B. Williams), and coach to the Monaco national team, he had joined the escape game by convincing the governor of the Fort de La Revère prison down the coast that his Allied PoWs needed some weekly sport. Thus he had enabled more than 50 to sail away to Gibraltar! He was being sent back to France by MI9 to co-ordinate OAKTREE, the maritime escape route from Brittany.[11]

This time the forecast was again poor and proved correct – fog prevented Mac detecting any ground features until south of the Loire. The fog persisted over the target airfield, and he was forced to bring his passenger home after an exhausting seven-and-a-half-hour flight.

Hugh Beresford Verity was another pre-war RAF entrant, arriving at 161 with experience and tales. Born in 1918 in Jamaica to Dorothy and George, a clergyman, Hugh's upbringing was eclectic. His parents brought young Hugh back to Great Britain most years on a banana boat to re-connect with their extended family. After school at Cheltenham College, Hugh won a Laming Scholarship to Queen's, Oxford, to read French and Spanish; he also learned to fly with the University Air Squadron. It was almost as though those two choices pre-destined him to end up at 161 a few years later. His life at Oxford could hardly have been more enjoy-able: he relished flying the Tutor – and the Hawker Audax even more so. His love of literature was evident in the lyrical descriptions he sent back home in frequent letters to his parents; during a summer camp at the busy Lympne aerodrome, it 'looks very lovely after dark, the silhouettes of the hangars and the fir trees around the edge with points of yellow light flick-ering off, on all round a yard above the ground and red lights on the top of 30 ft. posts along the edges…'[12]

Verity had visited France during his degree, and was drawn back to it for the summer of 1939, subbed by occasional cheques from his doting parents. He was quite relaxed about the prospect of being called up to the RAF if war was declared, as he loved flying and found the thought of serving in the infantry somewhat distasteful. In the first week of August he was sunning himself on the Atlantic coast near Bayonne, and a few days later had returned to his hosts by the Seine, downstream from Paris. By the middle of the month, this French family was seeming 'pretty scared' in Hugh's eyes. Having sent his address to his UAS, he had resolved to stay as long as possible 'as I am learning a lot, especially of the language'. Avidly scanning the newspapers each day, Hugh, who had been hoping for a career in the Foreign Office, was misreading the runes: 'I personally have a sort of feeling that Hitler is not a big enough fool to start a war.' He did not consider that 'Roosevelt's appeal to Victor Emmanuel will do the slightest good. He should have appealed to Mussolini.' There was no doubting Verity's patriotism: 'I look on the possibility of war like this: England is the greatest country in the world. Germany wants to be it. We have got to stop her, and will stop her too.'[13]

Once called up, during his advanced flying training at Cranwell Verity was lucky enough to be presented to Lord Trenchard. Young Verity was quizzed by the grizzled father of the RAF on his career aspirations: 'Twin engined fighter, Sir.'

Trenchard: 'You don't want to bomb the Ruhr, eh? Like to see it bombed though, I suppose, but you want to stop the Hun doing that here. Would you rather have eight machine guns or cannon?'

Verity: 'I would rather have both, Sir.' Trenchard's group all laughed and the young officer made his exit.[14]

In July 1940, he married his longstanding girlfriend 'Mog' (Audrey Stokes), and his first posting was one of the least exciting the RAF could offer a newly fledged pilot – flying slow old Coastal Command Ansons on convoy patrols over the North Sea. He survived that to go on to fly the considerably more sprightly Beaufighter with No. 252 Squadron in Northern Ireland. This unit was deployed to Malta for a few weeks, and Verity and his radar/wireless operator were one of the few crews to emerge unscathed from that escapade. However, on their return to Ulster in May 1941, Verity encountered engine problems whilst over the Irish Sea, and 'got away from a very sinister situation – a combination of wireless failure, impossible weather, and failing petrol supply made it seem inevitable that we would have to make a parachute descent through cloud, or spend a long time in the sea. As it happened we were astonishingly lucky to find land after our petrol gauges showed empty in a patch of visibility not so bad as the rest.'[15]

He emerged from the resulting forced landing and crash into a ten-foot concrete wall with just a slight scratch to his forehead, and some bruised teeth. The Irish looked after him and his fellow internees rather well at Internment Camp B at The Curragh racecourse.[16] But he managed to escape from the camp one day when his guards were occupied in celebrating their success on the horses. Verity simply caught a train to Belfast. (For years Audrey's Irish relatives would have little to do with him because they thought he had broken his parole.)

Once back in the UK, he had a spell on No. 29 Squadron with night-fighters, before being sent on a ground tour as an Intruder Controller at Bentley Priory, Fighter Command's HQ. His job was to vector RAF long-range fighters to catch the enemy night-fighters as they took off or landed on sorties attacking the Allied bomber streams. Like the better-known plotting room at Uxbridge that controlled the RAF's day fighters in the Battle of Britain, he had before him a large table covering southern England, the Channel and the near Continent. On a number of nights, he saw so-called special radar plots crossing the Channel. 'One night the Senior Air Traffic Control Officer from Tangmere, Dusty Millar, came and said "Do you know what those specials are?", and I said "No – I've no idea". He said "Well they're either parachuting agents into enemy-occupied Europe or they're going to pick them up in Lysanders."'[17] The controller told him the story about Sticky Murphy being shot in the neck – Verity was entranced, and requested a transfer to 161, which he believed was commanded 'by a rather eccentric character called Squadron Leader Guy Lockhart'.[18] In reality, Lockhart did not command 161; he was the Lysander flight commander. Verity's good knowledge of European languages meant he had been approached by an Air Commodore Pearson for a job as Assistant Air Attaché at a Spanish-speaking country in South America. But this sounded too far removed from the action for Verity – his French and operational experience secured him the job of Lysander flight commander at 161.

He arrived at Tempsford in November 1942, having cryptically told his parents that the 'job will be an astoundingly important one. It will involve a little operational flying', deliberately understating the dangers involved.[19] This squared a circle in Verity's wartime RAF career: he had spent the first year in Training Command, the second in Coastal Command, the third in Fighter Command, and now was due to spend the fourth in Bomber Command, albeit in a most un-bomber like role. In his new position, he carried a quasi-religious sense of purpose – 'Personal fears and hopes must shrink before the importance to millions of people of shortening the war.' Verity's underlying pomposity was not to go unnoticed by his new colleagues...[20]

When he had escaped from Ireland, he had left most of his personal belongings behind, including his log book. Thus by the time he arrived at Tempsford, he had had to guess his cumulative totals of flying hours; one night in the Tangmere bar he declared, 'I have to guess my totals but it's the assessments I miss' (his periodic reviews by his commanding officers had generally been of the highest order).[21] He soon christened his Lysander *Jiminy Cricket* because it was a 'suitable character from a Disney film of my youth, after all he was quite good at jumping around the place'.[22] His ground crew painted the creature on the Lysander's nose.

Verity's past had not included much pilot-navigation, and only 250 of his 850 flying hours were at night, so he had to work hard at his night-navigation skills during his bedding-in period. Bunny Rymills, who had found a billet at Joe Balls' farm near Tempsford, was also practising solo navigation assiduously as 1942 came to a close. The ground crew had little faith that Bunny would emerge safely from his training hutch, his rigger noting wryly, 'He needs a bit of practice because when we flew down here [from Tempsford to Tangmere] if we hadn't come to the Channel, we shouldn't have known where we were.'[23]

New Year's Day brought some welcome news for the squadron – Pick's wife Dorothy, who lived near Tempsford, had given birth to their son, Nicholas. The infant's head was well wetted at the Mess; Pick decided to perform his trick of folding the flesh of his forearm and inserting a couple of nappy pins through it. As the evening wore on, someone had the bright idea to traverse the bar by hanging from their toes on the wooden beam that ran its length. 161's commanding officer, who as ever had led the drinking, fell to the floor. The Tempsford medics diagnosed a broken left thumb, and put Pick's wrist in a plaster cast. Not that this stopped him flying...[24]

The doubts of Pears, Rymills' rigger, were to be proved misplaced. The ever optimistic Bunny carried out his first Lysander operation on 23 January. He set off from Tangmere with his usual vital equipment – two packets of Wills 'Ship' Woodbines, which against all regulations he assiduously smoked throughout the flight. But he saw no reception lights at the field at Le Grand Maleray, so came home empty-handed.[25] Mac encountered similar difficulties that night. Having earlier heard the message '*Les femmes sont parfois volages*' ('Women are sometimes fickle'!) on the BBC, Peter Churchill and Odette Hallowes were waiting for him at Basillac, the old aerodrome near Perigueux. Odette ('a shrewd cookie') had made a big impression on Selwyn Jepson, SOE's recruiting officer, although he 'was rather doubtful about her personality. It was so big. God help the Germans if we can ever get her near them.'[26] Well she was near – too near – to them now.

She and Peter Churchill (on whom she had made a great impression when they first met) had paced out their light positions, and marked them with handkerchiefs, and were consuming a picnic dinner of smoked ham washed down with Armagnac, when they heard the drone of Mac's Lysander at only 2230hrs. Churchill flashed the recognition signal, but received nothing back from Mac who flew straight on. A few minutes later Odette thought she heard voices; the duo fell to the ground as a pair of strangers brushed past. After they had disappeared, the two SOE agents hatched an escape plan if matters deteriorated. Mac returned in the Lysander when light signals were suddenly made from the direction of the old control tower. The would-be captors had played their hand too early; Churchill flashed some warning signals to Mac who then disappeared northwards.[27]

At the end of January, Verity organized a double for Rymills and McCairns, with himself as airborne back-up 'as I had not been able to do much that moon'.[28] *Prawn/Gurnard/Whitebait* was to a favoured field near Lons-le-Saunier, owned by the local mayor – who insisted on being present for their arrival, which was organized by the very competent operator Paul Rivière. As the trio were passing the French coast outbound, Tangmere issued a recall signal because of increasing fog. Only Mac heard it, and only he returned. For the remaining two, there was the usual welcome from the flak gunners at Carpiquet aerodrome. Verity later said, 'One always feels a little bit frightened when shot at by tracer, but we were generally too busy [to worry about it].'[29]

Bunny found the field despite 'a low blanket of fog practically covering the target'. He landed successfully at 0130hrs despite that fog, embarked his two passengers and departed. Only later was it found that his two outbound agents had forgotten to unload all the parcels destined for the reception committee. But after Verity landed in turn 'with a dull thud' (finding out later he had bent a longeron in his Lysander), he halted:

A scruffy looking Frenchman talked to me in English while I talked to him in French. He asked me where his passengers were, and I asked him where my passengers were. I explained that another aeroplane which had the outbound passengers had not appeared, and I wanted to take back two to England. He said they did not understand it was a double operation. My two passengers would not be there until the next day, as they were at the other aerodrome near Mâcon. I asked if any of the odds and sods on the field would like a free passage to England, but there were no takers.[30]

Three nights later, for SIS, Pick flew out the aquiline veteran of the CND network, Pierre Brosselette, and after struggling to spot the field in dark conditions, picked up René Massigli, the former French Ambassador to Turkey, and André Manuel, BCRA's Head of Intelligence, with no fewer than seven suitcases.[31]

On the return flight, Pick was discomfited not to be able to recognize where he was crossing the French coast, but stuck to his pre-determined compass course. With his fuel tanks showing empty, he crossed a craggy coastline on fumes and landed at the first aerodrome he saw, which turned out to be RAF Predannack on the tip of the Lizard peninsula in Cornwall. With only a slightly more westerly course he would have missed England altogether, and expired over the Atlantic.

Once back at Tangmere, drawing on his pipe, Pick was adamant that the Lysander's compass must have been faulty and berated the ground crew; in fact the cause of his near-disaster was entirely of his own making. The wing commander was in the habit of equipping himself like a pirate for his Lysander trips – the bayonet stuffed into his left flying boot understandably distracted the compass from Magnetic North! Strangely, this mistake did not feature in his description of the mission in the squadron's ORB.

Even the most talented pilots occasionally have a bad day – Mac, who by now had accumulated 536 flying hours (including 155 hours on the Lysander), had one such on 2 February. Whilst taxiing his machine R9106 in a strong wind, he left the tarmac taxiway, the wind lifted the tail, and the aircraft tipped onto its nose bending the propeller. In the official report, Pick attributed this to 'carelessness', whilst Fielden succinctly remarked 'Overconfidence'.

Lockhart's CV already featured a tour on Spitfires and a record of unauthorized low flying. With experience comes wisdom, but not in Guy's case. He took up a Lysander for an air test, and decided to perform a slow roll over Tempsford so his colleagues could witness his skill. Being a high-wing monoplane with the extra underslung fuel tank for added stability, Petter's design was hardly intended for this manoeuvre. He dived the poor machine to pick up speed and pulled up into a much less impressive barrel roll. On landing, the long-suffering 161 mechanics were not impressed – all the side glazing of the cockpit canopy had popped out due to the wings flexing when the aircraft was upside down.

Mac ribbed his flight commander about this, and attributed the canopy issue to Lockhart's poor technique. Pick heard the discussion, thought the same, and despite not having had the benefit of a tour on fighters, took off to show Lockhart how it should be done. Another dished-out barrel roll ensued: 'You're right Guy, all the windows dropped out.' He forbade anyone else to try the manoeuvre. Mac returned from a flight and tried a roll over the airfield. Afterwards the mechanics were running short of canopy glazing, and Mac was given the traditional punishment of a fortnight acting as duty officer.[32] The perils of audacious flying in Lysanders were brought home more vividly on 11 February when Sgt Witold Szott killed himself and his gunner, flying into the mast of a ship in the Irish Sea.

By the time he carried out his first Hudson operation, on 13 February 1943, with the Canadian Dicky Taylor as navigator, Pickard had flown a staggering 49 different aircraft types. This operation (*Sirène/Bérénice*) was the first successful Hudson operation for the squadron, which now had the ability to become truly Churchill's (small) European airline. Triple Lysander operations were now banned (because they required too long on the ground), so Hudson trips became the solution for larger groups of passengers. Whilst Pick only brought mail back (because the return passengers failed to arrive), the five outbound passengers included Henri Gorce (the only survivor of the blown Parisian network INTERALLIÉ), Fernand Gane, who was being sent out by Dewavrin to join Christian Pineau in the PHALANX network, and Felix Svagrovsky (*Gabriel*), a CND agent. Sadly the field, near Saint-Yan, was visited by a German patrol the following morning, who noticed both the obvious Hudson wheel marks in the turf, and a hat which had blown off Gane's head during disembarkation. They had the field ploughed immediately.

On the same night, Mac and Vaughan-Fowler mounted a very important double (*Porpoise* and *Prawn 2*). They encountered heavy flak when passing Caen's aerodrome, but this was a long trip, the destination being a meadow at Ruffey-sur-Seille, only 30 miles from the Swiss border, which was partially covered by low fog by the time they arrived at 0125hrs. Mac took out Colonel Henri Manhès, one of Moulin's senior commanders, but his return passenger was Moulin himself, whilst Fowler brought back the 62-year-old vehemently anti-Vichy General Charles Delestraint, to be anointed as head of the newly created Armée Secrète. Together they were possibly the most important cargo in the French Resistance at the time, and both were needed for consultations with de Gaulle and Dewavrin, when Moulin argued that 'de Gaulle and the Resistance should incorporate the political parties', and that these should be controlled through a national Conseil National de la Résistance (CNR, or Council of Resistance).[33] Such was the importance of this mission that Verity had been sent in a spare aircraft, but did not need to land. On meeting in London, Moulin and de Gaulle got on famously: both were sons of professors, and loved the Republic. Delestraint had brought to London the maps and (doomed) plans of Pierre Dalloz to militarize the plateau of Vercors. Under his new alias of *Vidal*, Delestraint issued an important order to all of the French Resistance, bringing them under his command.

On 23 February, there were no operations, so there was a party at the Cottage, with much badinage. The two sergeants had been digging four trenches, 'but we had to stop because the forks got so hot'. This stimulated the young Vaughan-Fowler into talking about gardening: 'I have more to show for it than any of you buggers have.' Meanwhile Bunny's mind was (again) on sex, specifically with a certain WAAF – 'I'll see what I can get out of her. If I can't get anything, no one else can.' After more beer and champagne had been consumed, he was moved to say cheekily of his flight commander (Hugh Verity), who was enjoying employing his excellent French on a rare young French WAAF, 'If he had a tool as big as mine, he wouldn't need to speak French.'[34]

The following night, Pickard, with the same Hudson crew as before, took Claude Lamirault to Arles, and returned with a full load of six passengers. His next Hudson operation, *Pampas*, was to prove much less straightforward. When Pickard took off just before 2230hrs on 24 February, he was feeling quite fresh, although his control of the Hudson was not helped by the plaster on his right wrist – the legacy of his high jinks at the party to celebrate the birth of his son. His crewman Henry Figg obliged in operating the throttles.

Pick had no idea of the anguished preparations at his destination. Peter Churchill was engaged in a leadership battle for control of the CARTE network with André Girard. For future operations, his team had found a field at Cuisery outside the small town of Tournus by the Saône, but when he went on his bicycle to inspect it one day, he was dismayed to see piles of bricks across it – clearly the Germans had also guessed its potential use. He decided that a team of ten or so men could dismantle enough piles to allow a landing strip to be created. He remained in Tournus to await his BBC message.

A few nights later, he cycled out to see how the field looked in moonlight and was very surprised to see lights flashing all over the place, and a team of men noisily throwing the bricks around. He was astonished that another Resistance group had chanced upon 'his' field. Churchill decided to hide behind a hedge and await events.

It was Claude Lamirault and his JADE-FITZROY team in action, and a prime example of the lack of co-ordination between SOE and SIS. By the time Pickard had reached the target area it was 0130hrs and fog was drifting about, with visibility only about 150 yards. He circled for a while as the brick heavers toiled, before the flarepath was illuminated and he made a prudent total of 20 circuits followed by a successful, if heavy, landing. If anyone in Cuisery had been sleeping through the hours of brick-throwing, they were awake now. The freshly escaped Pierre Hentic bumped into Churchill and exchanged a brief 'good evening'.

The Hudson bounced on landing, swerved off the line of the lights, touched down again with mud splattering the man at the second lamp, and disappeared from the sight of the operators. Pickard squelched past the ninth lamp, and turned back to his take-off point, slaloming through the brick piles. But then the Hudson ran into a boggier patch, and came to an abrupt halt. Pickard swung open his cockpit door and shouted at the top of his voice in a heavy English accent, '*Qui est le chef de cette bande de sauvages?*' ('Who is the leader of this band of savages?') When Lamirault reluctantly approached, a smiling Pickard added, 'Well you've got nothing to be proud about, not only have you landed me in the backyard of a brick factory, but in the centre of a bog into the bargain.'

The many people present on the field, including both sets of passengers, set to digging out the stricken Hudson. (Given the nervous state of the locals, and their possession of many sten guns, Churchill thought it best to remain behind the hedge.) By now, it was 0330hrs – the sound of the Hudson's straining engines produced more helpers from the nearby village, leading to a throng of about 50 people in Pickard's estimation. Whilst Pick chomped on his pipe, Flt Lt Putt did his best to control the work of this motley group; some of his colleagues grasped the opportunity to make post-war dates with the more audacious French women. The Hudson's tailwheel was not co-operating since every time Pickard gunned the throttles, the tail swung round and one main wheel dug in deeper. Eventually, Figg procured a stout branch and used that as a 'steering arm'. It was only when two horses arrived that the aircraft could be towed to better ground. Hitching them to the undercarriage, the pair needed little encouragement as the sound of the Hudson's Twin Wasp radial engines at full chat was enough to terrify them.

However, the fog had not dispersed and some of the flarepath had disappeared with the villagers who owned the torches, so one of Pickard's crew had to pace out the field to see whether a take-off was practicable.

He decided 'that there was a reasonable chance of becoming airborne', so they made an attempt, but by now it was 0530hrs. Pick had unfortunately allowed W/Cdrs Brooks and Lockhart on the trip entirely unofficially – because he had planned to bring back only four official passengers; so when a crowd arrived for their return to England, he had to turn two away, embarking Lamirault, Pierre Hentic and eight others.

Pick's Hudson did leave the ground – but only after losing 30 inches of its starboard wingtip in a battle with a tree at this cramped field. Churchill watched Pickard in the departing Hudson, raised his hip flask and thought to himself, 'To a Victoria Cross: for succeeding in accomplishing the impossible.' The leading edge of the Hudson's wing was badly dented, and both the autopilot and the undercarriage were damaged. As dawn was breaking by the time he re-crossed the French coast, he radioed for fighter protection, but 'none was forthcoming'; Pick limped nervously across the Channel.[35] He received a rare third bar to his DSO for this operation.

That night of 24 February was indeed dramatic for the squadron: Verity had also set off across the Channel in V9283, on an SIS trip to Le Grand Maleray near Châteauroux. His outbound passenger was of the most precious quality – Jean Moulin, returning to his mission. Once over France, Verity's problems started – the land was covered with interminable low stratus cloud. He flew on dead reckoning to where he thought his target field was, but finding no break reluctantly had to turn for home. Having had no landfall for over two hours, it was of little surprise that he was way off course by the time he reached the Channel again. Unfortunately, he had drifted westwards to Cherbourg which, as an important naval base, was well defended with searchlights and flak. Verity did a corkscrew dive to evade the lights and headed back to England. Sadly, by the time he reached the English coast, Tangmere too was covered in fog. He radioed for a steer from the Homer Direction Finding Station manned by WAAFs (in a field outside the airfield but in line with the runway); he also asked for the airfield defence searchlights to be illuminated at either end of the runway, and it was agreed that he would let down as far as 300 feet in the hope that the ground would be in sight.

The ground crews had also lit very bright 'Money' flares either side of the runway. He flew so-called racetrack circuits around the two bright searchlight beams, and started letting down to land. But each time he had not gained sight of the ground by the time he had reached 300 feet. Boredom, as well as fatigue, was creeping up on Verity. After 11 attempts he had had enough, so he determined that on the 12th, he would carry on in an instrument descent as slowly as possible until he reached terra firma. The problem was that at the last moment he sighted a Money flare, which made him think he was about to fly straight into the ground. He reacted by pulling the control column back and closing the throttle. Sadly, he was 30 feet too high and the Lysander smashed into the ground, breaking undercarriage and propeller, with the former absorbing most of the shock. Thankfully, there was no fire, and both Moulin and Verity extricated themselves without injury. Moulin thanked him 'for a very agreeable flight'!

Naturally, it took some time for the squadron ground crew to locate them. Verity's prime concern, possibly after the welfare of Moulin, was the whereabouts of his almost new Service Dress hat, which he had put away in the cockpit. An hour or so later, after being anaesthetized by a few beers, the squadron leader recalled, 'It was the sense of gentle deceleration which was so pleasant'! Two nights later, his rehabilitation was completed by a trip with two comrades to the Unicorn in Chichester where they dined on partridge casserole followed by a big omelette. The landlord, who doted on the Tangmere pilots, ensured there was plenty of good claret and burgundy. At the end of that week, Tangmere's morale was further improved by a visit by the women from the renowned Windmill Theatre in Soho. Despite the presence in the audience of the station commander and his guest the Duke of Norfolk from the nearby Arundel Castle, the infamous Phyllis Dixie performed to great applause her full fan dance.[36]

The 161 pilots were also concerned about what clothing to don and how to disrobe. When Nesbitt-Dufort crashed in January 1942, he was wearing uniform, with mechanic's overalls on top. In his view, wearing uniform meant that his chances of being shot as a spy were considerably reduced. Only having a uniform to wear, however, vastly increased his chances of arrest. So by the time the 161 Squadron boys had established themselves at Tangmere, it had been decided that it was best to fly in civilian gear, albeit usually with normal RAF flying boots, which were fashioned so that the fleece-lined upper boot could be cut away leaving a normal black shoe remaining. Webley service revolvers were the fashion accessory of choice. Mac, for example, with his experience of having been captured and being a PoW, held that it made no difference – if the Germans wanted to kill you, they would, regardless of garb. But he paid great attention to what he wore on operations – a suit made in Belgium, with all sorts of escape gear (including SOE's tear-gas fountain pen) concealed inside. Over this he would wear a black overall, with pockets containing more useful gadgets.³⁷

Bob Hodges, by now in charge of 161's Halifax flight, preferred to fly in uniform. In the mess one evening he once said, not entirely in jest, 'No, I couldn't walk into a prison camp without a tunic. They wouldn't know what rank you are.'³⁸ Bunny Rymills flew in uniform and carried a bag of civilian clothes with him – his height would have made it difficult for French peasants to find some suitable attire in a hurry!

At the beginning of February, a Frenchman with a most unusual background arrived at 161. Philippe Level had endured World War I in a French artillery regiment, and was commissioned in 1918. He celebrated peace by going on to father six children with Nicole, living in some style in Paris and his Normandy château, and learned to fly as a civil pilot. Rejoining his old regiment in 1939, he was wounded on the Maginot Line and demobbed. Not a man to rest in his armchair in such circumstances, he spent 1940 acting as a courier between several Resistance groups. Having left his large family at his Normandy château, he managed to make his way to Portugal, arriving in England in April 1941 on a KLM DC3, with the ambition of joining the Forces Aériennes des France Libres (FAFL, or Free French Air Forces). Level was of course subject to the usual grilling for aliens at the Royal Patriotic School in Wandsworth. De Gaulle's FAFL rejected the offer of his services since, at 42, he was seven years too old for their upper age limit. He pleaded with Anthony Eden, who offered him an intelligence-gathering role back in France. This held little appeal, so he added Livry (the name of a nearby village in Normandy) to his surname, reduced his age by 14 years, and presented himself at an RAF recruiting office in London! He passed his medical – when the doctor expressed surprise at the rather care-worn appearance of this '29-year-old', he replied, 'You know… life in Paris!' He qualified as a navigator and, instead of joining other French aircrew in the North African campaign, was posted to Hudsons in Coastal Command. This entailed a detachment to the eastern seaboard of the US on anti-U-boat duties for the second half of 1942 (enabling him during a brief period of leave to check on the startled staff of his company's New York office). He returned to England with No. 52 Squadron on New Year's Eve, still in French uniform.

When he joined 161 at Tempsford, he was reupholstered in RAF kit, and the elderly Frenchman with resplendent moustache became a navigator on Halifaxes. Pickard was aware that Level was in fact 42, and indeed only had 60 hours' night-flying experience; Pick told him not to worry as 'you can't see obstacles at night'![39] The old man with a 'voice like thunder', and 'a formidable presence' did many a mission to Scandinavia, but soon became the Hudson navigator of choice for Hugh Verity, with whom he became good friends. Indeed, he was warmly embraced by all the 'A' Flight team.

At the beginning of March, Verity and Bridger had disappeared to RAF Silloth in Cumberland to do a Hudson conversion course run by Coastal Command (the main user of the twin-engined American machine). It took less than a week, despite the two 161 pilots trialling approaching in the Hudsons at 20 knots slower than normal, in preparation for their arrival in diminutive French fields.

Meanwhile, Mac had flown down to Tangmere with his colleagues for the start of the moon period, but soon felt queasy. The doctor diagnosed jaundice, and he was sent to the station's sick bay. The previous month, he had tipped a wing of his Lysander onto the grass in strong wind – Pick attributed this to 'carelessness', so a rest was perhaps overdue.[40]

On 17 March, Vaughan-Fowler and Rymills carried out a double. Coastal fog had been left behind, and the weather was fine by the time they crossed the Loire. On reaching Poitiers, Bunny radioed Vaughan-Fowler, informing him he was not yet ready to fly to the field. Bunny circled for a while, but after midnight the lights of the city were gradually being turned off, so, with boredom setting in, he proceeded to the field south of Poitiers. Déricourt (the operator) flashed the code 'SC', and the pilot responded with the agreed 'RA'. Bunny landed without incident, and deposited John Goldsmith and Francine Agazarian to act as a courier for her husband. The former had worked in France in various equine industry roles; he had already done one mission entering by felucca, and operated around the Riviera. This very confident agent had slipped easily into his cover of being a black market operator. Now, within the allotted three minutes, Rymills had picked up two Mauritians,* Claude de Baissac and France Antelme (who had run an ice cream business in Madagascar), and returned to Tangmere safely. De Baissac had left behind Mary Herbert, his newly

---

*Mauritius had proven a propitious hunting ground for F Section since it was a French-speaking British colony and by now SOE had been barred from recruiting French nationals.

pregnant lover, and once back in London gave a rosy view of the strength of his network and that of his fellow network-leader Grandclément. His colleagues had, however, found working with him unpleasant.

Vaughan-Fowler, who had had some uncharacteristic navigational problems, was not quite so lucky: on landing in the long thin field bounded by trees, he hit a bump, after which flames streamed from his exhaust stack. His reaction to this unwanted and unexpected event was exemplary: he stopped in double-quick time, cut the fuel supply, dismounted, whipped off his Mae West lifejacket, and stuffed it into the exhaust. This did the trick; he restarted and taxied over to Lamp 'A', to disgorge his passengers with no further ado. Robert Dowlen was a sorely needed wireless operator for CHESTNUT; the other passenger was Pierre Lejeune, a very experienced soldier now working for F Section. Vaughan-Fowler picked up Robert Flower, who had proved a troublesome agent and was being retired from service in France, and André Dubois, a radio operator who required further training.

Two nights later, the quietly effective John Bridger squeezed three VIPs into V9353 – Jean Moulin, General Delestraint and Christian Pineau, returning to their homeland after their conferences with de Gaulle (and in the case of the first two, also with General Brooke). It was rather a risk to put three such notables into the same aircraft, which, together with 13 packages, was well laden. Bridger made it successfully to the field in between a canal and the Loire only 30 miles east of Vichy in south-east France, returning safely with one anonymous passenger for SIS. The three VIPs made their way by Citroën, bus and train to their safe house around Lyon. But it was a close shave – the Gestapo arrived at the field only ten minutes after Bridger had taken off.[41] In London before his departure, a British friend had wished Pineau good luck, to which he had replied sardonically, 'If the little pigs don't eat me!'[42] Pineau's return to French soil sparked an upsurge of activity for his PHALANX network, and Moulin started his mission of creating the CNR to try to bind the various organizations and political parties under one body (which de Gaulle hoped to control).

Moulin had been graced with several meetings with de Gaulle whilst in London, and on this return trip carried a letter from the general written, after much debate, to the Resistance in his homeland:

My Dear Friends,

I know the work you are doing, I know your worth. I know your great courage and the immense difficulties you face. Despite everything, you must continue your work and spread your influence. We who are lucky enough to be able to still fight with weapons, we need you now and in the future. Be proud and confident! France will win the war, and she will welcome us in her soil.

With all my heart, Charles de Gaulle.[43]

It was freighted with hope that Moulin would be able to use it to unite the still-warring factions. His other mission was to dampen French expectations that the Allied invasion was imminent.

The following night Pickard took back Léon Faye, and brought back three agents without incident. But perhaps he was by now beginning to feel the strain, for after landing back at Tangmere, he sighed into his beer, 'I think I am getting too old for this job!'

The strategic direction of the war continued to run anything but smoothly. It had taken much coercion to persuade de Gaulle to attend the Casablanca Conference of Allied leaders in order to meet his arch foe General Giraud. On his return to London, a tired Churchill confided to Ivan Maisky, the Soviet Ambassador to the Court of St James, 'I'm fed up with that Jeanne d'Arc in trousers. I have been looking for some bishops to burn him.'[44]

Verity had an important mission (*Jockey/Playwright*) on 23 March – a short flight to a hop farm at Estrées-Saint-Denis, east of Paris, owned by the aristocratic Mme Sainte-Beuve. The handsome and moustachioed Francis Cammaerts, the son of a Belgian poet and a pacifist by inclination, had started the war as a history teacher and a conscientious objector. But the death in action of his brother and the arrival of his first child spurred him to action. By 1943, he had been transformed into a 26-year-old SOE agent; during his training he had contracted jaundice, which SOE thought had weakened him too much to arrive into France by parachute. So that night, under the codename of *Roger*, he sat in the back of Verity's aircraft on his way to assess Peter Churchill's SPINDLE circuit in the south-east. Facing him in the back of the Lysander was Georges Dubourdin, who by now had already done one tour in France as an SOE agent. He was being sent back to run the PLAYWRIGHT network. The two passengers endured Verity's violent evasive action when some German night-fighters were spotted. Verity became 'hopelessly lost, but by a happy fluke' regained his track.[45]

On arrival, Cammaerts was greeted by '*Raoul*' (Peter Churchill) and '*Louba*' (the 46-year-old 'greying architect' Henri Frager) who were the patient return passengers, having waited three months (and crossed most of France) for this trip. The former slipped Cammaerts a message before mounting the Lysander ('Always carry a newspaper in France as they are a little short of toilet paper').[46] The pick-up had originally been scheduled for Tournus, many miles to the south, but had had to be relocated at only four days' notice due to German activity. Seven resisters took Cammaerts in a car to Paris – the driver, being a doctor, had the correct permits to drive at night. Cammaerts wondered about the wisdom of carrying so many men who did not. *En route* they threw his service revolver into the Oise, deeming it a liability.[47] Churchill and Frager, together with a briefcase full of the former's correspondence and *courier*, were going back to London to attempt to reconcile their differences with the truculent André Girard about the management of CARTE. Churchill's organization of the operation had been flawless and timely – the field was due to be ploughed up the following day. 'Congratulations on a perfect field,' said Verity, 'It's a piece of cake.'[48] Churchill was to return to his hide-out near Lake Annecy by Halifax and parachute less than three weeks later.

That night, Bunny Rymills and his chum Peter Vaughan-Fowler, who had clearly made an impression on some female members of SOE and the Resistance, had been philosophizing over a drink at the Cottage. Whilst discussing the hot topic of the moment – the possible opening of a Second Front – Rymills had a flash of inspiration – 'We could go over to Paris in the Oxford [a twin engine aircraft the squadron utilized as a hack]. Peter could have his woman, and I could fly it back in the morning.'[49]

12

Tangmere Life

If truth be the first casualty of war, then chastity is probably the second.

Ormond Burton[1]

Life in the RAF before the outbreak of the war could be magical; the so-called Expansion Era aerodromes were well constructed, with good facilities. None was in a more picturesque and idyllic location than Tangmere. It was regarded with great affection by those based there, an affection evidenced by their name for it of 'Tanglebury'.

From a 1943 perspective, the peacetime routine for the pilots had been very relaxed: 0700hrs (or 0600hrs in summer) – tea in bed served by one's batman. Work until 1300hrs, leaving the afternoon for sports: rugby, cricket and squash were favoured, whilst the officers were allowed to play golf at the nearby Goodwood estate. Mess kit was worn for dinners on Mondays, Tuesdays and three Thursdays a month. The remaining Thursday was a formal dinner, which required mess kit with white waistcoats. On Fridays, the officers wore dinner jackets, whilst on Wednesdays, Saturdays and Sundays, tweed jackets were the required rig. It all added up to what Fred Rosier, a pilot officer in No. 43 Squadron flying Furies, called 'one of the most exclusive flying clubs in the world'.[2]

Peter Townsend, who was to take over as commander of 'B' Flight from Rosier, and later to achieve greater notoriety for very different reasons,*

---

*For having a mutual romantic attachment to HRH Princess Margaret, younger sister of HRH Queen Elizabeth II. Whitehall and Buckingham Palace forced the break up of the relationship.

was even more lyrical, capturing the essence of the attraction of this Sussex jewel: 'the airfield at Tangmere was a broad meadow. The slender spire of Chichester Cathedral pointed the way there.' Landing his Fury in the long grass of summer, he noted the local farmers taking another crop of hay off the airfield, after which a herd of sheep would be set out to graze...

'Aircraft hangars... do not normally fit easily into the rustic scene. Ours did, with their wooden beams and uprights and their gently curving roofs.' They were built by German PoWs in World War I – ready for the next generation to demolish them with their bombs. 'Meanwhile life at Tangmere was peaceful, Pastoral. I loved the place; it was my home from home.'[3]

But even in peacetime, training accidents took their toll – F/O John Rotherham was one such. He was sent on his way by a big party in the Mess culminating in Fred Rosier taking out his violin to play *Orpheus in the Underworld*.

For the RAF men, the recreational possibilities were unparalleled. They could borrow the squadron's dinghy to sail in the vast Chichester Harbour, possibly from Itchenor or Bosham. Or perhaps go swimming from there or West Wittering. After which the young men were spoilt for choice of good pubs: the Old Ship at Bosham was a favoured spot to watch the sun disappear over the horizon, ale in hand. Even those without a car could walk the three miles into Chichester, where the Dolphin, opposite the Cathedral, was the tavern of choice. The Unicorn was also to become popular, largely because of the warm welcome given to pilots by its landlord, Arthur King. The walls of his upstairs bar were to be covered with signed photos of pilots and squadron groups, so it became known as the Heroes' Room. It was a favourite haunt of Douglas Bader when he was leading his fighter wing from Tangmere. Near the centre of the city was the Ship Hotel, once home to Admiral Sir George Murray. The 18th-century building was to become a popular choice of residence for officers' wives, including Audrey Verity.

This pre-war Laurie Lee idyll could not endure: the last hurrah was the evening war was declared. After they had been stood down for the day, Townsend and his chums hurried to the Old Ship, and at closing time went outside to fire their service revolvers towards the sea. 'What a party we had.' The locals rushed from their houses in the belief that the German invasion had started.[4]

German raids finally reached Tangmere on 16 August 1940, when Stuka dive-bombers dropped their loads on the unmistakeable aerodrome. Damage was widespread, and six Blenheims were destroyed on the ground. Ten civilians and three ground staff were killed. The officers' mess was then relocated to the elegant Shopwyke House, nearer Chichester. But then just before the Dieppe Raid (Operation *Jubilee*) in August 1942, this mansion was handed over to the 31st Fighter Group of the US Air Force (USAF), based at Westhampnett, and the officers' mess was relocated back to Tangmere.

From 161's professional viewpoint, Tangmere had two further attributes: it was as near to their destinations in France as possible, and it had one of the best weather records in the country. The first operation from Tangmere was carried out by Sticky Murphy on 8 December 1941. The airfield had been set up as a (day) fighter base. The needs of its fighter squadrons dictated its daily rhythms. 161 Squadron's needs were incompatible: the fighter boys flew from dawn till dusk, and partied into the night. 161 chaps slept until late morning (in theory), did some air tests and ground preparation in the afternoons, and flew operations after nightfall. Their after-operations partying might take them past dawn. To this clash of timetables was added the need to keep 161's activities a secret from the rest of the RAF. The answer was for the strange dark Lysanders to be housed on as remote dispersal as Tangmere was able to provide, and to remove the squadron's pilots and operations from the station to the Cottage. After its establishment, 161 pilots were no longer allowed officially to use the Tangmere Mess 'lest over a noggin of beer, we were pumped too much, and the odd secret was allowed to slip', as Mac later recalled.[5]

SIS laid out the rationale more prosaically:

For obvious reasons of security, agents, necessarily in plain clothes when leaving or arriving, could not use ordinary military or air force facilities. In the very early days the only solution was to drive direct from London to the aerodrome. This, especially on short winter days, might mean arriving to find the operation was cancelled. Similar abortive trips might be repeated many times. This was in every way clumsy, nerve racking and bad security… When the operation had succeeded, the new arrivals, probably dressed in a way that was conspicuous in England, perhaps mud-stained, certainly tired and not rarely in a state of nervous tension, had to be driven through the night and be disposed of in London. In addition there was the presence at the aerodrome of SIS officers, soldiers and sailors, which might well arouse the curiosity of the many strange pilots and crews who are liable to be found in any RAF mess.

After the experience of five operations carried out in the difficult circumstances [redacted] took rooms in a cottage at Tangmere aerodrome. This was in January 1942, and shortly afterwards the whole cottage was taken over.[6]

THE COTTAGE

So it was that the Lysander pilots of 161's 'A' Flight were, uniquely in the RAF of the time, to have their own officers' mess and operations centre. The Cottage was just over the road from the main entrance to the station, at its north-west corner. In late 1939, it had been annexed by the rather well-heeled members of No. 605 Squadron, Royal Auxiliary Air Force, as their party HQ. 'Cottage' was a misnomer: it was a five bedroomed house dating from 1750, with a low tile-hung roof, and four small bay windows to the right, all set in half an acre. It had many advantages, not the least a high hedge – which meant that any car-borne arrivals could be driven around the back and decanted in privacy.

It became the accommodation of 'A' Flight's pilots as they flew down from Tempsford a day or two before the start of the moon period. Initially, the station's Roman Catholic priest continued to occupy some rooms downstairs, but as 161's operations increased, he was banished.

The ground floor was dominated by the 20-foot-long dining room, now repurposed into the Operations Room, which also served as a crew room. The walls were covered in white lime wash; one was completely covered by a large map of France with red marks, mostly over the coastline, showing the disposition of enemy flak defences. On the desk was a black telephone; a green scrambler phone for conversations with the Air Ministry, Baker Street, and Orchard Court (the head office of SOE's F Section) was also soon installed by a bemused Post Office engineer. He could not comprehend why such a charming Sussex house should warrant such an instrument: 'Mr Churchill's got one of these; Mr Anthony Eden's got one of these. I don't know why you young buggers want one of these.'[7]

Next to this was the larger drawing room (more than 33 feet long) with the bay windows, which became the 'Recreation Room', and was used for messing at two simple trestle tables; it was also therefore the scene of the parties. On one of the walls was a prized trophy – the personal flag of the Gauleiter (Nazi regional leader) of Caen, taken from its flagpole by a brave French youth, and spirited back to England in a Lysander. One of 161's pilots was to discover faint pencilled markings (I to XIV) on the walls, which he deduced denoted the Stations of the Cross, probably inscribed by the Roman Catholic priest. At the east end was a coal fireplace, with its mantelpiece adorned by several (empty) bottles of champagne – the favoured gift of the Resistance passengers, and favoured drink at parties. A photo of Churchill was to the right, a portrait of Her Majesty to the left. A wooden Lysander sat on a bookshelf, and the pilots could sink into several deep leather armchairs. Upstairs were six bedrooms, crammed with beds. The whole set up at the Cottage all served to create, as SIS later observed, 'an atmosphere of friendly intimacy'.[8]

Outside, the large garden, which had hitherto included a vegetable patch which had supplemented the less than exciting RAF rations, was transformed with the erection of two Nissen huts, which had two silver birch trees as silent sentinels. The huts provided more sleeping accommodation, as agents and SIS/SOE minders were sometimes required to stay overnight if flights were scrubbed at the last minute. The whole operation was run by two stalwart 'Snowdrops' (RAF Police) – the indispensable Flt Sgt Bill Booker and Sgt Steve Blaber. 'Whoever selected them for that job was touched by inspiration.'[9] They generated great affection from the pilots; indeed the traditional social barriers between officers and men bore little relevance inside the walls of the Cottage. 'They acted as batmen to us, they brewed up mixed grills and coffee and so forth, they made up beds and they kept the security of the place – it was really the security of the agents we were worried about.'[10] Blaber and Booker were adept cooks. They also excelled in their primary role of security – the tall Blaber and the tubbier Booker were both physically tough. As if this were insufficient, Booker was also a natural poet – but of the sort you might find (if you were terminally unlucky) in the smoky tap room of a pub, late of an evening. Some examples of his oeuvre have survived: 'Old Ebenezer/Sat in his snuggery/Did he say 'Tea, sir'?/Did he b...[buggery]' and 'There goes Pickard who you have seen on many screens/All he fucking thinks about is toast and bloody beans'.[11]

They had been provided by the Deputy Assistant Provost Marshal at Group HQ and 'mothered by the area security officer supplied especially for the job by the Air Ministry.'[12] Notionally in charge of this duo was Flt Lt John Hunt, an intelligence officer; equally useful for the pilots, he was a pianist 'of international repute' – who had trained under Arthur Schnabel in Germany before the war. Now he would provide entertainment at the Cottage during those long hours before dawn as the team awaited the return of pilots and agents. On occasions he even played concerts in Chichester Cathedral.[13]

The 20 or so Lysander ground crew lived in Tangmere's normal airmen's accommodation, but needed little encouragement to come over to the Cottage when there was a party to celebrate a new medal or some such. Partying was not confined to the Cottage: sometimes when operations were cancelled due to the weather, the Bertrams invited the pilots of 'A' Flight over to Bignor Manor for high-spirited socializing, often with stranded agents. Thus were friendships made which outlasted the war – as did hazy memories of the parties. Barbara put her heart and soul into keeping a good house, tending the needs of her transient guests, and doing all she could to sustain the morale of both pilots and agents.

On 10 April, Verity led the Lysander flight on its 50-minute journey down to Tangmere for that month's moon period. The following evening, Mac could not wait to phone his chum Vaughan-Fowler extolling the virtues of the new beds that had just been installed in the Cottage: 'They are so beautiful we should have something to do in them'. The WAAF telephone operator interjected, 'Trying to connect you, Sir.'[14]

At this time, 'A' Flight comprised Verity, McCairns, Rymills, Vaughan-Fowler and Bridger. Pickard, the squadron boss, of course also elbowed his way into Lysander (and Hudson) sorties, but did not always position himself at Tangmere for the whole of the moon period. All these fellows, apart from the youthful Vaughan-Fowler and Mac, were married. But wives tended to be parked near Tempsford. So at the Cottage most of them were able to carry on an unfettered bachelor existence.

However, the carefree Mac started dealing close to home: from March 1943 he began dating Moira, a Special Duties WAAF, whose special duty at Tangmere was to move chips representing 161 aircraft across the chart table in the station's Operations Room. When Mac was not on duty, this moon pilot started to moon around the Operations Room watching his beloved in action. His choice received approval from his colleagues.[15] Most of the pilots, and certainly Bunny Rymills, enjoyed the freedom of action at Tangmere – they were well away from the supervision of Mouse Fielden, who was regarded as rather old school, and more reserved than his Lysander men. The putatively patrician Verity, perhaps because his wife Audrey was frequently ensconced in the Ship Hotel in Chichester, or perhaps because he had inherited a sense of propriety from his vicar father, or perhaps simply because he was the flight commander, was merely a detached observer and chronicler of 'A' Flight's more bawdy antics.

Operation *Salesman* on 14 April was too exciting. Mac's rigger gave him a Popeye the Sailor badge as a lucky charm; he took out André Dubois and Henri Frager to a field just outside Amboise in the lush Loire valley. As Bunny Rymills later noted, 'When God made the earth, he designed France with the Loire for we Lysander pilots, because without that we would have been lost.'[16] By now, Rymills had proved his worth to 'A' Flight, and his tour with 161 was extended indefinitely; this prompted him to claim after that operation, 'In forty years I'll tell my grandchildren that by my 300th trip I'd landed in one field so often they had to build me concrete runways'![17]

Vaughan-Fowler flew Philippe Liewer and Joseph Chartrand as part of this double. Liewer had suffered nine months in a French jail, but with the help of the redoubtable Virginia Hall had escaped back to England and had now completed his training. He was being sent back to set up the SALESMAN circuit around Rouen. The two pilots made a rendezvous at Blois, before heading up the Loire to the east. At midnight the reception lights were seen and Fowler went in first. After he took off, he signalled to Mac to land, who initially made a glide approach to the field, lights clearly in sight, but then he 'changed to a low motored approach, and just then realised there was an obstacle in front. In spite of opening the throttle the aircraft ploughed through the obstacle, nosed over, then lifted, and eventually settled down some yards after lamp A.' Henri Déricourt, the leader of the reception party, informed him that the 'obstacle' was a 12-foot poplar, which he had just destroyed, but that the only damage was to his radio aerial. A livid Mac (as he was supposed to be given obstacle-free approaches) disembarked his two passengers, and took on board Marcel Clech, a wireless operator who was being rested after several months in the field working for de Vomécourt and then Raymond Flower. Little did they know that the Germans were fully aware of this operation – Peter Churchill had been captured in April 1943 and had given the Germans the date and location of this delivery of Frager during his interrogation after his arrest. They arrived at the field an hour after the Lysanders had departed.[18]

On the return, Mac encountered heavy flak at Carpiquet aerodrome, but that was probably his own fault for straying too near a known dangerous area. He had been somewhat distracted by a rising oil temperature that forced a climb through cloud to colder air; moreover the stick was shaking in his hands. After ten minutes in cloud the engine failed – he had not noticed that his carb heat control had slipped to 'cold'. Another of the Lysander's faults was its proneness to carburettor icing – once Mac restored the control to its proper position, the engine spluttered back to life. As usual he was plotted on radar returning across the Channel; once in radio range of Tangmere he was asked what colour he was. This was code for whether he had been successful – 'Red' for success, 'Blue' for failure. Mac answered 'pale green'![19]

Once back at Tangmere, Mac's fitter found that the damage had been much worse than Déricourt's hurried inspection in the dark had indicated: the propeller spinner, air intakes, exhaust ring, the underslung fuel tank, the tailplane, an undercarriage leg – all had been re-arranged by the tree. Mac's post-flight report reveals some unwarranted satisfaction that he 'was able to land one seriously damaged Lysander complete with sticks of broken willow'. Pick's laconic addendum was, 'Perhaps this will teach the pilot to use his landing light' (the policy at the time was NOT to use the landing light, as this might alert any Germans in the vicinity).[20] Verity concluded that the underlying fault was Déricourt's choice of field, which had been caused by a degree of complacency on his part. Verity went back nine days later to bring back Déricourt for some rest in the UK, during which he had some Lysander flights to give him a better understanding of the issues. The dented spinner was removed and placed on a wall at the Cottage as a cautionary trophy. Surviving this operation gave Mac the encouragement (after discussion with his ground crew) to have a mascot painted on the side of his Lysander V9822; befitting his cheeky exuberance, and in celebration of his lucky token, he chose Popeye, the cartoon hero.

The following night, the 15th, saw the *White Rabbit* return to his British hutch. The family of Forest Yeo-Thomas had lived in France for more than a century; until the Occupation, he had worked as a director of the Parisian fashion house Molyneux. Fleeing the Nazis, he arrived in London with ambitions to be a pilot, but was regarded by the RAF as too old for flying duties (he was 40). After one or two diversions, he ended up as an adept circuit organizer at RF Section, where he impressed: Dewavrin later described him as 'one of the most magnificent heroes of the war, a valued comrade, a dear friend, with intelligence and quiet and determined courage'.[21] Known as 'Tommy', Yeo-Thomas' agent codename was the *White Rabbit* – chosen by himself because SOE and Baker Street had (quite understandably) reminded him of Lewis Carroll's *Mad Hatter's Tea Party*.

Bridger, Vaughan-Fowler, Mac and Verity were all outbound from Tangmere. Vaughan-Fowler and Mac were doing a double for SIS. Their outbound passengers included Jean Cavaillès and some BCRA agents, but they brought back a rich haul: Dewavrin, Pierre Brosselette, an escaping US pilot called Ryan complete with broken shoulder, *Jargon* (a wireless operator), and the *White Rabbit*.[22] Barbara Bertram, shrewd and diligent as ever, hosted Brosselette for a very late dinner that night, and did not like him, finding him 'quite cold'. The Bertrams had become a key part of the Tangmere infrastructure – both operational and social.

Verity had a slightly longer journey that night, taking out two agents, but bringing back Julienne Aisner, whose lustrous beauty was recognized on both sides of the Channel. The choice of field did not please Verity – it was small, and its 'soft and irregular surface' broke the Lysander's tailwheel oleo. After 20 minutes on the ground – much longer than desirable – he took off successfully.

Pickard piloted a Hudson that same night for *Dogfish*: as well as Broadley his navigator, and Cocker, he took along W/Cdrs Brooks and Lockhart 'for the ride', as he was only expecting to pick up four Frenchmen, but when he landed (between Uchizy and Pont-de-Vaux), 11 were clamouring to embark. He had to leave three disappointed souls behind. Two of them remained near the field for a Lysander expected the following night and were arrested by the Germans.

The moustachioed Bridger was in action again the next day, on a long run to collect two SIS agents from Issoire, in challenging terrain south of Clermont Ferrand, whose four aerodrome searchlights tried unsuccessfully to focus on his machine. Travelling down France, he had had to fly above cloud – never comfortable for an unarmed Lysander as it made recognition by night-fighters too easy – but started his descent through the murk just on dead reckoning.

He found the field easily. 'The flare path was laid from NW to SE on top of the plateau. The approach was over a scarp. On my first attempt I had a little difficulty in getting over the scarp due to a down current caused by a headwind.' He over-compensated in opening the throttle momentarily.

> As a result I landed with too much speed. I almost came to a stop but over-ran the plateau. I immediately opened up everything and tried to take off. The aircraft charged downhill and became almost airborne. It went through some high tension wires which gave off vivid flashes and staggered into the air. I passed over some buildings and bumped violently on the ground again. The engine then cut for a few seconds, but then picked up again. As I climbed away I examined the undercarriage as well as I could with a torch.

He made a slow circuit and on his second attempt landed very roughly. After dismounting and heaving a sigh of relief, Bridger inspected his Lysander and found that one tyre had been torn during one of his bounces – he now needed to deflate the other to balance his aircraft on take-off.[23] An attack with his commando knife failed, so he took out his service Smith & Wesson revolver, and after five bullets it finally expired with a hiss.[24] Yet the punctured Lysander needed only an extra 50 yards for its take-off, and the return flight with two SIS agents on board allowed the pilot to catch his breath. At dawn the following morning, Bridger's fitter got to work on the battered Lysander (V9353). His first task was to uncoil five feet of 3/16-inch copper wire that had wound itself behind the propeller.

Verity later summarized his team of Bridger, Vaughan-Fowler, Mac and Bunny thus: they 'were as pleasant and amusing a little group of young pilots as I had met anywhere. All were different, all had strong personalities. Not all would be ideally suited to a conventional career in a peace-time service.' Bridger would have been tickled to be called a 'young pilot'.

The same night as Bridger's eventful operation, Bunny had been set a mammoth task – a pick-up from Villefranche in Provence. He had tried for the same field in March but failed to find it; Pick had found it the following night (ALLIANCE was a demanding circuit at this time). Bunny took off from Tangmere fully loaded with three passengers and seven parcels, but had a 'violent swing', which was later helpfully ascribed to a tyre burst. He had to switch hastily to Verity's *Jiminy Cricket* and took off for the second time at 2300hrs. His agents included Pierre Dallas and Henri-Léopold Dor, from a wealthy Provence family, who had studied law at Cambridge, and like Dallas was a member of Fourcade's ALLIANCE network.

The flight down was more than four hours, thankfully in very good weather, following a by now traditional route, crossing the coast at Cabourg, checking his position by a bend in the Loire, Nevers, and then his field. He loaded three for the return – Commandant (Cmdt) Félix Cros, Robert Rivat and Pierre Berthomier, ALLIANCE agents who were being brought to London for training. Bunny's flight back to England was without incident, but he did not land back at Tangmere until after dawn had broken.

Mac had a sweaty time a few days later with Operation *Sabine*. He took out two SIS agents, and the flight down was normal enough. But on arrival at the target area in the Touraine, he was flashed the wrong recognition signal. When he flashed the right one, the reception team corrected their error, so he decided to land, despite his passengers telling him this was not the field that had been briefed – which was the one used five days earlier near Luzillé, when Mac had the encounter with a tree. (Verity had loftily told him afterwards, 'I am not in the business of collecting firewood.')[25] Tonight there was 'troublesome drizzle', and under heavy high cloud, the moon was 'completely obscured'. Mac approached a little high, and hit a bump when he landed long. Alarmingly, this caused the engine to cut. He restarted without difficulty, and taxied over to collect his passengers. To his surprise, the operator handed him 'an attaché case to nurse'. He took off successfully, but 25 minutes later, when he was flying through thick cloud at 7,000 feet, the engine cut again. Could his night get worse?

He lost 1,000 feet before it restarted after he had taken the precaution of switching fuel tanks. Moments later, one of the passengers in the back informed him on the intercom that there were four of them squeezed into a space where three was the normal absolute operational limit. Two were married (Colonel and Mme Valois), who hopefully did not mind being squeezed in together. One of the others was a French submarine captain.[26] Mac was very unhappy, and rebuked the operator, who explained he had had direct orders from Colonel *Passy*, head of the BCRA (who was somewhere on the field). The operator was later to argue 'but they were all small'![27] Mac's stress levels rose further when the French coast did not appear at his expected estimated time of arrival (ETA); an hour later, he found he had drifted westwards and was between the Cap de la Hague and Alderney. Flak batteries in both places opened up at him, and were then joined by naval ships. He evaded them by diving from 8,000 feet to sea level (with four in the back going downhill was easier than going uphill). Mac finally made it back to Tangmere at 0315hrs. After receiving Mac's report, Pickard was furious with the amateurish behaviour of the reception committee, and, having tried to carry out the same operation a few days earlier to find no reception, demanded an enquiry.

On 20 April, in a double with Vaughan-Fowler, Bunny brought back Agent *Émeraude* (Jacques Voyer), who was so grateful he gave his pistol to him. An unwelcome disruption to operations was the visit to Tempsford of Sir Archibald Sinclair, Secretary of State for Air, on the 21st. Sinclair knew Churchill of old – he had been second-in-command of the battalion of the Royal Scots Fusiliers that the Prime Minister had commanded on the Western Front for a few months in World War I – the pair had 'an unbreakable link'. With the air of a 'Spanish grandee', he had both a stammer and an original brain.[28]

This VIP visit meant that both Bridger and Pickard had to haul themselves from Tangmere to Tempsford just for the day. The interruption to operations was compounded by Sinclair's being three hours late. The bulk of the aircrew that greeted him were the Halifax men of 138 and 161. But he inspected a Hudson in the company of Pick, Mac and Ken Batchelor. Bridger was also to hand when Sinclair looked over a Lysander.

Pick was more content with his Hudson operation, *Zinnia*, to Florac in the tricky mountainous terrain of the Tarn. Even with his trusty navigator Alan Broadley at his side, the rather pebbly strip (the Plaine du Chanet) located on a small plateau was hard to find. Pickard was pleased there were no houses within 20 miles. He picked up eight passengers of whom Koenig and Petitjean were *Commissaires de Police* in the counter-espionage role; three others were senior French officers.[29] SIS judged that the operation 'went smoothly'. There had been a difference of opinion about the field: Fielden who had used it a few days earlier 'reported it as unfit for use', whereas Pick reported, 'I strongly recommend it be used again', but he admitted he had to take off downwind 'as there was a large hill at the upwind end of the flare path'. In consequence, he only cleared a hill by 20 feet.[30] Three days later, Pickard mounted another Hudson operation, but failed to find the target. His time in charge of 161 was drawing to a close.

With the hard-drinking Pickard in the vanguard, a raucous party started at the Cottage on 23 April to celebrate not only the end of that moon period but also the well-deserved award of DFCs to Vaughan-Fowler, McCairns and Broadley. It was the former's first award, and he confessed into his beer, 'You feel a bit naked with just one gong.' Mac, who had gained an MM before he was commissioned, could not resist the open goal – 'Well of course I do admit it's a nasty stage to pass through.'[31]

Two days later, Sqn Ldr Desmond Scott, the Kiwi commander of a squadron of ground attack Typhoons at Tangmere, had been invited into the sanctum of the Cottage – so much for keeping the activities of 161 at Tangmere secret. He could not resist bragging that his flying job was much more exciting than theirs: 'We had grass on our fucking pitot heads, and that's with our bloody wheels up too!'[32] 'A' Flight pilots, each with a couple of ground crew in the back, flew back with sore heads to Tempsford the following morning.

The importance of the activities at Tempsford was further underlined on 30 April by a visit of the RAF's Inspector General, Sir Ludlow Hewitt, who enjoyed it so much he returned four days later.

On 6 May, Lewis Hodges was promoted from squadron leader to acting wing commander to take over command of 161 from Pickard, who 'much against his wishes' six days later moved north to become the station commander at RAF Lissett in the East Riding of Yorkshire. 'Compared to war all other forms of endeavour shrink into insignificance. God, how I love it!' could have been spoken by Pickard, but was from the equally pugnacious General Patton. Pick had carried out five Hudson missions and seven in the Lysander. His success rate was below average for the squadron (see Appendix A). Pick was poor at mental arithmetic – which was a vital skill for flying a Lysander cross-country, particularly at night; he was better suited to flying with a navigator at his side. By this stage of the war, he had accumulated more than 2,000 flying hours – it was time for him to fly a desk. The role of Tempsford's station navigation officer was now filled by James 'Waggy' Wagland, complete with an archetypal RAF moustache. All 161 aircrew took with them on operations several photos for use should they need a (forged) identity card in a hurry. Given that young Frenchmen were not given to wearing RAF moustaches, this rendered Waggy's photos somewhat useless, even if he were to shave as soon as possible.

Lewis Macdonald Hodges, known to all as 'Bob', was 25 when, with a fresh bar to his DFC, he took over 161. He had already had an eventful war. Born in Richmond, and educated at the nearby St Paul's, he had joined the RAF at the age of 18. At school he had been far from a model pupil, the High Master acidly commenting on his recruitment by the RAF, 'They seem to be taking anyone these days.'³³ After Cranwell he was posted to Bomber Command, initially flying the underwhelming Wellesley at Finningley, before progressing to the marginally less obsolescent Hampden with No. 76 (B) Squadron.

On 4 September 1940, he was flying a night-bombing mission to Stettin, and must have become wildly lost for, at 0600hrs, out of fuel, he told his crew to bail out. Hodges made a successful crash landing in a field which turned out to be outside Saint-Brieuc in Brittany – miles from any sensible route to Stettin, which is on the Polish–German border. Accompanied by Sgt Wyatt, a crew member who had not heard the order to jump as his intercom had become disconnected, Hodges walked southwards in the direction of Spain. Using maps ripped from the back of calendars, the pair navigated their way through each *département* on minor roads. Once, when without such a map, and walking down a main road, they were stopped by two *gendarmes* who demanded their papers. Thankfully, after opening their peasant coats to show their RAF tunics, they were waved on their way. At Goven, south-west of Rennes, they were finally fully kitted out in civilian gear. They had by now been on the run for three weeks, but, having worn out two pairs of boots, their escape speeded up. At Antigny, on the southern border of Brittany, they caught a bus. At Limoges they took a train to Toulouse, and thence to Bagnères-sur-Luchon in the foothills of the Pyrenees. There the two RAF men were stopped by two *gendarmes*. The fliers claimed they were Belgian refugees who had lost their papers; the story was not bought, and they were arrested and put in a concentration camp at the Château Isle Jourdain, to the west of Toulouse. They were in good company – three other British officers were also incarcerated there including Captain Ian Garrow. Two weeks later, they were despatched to Fort Saint-Jean at Marseille, which was to figure in the lives of many SOE people.

Hodges, together with an international ragbag of other escapees, managed to stow away on a French cargo ship bound for Casablanca, but he was discovered and after a spell in prison in Oran, returned to Marseille, where he was again imprisoned. But the governor of Fort Saint-Jean managed to retrieve him and put him on parole, pending trial for the civilian offence of taking passage on a ship without a ticket. In January 1941, he was switched to Saint-Hypolite-du-Fort at Gard, but the wheels of the French legal system were grinding exceedingly slowly. He and another British prisoner forged passes, giving themselves five days' leave, during which they took a train to Perpignan with the help of SOE's Nancy Wake, and after a short taxi ride started their walk over the Pyrenees, the peaks of which there were 4,000 feet. He was caught by the Spanish at Figueras, and stayed in several prisons, but fortunately had made contact with a British consul, who secured his release after eight weeks. He left Gibraltar by the normal means of a Sunderland flying boat which brought him back to Plymouth on 14 June.[34] He returned to his squadron and continued bombing Germany, and was soon awarded a DFC. Hodges participated in the Hampden raid on the German cruiser *Gneisenau* when it was in dry dock in Kiel in February 1942. Two days later, he wangled his first flight in a Lysander.

Pickard knew Bob Hodges from being at the same training unit earlier in the war, and approached him for 161 to be one of the two flight commanders on the Halifax flight on agent-dropping missions; he 'jumped at the chance', and also soon qualified on the Havoc (which was used by 161 for missions to communicate with agents in France on the S-phone radio device). In November 1942, he skippered the fabled seven-hour 40-minute flight that dropped two Czech agents who successfully assassinated Heydrich in Operation *Anthropoid*.

Hodges had accumulated 1,600 hours by the time he assumed overall command of 161; he realized he needed to become operationally capable on the Lizzie, and started training on the type on 1 July. But the members of 'A' Flight noted that Hodges' first allegiance was to the Halifax crews in the squadron – as Mac wistfully noted, 'we ceased to be the blue-eyed boys'.[35]

The Halifax men regarded Hodges highly, but at this time were suffering serious losses. After taking command, Hodges lost two of his Halifax flight commanders within three days – he filled one vacancy by persuading his old chum Len Ratcliff, who had spent all the war in Hodges' slipstream, to move to Tempsford.[36] Hodges did not find the transition to flying Lysanders and solo navigation easy: 'on occasion it happened that as you were flying along looking at the map, one's torch fell on the floor and it was quite difficult to retrieve it sometimes.'[37]

The May moon period kicked off on the 13th with a double by Verity and Bunny. Their outbound passengers comprised the well-travelled SOE agent Julienne Aisner (now Mme Besnard), Sidney Jones, who had transmuted from a pre-war French representative for Elizabeth Arden cosmetics to an arms instructor, Marcel Clech, a Brittany taxi-driver, now a wireless operator, and the Yorkshire-born Vera Leigh of SOE, who was sent to form a sub-circuit named INVENTOR.[38] They brought back Major Francis Suttill; his family antecedents were in the Lancashire and Yorkshire textile industries, but he was born in Lille. Educated at Stonyhurst, the Catholic school in Lancashire, and then back in France, he read law in both Lille and London and then was called to the London Bar. On the outbreak of war he joined the East Surry Regiment, but soon moved into intelligence roles from which he was recruited into SOE.

Suttill was now a key agent, having formed and led the PROSPER network. Buckmaster needed to see him at Baker Street to encourage him to dampen down expectations amongst the Resistance that there would be Allied landings in France in 1943.[39]

The same night Mac brought back three from a favourite field near Tours, including Jeanette Guyot, who had already earned the admiration of her masters at SIS:

> [A] remarkable girl, who had worked with [redacted] since his earliest days and gone through the most astonishing series of cinema episodes, including roof chases... Guyot had been running an escape line, and much else. Although only twenty-four, her eyes bore witness to her many unpleasurable experiences at the hands of the Gestapo. She had already spent three months in jail, and her colleagues were now being arrested – Guyot's safety rested in her being in England... She was a quiet little thing who would not have looked out of place in one of Miss Charlotte Yonge's novels.[40]

Verity hired the 29-year-old Flt Lt Jack Edward Bartrum, a pilot with a similar upbringing to his own. A son of a vicar on the Isle of Wight, like Verity he had been up to Oxford (Keble College), where he gained a blue for rugby. Like Verity, he had been a keen member of the UAS before the war. After university he had toyed with the idea of becoming a banker, but instead pursued an entirely different career, becoming an assistant district commissioner in the Sudan Civil Service.

He had joined the RAF as an LAC after war was declared, being commissioned in March 1941. Verity found him at 51 OTU at Debden, and he started at 161 on 6 May 1943, a week before the start of the moon period. By this time, he was an experienced pilot with more than 1,200 hours; however he only had eight hours in a Lysander. Ten days later, he was landing back at Tempsford after a training flight in Lysander R9106, watched by his mentor Verity, when he stalled on final approach. Extracted from the wreckage, he was taken to Tempsford's sick quarters where he died within hours. The aircraft burnt out in the middle of the airfield. A subsequent investigation concluded that his inexperience on the type had led him to underestimate the angle of glide.[41] It is probable that he too had been bitten by Petter's design fault, having yet to master the arcane use of that wretched tail trim wheel.

Verity had only just returned to Tempsford in a Lysander with Mouse and Waggy on board. Verity later recalled that, during the recruitment process a few weeks before, he took Bartrum out to dinner; Jack had taken a card from his wallet with a list of all the pre-war members of Oxford UAS. Even by spring 1943, half the names had already been crossed off.

Mac and Bunny had the sad duty of attending the funeral in Ventnor on 20 May, which was led by Bartrum's grieving widow Gladys, and his mother, whose husband, the vicar there, had died only ten months earlier. Verity had the even sadder task of writing to her; he wrote beautifully:

It would be presumptuous for me to speak to you of his great qualities, which you must know far better than anyone else. He was a constant source of good humour and kindly influence on the other pilots. His glorious personality always cheered our hearts. He set a good example by his enthusiasm to fly and fight for his ideals, with no worry for himself, no thought of advancement, and no fear of danger. He was jubilantly pleased to be in an operational squadron. He will be a great loss to us and to the world after the war, especially to Africa, where his great-hearted administration was already highly valued.[42]

Jack's brother, Peter, was home on leave from his role in the RAF's boat service at the time of his death, whilst his other brother Bob was in pilot training in Canada.

A week before Bartrum's funeral, Verity and Rymills had carried out an important double. Navigation was easy – the field was just next to the Cher, to the east of Tours. Verity flew Marcel Clech and Juliette Aisner, whilst Bunny took out the fated Vera Leigh* and Sidney Jones, all to re-form the INVENTOR network. Whilst Vera was all of 40 years old, and a dress designer by profession, she had deeply impressed her SOE instructors with the best shooting scores of her course. Verity landed first and picked up Francis Suttill.[43] But whilst on the ground he had an argument with Déricourt and his assistant, who for some reason only wanted one Lysander to land. Verity prevailed, and by just after 0300hrs the two pilots and Suttill were back in the cosy embrace of Tangmere Cottage.[44]

The youthful and good looking Vaughan-Fowler had developed a reputation amongst his colleagues for not only having an eye for the women

---

*Arrested in October 1943, she was eventually executed at Natzweiler on 6 July 1944.

but acting on it. Whilst Rymills had a reputation for snaffling all the attractive female passengers, it was Vaughan-Fowler who, on 21 May, took Noor Inayat Khan and Jacques Courtaud to a field near Compiègne. Khan was desperately needed in Paris where there was an acute shortage of radio operators, so she was sent to Tangmere before having completed all her training. But Vaughan-Fowler had to bring them back when no reception lights were seen – the operator had failed to hear Baker Street's radio message due to jamming.

A complex character, Khan had a Sufi Indian father and an American mother. Already in the army as an Auxiliary Territorial Service (ATS) telegraphist, she was tailor-made to become a wireless operator, yet 'My first loyalty is to India. My second to Great Britain.'[45] This was somewhat against the mantra of Selwyn Jepson as head of recruitment that all candidates should have their prime loyalty to Britain, ideally through having a British father and a French mother. And if the prime requirement of an SOE agent was to blend in to French society, her Asian good looks counted heavily against her. Brought up in the Paris suburb of Suresnes, where the family was somewhat conspicuous, Noor stood out from her fellow students because of her dark skin and hair.[46]

That night, Bridger carried out his last mission for 161 – *Gauguin* for SIS. He had asked for a posting to somewhere more exciting! The Germans were prepared to give him a good send-off. His report reads: '2340 Observed heavy flak at Caen-Carpiquet and light flak near Bayeux.' Half an hour later: 'accurate and fair concentration of light flak at 6000'. Evaded by diving away. 0345 was off course and flew over Carpiquet at 8000'. Received a good concentration of heavy flak. Now between 10 and 20 guns firing. Fairly accurate... I evaded by diving and changing course'. He missed the reception because the target was covered in mist and he had to repeat the flight the following night.[47]

Bridger followed Pickard back to bombers, and achieved his wish for excitement, being shot down on his third mission, to become a PoW once again.[48] With Bridger gone, and Rymills up to speed operationally, 'A' Flight became a true band of brothers. With the slightly aloof Verity at their head, Rymills, Fowler and McCairns had a strong bond. Hugh had installed his wife and young son in the Ship Hotel in Chichester, but had little time to see them. Fresh back from an operation, he went back there in the early hours of the morning to greet his wife. All doors being locked, he had to make his way up the fire escape and climb into her room like a burglar. She was mollified by the handful of lipsticks he had brought back from France that night.

A few days later, bad weather prevented operations, and the Lysander team went on a bit of a bender at the Cottage. Claims became more outrageous as the evening wore on, until Bunny could not resist joshing Vaughan-Fowler about his comparative youth – 'I was doing three women a day before you reached puberty'![49] He may have been young, but the handsome Vaughan-Fowler had great flying skills, could speak French easily, and had a gentlemanly nature.

In June, Hodges departed for what was afterwards reported as 'a very successful tour' of the Middle East in the company of Sir James Marshall-Cornwall, a truculent general who had fallen out with his peers, retired from the Army in January, and was now occupied in trying to improve the fractious relationship between SIS and SOE. The depleted ranks of 161 were bolstered that month with the arrival of P/O Douglas Bell and Flt Lt Stephen Hankey, as well as, initially just on Halifaxes, Acting Sqn Ldr Len Ratcliff. Their paths would diverge…

On 23 April, the Germans had ramped up yet again their demands on the French population under the Service du Travail Obligatoire (STO), ordering Vichy to provide another 120,000 young male French workers for the Nazi war machine. A good proportion of those in the Germans' sights simply vanished from their family homes and joined the Maquis in the hills. This put further strain on Resistance organizations: the need for drops of arms and other supplies by the Halifaxes of 138 and 161 increased exponentially. At the same time, both SIS and de Gaulle needed to attempt to bring direction to these swelling bands by bringing leaders back to London for briefing before sending them back to the field.

When STO was first mooted at the beginning of March, de la Vigerie was so exercised he sent a telegram to de Gaulle:

FRANCE THREATENED WITH BEING EMPTIED OF ALL ABLE-BODIED MEN IN TWO WEEKS STOP AWAIT YOUR CALL FOR VIOLENT AND TOTAL RESISTANCE STOP HAVE DECIDED TO TAKE UP REPEAT TAKE UP IMMEDIATE ACTION STOP HOPE TO PRODUCE UNANIMOUS MOVEMENT OF DISOBEDIENCE AND REVOLT STOP REQUIRE HELP AID AGENTS AND ARMS.[50]

161 was about to become very busy indeed.

13

Treachery

Vaughan-Fowler had been unable to deliver Khan and Courtaud to Compiègne on 21 May, which at least allowed Khan to finish her training. She was sent to Bristol for her final multi-day exercise. At its conclusion, she did not handle the interrogation well – the police inspector in charge, when debriefed by SOE, said, 'If she's an agent, I'm Winston Churchill.'[1] Khan's suitability caused sharp debate amongst the team at SOE's finishing school at Beaulieu: the instructing staff worried she could not control her emotions and lacked a sense of security. Colonel Frank Spooner, the 'headmaster' of the Beaulieu schools, noted, 'Not overburdened with brains but has worked hard and shown keenness, part from some dislike of the security side of the course. She has an unstable and temperamental personality and it is very doubtful whether she is really suited to work in the field.' Buckmaster annotated this report 'nonsense'.[2] Buckmaster was swayed by pragmatism – there was an acute shortage of trained wireless operators at the time. They were both right, after a fashion. Spooner felt so strongly he sent a copy of his report to both Robin Brook and Mockler-Ferryman (affectionately known as 'The Moke').* Brook, the staff officer in charge of F Section at SOE, had represented Britain at the 1936 Berlin Olympics where it was an open secret that the Olympic village was to be an officer training camp after the event.

Vera Atkins, 'so exceptional in every way', once Romanian but now quintessentially English, had risen spectacularly within F Section to be

---

*Brook was SOE's Regional Controller for Western Europe at the time; Brigadier Eric Mockler-Ferryman was Director of Operations.

Buckmaster's number two. She inspired a slightly fearful awe amongst the agent fraternity, one of whom noted she 'knew she could master anyone in trousers'.³ On 16 June, the day after being commissioned as a WAAF, Khan was picked up by Vera in London and driven to Tangmere. It was a lovely summer's day, and the open-topped car allowed them to enjoy the fragrance of the Sussex hedgerows fresh with dog roses. But the putative agent was taciturn. The duo arrived at the Cottage late afternoon for Khan's outbound trip in a double. The BBC messages that evening included 'Jasmine is playing her flute' – Déricourt now knew the double was on.

Apart from Khan, Bunny took Cicely Lefort, a 40-year-old skilled Irish yachtswoman who owned a villa on the coast near Dinard, but was now serving in the WAAF – her appearance reminded Bunny of a vicar's wife or 'a miserable school teacher', and her French accent was questionable. Lefort was to become a courier for Cammaert's DONKEYMAN. 'A serious young man, a very pleasant person' in Verity's view, Cammaert had not requested her and had severe doubts about her suitability. Possibly a little harshly, he believed Lefort's main motivation in wanting to return to France was to see again her husband, a doctor in Paris; whilst Khan 'should never have been sent to France. She was a shy woman who was completely lost.'⁴ Bunny was entranced by Khan's beauty, 'a very attractive young lady, but nervous or pensive rather'; he was less impressed by her preparations to go to war – she was wearing a green oilskin coat for the flight.⁵

The pair of Lysanders left Tangmere on this shortest of nights at 2320hrs. Bunny's fur was ruffled twofold: after landing in his appointed field at Villevêque, north of Angers, the strut for the tailwheel oleo broke on some rough ground, and his engine cut. After restarting, and having disgorged his shy females, the operator's team turned off their lights as he set off to depart with Pierre Lejeune, Gaby Pierre-Bloch and a politician in the back.

On the same operation (*Teacher*), Mac took Diana Rowden and Charles Skepper, who was to become head of another troubled network, ACROBAT, for which Rowden was to be a courier. On the return flight he brought back husband and wife Jack and Francine Agazarian, who, having been in the field for three months, on Suttill's orders were fleeing the imminent collapse of his PROSPER network. Once back at Tangmere, Mac revelled in embarrassing Bunny by telling him that his smooching commentary to his two ladies on the way over had been overheard by him, as well as any German operators monitoring the frequency, 'Now

Mesdames, we are approaching your beautiful country, isn't it beautiful in the moonlight…' Rymills had left his transmission switch on.[6]

The squadron's 11 tons of Hudson were in operation for that moon period: the Prime Minister was most keen that the 68-year-old General Alphonse Georges be brought back to the UK. Georges had commanded the French field armies in the Battle of France, and then distinguished himself in Winston's eyes by refusing to join the Vichy regime. Churchill felt that if he could have a few words in his ear before Georges met de Gaulle, who was of course his junior in rank, de Gaulle might become less truculent. The French leader's position was still far from copper bottomed: on 7 July, he had a rally for 'his' Free French at London's Olympia, and only 500 putative troops appeared.[7]

Despite his own mixed record of successful pick-ups, this SIS mission was so important that Mouse Fielden felt compelled to take it on himself. On 15 May, he departed Tempsford, but even with Waggy, the squadron's navigation officer, on hand, weather conditions south of the Loire prevented his finding his pinpoint or their landing ground, which was again the Plaine de Chanet.

Four days later they set off again, with six French politicians in the back. This time they found the 'rather pebbly' landing ground, but had to wait ten minutes for the convoy to show up with its important cargo. As well as the general, there was Michel Thoraval, a Deuxième Bureau agent, and four other senior officers. Fielden had found the landing and approach tricky: 'This is a difficult landing ground, being 3000' above sea-level and surrounded by higher ground. The tops of the higher ground were covered by 8/10ths stratus which also obscured the landing lights except for brief glimpses.'[8] When on the ground waiting for the convoy, Fielden made a momentous decision – because of the delay he would carry on to Algeria rather than risk flying back over northern France after dawn had broken. He reached Maison Blanche successfully but, to his dismay, Georges decided to stay there – and ally himself to General Henri Giraud, who had taken command of Free French forces in North Africa. As SIS later drily noted, 'The public never seem to have wondered how he [Georges] got there.'[9]

So Fielden failed to bring his precious cargo back to Tangmere. He did however bring back a bottle of respectable French wine given him by one of his grateful passengers. As the bar stocks at the Cottage were as usual more than adequate, he gave the bottle to the King, who much enjoyed having it served the next time he entertained Churchill to lunch. The

Prime Minister could not understand how his monarch had obtained a bottle of the 1941 vintage – and his monarch was not about to tell him.

In the next moon period, Verity took a Hudson down to a field near Mâcon, organized by Bruno Larat, 'who was not a tremendously practical operator' – perhaps because he was a poet. Larat had undertaken to cut down a tree bordering the field, but had failed to do so. Outbound, Verity took Claude Serreulles who had been acting as de Gaulle's ADC, and was now to be a deputy for Jean Moulin. Apart from Paul Rivière, one of his key England-bound passengers was Henri Frenay who was livid after some security breaches had resulted in the arrest of General Delestraint six days earlier. Frenay would have been even more unbalanced had he been told that his lover (Berty Albrecht) had committed suicide in Fresnes prison a fortnight before. Fearing for Frenay's mental state, his friend Pierre de Bénouville had withheld the news from him.

There were a few delays, and like Fielden, Verity decided it was safer to fly his cargo down to Algiers. 'What the hell is the general direction of Algiers from where we are now', he thought. He had failed to bring the right maps with him; he racked his brain for his geography lessons and thought that a heading of due south would do. It did.[10]

Peter Churchill had been captured in April 1943 at his Saint-Jorioz hideout near Lake Annecy, and was now in the capable hands of Hugo Bleicher ('Colonel Henri'), the Abwehr's star Paris-based spy catcher. Or rather, he was in the hands of the Gestapo in the detested Fresnes prison in Paris. But Bleicher had convinced the Gestapo to allow him to take Churchill for an away day: he brought him to his own flat in the Rue Pergolèse, where he introduced Peter to his French mistress, Suzanne, and encouraged Churchill to have a bath and smarten himself with some borrowed clothing. They then progressed to the nearby flat of Charles and Biche Fol. Bleicher, Biche and Churchill were all pianists of some talent – Churchill managed a tune or two despite his fingers having suffered some rearrangement by the Gestapo. Bleicher entertained the small party with some Viennese waltzes.

On the way back to Fresnes, Bleicher suggested another day trip, but with the proviso that Peter Churchill could radio London (on a set that Bleicher had acquired) asking for a Lysander to land to take the two of them back to London (as part of his softening up act, Bleicher had been mouthing mildly anti-Nazi views in their discussions). Thankfully for the safety of the men of 161, Churchill responded that he could not live with himself if he was responsible for the capture of a Lysander and its pilot, and

Westland's Lysander production line at the Yeovil factory. (Leonardo)

The Mk III SCW Lysander as modified for the Special Duties squadrons. (Leonardo)

The Lysander preparing to take off. (Gus & Clara - Gusair)

The Lysander cockpit. (Author's collection)

161 Squadron Hudson departs from Tempsford. (IWM HU 60553)

161's crew room at Tangmere Cottage. (IWM HU 60563)

Edward 'Mouse' Fielden helps the Prince of Wales don his flying suit. (TQFA)

Lewis 'Bob' Hodges. (Photo by George W. Hales/Fox Photos/Hulton Archive/Getty Images)

Frank 'Bunny' Rymills.
(The National Archives HS9/1295/7)

Guy Lockhart.
(The National Archives HS9/932/8)

John Tonkin, leader of the SAS's *Bulbasket* raid. (John Tonkin Collection)

The 161 'Dream Team' outside the Cottage. From left to right, James 'Mac' McCairns, Hugh Verity, Percy 'Pick' Pickard, Peter Vaughan-Fowler and Bunny Rymills. Old English sheepdog Ming and cocker spaniel Henry are in front of them. (piemags/ww2archive/Alamy)

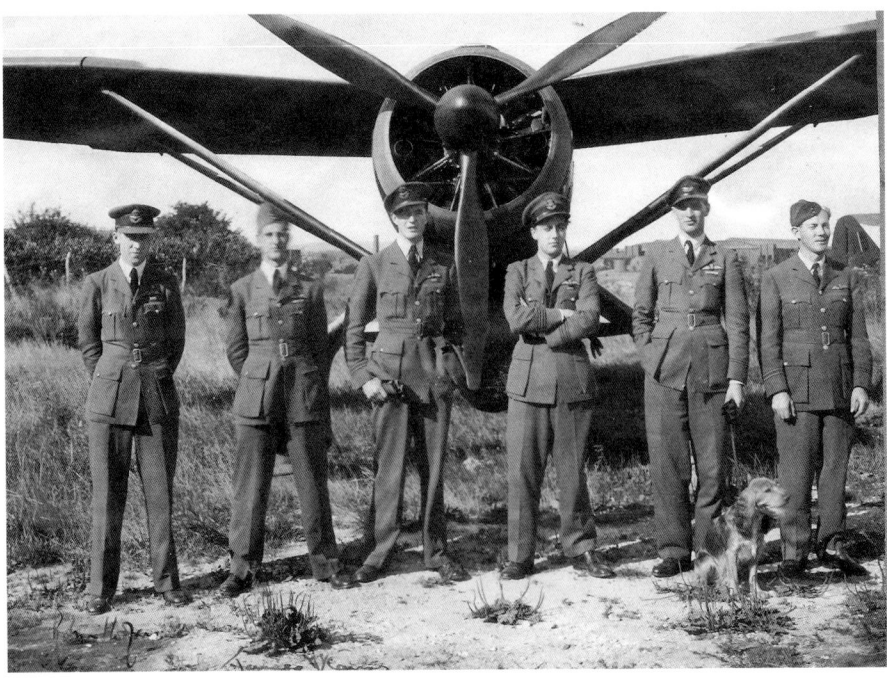

161 Lysander pilots at Tangmere. From left to right, Robin Hooper, Mac McCairns, Peter Vaughan-Fowler, Hugh Verity, Bunny Rymills and Stephen Hankey. (Simon Rymills)

John Nesbitt-Dufort's Lysander after his crash in France. (The National Archives AIR40/2659)

N.H. Attenborrow collects a wounded American officer in Friuli, Italy. (piemags/ww2archive/Alamy)

The graves of James Bathgate and his passenger, agent Emile Cossoneau, at La Ville-Aux-Bois cemetery, France. (Author's collection)

Leslie Whitaker's grave at Guillerval cemetery, France. (Author's collection)

anyway, the two of them could always trek to freedom over the Pyrenees. Bleicher swept that suggestion aside, and the idea was shelved.[11]

For some months, the central figure in 161's pick-up operations in France had been Henri Déricourt. Only 5 feet 8 inches, but of strong build, the 33-year-old pilot had been appointed by Maurice Buckmaster in 1942 to be the SOE's Air Movements Officer for F Section, and sent to France on 23 January 1943 by parachute, with a brief to find good landing grounds. This man would come to know more about 161's operations in and out of France than any other individual in the country. The problem for 161 pilots was that he was a 'wrong 'un'.

Born in 1909 in Coulognes-Cohan, on the western fringes of Champagne country, Déricourt popped up in Gibraltar in August 1942 together with Léon Doulet. As qualified pilots, the pair claimed they had presented themselves to BOAC in Syria when that country was overrun. Déricourt had qualified as a military pilot in France in 1930 and after a brief military career set up a firm giving joy rides, three years later becoming chief pilot for the Aero Club de Paris, before progressing to airline flying for Air Bleu. On the outbreak of war he was mobilized to fly small transport aircraft, and then became a test pilot in Marseille. Now on the books of Air France, he was tasked with flying spare parts to Aleppo, and was there when the British arrived. A well-connected RAF officer spoke to Déricourt and his colleagues at the hotel, and offered them roles with British Airways. He arrived back at Marseille on 27 August 1941 and began flying for Air France in the Unoccupied Zone, all the time maintaining contact with the US consulate with a view to coming to England. This was eventually arranged in August 1942 with a week's notice. He resigned from the Air France job, and, together with Doulet and some others, was extracted from a beach near Narbonne, before sailing for Gibraltar. On arrival in England, like all aliens he was interviewed at length at the London Reception Centre in the Royal Patriotic School. His interviewing officer, R.H. Osborne, immediately recognized that there was something strange in Déricourt's urge to serve the Allies now, when he could have taken up the offer a year earlier in Aleppo. He raised the question of whether Déricourt had been given some sort of mission by the Germans during those months.

Doulet and Déricourt rather oddly requested the authorities not to seek information about them from the BCRA, being keen to work just for the British. Air Commodore R. Chappell, the perceptive Director of Intelligence at the Air Ministry, summed up the pair thus: 'the men want to earn a fat salary and I am sceptical about their desire to "fight the Germans".'[12] At the beginning of December 1942, Vaudreuil, the counter-espionage head of BCRA in London, reported bluntly that 'One of his former pre-war comrades who had met him several times in London reported to us: "Since the armistice in France, Déricourt started frequenting German environments in Paris. Later he went often to Toulouse, meeting with ladies of dubious morals who were paid by the Germans. He is now telling people that he will be leaving shortly for France in the service of Britain."'[13]

The Home Office and MI5 were still discussing whether Déricourt and Doulet could be allowed to be employed by BOAC in late December 1942. Yet that month, Déricourt arrived at Tempsford for training in 161 Squadron operations, and indeed spent Christmas in the Tempsford mess in the uniform of a British Army officer. As an experienced flyer, and a confident outgoing chap, Déricourt was warmly welcomed into the fraternity of 161 pilots. Waggy Wagland and McMillan, who was navigator for Alan Boxer (who was then on Halifaxes), had quite a lot to do with him: 'he behaved in quite a normal fashion'. Verity, who had newly arrived at 'A' Flight at the time, found him 'a pleasant fellow', and enjoyed chatting to him in French; indeed, he effusively extolled the French pilot's virtues in letters home to his wife. Although he always treated him with caution, Rymills enjoyed taking Déricourt to a café down a small side street in Bedford, where they discussed their different routes to the skies, and the problems of avoiding the Germans.

Déricourt, now known as Agent *Farrier* or *Gilbert*, was dropped by Alan Boxer from his Halifax on 22 January 1943 near Montargis.[14] Perhaps as he mounted the Halifax in the Tempsford dusk, he noticed that Boxer, a Kiwi, had named his Halifax *Kia Ora* – not after the soft drinks brand, but after the Maori greeting for 'Good Health'. Déricourt made his way by train to Paris, and thence to his home village near Rheims where his mother lived. After some rest, he travelled to Marseille via Paris to retrieve Jeanne, his wife. (Verity, who was not prone to such blunt language, described Déricourt's wife as 'short, plump and had brassy hair'.) In Marseille, he also contacted his old flying pal, Remy Clément, and tried to persuade him to become his assistant in SOE work. Clément required time to consider the surprising offer, and to hand in his notice to his employers. The Déricourts returned to Paris to live in an apartment arranged for them by Julienne Aisner.

But in less than a week, Déricourt had met his pre-war friend Karl Bömelburg, now head of the Sicherheitsdienst (SD, the counter-intelligence branch of the Gestapo) in Paris, and briefed him on his new role in SOE. Known as 'no great thinker',[15] the German did not question this extraordinary turn of events, and arranged for the Déricourts to be installed in the Hotel Bristol (at the time requisitioned by the Nazis), where they stayed for three weeks until moving into a flat in the Rue Pergolèse, which happened to be adjacent to that of Hugo Bleicher, and within yards from the headquarters of the SD, at 84 Avenue Foch. Bömelburg had worked at the German Embassy in Paris before the war, no doubt in some sort of espionage role, and had met Déricourt and Nicholas Bodington (then a Reuters journalist but now a senior SOE officer in London) at dirt track race meetings outside Paris in the mid-1930s. Whilst Déricourt was *Gilbert* to Baker Street, he now became known as *BOE 48* by the Germans – indicating he was the 48th agent run directly by Bömelburg.[16] The agreement the stocky Frenchman made with his ostensible foe was that, in return for substantial amounts of cash (some sources ascribe £5,000 per British agent betrayed), he would give the Germans advance notice of all landings, and also lend them all outgoing *courier* that was to be picked up for Baker Street. This was then copied overnight and returned to him. The condition that *BOE 48* extracted was that no arriving agents were to be arrested within a reasonable distance of the landing field.[17]

February had been a quiet month for 161, but Déricourt was organizing pick-ups in March, his first being that flight where Vaughan-Fowler's engine caught fire on landing. But it was Mac's difficulty with trees on 15 April that gave the excuse to recall Déricourt to London. On the other hand, perhaps he was keen to return? He had had a meeting with Bömelburg in the third week of April when he had learned that the DONKEYMAN circuit had been penetrated, and felt that London needed to know this.[18] He was picked up by Verity (on Operation *Tony*) on 23 April from near Le Mans. Back at Tangmere, his innate self-confidence was undented, bragging, 'Give me a Comper Swift [a popular pre-war touring aircraft] and I'll garage it in my barn and fly myself back next time.'[19] Where he would keep the monoplane in France was left unsaid.

After his discussions at Baker Street, he was commissioned into the RAFVR as a flying officer, and returned by Halifax and silk on 5 May. But the more alert agents in France (not to mention those that had already been arrested) were becoming suspicious. A week later, Verity picked up Francis Suttill (*Prosper*), in an operation organized by Déricourt, because Suttill was desperate to go to London to express his doubts about Déricourt to Buckmaster in person.[20] Suttill had an intense round of meetings with Buckmaster: lunch in the SOE canteen on the 15th, lunch the following day at Carletta's restaurant, dinner at his Pelham Court flat on the 17th, lunch at the Park Lane Hotel the day after that, and a final lunch meeting in the canteen on the 19th, before he returned to France.[21] He told Buckmaster that he wanted nothing further to do with Déricourt, and moreover demanded that his own return to France be organized by someone else. Suttill was therefore parachuted into the hands of Pierre Culioli, and his ADOLPHE network in the Sologne.

The suspicions of agents in central France were further aroused in May. Marcel Clech (*Bastien*) arrived at Déricourt's flat with his cases, which were left temporarily in the custody of Déricourt's friend and assistant, Rémy Clément. 'When Clech retrieved them both his codes and his signals plan had disappeared.'[22]

Soon, Vaudreuil of the BCRA was becoming more worried about a possible security breach, writing to Major Younger that he gathered that Déricourt had recently left the UK for a mission in France: 'this seems to us particularly imprudent'. Discretion was difficult for Déricourt at times – all his chums in London were aware of his imminent departure, as were the Gestapo, who were keen to 'use' him. 'It seems to us inappropriate to use him as an agent.'[23]

Towards the end of the June moon period, Verity was charged with *Wrestler/Acolyte*, an operation to fly out Robert Lyon (an F Section agent) and Colonel Emile Bonoteaux. The latter was carrying orders from General Giraud in Algiers for the non-Gaullist element of the French Army resisters. Déricourt failed to set up a reception for the first flight. Verity tried again on the 22nd, but had to turn back to Tangmere when his generator and electrics failed. The following night he had more success: the target near the Loire was easy to find 'as the stars were bright', and the river stood out clearly. But Verity was over-confident, and decided that light conditions were so good that he was happy to land before the moon had risen. His approach was too fast and he only avoided the far hedge by a last-minute swing to port.[24]

Verity was very pleased with the quality of the field, and once stationary 'had a long chat with the agent (an old friend) [i.e. Déricourt], who told me he had an excellent Hudson ground near Angers'. Déricourt blamed his own absence three nights earlier on 'a mistake in the messages'. Verity picked up Richard Heslop, who was ending his 11-month run with the PRIVET circuit after some arrests; the SOE agent, who had broken his leg badly whilst training in Scotland, was only ever going to be inserted or extracted by boat or Lysander. His other passenger was RAF meteorologist P/O Robert Taylor, who had had an exciting fortnight. A navigator on a 1409 (Met) Flight Mosquito that had been shot down by two Fw 190s, he had parachuted safely into Normandy (his pilot having been killed), and was smuggled to Paris by the Resistance. Once sure of his credentials, they conveyed him to the Loire for the luxury of a Lysander pick-up. Heslop noted that his fellow passenger could not speak French and 'looked as English as roast beef'![25] Verity much later recalled this mission: 'I did a landing before moonrise once, just to see how frightening it was – it frightened me so much I never tried it again.'[26]

Robert Lyon left the field safely, but the Gestapo (possibly alerted by Déricourt) were waiting for Bonoteaux at Amboise station, and he was arrested. Whilst Picardy and north-east France were very much not conducive to SOS operations, neither was the Loire valley. With an absence of mountains, few forests, and poor communications, the local head of the Organisation de Résistance Armée (a Resistance organization opposed to de Gaulle, which later became one of the founder members of the FFI) described Anjou thus: 'there is no solitude, no isolated shelter, or defensible hiding place. Such factors ensured that in this department the Resistance did not take the form of the Maquis [a more urban-based grouping, not relying on peasants or farm labourers].'[27] But it was primarily the treachery of Déricourt that enabled the Gestapo to roll up the PROSPER circuit in the Sologne area of the Loire valley after the 23 June arrest of Bonoteaux. The reaction of Dansey, head of SIS, was illuminating. As Patrick Reilly (who was Private Secretary to Menzies) noted:

> My own most vivid memory of Dansey is of seeing him come into my room opposite Menzies', rubbing his hands with glee. 'Great news', he said, 'great news!' I expected to hear news of some splendid intelligence coup. The cause of the great glee was the destruction of a major SOE network in France... Misery, torture and death for many brave men and women, British and French, and Dansey gloated. I remember feeling physically sick.[28]

That week had also been disastrous for the high command of the Resistance, for on 21 June, Jean Moulin had summoned the leaders of all major Resistance factions to a house in Caluire, a northern suburb of Lyon. Thirteen men sat around a long table in order to discuss who would replace the captured Delestraint as head of the Armée Secrète. It was an amazing technicolour dreamcoat of French politics with representatives of no fewer than 15 organizations present.[29]

In perhaps the most cataclysmic act of betrayal in the history of the Resistance, a traitor had notified the meeting to the Gestapo, and all were arrested. By the beginning of 1943, it had looked as though de Gaulle had successfully unified the disparate elements of French resistance; this was now split asunder. As Pineau later described Moulin's loss: 'He held so many strings in his hands, that the task of retying them would be difficult.'[30] Selborne submitted insightful and occasionally witty quarterly reports to Churchill on the activities of SOE. Covering this quarter, Selborne noted that 'the incident shows once more the chronic French incapacity in security', thereby underlining the wisdom in having created a separate F Section.[31]

The forecast for 19 July was terrible; nonetheless, Mac was sent forth in V9822. He took out two 'bods' including Pepe, a wireless operator. Persevering through a strong weather front across the Channel, he made the field at Azay-sur-Cher. There was a 'rather lengthy turnabout' (14 minutes) and 'a hurried conference with the operator' (Déricourt again). Whether he took three or four passengers back to the UK is open to question. His main passengers were France Antelme and his colleague in BRICKLAYER, the Paris barrister Jean Savy, both being on the run. However, this was an SIS flight. It is of note that in his handwritten report of the operation Mac crossed out the original entry for the number of passengers on the return flight, and amended it to three.

Mac's flight was urgent – it was the RAF's only offensive operation that night, the rest of the RAF having been stood down due to the weather. This was a fleeting visit to London for Déricourt, who was taken back to France on 21 July by a Verity and Vaughan-Fowler double – *Floride*. That Déricourt was taken back to France on an SIS mission leads some to conclude that he had been recalled to London for this brief visit by SIS and not his ostensible employers, SOE (who were unaware of this visit), adding credence to the later theory of his being a triple agent (F Section/the Nazis/SIS). He spent his single night in London at the home of André Simon of the wine family, who was one of the few agents to work for both SOE (as a conducting officer) and SIS in London.[32] For the return Verity brought back the wife of the agent Jacques Robert, together with their two small daughters Marianne and Chantal. One of them had asked their mother how they were going to be transported to England. The response was 'The Holy Ghost'. Many years later, Verity received a letter of thanks addressed 'Dear Holy Ghost'.[33]

Again this was an SIS mission, with Déricourt's dubious social circle in danger of polluting that organization as well. But he was back in business immediately, organizing the following night a Hudson pick-up flown by Hodges (Operation *Gamekeeper*). This took out the fated Jack Agazarian, Nicholas Bodington and a Frenchman for SIS. Bodington, who was at the time Buckmaster's deputy in Baker Street, had persuaded his boss (against all norms of military common sense, and despite the fact he had panoramic knowledge of all the French circuits) to allow him to go to France himself to investigate the collapse of the PROSPER network; he took Agazarian (who by now also had wide knowledge) as his wireless operator.

At the beginning of August 1943, Frager (*Louba*) and Cammaerts (*Roger*), whilst on their way to a café in Paris, 'happened' to bump into Bleicher. Frager introduced Cammaerts to Bleicher as his uncle 'who was interested, but not active, in the Resistance'. Bleicher informed them (*inter alia*) 'that the chief source of the Gestapo's information was the agent in charge of receptions' (i.e. Déricourt).[34] Cammaerts immediately informed Bodington of this – who in turn fed this back to Déricourt.

Major Geoffrey Wethered, a counter-intelligence expert in MI5, was appointed by the Director General of MI5 in March 1943 to investigate the enemy penetration of SIS and SOE (although he was placed within the latter organization).[35] Wethered reported on a meeting at Baker Street on 18 November to discuss Déricourt's status. Buckmaster, true to form, 'was inclined to regard Déricourt as genuine, his work had been carried out without a single apparent failure and was, on the face of it, so well regarded that a move had been made before the report by *Louba* [Henri Frager] to have Déricourt decorated'. Frager was to be sent back to France – but without contact with Déricourt's circuits. Within a week, Wethered was also made aware that Roger Bardet was 'a dangerous man', whose several escapes from German hands were implausible. By December 1943, SOE had also been told from SIS sources that Déricourt was working for the Germans.

SIS took some comfort in the chaos that Déricourt had sown in Baker Street, yet its cockiness was unwarranted because it had had its own traitor.

Arthur Bradley Davies, better known as Agent *Bla* or *Blanchet*, worked for Marie-Madeleine Fourcade's ALLIANCE network. He had been parachuted in on 12 August 1941 to teach the network how to use the new radios they were receiving and new enciphering methods, after which he was to set up his own network in Normandy.[36] A Cockney (with a Welsh surname and fluent French, albeit with a Cockney accent), he caused alarm on his arrival by wearing an outfit complete with bowler hat that invited suspicion in rural France. He talked too freely in English and displayed very lax security, preferring, for example, to give his coding lessons in a loud voice in public places such as parks. Aged 39, he had accrued his French working as a farm manager in Normandy for 20 years.

He betrayed nine agents, who were executed by the Germans on 30 November 1942.[37] But the steely Fourcade was on his tail. One of her agents, Arthur Gachet, had uncovered evidence that *Bla* had given his radio set over to the Germans, and was transmitting on their behalf from Paris (rather than Normandy). SIS was reluctant to concede their man was a traitor, but eventually did so, and uncovered failings in its recruitment process – before the war, Davies/*Bla* had been a member of the British Union of Fascists, Oswald Mosley's proto-Nazi organization. *Bla* had been in cahoots with the Germans from the outset. London gave the order for execution. The ALLIANCE members tried to be subtle, but there followed a comedy show. When *Bla* consumed a bowl of soup laced with a cyanide tablet it merely gave him stomach ache; when he was given a cup of tea, he noticed it tasted rather strange, which was true as it contained another tablet. He now realized what was happening – and accepted his fate. After an attempt to drown him at sea failed when the boat did not appear, he was hauled back to Marseille and confessed his treachery in front of an ALLIANCE 'court'. It is thought that the following day he was executed by Lucien Poulard (a leader in ALLIANCE) and his team.[38]

On 17 July, Vaughan-Fowler carried out a notable SIS mission – *Renoir*. Pierre Dallas had organized it to the old aerodrome at Betz/Boullancy near Soissons. The prime objective was to bring Marie-Madeleine Fourcade back to London to save herself and to discuss whether her crumbling ALLIANCE network could be preserved. She had been loath to leave her treasured colleagues, but the arrest of *Elephant*, her head of security,

persuaded her to flee. Vaughan-Fowler crossed the French coast north-east of Dieppe just after midnight. On board were Georges Lamarque (known as *Pétrel*, who ran the ALLIANCE sub-circuit DRUIDS and was returning to the field after training), and two other agents.³⁹

Fourcade left her Paris flat shortly before 1900hrs, and at the Gare de L'Est spotted Pierre Dallas who was holding her *courier* for London in a suitcase. She hopped off her train at Nanteuil, and followed some way behind Pierre Dallas until they found crepuscular shelter in a ditch to await nightfall. Once shrouded in darkness, they were picked up in his car by Dr Maurice Gilbert, a local GP who moonlighted for ALLIANCE. She noticed the somewhat selfless Gilbert's poor attire, and asked him if he wished for anything she could procure in London and have sent out to him – just some decent soap was his reply. He drove them to the boundary of the airfield, and Dallas' team set up the flarepath.

Vaughan-Fowler arrived at 0100hrs; the operation went very smoothly, and she together with two friends – Lucien Poulard, who had recently narrowly avoided arrest, and another agent – were soon in the bosom of Mrs Bertram at Bignor.⁴⁰

At the beginning of July, to replace the departing Bunny, the elegant and patrician Robin Hooper arrived from 138 Squadron the other side of Tempsford, having done a full tour on Halifaxes dropping agents and supplies around Europe. Older than most 'A' Flight pilots at 29, he had married two years earlier; like Verity, he had a good command of some European languages, had been up at Oxford and was a member of its UAS. But on graduation he had entered the Foreign Office. At the declaration of war he decided that life as a diplomat was inappropriate in the circumstances, and used his UAS experience to re-enter the RAF.

Hooper's debuts were not easy: he had to return from his first operation (*Aster*) due to violent storms in north-west France; on his second attempt the following night, he flew too close to a German night-fighter base, but luckily they showed no hostile interest, and flashed him a green light indicating he could land. Declining that offer, in the clear sky he found his field to the south-east easily but aborted his first attempt at landing; his second was successful, but Pierre Hentic, the operator, shouted to him that an obviously German car was barrelling down a nearby lane. Hooper disgorged his SIS agent (Robert Champion) quickly, Hentic threw in the sacks of *courier*, and Hooper started his take-off before Paul Fortier (who had taken out insurance by attending an Assumption Day service the previous day) and Cmdt Feyfan had time to pull the canopy shut. Hentic successfully evaded the approaching car, but in his haste had left behind the bottles of champagne and Chanel No. 5 meant for Hooper.

That same night (15 August), Vaughan-Fowler carried out an important mission for SIS. He was to return Marie-Madeleine Fourcade's star agent, the furrow-browed Lucien Poulard, to the field (together with a sack of gifts for her other agents), and bring back two of her most important subordinates in ALLIANCE – Leon Faye and Ferdinand Rodriguez. There was a warm welcome from the Bertrams and Fourcade on their return to Bignor.[41] In a double with Mac (*Popgun*), Verity took out de Gaulle's deputy for the Southern Zone, Jacques Bingen. The young man had written a highly charged letter to his mother on the eve of his departure from Tangmere:

> My departure... may help France as much as many soldiers, I hope that, before my end, I will have rendered many of these services. Finally there is the additional desire to avenge so many Jewish friends who have been tortured or assassinated by a barbarism such as we have not seen for centuries. One more Jew (there are so many of us, if only you knew) will have taken his part. There you have it, dear Mother, that's why I'm leaving, fully aware of the danger, and having weighed the risks.[42]

A sadly high proportion of flights at this time were required to extract agents who were in imminent danger of arrest. On 19 July (Operation *Athlete*), Mac had brought back France Antelme, who had witnessed many of his colleagues in BRICKLAYER arrested at the end of June. Déricourt took advantage of this flight to have a 24-hour visit to London. The collapse of PROSPER meant that Verity had to extract the siblings Claude and Lise de Baissac, whose circuit was being mopped up by the Gestapo, and Nicholas Bodington on 16 August on Operation *Diplomat*. This had been hurriedly arranged by Déricourt after Noor Inyat Khan had sent messages from the Benoist family estate at Auffargis outside Paris, where she was holed up with Maurice Benoist, William Grover-Williams, and their wives. Despite the presence of her brother alongside her, Lise confessed to nerves whilst waiting in the field for Verity's Lysander to growl over the horizon – 'Will the plane come, will it?'[43]

VCAS Air Marshal Sir Douglas Evill had sanctioned a transfer of a further two Hudson Mk IIIs to 161 Squadron from a reserve pool held for Coastal Command.[44] After the normal quick conversion – rip out the seats, remove gun turret – they were put to immediate use. The autocratic Mouse Fielden's chequered operational record took a further hit in July. On the 16th, he took off in a Hudson for a field east of Lyon with two agents on board. No reception was seen, and he worried about gaining the French coast before dawn so he carried on to Maison Blanche in Algeria. After refuelling he continued to Blida to meet some former SOE staff. Whilst parked there, his Hudson was destroyed when a Blenheim made a forced landing and swung into it. Fielden and crew now had to endure an uncomfortable journey back to England in the rear of a Lancaster.

Hugh Verity carried out the same mission (*Buckler*) eight days later, on 24 July. He had more success, dropping off the same two agents (Emmanuel d'Astier de la Vigerie, and Jean-Pierre Lévy). The pair had unusual cargo – the lyrics of *Le Chant des Partisans*, written in London by Anna Marly, which was destined to be the totemic anthem of the Résistance.

Verity picked up six senior political and Resistance figures including André Déglise-Favre, together with two Air France pilots. On take-off, disaster was mere feet away – the Hudson's port engine started to misfire which caused a swing in that direction, and Verity narrowly missed the boundary hedge.

But he had the same problem as Fielden with a pick-up location so far south and it being the height of summer. So he carried on to Blida, where the group stayed 24 hours before heading home.

The Lyon Gestapo were by now hot on the heels of the SPRUCE network, which included Robert Boiteaux-Burdett (Agent *Nicolas*). Burdett had had a colourful pre-war career – Bond Street hairdresser, gold prospector and boxing champion were not typical even in SOE CVs. His strong but delicate hands had latterly been used to assemble explosives. All SPRUCE members including Joseph Marchand were now recalled to London for their own safety. For Burdett, the experience was like a hush-hush airline: he had met a man in a café in Paris, who had given him a map reference and told him to be there at 2200hrs on 19 August. Déricourt had assembled a full complement: Burdett and Marchand had already hooked up in Paris with a distant relative of the former's, Marie-Thérèse Le Chêne (*Adèle*), the oldest female agent to be sent to France by SOE. Also on the passenger list was the star SOE agent Tony Brooks, who needed to come to London for re-briefing and, more importantly, to be married; the remainder were agents on the run in varying states of anxiety. The craggy-faced former Bugatti racing driver, Robert Benoist, was perhaps in the most mortal danger of them all, having made an astonishing escape from the Gestapo's clutches.[45] With customary sang-froid he had managed a relaxing dinner at Briollay, some three miles south-east of the field, before walking over after dusk. Déricourt told them all to be at the field at 2200hrs. They were all surprised that there were so many as they bumped into each other at the rendezvous.

A relaxed Déricourt arrived last of all at 2315hrs. The field was blighted by gaggles of horses and a herd of cows; the former soon bolted to the tree line, but the latter were reluctant to obey the agents' earnest shepherding efforts. 'After much goading and persuasion, we managed to move them to the perimeter of the field and then all ears strained to listen to the plane', remembered Boiteux.[46] Another of the would-be passengers later recalled the sight of the stampeding livestock as 'the worst fright of my life'.[47]

For this operation (Operation *Dyer*), Bob Hodges used the field (*Achille*), a water meadow north of Angers at which he had landed successfully only four weeks earlier. Mist – the curse of water meadow sites – descended, but eventually after midnight Hodges' engines burst the silence, scattering cows in all directions. After one circuit when he was put off by the mist, he thought, 'Now if I just line up properly, just motor gently down into the fog, I'll be alright.'[48] He landed, managing to avoid both animals and humans, but could not see where to taxi because of the fog, so stopped. Eventually, Déricourt found him. Only one agent, Erwin Deman, an Austrian Jew now working for MI9, emerged from the Hudson. Despite being 52, Marie-Thérèse le Chêne managed to climb nimbly aboard. The other much younger female, Raymonde Menessier, although only 29, was not so agile, encumbered by a fashionably tight skirt. Brooks encouraged her into the Hudson's interior with a shoulder to her rump.[49]

Ten agents in all had clambered into the Hudson. Déricourt pointed Hodges in the right direction for his take-off and said, 'Alright. You take off in that direction on your compass and you'll be alright; by the way, mind the horses.'[50] Hodges pushed forward the throttles and *'O' for Orange*, despite its full load, quickly lifted through the gossamer layer of stratus. Lulled by the symphony of the pair of Twin Wasps, and their own exhaustion, the passengers soon fell asleep. Buckmaster was there to greet them on arrival back at Tangmere soon after dawn, and chatted to them over a cooked breakfast at 0600hrs.[51]

Three days later, Verity tried to carry out another Hudson trip (*Trojan Horse*) to the Saône valley but by the time he arrived in the area at 0330hrs the fog was too thick for a landing. The operator, Paul Rivière, was frustrated that Verity had arrived so late, a mere half an hour after the fog had started, and also that the Hudson had not been equipped with an S-Phone so that alternative arrangements could have been made immediately.[52] Hodges successfully carried it out the following night.

The pilots of 161 worked hard and played hard, and when they wanted to party at the Cottage they naturally liked to have some women for company from time to time. But clearly only people who were privy to the secret nature of the Special Duties squadrons could be admitted to the inner sanctum. There were quite a few WAAFs at Tangmere who passed muster on that basis. One was F/O Faith Townson. University educated, she worked in Air Liaison at Baker Street and could hold her own with the men of 161 and could speak a little Russian as a party trick.[53] Her experience in dealing with alpha males at Tangmere was to stand this 29-year-old in good stead. For in 1945, she was posted to the Far East with SOE, where she met the buccaneering Freddy Spencer Chapman, who performed acts of derring-do behind the lines in Malaya. They married in Delhi in 1946.

Although 28, with his receding fair hair and confident patrician manner, Stephen Hankey had the air of someone older. Moreover he was a local boy, local to Tangmere that is. Although known in the RAF as plain Stephen Hankey, he came from a wealthy Sussex family, more generally known as Alers-Hankey, who had lived in the glorious Binderton, just over Tangmere's hedge at Westhampnett. The 17th-century house, remodelled in the 18th in the Regency style, was now loaned to Anthony Eden as his country retreat for the duration.[54]

After school at Lancing up the coast, he commissioned with the Royal Sussex Regiment (the former unit of his father, who had retired as a colonel), and excelled at Sandhurst in boxing. This was how he gained a broken nose which was to give him agonizing bouts of sinus pain during his future career. He swiftly gave up the Army to become a salesman of Delahaye sports cars. That lasted less than a year before he gained a short service commission in the RAF in June 1938, and married Elizabeth Papillon a month later. By the time war was declared, he was flying Lysanders with

Geddes' II Squadron. He survived the Battle of France with only one crash, shot down over Belgium. Elizabeth had refused to be separated from him, and had installed herself in Paris for the period, which made for a narrow escape from the capital before its fall.[55]

Thereafter Stephen spent some time in the Middle East on photo recce work, and acquired a collection of buttons from the various air forces out there, with which he adorned his own tunic, in contravention of regulations, of course. When he joined 161, camp follower Elizabeth took up residence at Dell Quay near Tangmere so as to be close to him. Against regulations again. A later colleague described him as 'the sort who enjoys tooling around in an open sports car, with his dog and his wife'. The hospitality he and Elizabeth gave his squadron colleagues at their cottage was much appreciated, and his bonhomie and sense of humour soon earned him the affection of his colleagues.[56]

By the time he arrived at 161 in June 1943, although vastly experienced, including a tour on Lysanders, he had not gained many night hours, which left him at a disadvantage with his new peers. Consequently, he had to spend three months training at 161, accompanying Verity as a passenger on Operation *Athalie* on 14 July, before starting operations in September. This debut trip for SIS to the south of Bourges in the Cher was uneventful.

Late that summer, he invited the Edens over to the Cottage at Tangmere for tea to discuss some matters in connection with Binderton (or 'Old Binders' as Sir Anthony called it). Once Stephen had explained what they were up to, the Foreign Secretary expressed total surprise – he had had no idea of 161's operations. At that point, Henry (Bunny Rymills' cocker spaniel) jumped through an open window to land with muddy paws on the lap of Beatrice Eden, adding to the amusement.[57]

Before the start of August moon period operations, Mac, who had recently acquired a bar to his DFC, had popped down to the 'Old Uni' (the Unicorn) for a few beers. The following day he reported his outing to his colleagues: 'There were three Group Captains talking to each other [in the bar]. They did not have a gong between them. Boy, did I feel good! There is no need to cut my citation out of the Times. My press cutting agency takes the London Gazette regularly.'[58]

In September, soon after Hankey's arrival, 'A' Flight pilots assembled for a photo in front of one of their Lysanders parked on the sandy fringes of Tangmere. Hooper, with only a month of operations under his belt, looks pensive; Mac looks like an airman on parade; Vaughan-Fowler, with only a few missions to go, looks suavely confident; Verity is attempting gravitas; Bunny, with his faithful spaniel, is quizzical; whilst Stephen Hankey is staring into the future.

Robin Hooper's bumpy initiation into 161's ways continued in September: he was tasked with *Californie* on the night of the 10th down to Bourges. With three agents in the back, he encountered widespread violent thunderstorms that only cleared around the Loire valley. In Hooper's laconic style, he afterwards only reported the weather as 'indifferent'. But then he dropped his map and flight plan into the bowels of the cockpit and was unable to retrieve them. He managed to find his pinpoint on the Loire from memory, but then became lost and returned to Tangmere with his tail between his legs. Verity drily noted that 'Pilots in this flight generally carry spare maps and flight plans to avoid misfortunes of this type. The practice has [now] been crystallised in a Pilots Order.'[59]

James Robertson Grant Bathgate had joined 'A' Flight at the end of July 1943 – the first Kiwi to do so. Born in Outram in 1920, he was educated in Otago, and applied for pilot training in February 1939. He earned his wings as a sergeant in April 1941, and was immediately despatched to the UK via Canada, and was streamed onto bombers. Qualified as a second pilot on Wellingtons, after one raid from Stradishall he was sent to Malta in October, from where he carried out 14 operations over Italy and North Africa with No. 104 Squadron. Jimmy did a further four operations from landing grounds in the Western Desert, before returning to the UK. He met a 21-year-old Welsh woman, Dorothea Valentia Valess, whom he married on 31 October 1942.

The quietly affable, slightly jug-eared pilot spent 1943 ferrying Whitley, Wellington and Halifax aircraft within Transport Command. He narrowly avoided being part of the Liberator crew bringing the Polish General Sikorski back from Gibraltar, which crashed into the Atlantic soon after take-off, killing all on board.[60] After arriving at 161, he soon impressed Verity as a diligent navigator. His first operation (*Gladiola*), a double with Stephen Hankey, was in the September moon period on the 14th. This was a harvest moon, which enabled the squadron to mount operations on 12 successive nights, with 25 operations in all, of which 19 were successful. On his debut trip Jimmy found the field and brought back three SIS agents, but Hankey missed his destination, and could not raise his equally inexperienced colleague on the radio.

The previous night, Verity had carried out a rare mission – bringing back two evading Allied aircrew for MI9's POSSUM line, which was based in Belgium, and therefore a handier starting point for evaders from crews who had parachuted or crashed in the Netherlands. Hugh found Operation *Brasenose* 'rather dodgy' for two reasons: firstly, there was no reception waiting for him when he arrived at the field near Rheims. He circled for more than an hour flashing his recognition lights. The two aircrew had been joined by *Grand Pierre* (SOE agent Pierre Geelen), and were most disconcerted to see these lights when they were still half a mile from the field. They ran towards it, and hurriedly set up the flarepath on a narrow strip of stubble – the rest of the field had been ploughed since it had been selected. Flt Sgt Herbert Pond, a Kiwi, was one prospective homeward passenger; another was Sgt Fred Gardiner, a wireless operator whose Lancaster had been shot from under him over Belgium. Gardiner had found the Resistance, and a friendly priest had aided his disguise by giving him a cassock, in which he crossed the country into France. Once at the strip, with his Morse skills he was deputed to flash the letter 'R' at Verity, whose patience was nearing its end. Secondly, on final approach as he turned his landing light on, the flight commander was further dismayed to see a haystack bordering the field. Nonetheless, after 'a considerable bounce', he made a safe landing and embarked his trio of relieved passengers.

Gardiner recalled, 'we had quite a reasonable flight home, and when I looked down at Brighton I could almost pick out my grandmother's house at Portslade'. Given the variable navigation he had witnessed on Bomber Command missions, he was in awe of Verity's navigation skills in finding a solitary field in rural France.[61]

The hectic pace continued. Decent landing sites in the rolling country of Champagne were hard to find, but Pierre Hentic, having much enjoyed his training at Tempsford and Somersham, was now in charge of air operations for the JADE-FITZROY network. He had discovered a good field (formerly used as an airfield by the French in World War I) for *Larkspur* on 10 September. Vaughan-Fowler extracted three SIS agents. Hooper had to carry out *Ingres* on the 11th with some important outbound passengers (Leon Faye, Frederick Rodriguez and Marie-Madeleine Fourcade). But Dallas, the operator on the field near Compiègne, was having a bad night. He signalled recognition signals at two separate aircraft that flew over with no response. Spooked by that, he waited for a positive identification until he could recognize the shape of Hooper's Lysander overhead. The 161 pilot could not of course see the signal, since it was masked by the fuselage. So he returned to Tangmere empty-handed, having to repeat the flight two nights later; at least it was one of the shorter trips.[62]

Verity had been out on 12 September as part of a rare triple (*Battering Ram*), with Mac and Vaughan-Fowler. Verity gave them call signs – 'Freeman' (for himself), 'Hardy' for Mac and 'Willis' for Vaughan-Fowler, after the large British footwear retailer. Between them, the three had taken out eight agents and politicians, and brought another eight back from a field south-west of Tours that was too small for a Hudson. A measure of the peak efficiency of these experienced Lysander jockeys was that only nine minutes elapsed from the first landing to the last take-off. On the way down, Mac had a nasty scare: he was rashly circling at only 300 feet just south of the Loire, waiting for his colleagues, when the perspex in his cockpit glazing splintered. He had been fired at by a light machine gun, and the German had unsportingly failed to use tracer, so the first Mac knew about it was the shattering plastic after the bullet had passed just 20 inches from his head. Mac was the last of the trio to land and soon regained his composure.

Hodges and Bathgate did a Lysander double (*Milliner*) on the 17th, for Déricourt. Hodges was always more comfortable in the Hudson – 'Navigation in the Lysander was quite difficult, one had to have one's maps on one's knee, they would fall to the floor. [We had] a torch and so on – it was quite tricky.'[63] He carried some key personnel: outbound, he took Harry Peulevé and Yolande Unternährer (a wireless operator who had married Jacob Beekman (another wireless operator; he was 23 years old and from Zwolle) during her training, and who was going out to assist the Canadian Major Biéler). Peulevé was very security conscious and made sure he fled the field alone. This was well advised since this was one of the operations that Déricourt had briefed his Germans friends about, and they were hovering behind hedges in the vicinity. Yolande and Biéler only lasted until the following January. For the return, Hodges took on board Benjamin Cowburn (who had been in France for four months on this trip, and was another fleeing the collapse of the PROSPER network), John Goldsmith (a race horse trainer in more peaceful times), and Colonel Henri Zeller. Bathgate took out Henri Derringer and Harry Despaigne, a wireless operator who made his way to Marseille. Coming out of the station, he was tapped on the back and asked (in French), 'What are you doing there, my little pig?' by an old friend who was now working for the Vichy police. He was given 48 hours to leave town; and made his way to Arles where the town gossip soon reported a British officer was in town. He was not having much luck.[64] Amongst Bathgate's returning passengers was Déricourt's number two, Remy Clément.

Verity retrieved four Allied airmen from a field in quiet countryside east of Rouen on the appropriately named Operation *Wings* on 17 September. One was a most fortunate young fighter pilot: the previous Saturday, he had become engaged to a very attractive woman at a dance at the Savoy Hotel, and had made a date for a week hence. Shot down whilst doing a fighter sweep over northern France on the following Monday, he parachuted onto the roof of a château's greenhouse. Fortunately, the head gardener was a member of the Resistance, and the count who owned the place was also sympathetic, and took him in as a guest. Two nights later he was summoned to a field and brought home by Lysander. He kept his date at the weekend, but was despatched to SOE's cooler at Inverlair in the Highlands for six months, as he now knew too much about SOE and 161. Marriage followed.[65]

On the following night, the languid Peter Vaughan-Fowler carried out his last mission for 161 (*Bomb*) – taking out the famous Yeo-Thomas (the *White Rabbit*) and Pierre Brosselette, in a double with Mac. He had been on Lysanders for 12 months, becoming a rock of 'A' Flight. Yeo-Thomas had been tasked (as Operation *Marie-Claire*) with assessing the strengths of all the *réseaux*. Mac's return passengers made an odd couple: André Mercier, who was not from the Champagne house, but was a *député* in Paris; and André Le Troquer, a jowly left-wing lawyer of humble background who was on the run from the Gestapo, having been a senator and latterly the Parti Socialiste's representative on Moulin's CNR. The operator had allowed his deputy to lay out the flarepath: it was far too close to some trees, and both pilots had to use a near stalled approach descending like a lift at an angle of 1 in 7 (against the more usual 1 in 50) to squeeze into the field near Angoulême. Neither they nor Bob Hodges were impressed.

The pace that week was relentless. On the 19th, Hooper had to return from a mission when he again dropped his map into the bowels of his Lysander and became lost in bad weather. The operation was repeated the following night by Bathgate who flew out empty, but was disconcerted on landing to have to embark four male passengers. The normal limit was three, and the operator (*Gabriel*) had pulled this stunt before. His excuse was again that he had direct orders from Colonel *Passy*, who he claimed was somewhere on the field. On Bathgate's safe return, a discomfited 161 sent a signal that this operator would not be accepted 'as a responsible agent in charge' again.[66]

A few days later, Verity completed a Hudson mission (*Peashooter*): 'had I known what the weather was really going to be like, I would not willingly have undertaken this operation at this stage of the moon'.[67] 'It was only by a few breaks in the low cloud over one of the main rivers enroute, that navigation could be checked. The target area [in the favoured fields east of the Saône] was totally black.' Low cloud was drifting in, forcing him to land quickly, with no moon percolating the cloud layers above. 'On my third approach I managed to get in. Because of the rain on my landing light and on my windscreen, and the pitch darkness, I had the greatest difficulty.' It was only on his third approach that he managed to land. He had rounded out 20 feet too high, but caught a dropping port wing with some throttle, arriving with a thud on French soil. Amongst his seven grateful return passengers was Michel Dumesnil de Grammont, leader of French Freemasons, and a former cabinet minister in Daladier's government who was now working with LIBÉRATION SUD. He was being recalled to London by Emmanuel d'Astier de la Vigerie for briefing prior to appointment to the new French government-in-exile to be located in Algiers.

In October, the squadron's Hudson was busy operating its VIP transport service, with flights organized by Paul Rivière, BCRA's main operator. On the 16th, Verity, aided by Philippe Livry-Level (who had a habit of shifting to 'completely unintelligible' French when under stress) as navigator, took out two, and retrieved eight, of whom the most important was General Jean de Lattre de Tassigny. The cheery commander of the French First Army looked most unmilitary with a black beard, shoddy clothes and a cloth cap; this was explained by his recent travails. The only French general to have refused Vichy's order to lay down arms, he and his men had carried on the fight, but he had been picked up by the Garde Mobile on his way to the Pyrenees, and locked up in Riom's prison; having escaped, he was now keen to enrol with de Gaulle's Forces Françaises de l'Intérieur (FFI) in London.[68] After take-off Verity handed over the controls to his

Aberdeenshire co-pilot Johnny Affleck, and went back into the cabin with some thermos flasks of coffee 'and I shone my little torch on the cabin roof and in the dark, dim light I saw about nine of the roughest looking tramps you could possibly imagine (through hiding up in ditches). One of them came forward and said in French "Captain, Sir, I have the great honour in presenting you to General Jean de Lattre de Tassigny."'[69]

Two nights later, the squadron excelled itself with a Hudson double (*Helm*): Bob Hodges (who had just been awarded a DSO; 'his efficiency and personal example, both in the air and on the ground, have been outstanding'[70]) and John Affleck each captained a Hudson to a field near Bletterans. Affleck had been commissioned from the ranks, despite an occasional argumentative nature and a poor disciplinary record. He had been rescued from being thrust back into Bomber Command operations by Bob Hodges and invited to Tempsford. Outbound they only carried two passengers each. But Rivière had 18 passengers lined up to return to Tangmere. Whilst Hodges landed in France without incident despite a strong cross-wind, Affleck only made it at the second attempt, and that after carving a path through some tall poplars bordering the field. His crabbed approach had left Rivière perplexed about where the Hudson was going to touch down. In the event, Affleck landed on top of him, and the Frenchman was lucky not to have been clobbered by the Hudson's tail-wheel. If he had not attended Mass the previous Sunday, he would surely do so the next weekend.

One of Hodges' passengers was the politician Vincent Auriol. In 1948, when President of France, Auriol returned the favour by appointing Hodges, and his navigator Waggy, Companions of the Légion d'Honneur. (François Mitterand, whom he also carried that night, later made him Grand Officer of that order.)[71] Another passenger was Emmanuel d'Astier de la Vigerie on a further trip to London to lobby for more arms. When Affleck's ground crew checked his aircraft in the morning, foliage was extracted from one of the air intakes. Hodges had felt uncomfortable having to loiter (or 'stooge' in pilot parlance) in the target area for 45 minutes to await Affleck; he decided that Hudson doubles were not to be repeated.

Two nights later, on *Mate*, Affleck took out the craggy Bugatti racing driver Robert Benoist, who was courageously putting his head in the lion's mouth again; Affleck brought back four passengers in another Hudson pick-up, this time organized by Déricourt. Amongst them were Eileen Nearne and Paul Frager, who detested Déricourt, whom he had already identified as a German agent. The loathing was mutual, exacerbated in this case by Frager's bringing his friend Roger Bardet to the field near Angers 'to see him off'. Bardet had only just been released from prison by the Germans, for whom he was now acting as an informant; but Déricourt's objection was simpler – that bringing friends to a pick-up field was a needless breach of security. Frager was keen to return to London so as to denounce Déricourt to his masters in Baker Street. The argument between the two reached such a pitch that Frager clenched his fingers around his revolver in his pocket.[72] Affleck was thankfully unaware of the compromised nature of his reception party. Albert Browne-Bartoli, one of Benoist's fellow outbound passengers, was so disconcerted by Déricourt's behaviour that he then left the reception party immediately, and made his own way to Burgundy to set up the DITCHER circuit. He was in good company – Pickard's sheepdog Ming took a dislike to Déricourt and refused to go near him.

Bunny had left for 38 Wing with a new DFC, while Mac was given a bar to his existing DFC; Pickard had put them both forward for a DSO, but Fielden vetoed this on the grounds that it was given to senior officers who were in command. Nonetheless, a DSO was awarded to their flight commander, Hugh Verity, in August.[73] The path from Tempsford to the Palace was becoming well worn.

By now the requirements for selection of possible landing grounds were formalized. Essentially, the area needed three strips 600m long by 150m broad, set 60 degrees apart, enabling a landing to be made into wind, or nearly so. The strips could be in adjacent fields if necessary; a slope of no more than 1 in 100 was required, although slightly uphill landings would be allowed. The surface had to be firm and grass or stubble no higher than 30cm, and obviously devoid of ruts or ditches. The zone at either end of each strip extending 300m had to be free of obstacles. Further requirements detailed the layout of the torches.[74]

14

A Mission

For at least two years the moon was as much a goddess [to 161] as she ever was in a near-eastern religion.

Sir Robin Brook[1]

THE BIG PICTURE

161 and 138 continued to suffer from strategic turbulence above, although the Lysander flight remained well insulated. Portal had submitted a paper to the Chiefs of Staff Committee on 25 July 1943 rebutting SOE's request for more air assets. After some well-laid-out arguments, he concluded:

> While I feel that there is a very good case for providing aircraft to back SOE activities in the Balkans, even at the cost, as it must be, of some small detraction from the direct attack on Germany, I feel that it would be a serious mistake to divert any more aircraft to supply Resistance groups in Western Europe which will only be of <u>potential</u> value next year, when these aircraft could be of <u>immediate and actual</u> value in accelerating the defeat of Germany by direct attack.[2]

At a subsequent meeting of the Defence Operations Committee, Selborne made his case again: 'he was convinced of the increasing value of the contribution that his organisation could make. When the time came for the invasion of Western Europe the Resistance Groups should be capable of vitally important work in the destruction of enemy communications.' Churchill had 'no doubt of the value of operations of this nature.'[3]

Arthur Harris received an early Christmas present in August. His lobbying and whining led Bottomley as DCAS to put him in overall control of air operations for SOE and SIS. Both organizations had to come cap in hand to secure his assets. The stated intention was to make available more of the heavies used by the two Special Duties squadrons to supplement the Command's bombing offensive.[4] They also reiterated that 'the [air] requirements of SIS should be accorded propriety over SOE operations in Norway, France, the Low Countries, and other areas' (later detailed as Sweden and the Italian mainland).

Acting Air Commodore Lionel Payne had been Director of Intelligence three years earlier, but was now the RAF representative in SIS. On 10 January 1944, he wrote to Portal setting out that he had told Medhurst eight months earlier of his concerns that Dutch SOE operations had been controlled by the enemy (he had been struck by pilots' reports that reception committees and their lights had been just too perfect). He was exercised by the fact that 'all the initial planning of clandestine air operations is done in these country sections by naval or military officers or civilians'. He advocated putting senior RAF officers into SIS and SOE 'with executive, instead of purely advisory, duties', and that there should be an Assistant Chief of the Air Staff for Special Operations supervising this activity.[5] This succeeded in putting Bomber Harris' nose quite out of joint, more so when it was decided within days that operational control of the two Special Duties squadrons should be transferred to 38 Group, Allied Expeditionary Air Force (under ACM Leslie Hollinghurst). This was delayed until March for logistical reasons. The avuncular AVM Alan Ritchie was appointed as the Air Member on the SOE Council as from the end of February, which made Selborne happy: 'it seems he is just the man we want. We are very glad to have him.'[6]

Moves had been made to make SOE and SIS more militaristic and professional organizations. Despite having Churchill's endorsement, this did not go down well with the existing staff. The Prime Minister's amanuensis at No. 10, Desmond Morton, wrote to Brigadier Hollis in the Cabinet Office on 5 November (a propitious date for sedition) that 'I gather privately that the PM's minute has created an uproar in these two august bodies, half of which have been in state of mutiny on being forced to wear uniform by their respective Chiefs, while the other half have been attending the office in pyjamas as a protest against not being allowed to wear uniform.' Morton concluded, 'We shall have some fun.'[7]

Relations between the UK and French leaderships remained strained. An anonymous senior civil servant wrote to Churchill in November 1943 outlining the state of play:

> In 1940 SOE found it necessary to infiltrate British officers into France because the French were not playing. In 1941 the French Resistance groups started, and made an alliance with General De Gaulle. SOE created a new organisation to contact and service these movements. Ever since then we have maintained two organisations in France, one British and one French.
>
> General de Gaulle was well aware that SOE was also marinating a parallel British organisation and more than once protested against it. The Foreign Office and the Chiefs of Staff, however, have throughout supported SOE in their desire to maintain a separate organisation. Since the formation of the French Committee of Liberation in Algiers the matter has again been raised on several occasions, of which M. Massigli's conversation is the latest example.
>
> The reasons why SOE has found it necessary to maintain its British organisation are:
>
> 1. The Gaullist organisations are partisan in internal French politics, and tend to bayonet anyone who will not bow to the Cross of Lorraine.
> 2. The security of the Gaullist organisations is lamentable. They have repeatedly been penetrated by the Germans, and in spite of all SOE protests insist on maintaining centralised machinery in violation of the primary canons of Secret Service.
>
> SOE now has some 70 British officers in France, each with his own circle of workers. This organisation has never been penetrated by the Germans, although individual cells have occasionally been scuppered. The SOE organisation is playing an essential part in the plans of COSSAC [the Allied committee in oversight of plans for D-Day]. If we abandon it, and entrust all COSSAC sabotage work to the Gaullist organisations, there would be every likelihood of the agents being mopped up by the Germans on the eve of D Day.[8]

There was now demand to extend the scope of 161's activities. In the middle of November, Sqn Ldr de Laszlo was asking AI2(c) to consider doing Hudson agent pick-ups in Denmark. Elsewhere in Europe, SOE finally realized that the Germans had indeed infected their Dutch networks and captured many agents and supplies. Two agents had managed to escape from prison to

Switzerland where they went to the Dutch Embassy to relate the scale of the disaster. The SIS man in Berne made sure the news reached London quickly. On 1 December, the RAF said it was considering suspending all SOE flights in Europe. In London, Clement Attlee, the Labour Deputy Prime Minister, was in charge as Churchill was meeting with Roosevelt and Stalin in Tehran. Attlee told Selborne he was asking the Joint Intelligence Committee to conduct an investigation into SOE's activities in Holland, Denmark and Poland, and flights to all three territories were immediately suspended. Desmond Morton (a former SIS man) took the opportunity to reinforce the idea that SIS should take control of the young upstart. Selborne's report did an admirable job in preserving the status quo.

The essence of 161's flights for SOE or SIS was that each operation was complex (involving several services and agencies), and individualistic. It was an intricate dance between AI2(c), Tempsford, Tangmere and the field.[9] And of course, weather – the ever present enemy.

For the Special Duties squadrons, the biggest obstacle to completing a drop or pick-up successfully was the weather at the destination – and also at Tempsford and Tangmere. The pilots were expected to venture forth in very inclement weather – and did so. For example in the moon period of December 1941 into January 1942, 138 Squadron carried out sorties on five nights against Bomber Command's two, and this was at a time when 138 was critically short of serviceable aircraft and trained crews.[10]

So how to give some weather guidance to Lysander pilots? They benefited from the meteorological forecasting infrastructure of their parent – Bomber Command. The Central Forecasting Office and the Meteorological Communications Office were collectively known as ETA, which disseminated its wisdom to the various Bomber Command Groups via teleprinter, and onwards to the stations. As might be expected, the failings of the rather relaxed nature of peacetime arrangements were soon exposed once operations started in 1939 – even during those leaflet-dropping Whitley operations of the Phoney War. From 1942, Tempsford and Tangmere would have a dedicated forecaster; he would be in constant communication with his counterpart at 3 Group's HQ at Exning just outside Newmarket.[11]

European weather is of course very influenced by systems travelling eastwards across the Atlantic. When the US entered the war, it established a network of fixed weather patrol ships in the Atlantic to provide real-time weather observations. This was supplemented by weather reports from the increasing number of US and British transport and ferry aircraft crossing the Pond. The absence of such an extensive network of weather ships (and trans-Atlantic flights) meant that the Germans were more blind to Europe's approaching weather. This cost the Nazis dearly on D-Day, when they assumed that the storm that caused Eisenhower to postpone the invasion by 24 hours was destined to be more sustained than Gp Capt James Stagg (accurately) forecast.[12]

So at Tempsford and Tangmere, the Special Duties pilots received the usual thorough forecasts of likely meteorological conditions over the UK. But how to assess the weather at a destination which was a remote field in the middle of France?

Most Resistance networks did not have any trained weather observers or forecasters in their ranks. It would be difficult to ask them to communicate conditions to the SOE radio operators in England during the evening immediately prior to a mission. Firstly, the teams were busy assembling men to collect containers and secure the field. Secondly, and more importantly, a radio transmission from near the chosen field might alert the German direction-finding teams to the location of an imminent landing. And finally, the Maquis would only have been able to communicate the actual evening weather conditions, which would be of limited value if falling temperatures during the night subsequently brought in blankets of low stratus cloud or a miasma of fog. McCairns describes the few groups who could assist: 'Some groups of operators were so well organised that they had radio transmitters within ten miles of the field and could send a last minute message giving details of local weather and general security. News of that kind was unfortunately rare, but when it did arrive it was most reassuring to the pilot.'[13]

There was, however, one Resistance group that did send weather reports back to the UK; indeed that was their primary role. The group operated between 1942 and 1944, and was named BEAGLE, the codename for its founder Albert Toussaint. Sadly, it operated in Belgium. This country was too densely populated to be much use as an objective of the Lysander pilots. And the less populous areas such as the Ardennes were too steeply ravined or wooded to provide landing grounds. Toussaint was a trained meteorologist; after his recovery back to the UK after Dunkirk, it was decided he would be of most use by fulfilling his former role back in his home country. So he was parachuted back into Belgium in August 1942 together with two wireless operators. Eventually, three agent networks were assembled, and 40 agents trained in meteorological reporting. It carried on sending much useful information back to Bomber Command until Belgium was liberated in August 1944.[14]

The Tangmere forecaster or one of the 161 pilots assembled down there would phone Group Fighter Command Headquarters, and the photo reconnaissance units (PRUs) trying to retrieve any meteorological feedback from that day's missions.[15] But this had to be done discreetly so as not to alert the wider Air Force to the location of 161's missions that night.

Apart from cloud cover at the destination, the 131 and 168 Squadron pilots were also interested in forecast winds. Bomber Command crews would be interested in upper air winds, since they generally flew to their targets above 10,000 feet. The Lysander boys were much less predictable: whilst they would typically climb towards that level whilst crossing the French coast – in order to avoid light flak – they would usually descend to no more than 2,000 feet in order to avoid the German radar systems. So both medium- and low-level wind forecasts were needed for their pre-flight planning.

OPERATION *SWORD*

Wednesday 20 October: the daily routine at Tempsford was set in stone – at 0900hrs, the morning conference convened with station commander Mouse Fielden, the leaders of his two squadrons (Dickie Speare of 138 and Bob Hodges of 161), together with the station metman, and Tempsford's navigation officer Waggy Wagland. The picture they discussed was not looking propitious for that night's operations. A very deep low-pressure system was sitting off the north-west coast of Ireland.

As Mac awoke mid-morning and opened the door at Tangmere's Cottage, he sniffed a damp south-westerly breeze, with the cloud base at only 1,800 feet in a pewter sky. Having done operations on three of the last four nights, each one of around five hours' duration, he was weary, and would welcome a respite. But the 20th was the last night of the October moon period, and the Lysander flight's customers were needy. As well as the double Mac had been allocated with Hankey, Hooper and Bathgate were setting off on *Waterpistol* towards Angoulême, whilst Verity was scheduled for a solo mission (*Frederick*) for SIS to a field north of Chartres. Additionally, Affleck was doing a Hudson mission (*Mate*) from Tempsford to Angers with some high-profile passengers in both directions. This group of operational pilots assembled at 1000hrs to enjoy Blaber and Booker's mixed grill together.

The forecast was for 'moderate or fresh south to south west winds, bright periods with showers, but local thunderstorms near the south coast, rather cold'. Towards Cornwall was even worse with a threat of hail in the thunderstorms.

SOE operations staff requested AI2(c) to mount operations in a given order of priority. AI2(c) then sent Verity so-called Air Transport Forms

A MISSION

(ATFs) for that night's operations – these, which essentially represented the customers' demands, gave the location of the pick-up fields, the Morse code recognition signals to be exchanged between ground and air, the name of the operator, the identity of their trainer at Somersham, the load both ways, and what the BBC's personal message to initiate the operation would be.

The Air Liaison sections of SOE and SIS sent AI2(c) the details of the landing grounds their field agents had found. In addition to the photographic archive of fields AI2(c) married these with ground intelligence such as the location of nearby German garrisons, which might otherwise prejudice the suitability of the field. Around a hundred fields would have to be assessed in order to provide 15 suitable fields for a month's operations.[16]

Verity then handed his pilots photos of the fields, which had been taken by PRU Spitfires. These were in sufficient detail to highlight potential obstacles such as trees, bushes or cart tracks.[17] The Resistance groups nominated fields using grid references from the popular Michelin road maps; these were converted into British military grid references by a dedicated team of WAAFs back at Baker Street. The card files of approved fields were sorted using a sophisticated hole and knitting needle system! Any queries were resolved with a call to the Ministry on the scrambler phone.

After breakfast, Mac and Hankey went to the Intelligence Room in the Cottage, and picked up their maps: half-million maps to cover each side of the intended track, and a quarter-million map for the run in from the pinpoint to the target field. Mac folded these concertina-fashion so they could be stuffed into either the legs of his flying boots or the map pocket on the Lysander's port cockpit wall. The morning's next task was to calculate the key times of the mission on these and also begin to complete the so-called 'gen card' with the details of track, mileage and so on for each leg, not forgetting the recognition letters to be signalled between air and ground. Tonight's target field had not been used before – if it had been, they would have read the pilot's comments from the previous mission to see if it harboured any hazards.

After lunch all the operational pilots crossed the road to perform a short air test on their steed for the night – the Typhoon pilots at Tangmere would have known that the Special Duties men were going to have a busy night simply by the number of Lysanders being so tested. 161's mechanics were so skilled and diligent that these short flights rarely revealed any problems. Following a meteorological update, Mac and his colleagues went to Stores to pick up their escape kit, a shoebox full of coffee and other goodies for the French operator, and handguns. Given his fatigue, it was not difficult for Mac then to have a nap once back at the Cottage.

By 1900hrs, the humidity had increased; the cloud base had risen to 2,500 feet. But the forecast had not changed much: the depression off Ireland was only moving slowly northwards, and the threat of thunderstorms and hail remained. The pilots updated their maps and gen cards with headings and timings to take account of the latest winds.

Mac was to take out André Schock and Dr José Aboulker: the 30-year-old Schock had been recruited by Dewavrin's BCRA and brought to London. Under the agent name of *Voltigeur* (which could be translated as 'aerobatic pilot'!), he was being taken back into France to take charge of the military region between Rheims and Nancy.

Aboulker was an Algerian Jew who had already had an eventful couple of years in senior roles in the Resistance in North Africa. Coming from a medical family (but yet to complete his own medical training), he was being sent back to France to supervise the rudimentary healthcare of Resistance members. With their escorting officers, they arrived at the Cottage late in the afternoon from London, chauffeured of course by FANY drivers. It being an SOE operation, there had been no need to liaise with the Bertrams of Bignor. All the outbound passengers joined the pilots for dinner at two trestle tables. Usually there were some pilots not delegated to fly that night who would hit the wine, which was in plentiful supply to ease the nerves of the agents. Tonight every 161 'A' Flight operational pilot was due to fly, so it was just their ten agents who were partaking. The agents were then issued with lifejackets and given their allocation of chemicals, the most important of which were suicide pills. Meanwhile, Mac and Hankey changed into the strange mix of civil and military attire which 161 had come to agree was the best for survival in the event of having to evade in France: plenty of civilian outer garments for disguise, but enough military attire to avoid being shot as a spy.

In contrast with the Whitley, Stirling and Halifax pilots who were only introduced to their agents just before departure at Tempsford, the 'A' Flight boys knew most of their outbound passengers by name. If the agents were operators they would have spent a week training them at Somersham; if they were agents of long standing, the chances were that one of the Flight would have brought them back from France.

There was now solid cloud at 3,000 feet. Mac's was to be a relatively short mission – the destination was some 46 miles south-east of Paris. After they had been dropped at 'A' Flight's secluded dispersal, Mac showed his two passengers where to stow the parcels of *courier*, and the button in the rear cockpit they had to press if they wanted to communicate with him on the intercom. After he had clambered up to the cockpit some 14 feet off the ground, the ground crew passed Mac his pistol, maps and a thermos of fresh coffee. His nostrils met the familiar perfume of his Lysander V9822 – a cocktail of aviation fuel, oil (plenty of that), burnished leather and sweat.

Having stowed all the tools of his trade, he perused the cockpit carrying out his checks from memory. Then to start the Mercury engine he opened the throttle just half an inch, pushed the mixture control to normal, pulled out the red propeller control knob on the left side of the panel for coarse pitch, opened the fuel cock and coolant gills, pushed the carburettor heat control to COLD, and then with his right hand primed the carb with eight strokes of the pump. Shouting 'All Clear!', then mag switches to ON, and 'Contact!', he flipped the protective cover and pressed the starter button. The Mercury wound up, ticking over a little lumpily at first before settling into its accustomed rhythm at 1,200rpm. Mac pulled out the knob to operate the oil heater, and after five minutes gave the engine a few hundred RPM more to warm it further. He was cheered by the smell of warm oil. The two passengers made themselves as comfortable as possible in the third class accommodation at the back, and Mac radioed the control tower for permission to taxi. Swiftly given, he set off round the northern perimeter track to the end of the south-westerly runway. There he tested the engine and completed his pre-take-off checks, the most important being to verify that the tail actuating wheel was set to the take-off position (it was always wound fully back for any ground manoeuvring), cooling gills open, and flaps unlocked, followed by a peek over his left shoulder for a final check that the fuel gauges were registering the correct amount.

As Mac lined up on runway 25, the wind had increased to more than 20 knots. Holding the Lizzie on the brakes, he opened the throttle to +1lb/sq in of boost, released the brakes keeping the stick neutral – and apart from a little dancing on the rudder pedals, he just waited. The Lysander's desire to become airborne was understated; it simply levitated into the air at a time of its choosing. Similarly, the wings' slots and flaps retracted when they wanted to.

Bathgate had taken off at 2307hrs, Hooper and Hankey almost in tandem at 2315hrs, and Mac left the Tangmere tarmac at 2320hrs. Verity followed him into the skies 15 minutes later – 161 was providing plenty of targets for German radar operators. Whilst still in the climb, Mac turned to port onto his heading for the first cross-Channel leg, and after leaving the Tangmere frequency retuned to 'Blackgang' (a RAF wireless and radar unit at Ventnor on the Isle of Wight) who were following his progress on their radar sets. Levelling below the cloud base by mid-Channel, he was allowed one call to them for a back bearing. This gave him his drift. Some rapid mental arithmetic told him whether the wind he was enduring was as forecast, and enabled him to update his flight plan for the rest of his trip.

The usual coasting in point was Cabourg, not because it was the charming resort chosen by Marcel Proust to write his novels, but because it was largely free of flak batteries. And, by happy coincidence, almost exactly 90 nautical miles from Tangmere. This enabled the pilots to use the '1 in 60' rule beloved of aviators. (If you are one mile left of track after 60 miles you have drifted one degree to port. A correction of two degrees to starboard should bring you back on track after another 60 miles.)

He climbed as usual to 4,000 feet before the French coast to avoid any light flak before descending as soon as possible back to as low as 500 feet. He encountered low cloud over most of his journey.[18] There was no safe route to his destination. He had to avoid Paris, the obvious routing being to the west of the capital, but both he and Hankey had to avoid the fighter airfields clustered around the city, Étampes Montdésir being the nearest and most important. In the moments when the ground was visible, Mac looked to identify water features such as rivers and lakes; the next most easily recognized landmarks in moonlight were forests, woods and railway lines. In spare moments when not searching for landmarks, he was mentally recomputing his ETA at the field.

Mac called up Hankey 45 minutes before he arrived at their appointed rendezvous point at Montereau; the town was relatively easy to find because of its location at the confluence of the Seine and Yonne rivers, and an unusual pattern of railway tracks. He reached it at 0215hrs. Twenty-five minutes later, Hankey called up Mac to tell him to proceed on his own to the landing field. After passing the Loire, Stephen had found the conditions trying – 'extremely dark, and full of rain and low clouds'. After half an hour of attempting to establish his position, he gave up and turned northwards for Tangmere.

As Mac neared his destination, solid medium-level cloud and rain reduced visibility to less than a mile. He had been doing gentle orbits of Montereau since it was only six minutes' flying time to the field. As was his habit before landing, Mac wound back the left-hand-side cockpit window and stuck his arm out into the 150mph slipstream to wipe some oil off the windscreen.

From Montereau, his destination was not too difficult to find (just as well given the poor weather) – he followed the twisting Seine upstream north-eastwards from Bray, and the D road to Nogent took him to where the operator, Pierre Delahayes, and his team were waiting. As soon as he heard the Lysander, Delahayes flashed up 'Y' from his torch; as Verity later noted, 'it was always quite a thrill to see the correct letter' flashed through the gloom. Mac responded with 'G' from the signalling lamp under the fuselage. Delahayes' colleagues turned on the other torches of the inverted 'L' flarepath. Passing over the Resistance men at 400 feet, noting the direction of landing on his directional gyro, he headed east before doing a descending turn towards the glimmers of light. Mac was hoping they had laid out the flarepath correctly into wind – the Lysander hated cross-winds, and its 'horrifically bad' brakes would fade given half the chance. Before he started his final descent, Mac wound the tail trimmer forward; this increased the load on the stick as he pulled it back to slow down the Lysander. But it was an insurance policy – if he had to go around from this landing, when he opened the throttle the nose would not rear up and produce a fatal stall. He knew Petter's main design flaw, and was not going to be caught out by it.

Flipping on his landing light at the last moment, it was 0147hrs by the time he landed. He touched down by Lamp 'A' and, despite the absence of wind, came to an abrupt halt by Lamp 'B' (see Appendix F). He needed full throttle to taxi back to Lamp 'A', but as he tried to swing the aircraft back into position for a take-off run, it became completely bogged. Schock and Aboulker disembarked, probably not realizing the extent of Mac's skill in bringing them to their destination. Leaving the engine ticking over, Mac hopped out too, sinking straightaway into the wet clay soil. He called over to Delahayes to tell him what he thought of his choice of field; the Frenchman retorted that a week earlier it had been flat harrowed soil with no bumps, but solid rain for the last 48 hours had changed it more than somewhat. Mac told him a take-off was impossible. Delahayes, having drunk deep from the flagon of optimism that evening, said '*Eh oui, ça va*'. It will be all right.

Mac organized the assembled party to swing the Lysander round, and paced the distance to the far fence – its 500 yards would have been more than ample in normal conditions (Sticky Murphy's personal best was 35 yards), but tonight? The three passengers[19] for the return pushed through the slipstream of the idling Mercury and after the exchange of suitcases and sacks of *courier* packed themselves into the rear cockpit. Mac picked up some clay from the field, rolled it into a ball and took it back to show to his chums at the Cottage. Kicking as much clay as possible off his boots, he clambered back up to the cockpit. As he opened the throttle, he gave the Lysander boost over-ride, but by Lamp 'B' he was only doing

20mph rather than the normal 70. He eventually unglued from French soil after 300–400 yards. Delahayes and his men stomped off to escort Schock and Aboulker to their refuge.

Mid-Channel, Mac was called by 'Blackgang' again and asked if he had 'joy' (and given a bearing to aid his heading back to Tangmere). Mac answered with one word – 'Red', to indicate success. Hankey had had of course to respond 'Blue', meaning failure. The return flight lasted only just over two hours, by which time the cloud base at Tangmere had descended to 1,500 feet. After landing uneventfully he taxied to 161's special dispersal, and cut the engine. The silence was barely interrupted by the clicking of cooling metal. Mac entrusted his Lysander once more to Pankhurst and Prentice (his ground crew); it was by now after 0500hrs. Once back in the Cottage for some coffee, he took the ball of clay out and threw it at an Air Ministry type with the caustic comment, 'Is this what we are supposed to land on?'[20]

Checking his briefing folder later that day he realized that the field into which he had been ushered was not the one that had been recced by the PRU Spitfire and approved by the Ministry, but was just to the west of it. A further source of irritation to Mac and his squadron commander arose when they discovered that Delahayes had not been expecting a double, and had no passengers for Hankey even had he landed.

Mac wrote up his operational report in longhand and passed it to Verity for his comments and approval, before it was typed up by a WAAF, and sent up to Tempsford and the chain of command. To his cost, Mac had by now learned not to be flippant when describing his missions, so few editorial changes were needed.

Had it been an operation for SIS the treatment of the agents would have been slightly different: 'The new arrivals after a drink and talk with the pilots at the Cottage, were taken to Bignor where they were given a meal. *Courier* was, when urgent, sent straight to London, but the party went to bed and, during a leisurely morning, each member was interviewed by the administrative officer as he came down. Some, whose affairs were not in order, were able to remain at Bignor until they were.'[21] Of the operations that night, only Verity's was for SIS.

That marked the end of the October moon period. A day or so later the weary five flew their Lysanders back to Tempsford for a few days of the more relaxed routine of operator training, admin and rest, before the cycle started again on 9 November.

15

Tangmere Death

The start of the next cycle, 9 November, was also a special day for the Special Duties pilots – King George and Queen Elizabeth arrived at Sandy station to be greeted by Fielden, their former equerry. The monarchs toured those parts of RAF Tempsford 'which were unique to the station', before having tea in the officers' mess. A very proud Hugh Verity was presented to His Majesty, whilst the Queen chatted away in French to Philippe Livry-Level. The royal visit did not ruffle that day's operations too much – there were eight Halifax operations that night. Flying Officer James McAllister McBride took his Lysander to Tangmere afterwards, but suffered a burst tyre; the Lysander developed a wild swing, and was written off. Only his pride was hurt.

McBride joined on 4 October from No. 85 Squadron where he had been flying Mosquito night-fighters. Aged 25, he was 'tall, well-built, with the face of a boxer', and, unlike most of his new colleagues, tended to be quiet and shy.[1] His father ran a plantation in Port of Spain, Trinidad, so together with his elder brother he was sent to Strathallan School in Perthshire. Its founding headmaster had some sensible but unusual ideals including that education should be enjoyed and not a drudgery. McBride was Captain of School in his last year and went up to St Catherine's, Cambridge, to read Agriculture in 1937. When the war called, he left his studies prematurely in 1940 to join the RAF.

The night of 9 November, Mac brought back a scarcely believable four US airmen from a field north-west of Soissons; on landing at Tangmere the grateful evaders uncoiled themselves from the bowels of the rear cockpit, and kissed the Sussex soil: 'Christopher Columbus! We are in England!'[2]

Another Lysander treble (*Oriel*) was mounted that night, with Hodges, Hooper and Hankey. Yves Henri-Léon Le Hénaff, a vehemently anti-Nazi former French Navy lieutenant and now an MI9 operator, had picked up Sgt P.V. Matthews in Paris with another member of his crew, and an Intelligence Corps captain. The group made their way in a truck to a field east of Poitiers. But the three 161 pilots were thwarted by solid cloud over the coast and dense fog from the north of the Loire valley to their target. Not seeing the ground at their ETA, they turned for home; their mood was not enhanced by some radar-directed flak popping through the cloud at them near Cherbourg. The disappointed Matthews and his colleagues retreated to a town a few miles to the north.

Two days later another attempt was made, with Hooper this time being accompanied on *Oriel* by Bathgate and Mac. The weather was as perfect as November in northern Europe can be. The three pilots made their aerial rendezvous as planned. As leader, Hooper landed first and stopped in only 30 yards – the ground was so soft that he had to use all of the Bristol Mercury engine's 810 horses to taxi back to his reception party, and only just avoided becoming stuck when turning round. After embarking Matthews and two French airmen, he could only take off from the sticky field by using the emergency over-ride on the engine. Hooper radioed his colleagues, 'Do not go in!' Le Hénaff was amongst the party who missed their flight back to England. When Hooper's ground crew examined the Lysander the following morning, they found enough French mud to fill a wheelbarrow. They deposited this in the garden at the Cottage, proclaiming 'there is some corner of an English field that is forever foreign'.[3]

The following day, Verity was planning *Gloxinia*, but a late change in the weather forecast necessitated a change in his routing, and therefore charts. Everything became a little rushed, and this no doubt accounted for his forgetting to extinguish his navigation lights after leaving Tangmere. On arriving at his field, this alarmed the agents he was picking up who thought he must be a German aircraft.

On 11 November, Verity and Hankey carried out a double (*Salvia*): amongst the return passengers was M Potelette and his wife. He was an engineer with the national railways and wanted to lobby in London for the destruction of the railway system by sabotage rather than RAF bombing, with attendant collateral damage. The ground party was unnerved by the appearance of a German Dornier from an airfield less than two miles away. Verity was relatively relaxed – he had identified it as an unarmed Do 217. Hentic climbed aboard Verity's Lysander for some debriefing in London.

The ability of the squadron's Hudsons to extract evaders and threatened agents from the jaws of the Germans was again in evidence in that moon period. On 15 November with Waggy at the maps, Bob Hodges took a Hudson down to Angers on Operation *Conjurer*, with five agents on board; on arrival at the field, they split into two parties to make their way to Paris. With Déricourt having betrayed the operation to Sturmbahnführer Josef Kieffer (head of the SD in Paris), French thugs working for the Germans monitored the landing, and followed one of the groups to Paris where Jean Manesson, Paul Pardi and André Maugenet were arrested at the Gare Montparnasse. Their place in subsequent meetings with fellow agents was taken by German stooges, causing more mayhem.[4]

Bob embarked a full plane load of at least ten passengers, amongst whom was Francis Cammaerts, now an increasingly important cog in the DONKEYMAN circuit, who had cycled the last seven miles to the field in the company of Rémy Clément. Another passenger was 'Captain Moreland', more commonly known as François Mitterand. There was also a group of evading pilots. Hodges was blissfully unaware of the fate of his outbound passengers and the part of Déricourt, and considered the three-hour flight 'a very straightforward operation'.[5]

When Mac heard the title of Operation *Tommy Gun*, he knew it would require the greatest effort. He was a little perturbed to find that it was a novice operator, Pierre Deshayes, who was running it that night – he had been in the field for several months yet this was his first pick-up. Further, Deshayes had actually chosen a field within an artillery shell's flight of the V-weapon sites – it was a mile or so from Frévent in the Pas de Calais. The Cabinet and Britain's intelligence agencies had been becoming increasingly concerned about the Germans' preparations to launch secret weapons at England from northern France and the Benelux countries. The code word *Crossbow* was attributed to this intelligence, and it was accorded the highest propriety.

The objective of *Tommy Gun* was to bring home one of RF Section's best operatives – the *White Rabbit* himself, Sqn Ldr Forest ('Tommy') Yeo-Thomas. He had been scouting around northern France and had acquired much valuable knowledge about the V1 and V2 programmes and their launch installations. Dizzy Dismore, RF's head, needed him back in London for debriefing. Yeo-Thomas returned to Paris by train to warn Pierre Brosselette of the latest arrests, and to await pick-up. Space in the carriages was at a premium, and he squatted on his suitcases next to a German private, whom he charmed with simple banter, enhanced by offers of cigarettes, Mirabelle brandy, and then, opening one of his suitcases full of PARSIFAL circuit's blueprints and notes, some scarce chocolate for the soldier's children back in the Fatherland. Yeo-Thomas explained to the by now intoxicated German that the case was full of his black market contraband, which he was taking to sell in Paris to sustain his own family, and would he mind keeping it for the imminent arrival of the team of police inspectors? Of course not. With his new German friend he passed the Gestapo checks at the station exit too, before parting company.

Hearing the message from London, he journeyed by train back to Picardy, with a shopping list of matériel requirements of the local Resistance groups. On arrival in Arras he was disheartened to hear that a new Wehrmacht division had installed itself in the area of Frévent. Deshayes was saved by the ingenuity and bravery of one Berthe Fraser, an Anglo-Frenchwoman of formidable guile. Having noticed a cemetery on the route, she organized M Bisieux, a local undertaker, to provide a hearse, petrol and a team of his staff dressed in appropriate mourning gear. Yeo-Thomas, already with a pistol in his shoulder holster, was given a Sten gun; together with his vital suitcase, all was spirited into the hearse, and covered in enough flowers to stock a florist. From his coffin, Yeo-Thomas heard at least one German officer interrogating the team at a roadblock – he was ready to shoot his way out. But the group made it to the safety of a nearby farm for supper and to await nightfall. Alex, the leader of this Resistance group, made a heartfelt speech: *'Mon Commandant, c'est un grand honneur pour nous tous d'assurer la protection d'un officier anglais, surtout d'un anglais si grand ami de notre pays.'* ('Commandant, it is a great honour for us to ensure the protection of an English officer, especially one who is such a great friend of our country.') Moved by such emotions, Tommy gave him his cufflinks as a souvenir. After a hearty dinner at a nearby farmhouse, at midnight the group stepped over the frozen fields to the strip where Deshayes' men had already laid out the stakes for the torches. As they waited in the bitter cold, the moon gradually became visible in the improving weather, and their spirits lifted.

When Mac was briefed about this mission, he was told he had to bring Yeo-Thomas back 'conscious or otherwise'. So he was in a state of high tension when at 2000hrs, having read the latest meteorological reports, Bob Hodges cancelled it. After working his 'mind and body to such a pitch', Mac felt 'I could press on regardless of weather', and was 'so disappointed that I pleaded to be allowed to go and do a weather reconnaissance'. Mac was writing a script for a fatal accident report. Hodges finally relented, and in a state of anxiety Mac took off from Tangmere a minute after midnight. The outbound passengers were René Houze and Georges Broussine of SOE's RF Section.

'Halfway across the Channel cumulo-nimbus [i.e. thunder] clouds became 10/10ths, [with a] base 1500' with heavy showers.' He crossed the French coast somewhere, but in the murky weather he had failed to find his appointed crossing point at Cayeux, just south of the mouth of the Somme estuary, which would give him an infallible landmark. Turning the Lysander to port, he followed the French coast. Luckily his instinct had proved correct, and he soon found the gaping mouth of the Somme, turned to starboard and proceeded to Frévent. Flying over that town, he saw the operator two miles away flashing the appointed 'X' – 'the signalling was magnificent, and the flare path brilliant', he noted. The weather had improved sufficiently for him to notice that as soon as he had touched down the colour of the ground ahead changed. He recognized that this was likely to mean plough and not meadow, so he stood on the brakes, and pulled up just before he would have tippled into the plough. Mac turned the Lysander round and taxied to the reception party. A man came up and said in English, 'Nice work. It was pouring with rain thirty minutes ago. I am returning with you.' It was Yeo-Thomas, with fellow passengers Mme Virolle and Jacqueline Pichard at his side. Mac had to stay on French soil for a full ten minutes as Yeo-Thomas' 14 cases and parcels of mail required so much packing. As they chatted over the intercom on the way back, Tommy, encumbered by a woman on each knee, revealed that Mac had had nothing to fear about the security of the field – it had been guarded by 50 Resistance men.

The return flight, via the same route (with doglegs omitted), passed safely albeit very low below the lingering cloud base, and after an hour Yeo-Thomas was welcomed into the bosom of a party at the Cottage to celebrate his arrival. The following day he was ushered up to London's Air Ministry for a series of debriefings, which a few weeks later included meeting with Churchill in person. It gave Tommy an opportunity to return to his favourite theme of demanding more arms and support.[6]

That same night Jimmy Bathgate took on *Waterpistol*, flying two agents to a field near Angoulême (with McBride as his partner). Claude Bonnier was the most important cargo. This 46-year-old former aeronautical engineer had been tasked by de Gaulle as one of 12 military delegates of his French government-in-exile. Bathgate's other outbound passenger was Jacques Nancy, a military instructor and explosives expert.

'A' Flight's 15-month run of safe operations (deriving from both skill and luck) was about to come to an end. The following night, 16 November, Stephen Hankey ventured to the Vierzon area in his Lysander but returned home empty handed, finding the cloud on his route too impenetrable. *Magdalen* for MI9 to the east of Compiègne was to be swansong at 161 for both Verity and Mac. The latter's initial reluctance in view of the weather was overcome by his desire for this last evening in the moon period to allow him to reach the magic total of 35 operations before he completed his tour. They encountered the same unhelpful weather as Hankey with cumulonimbus clouds over the Channel, and needed to be bang on their waypoint crossing the French coast because the flak batteries in the Pas de Calais were very dense. They clawed their way over northern France still at very low level.

The pair arrived at the target area but had to stooge around for ten minutes trying to locate the field. Capt Edgar Potier, the middle-aged and deeply religious Belgian Air Force operator, for some unfathomable reason had ordered his team to put paper discs over their torches, making them very difficult to discern from the air. They dropped off two French-Canadians (Labrosse and Dumais) who were to set up the SHELBURNE escape line in Brittany, and they brought back Sgt Johnson RAF, and three American airmen. Potier ran the POSSUM line; they were also welcomed on the ground by Georges d'Oultremont, or more properly Comte Georges Albert Ferdinand Paul Marie Ghislain d'Oultremont, who, together with his brother Edouard, was a guide for the COMET line on the Belgium to Paris section, handing over five of his '*enfants*' (as the evaders were often termed in radio messages).[7] Potier himself boarded Mac's aircraft as he was London-bound for some refresher training – which would include not masking torches – making three in each Lysander.

In his operational report, Verity stiffly noted that although Potier had previously been admonished for piling four 'Joes' into the back of a 161 machine, 'my view is that four medium sized passengers may safely be carried in a Lysander if no luggage is carried'. Hodges as CO had agreed: 'in the case of escaped POW's four can be carried as there is no luggage, but I do not think it is a good thing to make a general practice of it.'[8]

For Mac, his 35 Lysander missions (plus one recce flight over France) represented a total that would not be matched or surpassed by any other Special Duties pilot. However, with six Hudson trips, Verity carried out 36 operations for 161 in all. In their year on the squadron, every month had meant a moon period of night work fuelled by adrenaline. Their circadian rhythms were shot. Verity was drained by the particularly intense pressure of operations in this November moon period, and a medical examination confirmed he was totally exhausted. After a rest, he was posted – as an acting wing commander – up to SOE HQ (coyly described in the Squadron's ORB as an 'Air Ministry unit') in Baker Street to act as Air Liaison – Operations, to supervise SOE's aviation activities across Western Europe.

Mac, who had arrived at 161 as a newly commissioned pilot officer, was despatched as a grizzled flying officer to AI2(c) at the Air Ministry, to oversee 161's operations from the ground. For a short period, he helped Tony Bertram train potential new landing field operators in the UK. From his standpoint at both Tangmere and the Ministry, Mac judged that the smooth running and success of 'A' Flight owed a lot to Verity's skills and experience. The flight commander had sought to recruit pilots into the Flight who had at least some French, in order to make the training of operators easier (and facilitate communication in a French field in the middle of the night).[9] Hodges also gave him a glowing testimony: 'Hugh was an expert pilot at night flying and had the ability to weld the Flight into an extremely close-knit operation, and led it from the front.'[10]

In the middle of November, as Verity and Mac had dropped off the end of the 161 conveyor belt, Flt Lts Anderson and Whitaker, together with F/O Milsted, joined it. There was another RAF unit whose pilots operated solo deep into enemy territory – the photo-reconnaissance pilots who flew gunless Spitfires, usually at high altitude, all over Western Europe. They were based for the most part at RAF Benson in Oxfordshire. Flt Lts Leslie Whitaker and Murray Anderson had completed several months on No. 542 Squadron. Although 161 kept its activities restricted to those with a 'need to know', this included the PRU pilots since every possible landing field put forward by either Baker Street or the Resistance needed to be captured on film before it could be used. Anderson and Whitaker were becoming restless in their PR role, and when 542's intelligence officer told them that Verity was in charge of the Lysander flight, Anderson phoned him up – he had been to school with Verity at Cheltenham. An invitation was immediate, thus the 542 pair took their Spitfires on the short hop to Tangmere, parked in the north-west corner, and walked to the Cottage where they met up with not only Verity, but Hooper, Hankey and Mac. Unsurprisingly, the duo passed muster, and started their tours on Lysanders in the middle of November. Building confidence in night navigation was the first priority. Anderson had the advantage of already having been taught to fly the Lysander by the Army at Old Sarum.

Leslie Whitaker was an undoubted addition to the list of characters that were to pass through the Cottage – a reporter on the *Keighley News* before the war, he could hold his own at the bar against all comers, and was a prolific smoker. The evidence was there on his fingers and vast stained RAF moustache. His wartime career had had its moments: landing down-wind on one occasion at Benson he had put his Spitfire through the far hedge and overturned. More critically, he had been shot down over the Norwegian fjords. Spirited by the local Resistance into Sweden, he was fortunate to be flown back to England.

Once at Tangmere, Anderson secured a WAAF girlfriend who worked in the Ops Room, and whose looks garnered the admiration of his new colleagues. Less welcome was the fact she lived with her parents in nearby Bosham. It was possibly her order that caused him to shave off his luxuriant moustache.[11]

Now approaching 24, he had a direct manner and a DFC with Bar. Although deeply religious, he carried an inbred distrust of authority – which was to cause him problems later in his RAF career. Brought up in India, after his parents' divorce he was despatched to Cheltenham College. When war was declared, he joined the Royal Tank Regiment, but soon found life as a 'tankie' was not for him, and plumped for the RAF. Robin Hooper considered him 'brave as a lion and very good at his work'.[12]

The new boys practised circuits at Somersham for eight nights running, determined to be operationally ready before the end of the year. A week was spent at Gaynes Hall helping to train embryonic French agents, and also, in the case of Anderson, falling in love (or so he thought) with a leggy and unattainable FANY. His skill with his bagpipes was perhaps a handicap.

Bob Hodges had only limited hopes for the success of Whitaker and Anderson. In November, he wrote to Sqn Ldr Kynoch at the Air Ministry, 'We are having considerable difficulty in finding replacements for our Lysander pilots. We are running out of French-speaking pilots... I have just got two pilots from PRU but unfortunately they are Flight Lieutenants and don't speak French.'[13]

The pair, having spent a week at Somersham, also went down to Tangmere to observe operations, and help where they could. F/O Eric Milstead had arrived at 161 from 42 OTU on 15 November – the patrician Robin Hooper thought he looked like a spiv, not helped by a rather dodgy moustache. He also did not impress his colleagues with his one-track mind. This was a short-lived problem, for he was to be posted out in February –

he 'was unfortunately found unsuitable for the type of work required', as the ORB bluntly described. His first operation (*Gitane* on 10 February) had been ostensibly foiled by cloud near the target – Hodges wanted a little more determination from his team.

Having been foiled by low cloud and heavy icing conditions the previous night, Robin Hooper set off again in the third operation on the night of the 16th.[14] For *Scenery* for SIS, he embarked the Duc de Magenta (Maurice McMahon, a French Air Force pilot of Irish descent) at Tangmere, his destination a field 24 miles east of Poitiers – the same meadow in which he had nearly become stuck five days earlier. Alarm bells should have started to peal:

> The outward trip was completely uneventful. We were on track the entire way from Cabourg down to Montsoreau on the Loire, every landmark on that fairly familiar milk run visible at the expected time. The sky cleared and the moon came out. South of the Loire, and Chatellerault and Parthenay showed up beautifully. I turned east just south of Parthenay and saw the reception signalling at me from at least two miles away. There were drifts of ground mist lying over the field. Although the lights were intermittently visible, the mist was surprisingly thick, white and milky when one descended into it. However, I had had what I looked upon as rather a succession of unsuccessful ops: the photograph had shown at least 1,000 metres run in the direction in which the flare path was laid; and the agents assured us that the ground was 'very hard'. Anyway, I decided to go in.
>
> After two unsuccessful attempts I got down off a very tight low circuit (even for a Lizzie!) dropping in rather fast and rather late through the mist. I soon realised that the ground was very soft indeed – softer than it had been on *Oriel* a few nights before. At first, when I braked, the wheels just locked and slid; but very soon it was a question of using quite a lot of throttle to keep moving and it seemed best to keep moving at all costs. Turning was all but impossible since the wheels dug into deep grooves. Finally we managed to turn 90 degrees to port and there stuck.
>
> The aircraft was immovable even with +6 boost, so I told the passengers to get out and got down myself to inspect. We were bogged to

spat level; the ground appeared to be a wet, soggy water meadow. The reception committee came running up: I organised them to push and we attempted some more +6 boost without the slightest effect except perhaps to settle the wheels a little more firmly in their ruts. 'Georges' the operator (a Belgian agent, Jean Depraetere), was in a state of great nerves and it was Albert, his second-in-command (who had been failed on the Lizzie course for over-impetuosity), who really took charge.

At this point someone suggested getting some oxen from the nearest farm; after a certain amount of fuss this was agreed and a small well-armed party set off to collect oxen, spades and some planks or brushwood (my idea, as far as I remember). The rest of us continued to dig trenches in front of the wheels with the idea of making an inclined plane up which they could be pulled. About 20 minutes later an odd procession loomed up out of the mist: two very large bullocks, trailing clanking chains, the farmer, his wife, his two daughters, and the three chaps from the reception committee. The farmer [Marcel Pairault, aka M. Bouillon] shook me warmly by the hand and asked me when the British were going to land in France, and got to work. He hitched the oxen [named Fridolin and Julot] to the legs of the undercarriage and we all heaved.[15]

This continued in the dark for another two hours, with another two oxen brought in by Adolphe Fournier as reinforcements. But with the approach of dawn finally we decided to abandon the struggle. Georges burst into tears on my shoulder. I patted him on the back and said 'There, there. Allons, voyons mon vieux', and generally tried to convey the impression that mucking around in several inches of mud, some hundreds of miles inside enemy territory, with a bogged Lysander, four bullocks and thirteen excited Belgians and Frenchmen was an experience that any officer of the RAF would take in his stride. I got out my parachute, pulled it, piled my secret papers on top, and then, with the greatest reluctance, started hacking holes in the petrol and oil tanks of poor old 'D for Dog', in which I had done all my trips and which no one else had ever flown on ops. The petrol spurted out of the bottom tank and soaked my trousers, so I thought it prudent to get Victor to apply the match. The aircraft burnt well, but as the fog was really thick by now the fire can only have been visible from any distance as a diffused glow. We ran (in my case at a very steady beagling pace indeed) to the car and piled in: nine people encumbered with suitcases, sten guns, pigeons, pistols and what-not in a small Citroen designed to hold at most five…

We drove rather slowly home – at one point past a German aerodrome, which shook me a little. Gradually we shed most of the party at their various homes or hide-outs, and at last it was our turn. As we relieved nature in a ditch by the side of the road, Albert explained that he was taking me and Jean Weber, the agent who should have left with me, to stay in the farmhouse where he himself lived.[16]

The party was well fed and watered, after which Hooper, in a state of physical and nervous exhaustion, spent most of the next 36 hours sleeping. He popped a short message into the tube of his pigeon and wished it well on its flight back to London (the bird never made it). Staff at Tangmere and Baker Street were extremely concerned about Hooper's absence. He and Mac had spent days compiling a filing system of all landing grounds put forward for 'A' Flight's use – the knowledge that Hooper now had was such that it was decided that he should never be allowed to be taken alive by the Gestapo to be submitted to torture. Hooper was to have been the commander of 'A' Flight after Verity's departure. On both counts it was imperative to retrieve him. The effort to do so was in the capable hands of Mac, in his new role at the Air Ministry tending to 161's needs.[17] 'A' Flight at Tangmere was agog at the urgency: 'If more than two members of this flight were simultaneously bogged in France, they'd start a Second Front to get them out', opined Stephen Hankey.[18] 'Georges', the operator of the fateful pick-up, was mortified by his contribution to the disaster, and sent a message to Baker Street announcing the failed take-off and the safety of all concerned: '*Après cet accident je ne me considère plus de votre confiance*' ('After this accident I no longer consider I have your confidence').[19]

Meanwhile, the Germans were equally keen to arrest the pilot, passengers and helpers of the burnt out Lysander. To Hooper's later amusement, the lorry which they sent to retrieve the charred remains also bogged down in the field. Local gossip held various explanations for the night's events, and the whereabouts of the crew. But the local *gendarmes* were on the case:

They came to the house, to everyone's dismay, the day after I arrived. After a glass of eau-de vie, the larger gendarme began to ask questions. Any trouble round here lately? No, M. Bellot, the farmer, hastened to assure them; it had never been so quiet. M. Bellot was quite sure? But of course. Funny, everyone else had been complaining about their rabbits being stolen. The smaller gendarme looked at his watch. A quarter past twelve. Someone in the town had been saying that Marshal Pétain had resigned: what about listening to the BBC [which was of course prohibited] and finding out if it was true? The BBC was turned on, and another round went its way, and the gendarmes departed in an atmosphere of amity and alcohol.[20]

Georges' team put forward a potential landing ground in Normandy for the rescue, but that proved unsuitable. London's two suggestions proved too wet; Hooper's innate cheerfulness was taking a dent. However, his stomach was swelling: Madame Bellot insisted on feeding him very well, and, being incarcerated within the confines of the farmhouse, he was unable to walk it off, at least during the daytime.

The November moon period concluded with the irrepressible Mac travelling to the Palace to receive a bar to his DFC. On returning to Tangmere he told his colleagues, 'It was damned decent of the King to be out of the country for my investiture, and let me have it with the Queen – knowing my taste for females.'[21]

On 1 December, VCAS Air Marshal Bottomley cancelled all further flights for SOE. HQ Bomber Command issued a *Most Secret* cypher message to Tempsford and 3 Group: 'All SOE operations are to be suspended until further orders. SIS operations are however to be undertaken as and when required.' This was a reaction to the discovery that all SOE agents in the Netherlands had been captured by the Germans as a result of Baker Street failing to notice that some of their radios were being played back to them – the infamous *Englandspiel*.[22]

This potentially was a major change in the demands for 161's services since by now two of SIS's three major chains (INTERALLIÉ and ALLIANCE) had been wound down in September, leaving only JADE/AMICOL operating at full tilt.[23]

In Hooper's absence, operations back at Tangmere had to carry on as normal. The start of the December moon period on the 10th marked a double for McBride and Bathgate. Although they had done a double together in November, neither could be called seasoned Special Duties pilots. For *Sten*, they set off at 2105hrs for a field in between Saint-Quentin and Reims. McBride found the weather over France increasingly difficult, failed to find the river that would take him to his pinpoint and could not contact his colleague on the radio; frustrated, he returned to base at 0050hrs. Hankey had also abandoned a solo trip to Compiègne that night because of adverse weather.

But Bathgate had in the back a 48-year-old BCRA agent, Claudius Four (alias *Duc*), and Communist deputy Emile Cossoneau (*Moreau*), even older at 50. Jimmy must have become somewhat uncertain of his position because he overshot his target field and was over Berry au Bac, 17 miles to the south, when he was shot from the sky by German night-fighters. Pierre Brosselette, the operator Pierre Deshayes and six Allied aircrew hoping for a speedy flight home had a miserable night waiting in vain for Bathgate at the field, and then searching for new sanctuary after the Germans raided their shelter in Vervins only 15 minutes after they had left it.[24] Another agent later reported that Bathgate's aircraft had been damaged 'trying to land but caught fire when it touched the ground. Its three occupants including the pilot were burned to ashes but one suitcase containing money and provisions had been flung out.'[25]

Four days later, the Kiwi was awarded a posthumous DFC, largely for his work with 161, although, as usual, the citation made no mention of that: 'F/O Bathgate has taken part in a very large number of sorties, many of them in the Middle East. He has displayed exceptional skill, keenness and determination, qualities which have earned him many successes. He is a very efficient captain and his example has proved inspiring.'[26]

Meanwhile, many miles away in Nouvelle Aquitaine, due to his own diligence and bravery, a young lad who worked for Georges, Louis Michaud, in a Citroen owned by his employer, the Ponts et Chaussées, had ventured far to come up with another potential landing ground for Hooper's retrieval. The RAF pilot had a very long trip in the Citroen to inspect it, but Louis and Georges had been overcome by optimism or lack of judgment, and Hooper turned it down. Georges' next effort was accepted, and the party celebrated with a lunch in a local hotel. After some bargaining with London about the state of the field, and a wait of several days, Georges received the message that the rescue mission was on. They left the sanctuary of the farmhouse in the Citroen again on a cloudless night, and consumed a bottle of M Bellot's home-made hooch in a fruitless attempt to stave off the biting cold. They waited until 0300hrs, but the Lysander never came.

Bob Hodges had by now grown into the role of squadron commander, and earned the respect and affection of all of his 'A' Flight team. It was entirely in character that he went down to Tangmere to take Hooper's place for the December moon period, and also to take on the mission to rescue him. 'Unflappable, completely in charge, and absolutely approachable' was the verdict of one of his men.[27]

Hodges' vital rescue flight of Hooper was scheduled for 16 December; Hankey and McBride were to set off later that night for a double to Issoudun. For 'MacB', as he was known (to differentiate him from Mac/McCairns), this was only his third mission for 161.

From his role at the Air Ministry, Mac was orchestrating the rescue mission; he and Verity wanted to be at Tangmere to welcome Hooper and were driven from London in a well-appointed staff car. Despite the influx of these old boys of 'A' Flight and the recent arrivals, there was the normal rhythm of an operational afternoon at the Cottage: at 1800hrs, the scrambler phone in the Ops Room rang, and AI2(c) confirmed the three flights were on. Some of the outbound agents arrived at Bignor rather late before being ferried to Tangmere. Barbara Bertram was asked by the conducting officer to show him the way, and had a drink at the Cottage before returning home to prepare a meal for the inbound passengers.

Met forecasts had of course been updated through the day, and Hodges checked them again – a clear night over England and northern France, with a slight risk of fog approaching by dawn – well after the last landing time. After a rest, Hodges came down to the Ops Room at 1900hrs, already togged up in the strange mix of civilian and military attire popular with 'A' Flight. Sgt Booker brought the boss his pre-flight bacon and eggs. The previous night Hodges had set off from Tangmere but had been thwarted by solid cloud over the Channel and northern France, and another, more avoidable, issue: Hodges had decided to have Bomber Command's new Gee system (developed to improve bombing accuracy) fitted to his Lysander to use as a navigational aid. His Gee signal faded a short way across the Channel, and moreover caused the compass to swing through 20 degrees – a problem which had not appeared in trials over the UK in the preceding days. The importance of the operation had meant that Wagland had joined Hodges in the back of the Lysander, but even his navigational skills could not pull triumph from this disaster.

Tonight, Hodges was to try again. His outbound passenger François de Kinder, brother-in-law of the Belgian Prime Minster, had arrived at the Cottage. Anderson collected Hodges' parachute from the store and walked with him the short distance to the Lysander dispersal. He helped strap his CO into his seat. John Hunt sorted out de Kinder in the back, and they left the Sussex earth at 2045hrs without Gee, but with Wagland onboard as well. Apart from some light mist north of the Loire, the weather was benign. But solid cloud above them dulled the light of the full moon which made map reading difficult. Hodges had chosen the town of Saumur for his main pinpoint – its island in the middle of the Loire was unmistakeable that night.

The field, north-west of Poitiers, was 48 miles from where Hooper had landed, and in his view the weather was no better than the previous night. Gentle rain was falling. The party's journey in the faithful Citroen had been impeded by a lorry, and when they arrived at the field Hodges had been orbiting at only 200 feet for a few minutes. The boss was concerned when he saw his target field was dark, but with a car's headlights approaching. 'The car suddenly turned off the road and I could see people running in all directions.'[28]

Hooper told Georges to signal a delay, and hurriedly laid out the torches. Hodges landed without incident; de Kinder stepped down and shook hands with a very relieved Hooper and Depraetere. The pair mounted the ladder, and squeezed into the back to be greeted by a grinning Wagland. The turnaround was particularly rapid.

Back at the Cottage, Mac took a call – it was the met man: 'Base is closing in rapidly. Thick fog will be expected in one hour's time.' Mac asked 'What about diversion bases?' 'Every base in Southern England is already out of action. One might hold good in North Wales or Yorkshire. Your present base at Tempsford is rapidly deteriorating.'[29] Both alternatives were of course beyond the range of the returning Lysanders.

Hooper spent the return flight in the unaccustomed position of lying on the floor of the rear cockpit: 'I was absolutely terrified little Jean was going to be sick all over me,' he later recalled.[30] The flight was uneventful until Hodges reached the Sussex coast where the weather had indeed worsened. As soon as his blip had been seen on radar, he was instructed on the radio to open his throttle to arrive as soon as possible. Mac and Verity left the warmth of the Cottage and hastened to the Lysander dispersal. Hodges had no option but to attempt a ZZ (radio assisted) landing to descend through the layer of low cloud that had drifted in. Verity and Mac heard him overhead. Hodges then descended through the murk which started at 1,500 feet, turned inbound still in the descent, and finally broke out of the cloud at 300 feet above the ground. The very bright sodium flares along the runway were a welcome sight. The boss thumped his Lysander down at 0130hrs and changed out of his flying clothing into his battledress, making small talk in the drawing room with Major Bertram, who was waiting to welcome his charges.[31]

After Hodges had taken off, Hankey and McBride had enjoyed a quick nap upstairs, then came down for some beans on toast by the fire. The crews at the Cottage only possessed three records: Hankey put on his favourite – '*Venez donc chez moi, je vous invite*', a hot swing number. Their six agents arrived in exuberant mood. Again Anderson and Whitaker took the pilots' chutes over to their waiting machines. Pilots and passengers arrived, and the duo left Tangmere an hour after Hodges. In France they picked up two agents each – Hankey had particularly requested to bring back a White Russian, Albert Kohan, who at 57 was a little old to be gallivanting around France as a BCRA agent. Hankey had become great friends with him whilst training him; Elizabeth Hankey too was fond of Kohan's fiancée.

Around 0300hrs, the Cottage's Ops Room phone rang. Anderson answered – it was the controller in the Tangmere control tower to inform him that the cloud had indeed descended to 100 feet and that fog had already reduced visibility to 500 yards. By now Hodges had fallen asleep – the strain of his own mission had caught up with him. Anderson had to wake him with the bad news. They both went to the front door of the Cottage – the cold humidity was immediately apparent; they could not even see the tops of the trees next to the road. They returned in silence to the Cottage's Ops Room. When the phone rang again, Anderson answered once more. The controller's update was even worse, the moon had now disappeared, and there was no visibility at all. A pale Hodges asked the controller the obvious question, 'Where's the nearest diversion aerodrome?' The response was Woodbridge in Suffolk, which had a long, wide runway and a petrol-fuelled system (FIDO) to disperse fog, but far too far away for a Lysander heading for Sussex back from central France. The CO was lost in thought for a few moments: the pilots could simply bail out over land, but that would condemn their chute-less agents to death, and was against 'A' Flight's code of conduct. So he took the only option available and instructed the controller to send the first returning aircraft into the circuit at the nearby naval airfield at Ford, and the second one into Tangmere – 'Let's hope we can talk them down.'[32]

Mac and the other occupants of the Cottage went outside. The fog was so thick that the flarepath was no longer visible, but they could hear McBride rumble overhead. With no wind, he had been given the longest runway (07) for his approach. The WAAF women, as ever, were on duty in the Homer Direction Finding Station, a hut a mile or so from the end of the runway; they had an open phone line to the controller, and fed the bearing of MacB's transmission to him each time. Trying to suppress his own anxiety, the controller talked MacB down to a good position for the runway, and told him to land straight ahead. It was more than six hours since MacB had departed Tangmere – reflexes were dulled with fatigue. He was spooked by the red light atop the runway controller's caravan, and shouted, 'You are flying me into the hangars', opening up the engine for another attempt.[33] Although no longer on the same radio frequency as Stephen, he knew his colleague was in the same plight. Had Harald Penrose been at hand he would have advised the two struggling pilots simply to pre-set the throttle and let their machines descend at five feet a second and 'wait until the ground hits you gently'.[34]

The Cottage crew heard MacB make another two attempts to fumble for the runway. Then someone heard a 'distant thud', so the tower was called – the controller believed that MacB was two miles west of the field (and just to the east of Chichester), very low and descending for landing.

Moments later the tower at Ford phoned to say they could no longer reach Hankey on the radio. After a few minutes the phone rang again and Anderson answered it. The Tangmere controller confirmed that Hankey had crashed near Ford and was on fire. Under the strain, Anderson's voice had all but disappeared, but he croaked the news to Hodges. Again the phone rang – the Tangmere controller said he could see a red glow to the south-west. Whitaker and Anderson were paralysed with shock; by force of habit Whitaker put '*Venez donc...*' on the gramophone yet again (the tune was to be tainted in Anderson's mind ever after). Hodges grabbed the keys to the Humber staff car and headed for the tower.[35]

'Sophy' (Gp Capt Victor Sofiano), an SIS man responsible for 161 activities, was a frequent visitor to the Cottage. Rather old school, with in Verity's view 'infallibly good humoured courtesy', together with Mac and Hooper he summoned another staff car and driver,[36] and set off from the main gates to try to find their stricken colleagues. The fog was so dense that almost immediately they drove the car into an anti-tank ditch, so set off on foot, 'jumping ditches, scrambling over barbed wire fences, and sinking up to my ankles in ploughed fields.' Eventually, they found the red glow of a dying Lysander. Nearby there was a small group of people watching the conflagration. Mac cried out, 'Where is the pilot?' A small man in civilian garb pointed to the flames and said, '*La bas*'. 'You were a passenger?'; 'Yes,' he answered, 'and my wife here.' It was Marcel Sandeyron and Denise Rocher (also known as *Atalas*). The two BCRA agents had somehow managed to break out of the side of the stricken Lysander after it had bounced to its grave. They had tried to extricate the unconscious McBride, but he was pinned by his legs.[37] The crash site was at Drayton, little more than a mile from the end of the runway and the sanctuary of the Cottage. Robin Hooper requisitioned a van and took the two shocked agents back to the Cottage before summoning a doctor to attend to the burns on their hands sustained in their rescue attempts.

Tony Bertram and John Hunt took another staff car to try to discover Hankey's fate. The fair-haired pilot had flown at some speed into the ground at Yapton, just north-west of Ford, possibly having lost control in the cursed cloud.[38] Debris was scattered over a wide area, but it included some parcels of *courier* remarkably intact. Amongst these were some of the plans of the Germans' V1 installations which SIS was most anxious to see. Also amongst the debris was a large package found to be containing diamonds – the police were warned off investigating this strange cargo.[39]

Bertram and Hunt's search ended at Arundel Hospital where both Hankey and Jacques Tayar, a Basque known as *Cazenave*, were in the morgue. Tayar was another BCRA agent, and had been awarded the Croix de Guerre in London in July. Bertram returned to Bignor Manor with Sandeyron and Rocher, greeting his wife with 'They're very tired.' The meal was eaten in glum silence; after relating the events to Barbara, he slumped asleep.

However Hankey's friend, Albert Kohan, was clutching at life. A son of a rich Russian businessman, he had studied at the University of Liège. Having fought in World War I, he was naturalized as a Frenchman in 1924. Arriving in London in April 1943, he joined the BCRA as agent *Albert Berthaud* – one of the oldest to undergo training. But he succumbed to his wounds before the fated night was done. It fell to Tony Bertram to identify Kohan's body by the small copy of Baudelaire about his person – before his departure he had given his copy to Kohan, and told him he 'could easily get another'. Kohan's face was unrecognizable. Tony's wife, Barbara, was most upset about the news about Stephen Hankey – she was close to his family, and had known him since he was a baby.[40]

Perhaps the omens had always been unfavourable for that night. During Hankey's training with 161 before becoming operational, he had rashly claimed, 'After my BAT [blind landing] course I shall be able to operate on the darkest night or wear dark glasses on a good night.'[41] And this, his 13th sortie, had been called Operation *Diable* ('Devil').

TANGMERE DEATH

THE AFTERMATH

Hooper phoned Hankey's mother-in-law, then, together with Mac, went to see Elizabeth, Stephen's wife – 'a harrowing business'. After breakfast on the 17th, Captain John Golding (another SIS conducting officer, alongside Bertram) drove Hooper and Monique le Bail (*Little Ben*), a female agent who had failed to make the outbound journey, up to London. Hooper had been away exactly a month, and was reunited with his wife before enduring days of intensive debriefing.

The burden of command weighed very heavily on Bob Hodges not just that night but in the ensuing days. The CO was to write many letters of tribute to grieving families. It was not just the two Lysander pilots and two agents who were killed. The weather had caused havoc amongst the Halifax crews in 161 on Operation *Wheelwright* as well: Flt Lt Gray and two of his crew died after he attempted a landing on the FIDO runway at Woodbridge. In another Halifax, skippered by F/O Harborrow, the navigator drowned after a ditching off Woodbridge. Two of the three Lancasters on secondment from No. 617 (Dambusters) Squadron were also lost that night. The sister squadron at Tempsford, 138, lost three Halifaxes that night too.[42] In all that night 3 Group lost 29 Lancasters of almost 500 which had been despatched to Berlin; they had either been abandoned by their crews after trying to land in the fog, or crashed whilst doing so. For Bomber Command, that night became known as 'Black Thursday'.[43] Christmas suddenly seemed not so merry.

Meanwhile, SIS had a problem – how to explain the deaths of two Frenchmen on British soil? The local constabulary registered the death of McBride, but did nothing to record Hankey's crash. All four deaths were registered separately, in order to avoid the association of Tayar and Kohan with any Lysander operations. A conducting officer came down to collect their bodies, and they were interred at the enormous Brookwood Military Cemetery in Surrey. Barbara Bertram accompanied Elizabeth Hankey who had expressed a desire to attend their funeral, which was conducted by Catholic and Anglican priests and a rabbi. Stephen was buried at Crowhurst, 'Greater Love Hath No Man Than This' on his tombstone. McBride was interred at Chichester. The accident investigation into Hankey's demise also sought to disguise the true facts (including that he was carrying passengers), noting that 'technical reasons prevented parachute use'.

The cost to 161 was felt deeply by its clients. 'The Moke' (Colonel Eric Mockler-Ferryman, SOE's Director of Operations, North-west Europe) wrote a touching letter to Fielden shortly afterwards: 'Thank you for the most delightful party you invited me to the other night. I do hope you will fully realise how much we deplore the very big losses you suffered the other night… From the reports I have had, the esteem and respect by the men in France for your pilots is beyond praise. In particular the two men who jumped safely over Brightlingsea are unable really to express themselves in their praise for the crew of the bomber that was lost…'[44]

As 1943 drew to a close, the war seemed to be swinging in favour of the Allies. Portal and Harris remained focused on conserving Bomber Command's assets for the preparation of the invasion. 161's Lysander operations had ended 1943 in very poor shape: morale had taken a knock, and the latest recruits were not yet operationally capable. The dismal sortie rates for 'A' and 'B' Flights in December were directly attributable to this personnel hiatus and their other traditional bugbear – poor weather over Western Europe.[45]

Hodges had to rebuild his team as soon as possible as 161's contribution would be crucial in the preparations for the invasion of Europe.

16

1944 and The Déricourt Dénouement

The events of December had deflated 'A' Flight, now denuded of operational pilots. So it was decided that:

> January operations should be reduced to a minimum. All operations to help brulé [compromised] agents or RAF crews were banned. It was not only that, from so small an establishment, we had lost two pilots who were experienced but also, by unhappy coincidence, our most experienced pilots had about the same time finished their tours of duty. The practice hitherto had been to break-in new pilots with the easier jobs. They now had to step straight up to the most difficult.[1]

In the event, the weather was so severe that no operations would have been possible in the January moon period anyway.

Across the Channel, the Resistance was having a tough time. One of the passengers due to board McBride's Lysander in the fated December mission was Emile Bollaert, whom de Gaulle had despatched to France to replace Jean Moulin. His control of the networks was troubled, and he needed extracting for his own safety. The fogs of January were against him.[2]

Meanwhile, an agitated Yeo-Thomas was bouncing around England, complaining that 161 and 138 had insufficient resources to provide a good service to SOE. His mental state was not helped by the inability of his friend Brosselette to secure a passage from France. He collared a friend, the retired Major-General Sir Ernest Swinton, who secured him a meeting with Churchill on 1 February, perhaps by telling the Prime Minister that Yeo-Thomas 'knew France better than any other Englishman'.[3] Given an audience of only a few minutes, the SOE stalwart outlined the impoverished state of resources of most Resistance groups, and that, to rectify this, 'it is necessary for a hundred aircraft to be serviceable and to do at least 250 sorties in each moon period'. 161 had started 1944 with ten Lysanders and five Hudsons. By the time of the invasion, this was only to increase to 13 and six.[4]

Verity's chum network had by now been exhausted as a source of recruits; in the January dark (non-moon) period, the raft of replacements had been procured via different channels. Flt Lts Bob Large DFC, Per Hysing-Dahl DFC, and F/Os Bell, McDonald, Bruce, Turner, Milstead and Alexander arrived at Tempsford. Not all of them would succeed.

Although not initially a Lysander pilot, Leonard Fitch Ratcliff was to become an important figure at 161, indeed in due course commanding it. Conceived, he later claimed, on Armistice Day 1918, and son of an Essex farmer, he grew up as an avid reader of World War I aviation stories, with Baron von Richthofen a particular hero. From the age of eight he boarded at Felsted, where he acquired a degree of resilience. Having left there at 17, he spent a couple of years in the agricultural industry.

By the beginning of 1939, with the threat of war mounting, Len's two elder brothers were working on the family farm, and therefore in reserved occupations. But Len had no such ties and applied to join the RAFVR in February at Southend Airport. After being given uniform he was then returned home to kick his heels, feeling something of a fraud. The outbreak of war caused him to reconsider his personal situation: Len had been dating a Scots woman, Bet, for some while, and they married at Middleton on Sea, on 26 September, spending the first night of married life at London's Cumberland Hotel.

On 1 February 1940, the Air Ministry finally realized it was wasting the talents of young Ratcliff and sent him a telegram recalling him urgently to Southend, where he was sent to the Initial Training Unit at Hastings for his militarization by former Army officers and NCOs. Always a keen sportsman in his youth (he went on to represent the RAF at cricket and rugby), at Hastings he took instruction early each morning from the world boxing champion contender Eddy Phillips, who was one of the unit's physical training instructors. His advice to Len was 'Never have sex more than three times a day, and never drink more than eight pints of beer a day.' Later, in his dotage, Len said, 'I've tried to stick to that.'[5] In May, he progressed to his flying training (at 4 EFTS at Brough in East Yorkshire) where, unusually, he actually enjoyed the ground school tuition element. He was lucky in his choice of flying instructor; P/O Jackson treated him to aerobatics on his first ever flight. Len went solo in a Tiger Moth after just five and a half hours, and finished the course with an 'Above Average' rating.

Like many an RAF trainee in 1940 he desperately wanted to become a fighter pilot, but was given multi-engine training on the Anson at 10 Service Flying Training School (SFTS) at Ternhill. By the end of that course, he gained his wings and the rank of flight sergeant, and a prescient instructor told him, 'I have studied your talents. You have organisational skills and could lead a crew. I'm going to recommend you be commissioned.' Len was stunned: 'I was considered not to be a daredevil fighter ace.'[6]

A posting to No. 2 Advanced Navigation School honed skills which would later be very useful at 161. Whilst at the Upper Heyford OTU for the twin-engined Hampden bomber, he encountered Robin Hooper for the first time. On one trip they were paired up with an instruction to swap pilot roles mid-flight. This caused some difficulty as Ratcliff was short of stature and sometimes needed blocks on the rudder pedals to compensate – the aquiline Hooper was tall. Hooper later commented that 'We achieved our objective [of swapping seats] with the loss of only 5,000 feet.'[7]

Len carried out 29 operations with No. 49 Squadron, mainly across northern Germany, where 'losses were pretty awful', after which he was promoted to flight lieutenant, and sent back, complete with DFC, to 24 OTU at Honeybourne as an instructor. This unit was commanded by one Bob Hodges. This was the time that 161's Halifax crews were suffering heavy attrition, and after Hodges was appointed squadron commander, Len was promoted to command the OTU in Hodges' stead, soon being awarded the AFC 'for services to training'. But he hankered after operational flying. Having heard that Hodges had lost two of his Halifax flight commanders in a matter of days, he phoned him up at Tempsford – 'Bob, I'm terribly sorry you've had a lot of bad luck, but I'm ready to come back on ops and I'd very much like to work with you again.' Music to Hodges' ears: 'That's a jolly good idea. I would love that.'[8]

Two days later, Midsummer's Day in 1943, he was warmly welcomed to the Halifax flight, and was soon given Philippe Livry as his navigator, who was later described as 'an extremely patriotic officer – a great asset in every way'.[9] His wife and one-year-old son joined him in a house near

Tempsford. Len's training on the Halifax was cursory, and he flew his first op on 12 July. His Halifax lost an engine on the outbound journey; since the agents on board told him their mission was urgent, Ratcliff decided to persevere but then carry on to Algiers rather than limp back across France. The French air traffic controllers at Algiers never answered his Mayday call 'because we were English'! After repairs he routed back to the UK via Gibraltar where the bomb bay was loaded with Dry Sack sherry at 4s/6d a bottle, some exotic fruits – and a large bunch of garlic for Mouse Fielden, still at Tempsford as station commander.[10] He shared a room at Hassells Hall with Hugh Verity, who was of course only there for half the time, being at Tangmere during moon periods.

With an acknowledgement from the Air Ministry that demands on it were increasing in the build-up to the invasion, Hodges had succeeded in building up the complement of 161 to ten Halifaxes, a trio of Hudsons and six Lysanders. This followed a 'hell of a row' between Gubbins ('Churchill's blue-eyed boy') and Bomber Harris; clearly the former won the argument. The extra three Lysanders had been purloined from the Target Towing Flights. VCAS was most keen that this increase in resource be communicated to Emmanuel D'Astier at the BCRA, as de Gaulle's whining was trying the patience of the RAF chiefs.[11]

Air Marshal Sir Douglas Morris noted that 'the most striking characteristic of the Norge [Norwegian] pilots was their intense desire to engage the enemy. The Norges were, possibly, the easiest of the Allies to handle. Their sense of humour – or sense of the ridiculous – and their reaction to any form of pomposity, was easily understood and accepted.'[12] Like most Scandinavians, their English was good, and their more outdoors upbringing made Norwegians naturally self-reliant.

Every battlefield tale needs a Viking warrior. For 161, the moon-faced Per Hysing-Dahl was it: he had escaped from Norway in 1941 from Bergen with two school friends. Like most Norwegians he was filled with a visceral need to rid his homeland of the Nazis. With the help of locals in islands off the Norwegian coast a boat was procured for their trip across the North Sea. Carrying a total of 28 escapers, M/B Soløy left Værlandet on 2 August. After 36 hours at sea the boat arrived at Unst in the Shetlands, coincidentally on the birthday of King Haakon.[13]

1944 AND THE DÉRICOURT DÉNOUEMENT

Per was commissioned into the RAF and trained on Oxfords at 34 SFTS, Medicine Hat, in Canada. He progressed onto the Anson twin-engined trainer at 34 General Reconnaissance School at Charlottetown. The Norwegian had some time on single-engined Stinsons and Fairchilds, which had more relevance for his ultimate Lysander flying career. Once back in the UK he was despatched to 11 Advanced Flying Unit at Shawbury, for flying on Oxfords, thence to 24 OTU Honeybourne, for conversion to the Whitley bomber where he was taught by Len Ratcliff and graded 'Above Average'. Once at Tempsford, Len had judged that 161 pilots (apart from requiring great flying skills) needed to be 'entrepreneurs that could think and act for themselves'.[14] Hysing-Dahl fitted that mould and was recruited. Per had arrived at Tempsford in July 1943 to join 161 Squadron's 'B' Flight on the Halifax. For his crew, he managed to find two other Norwegians, one of whom, Edvard Rieber-Mohn, had come over in the boat to the Shetlands with him. He completed a full tour of 30 operations parachuting agents and supplies into Western Europe before Hodges shuffled him to Lysanders; he had his first flight on type on 19 January 1944.[15] On the 30th, a station parade was held for the AOC's visit to Tempsford, who presented the Norwegian with his DFC. His baptism was in the February moon period when he acted as co-pilot to Scragg on a Hudson mission.

When Douglas Stuartson Bell arrived at Tempsford, he was a callow flying officer of only 20 – in danger of making the now war-worn Vaughan-Fowler look like an old man. He had become an electrical engineer for the Post Office on leaving school, but enlisted in the RAF soon after the declaration of war. Known variously in the Air Force as Dougie, or the inevitable 'Dinger', he was streamed onto bombers, and 161 appears to be his first operational tour. 'Tall, fair and very good-looking',[16] he was despatched to the Halifax flight and started operations very quickly.

As a Spitfire pilot in No. 92 Squadron, P/O Tony Bruce was injured in combat and crashed in October 1941. By April 1943, he was a squadron leader. A 'tall, lanky, horsey type, who stood at the bar with one hand in his pocket, the other holding a tankard of beer – the hunting squire at The Bruce Arms, amidst his lackeys'.[17] In quieter moments, he liked to play cards.

A former policeman, George Turner arrived in the middle of February from 60 OTU, a Mosquito intruder training unit. His *pièce de résistance* was to hold a clenched fist to his lips and play a range of light opera and classical renditions, including Purcell's *Trumpet Voluntary*.[18]

For the January moon period all the 'A' Flight pilots crowded into three Lysanders and flew down to Tangmere. The foul weather meant they were kicking their heels, and even training for the new boys was severely restricted. The parents of Whitaker's WAAF girlfriend hosted the bored pilots for tea on a couple of occasions at nearby Bosham. But more typically, given their evenings were unoccupied with operations, the pilots decamped to the Unicorn and the Dolphin in Chichester.[19]

Now off the squadron, Hooper was appointed acting squadron leader at the end of 1943, and was awarded a DSO. A Hudson operation (*Bludgeon*) was scheduled for 5 January – feathers were more than ruffled when eight passengers turned up at Tangmere with 35 suitcases, some of which were extremely heavy. The flight was cancelled and an apoplectic Fielden fired off a salvo to HQ Bomber Command.[20]

Meanwhile, on 7 January, Tony Bertram tried to boost the morale and cohesiveness of 'A' Flight by hosting a dinner at Bignor for Hooper, Dinger Bell, Rickie Milson and Mac. Ten days later, he gave another dinner for Hooper, Bell, Milson and new boys Whitaker and McDonald.[21] Operations resumed on 4 February when new boys Anderson and Whitaker mounted a double (*Roumanie*) for SIS – one of the outbound passengers was Marcel Sandeyron, recovered in body, if not in mind, from the trauma of the McBride crash that had brought him to England.

Len Ratcliff was now placed in charge of the expanding Hudson flight. However, he should never have been allowed to go on operations, since when he had been at AI2(c) he had been inculcated in the Ultra secret – 'I broke a rule.'[22] Flt Lt (Acting Sqn Ldr) Guy de Grave Sells arrived from 3 Lancaster Finishing School at RAF Feltwell to take charge of the Lysander Flight. The ORB noted that the many new arrivals (including eight Coastal Command Hudson crews) needed much training on type and role, and there were insufficient aircraft available for this. Two of the Hudson pilots (Flt Lt Craig and F/O Battles) were quickly found unsuitable and sent on their way. Another Hudson crew (including an air cadet along for the ride) disappeared in April in the most bizarre circumstances. Sgt Vear departed at lunchtime on the 19th for a cross-country training flight around England and Wales. Successive mis-setting of the directional gyro, flying north-east instead of north-west, combined with basic navigation mistakes and radio failure, left them lost. The water underneath them, which they thought to be the Irish Sea, turned out to be the Baltic. They were intercepted by Swedish J 22 fighters and forced to land at Gothenburg – not that their fuel state would have allowed much else. Prior to landing they decided to burn all maps and the aircraft documents, but the smoke blew forward into the eyes of the hapless pilot! After six months' internment, they were flown back to the UK.[23]

Scotsman John Affleck had come to 161 by the now well-worn route of the OTU at Honeybourne, but was destined to remain a multi-engine pilot at 161, in September 1943 gaining a DFC. For the February moon period there was a big backlog of work. On 4 February, now promoted to acting flight lieutenant and with a freshly minted DSO, he was detailed to do a Hudson pick-up (the revived *Bludgeon*) from a field at Chalon-sur-Saône, but the mission failed because the reception team was waiting in a different field. An investigation by AI2(c), initiated by Verity who was now working there, discovered that the operator had been sent details of a different operation.

Four nights later, Affleck tried *Bludgeon* again and departed Tempsford at 2115hrs. He located the field west of Bletterans without difficulty and landed at 2330hrs with seven passengers from RF Section and the BCRA, including Lt Col Pierre Fourcaud, and 54 million francs on board. He found the landing surface extremely wet and skidded for 'well over 100 yards'. Taxiing back to the take-off point, the Hudson came to an abrupt halt in some mud. Affleck cut the engines, dismounted, and the reception team was summoned to manhandle the aircraft back. The Hudson was sinking further into the mud with every passing minute.

Communication was severely hampered by the fact that none of the Hudson's crew spoke French, the work also impeded by the disorganization of the operator Paul Rivière (*Galvani*) and his team. As was now the pattern on such occasions, many villagers arrived on the scene, having been alerted by the commotion. A team of horses and oxen was prepared, but a German aircraft flying over caused some moments of panic. Affleck had sensibly given himself a deadline of 0300hrs for take-off – if he had not managed to depart by then the Hudson would be torched, and he and his crew members would place themselves for evasion in the hands of Rivière.

Channels were dug under the mainwheels, and the Hudson was liberated from the quagmire, but on his attempt at take-off Affleck could not accelerate quickly enough. Whilst taxiing back for another go, it sank into the mud again. In these circumstances the returning passenger load was cut to the minimum to comprise just Sgt John Brough, and Raymond Aubrac, a Jewish French politician and Resistance member, with his very pregnant wife Lucie and Jean-Pierre, their three-year-old son. Days earlier, she had liberated her husband from a Gestapo van at gunpoint; the family had been trying to escape France since December.[24]

Brough was a Halifax gunner from the other Tempsford squadron, 138, whose machine had crashed in November, and of which he was the sole survivor. 161 felt duty bound to retrieve him. The excitement was not over. As Affleck later reported:

> Having taxied the aircraft into a suitable position for take-off, [I] received the OK from Flt Lt Corner who was in charge of the loading. As the flare path had not been lit, I told him to go back and inform the ground party. On opening the door, he shouted to the men standing near the aircraft to put on the lights, but on seeing the door open, a number of men rushed up to the aircraft and endeavoured to throw a number of suitcases inside. Corner tried to stop this action and was more or less successful. He several times made a request for the lights and each time his request was met with a negative answer and shouts of 'The Mail', 'The Luggage' etc., also a Frenchman who said he was 'No. 1 priority' attempted to force his way into the aircraft, but was ejected by Corner and the Navigator, Flt Lt Richards, who had come to his assistance.[25]

Having been on the ground for more than two hours, and moved by the plight of the Aubracs, Affleck made a final attempt at 0205hrs; as he neared the far boundary, his machine hit a bump and lurched into the air at 50 knots – the lowest possible air speed. He clawed his way up to a sensible altitude but the Hudson was very sluggish. Damp, muddy and exhausted, Affleck had forgotten to raise the flaps after take-off.

As they neared the British coast, Richards could not raise anyone on the radio – the aerials had been ripped off during the attempts to shift the Hudson from the mud. So there was a distinct chance that they would be greeted by unfriendly but British anti-aircraft fire. In the event, they managed to land at Tempsford at 0640hrs – the mud-laden Hudson had been flying like a cart horse that night. No doubt hastened by the drama of the preceding 24 hours, Mme Aubrac gave birth to her second child in London later that same day; she was christened Catherine Mitraillette

('Submachine Gun')! Affleck recommended that all Hudsons on pick-up duties henceforth carry wooden planks.

Hodges had been deeply unimpressed with Rivière's organization at the field; the CO later noted that the operation 'was successful, but only due to the skill and determination of the pilot'; he recommended Affleck for a DSO, and promoted him to acting flight lieutenant.[26] The fallout was substantial: DDI 2 and 161 decided to ban Rivière from acting as an operator. His defence was that 'in his opinion he had undertaken no greater risks on that particular night than in the previous landing operations, he had been obliged to wait for this operation for four months when landing conditions were really excellent... he was being reproached for something which never should have occurred.'[27] AI2(c) were unimpressed: 'In banning MARQUIS [one of Rivière's codenames] we are doing more than deny ourselves the services of a brave and skilful organiser with an excellent record. We are depriving ourselves at a very vital time of the great personal influence of this man, whose name inspires the highest confidence among the large cross-section of the French Resistance.' The undated and unsigned memo's style smacks of Verity, who had known Rivière for some time, but W/Cdr Laszlo was of the same opinion.[28] Strong views flowed back and forth; it was decided that at the very least Rivière should be brought back for some more training, but this was impractical in the short-term as all the Saône valley fields were now too waterlogged for use. Rivière was himself keen to come to London to exculpate himself. He was told to prepare a landing ground – for Lysanders and anywhere but the Saône valley![29]

More Hudsons were delivered to 161, and some were now modified to allow the dropping of agents by parachute; John Scragg carried out the first such operation on 10 February. He had flown as a sergeant pilot since 1941, had some adventures in North Africa, been commissioned in August 1943, and was awarded the DFC in January 1944. He went on to fly only three Hudson sorties, all of which were parachute operations.

The volume of *courier* was mounting as more intelligence was coming through in advance of the invasion. So after some months of deliberation, a handful of Lysanders were adapted at White Waltham to carry out so-called mail pick-ups (MPUs). An arrester hook on a pole was fitted at the tail, connected via cable to a winch in the rear cockpit. The pilot flew at about 12 feet over the chosen field where the Resistance operator's team had strung a rope between two vertical poles; this was collected by the arrestor hook and a sergeant in the back of the Lysander operated the winch to bring the sack of mail on board. The advantage was that, without a touchdown, the condition of the field was immaterial – but a clear approach and departure lane was still needed.

That spring, SOE's Belgian section received an unusual request for an extraction. Prince Charles, Count of Flanders (and the brother of King Leopold III) was rather loosely confined by the Germans at a private estate in the Ardennes, and was in touch from time to time with members of his government. He decided he would rather spend the rest of the war in London, and it was thought that springing him from the Château de Halloy would be fairly easy. Although towards the limit of its range, a Lysander could land in the grounds and whisk him to Tangmere. Some planning for this operation took place, but in the event Charles was afflicted from some arthritis (despite being only 40) which he thought would make a Lysander ride too uncomfortable.[30]

A North London boy, Ronald Geoffrey Large (always known as 'Bob') was not a glass half full man – his was at least three-quarters full; he was 'irrepressibly ebullient' in the opinion of Anderson and most who encountered him. He had joined the RAF in July 1940 aged 18, and was fortunate to have his first posting after training to fly Spitfires for 616 Squadron. Even better, this was from the lovely airfield of Westhampnett (just up the road from Tangmere), where he was awarded the DFC for outstanding bravery in going to the aid of a downed colleague (Sgt Mike Cooper) in the Channel, despite being out of ammunition.

With 616 being part of the infamous Bader Wing, when the legless ace was shot down, Large was involved in the search for the missing Bader, and in the sortie to parachute a spare leg to him when in German captivity in Saint-Omer's hospital. In July 1942, with the squadron now flying from West Malling, Large was himself shot down over the Channel, but was rescued by an RAF launch, a fellow squadron member flying over him to keep a hostile Fw 190 at bay.

By the time his tour with 616 had come to an end, Large had flown 188 missions, and was posted to act as personal staff officer to AOC 9 Group. This was not to his liking at all, and he soon pleaded with AVM Hollinghurst to be allowed to return to operations. The Air Vice-Marshal was to the point: 'Bob, you are not only the worst PA I have

1944 AND THE DÉRICOURT DÉNOUEMENT

ever had; you are the worst I've ever heard of.'[31] In his keenness to rid himself of Large, Hollinghurst offered him 'any fighter squadron you want'. But this was not good enough for Large, who 'was very intrigued by this cloak and dagger business'. He was attracted by the concept of landing at night to bring people out – it was 'like thumbing your nose at the Germans'. So he contacted a chum at Tempsford and secured an invitation to join 161 despite the fact he only had 14 hours' experience of flying at night. On arrival at 161 at the end of February, he remained proud of his fighter heritage – 'We had the highest birth rate in Fighter Command'![32] He made a strong impression on the men of 161; Verity, who in his current role was still visiting Tangmere, described him as 'a fantastic character. Not the most disciplined man (in a military sense) that I have met, but an extremely good fellow, with unusual ability as a pilot.'[33]

After the end of February's moon period, the Lysander pilots and ground crew retreated as usual to Tempsford. Meanwhile their former CO, Pick Pickard, had jostled to lead a vital mission for his 140 Wing of Mosquitos. Air Vice-Marshal Basil Embry, his boss as OC 2 Group, had wanted to lead it, but had been forbidden to do so as he was privy to Ultra communications and had too much knowledge of D-Day preparations. The weather was foul on the chosen day of 18 February, but the operation – to break down the walls of Amiens prison to allow many Resistance fighters to escape – was time critical as many were due for imminent execution. With Broadley at his side, Pickard, as was his way, led from the front. After dropping his bombs, he carried on circling the town amidst snow flurries under the very low cloud base to check his colleagues' fall of bombs. Whilst doing so he was picked off by an Fw 190. The men of 161, like all RAF squadrons, were somewhat inured to the loss of comrades, but when the news of the death of the seemingly invincible Pickard reached Tempsford, the mood was very sombre.

Déricourt's position as a double agent in France had been weakened by the move of his guardian angel and friend Bömelburg, who had been posted at the end of October to Vichy, where his new role was to liaise with Pétain. Déricourt henceforth would have to deal directly with Kieffer, who held the French pilot in low esteem.[34]

Back at Baker Street, moves had been continuing to bring Déricourt back to England – both for interrogation, and to prevent his further damaging Resistance networks.[35] Henri Frager's denunciations of him had become so strident that even Buckmaster, hitherto his arch-defendant, was forced to concede that removing him from the field of play was the sensible option.

So the same night as Anderson and Whitaker's double (4 February), a crucial Hudson operation, quaintly termed *Knacker*, was mounted to the favourite field just north-east of Angers to bring Déricourt back to England. Gerry Morel, the operations officer of F Section, had volunteered to go in Len Ratcliff's Hudson, to secure the prey. Déricourt was the operator for this flight, but was of course unaware of its real purpose. Morel, now armed with a pistol, had dressed up in RAF uniform to add authority to his mission, but as he jumped down from the Hudson's rear door, his forage cap blew off in the slipstream. His undignified search for it in the moonlight took the impetus from his order to Déricourt to join the eight returning passengers on board. When Déricourt enquired as to the reason for this sudden order, Morel explained it was so that Buckmaster could tell him he had been awarded a DSO.[36]

Déricourt gave the plausible excuse that he needed a few days to inform his wife and settle his affairs; moreover he needed to dispose of the ten bicycles he had secreted around the landing site in the expectation of needing to transport ten inbound agents. Ratcliff stewed in the Hudson's cockpit as the discussion became more fraught – punches may have been thrown. After a few minutes, Déricourt gave his word he would return if another aircraft was sent in a week or so. Morel holstered his pistol. Yet that night, for it was now the 5th, the Frenchman returned to Paris to dine with Kieffer, Bömelburg and Josef Goetz, who headed Kieffer's wireless sub-section (and who later described the evening as 'cordial'), to explain his recall to England. An envelope containing two million francs was handed over to the traitor.[37]

There was an illustrious group for the return flight with Morel and Ratcliff: Robert Benoist, Phillippe Liewer and the badly wounded Bob Maloubier who had been shot in the lung, liver and intestines when fleeing from the Germans. (It was only falling into a freezing stream which had stemmed his blood loss.) The trio had assembled at Angers train station. Also on board was Col. Jean Valette d'Osia, who had been in charge of the Armée Secrète in Haute-Savoie, but had become too well known for his own safety, and was coming to London to work for de Gaulle.[38]

1944 AND THE DÉRICOURT DÉNOUEMENT

Three nights later, on 8 February, on *Grower* Leslie Whitaker took out two SOE agents to a field east of Tours, where Déricourt dutifully embarked in his Lysander, together with his wife wrapped in an expensive fur coat, to return to Tangmere. There was no great reception at the Sussex airfield – the couple were whisked to London by breakfast time. She was installed in a room at the Savoy, whilst Henri was taken to be interviewed by Buckmaster and Verity at F Section's flat at Orchard Court. As Verity later recalled:

> We were all sitting around in comfortable armchairs and Buckmaster told him that he'd had reports that he was working with the Germans in Paris. Déricourt was very dead pan and said 'Well of course I have to co-operate with the Germans and give them some black market oranges from Spain and be friendly towards them so that I can get on with my work for you'. He denied giving them any information of value but of course that proved to be untrue.[39]

Verity's conflicted state of mind is revealed by the fact that he and Audrey arranged a 'small party' at the Savoy for dinner and dancing for the Déricourts, and a young Belgian agent who had been one of his passengers. The Frenchman arrived in a new RAF uniform complete with a DSO medal ribbon (to which he was not entitled, as the award was rescinded before it was made). Audrey found him 'dour, silent and boot-faced' – perhaps understandable after being challenged for the first time.[40]

Verity was 'really pretty confident that Déricourt was one of our best men in France for us and laying on our landings'. As they had become good friends 'it was a very serious shock when I discovered that he had been working fairly closely with the German counter-espionage people in Paris and had given away a lot of our secrets, but certainly during the time that I was doing landings on his fields, I had every confidence in him.'[41] As the agent Bob Maloubier later noted, 'He could seduce men and women with his character.'[42]

SOE made disastrous errors in trying to install a tap on the telephone in the Déricourts' room at the Savoy, which only served to put the agent on his guard. MI5 was ostensibly in charge of the investigation, and a draft unsigned letter dated 16 February 1944 to Major Guy Liddell of that organization exists, probably penned by Buckmaster; in it, the author continues to claim Déricourt's innocence of Frager's accusations, believes 'Colonel Heinrich' (in reality Bleicher) 'either does not exist at all, or is a perfectly [unreadable] agent provocateur'. He bizarrely concludes by recommending that Major Nicholas Bodington, Frager and Déricourt be interviewed together to iron out inconsistencies.[43]

In February, SOE would still 'strongly oppose detention of GILBERT [Déricourt] in any circumstances'.[44] Various locations for his exile were discussed; in the end, Stratford-upon-Avon was chosen. One can only imagine Mme Déricourt's *froideur* at being removed from her favourite shopping and dining haunts. Within a fortnight he was back in London telling F Section he wanted to return to London permanently – and resign his RAF commission. By 20 June, he was demanding to be allowed to immigrate to Dakar – this was denied. Decisions were taken at the highest level – Archie Boyle (SOE's Director of Intelligence and Security) and the owlish Harry Sporborg, Gubbins' deputy. Buckmaster continued to defend Déricourt's corner.

For whom was Déricourt really working? Douglas Boyd asserted, 'What Bömelburg did not know was that his double agent was in fact a triple agent acting under instructions from Col. Bevan [a senior officer in deception operations organized from London] that overrode his duties for Section F. This was the real dirt of Operation *Cockade*' (the deception operation in late 1943 regarding the Allied invasion of Sicily).[45] Bunny Rymills also concluded that Déricourt was in fact a triple agent who had been in the employ of SIS to enable their keeping an eye on SOE's activities in France.[46]

In any event, by spring 1944 when events were moving rapidly in preparation for the Allied invasion, Déricourt was now safely out of the way in England, albeit that current and former members of 161 had had their confidence shaken by the episode. Verity acknowledged, 'I was completely conned by him.'[47]

The day after Leslie Whitaker had brought back the traitorous couple, he and his chum Murray Anderson flew back to RAF Benson to have lunch with their former colleagues. Once back at Tempsford for the non-moon period they dropped back into the routine of agent training, which now took place not just at Somersham but also at the relief landing ground at Caxton Gibbet, hard by the Romans' Ermine Street.

F/O John Walter McDonald was a 26-year-old from Queensland. Having enlisted in Brisbane, he had married his sweetheart Daphne. Arriving at Tempsford at the end of January 1944 from Bomber Command's Heavy Conversion Unit at RAF Topcliffe, he hurried onto Lysanders. The Aussie carried out *Canari* with two flights – he had to return from his first after radio failure, but the nights were long, so he had a second attempt, not finding a reception at his destination. Six days later and only a couple of nights after Déricourt had been retrieved, he was sent out on *Serbie*, a double with Dinger Bell, to a popular field south-east of Bourges. Although he had, somewhat oddly, acted as second pilot for Bob Hodges during a Hudson operation the previous October, he had by now only completed two Lysander operations. For this double, each pilot took out two SIS agents, and they met at the agreed rendezvous at Vierzon on time at 2315hrs. Bell arrived at the field first but circled for three minutes or so to await McDonald's arrival as it had been agreed he would be the first to land. Recognition signals were exchanged and the flarepath torches illuminated.

McDonald turned on V9822's landing light and made an approach, but overshot for another attempt. He went round again from his second circuit. Third time round he did not illuminate his landing light, 'but appeared to touch down, beside or past lights B & C, then ran on down the field very quickly until he tipped over and burst into flames. During the time in which he was trying to land he made no attempt to tell me if anything was wrong', noted Bell. 'The flare path was very bright and well laid, and there was ample room.'[48]

The operator, Felix Svagrovsky (*Gabriel*), considered that McDonald came in 'much too fast on all three approaches and that on the last it came in one wing low'. Hooper, in charge of 'A' Flight at this time, could only think that either there was a defect in McDonald's air speed indicator, or he had 'omitted to return his mixture control to "normal", and was therefore unable to throttle right back.'[49] Hodges concurred. The fact that the Lysander's unusual low-speed handling characteristics might have conspired with McDonald's very few hours on the type, was not considered.

A distressed Svagrovsky sent a signal to SIS in which he said the accident occurred at the fourth attempt; McDonald 'touched down 100 metres beyond Light B at an angle of 25 degrees, bounced 10 metres, hit the ground again and caught fire. The landing ground was 780 metres long and absolutely free of obstacles.' A passenger waiting to depart later sent a signal confirming these observations.[50]

McDonald died immediately, but of his three agents, radio operator Jean Lacroix (*Jean Lestanges*) extricated himself from the wreckage with bad burns on both arms and was treated in Bourges Hospital. Jean Aimon, McDonald's other passenger, was less badly injured.[51]

A horrified Dinger Bell returned to Tangmere without landing in France. He later talked through the incident with his new colleague Murray Anderson, telling how he had seen the Lysander 'belch a huge plume of flame from its exhaust'. (A bumpy landing could easily cause a pool of fuel in the carburettor.) 'Suddenly the whole engine nacelle burst into flames, and the wind blew the fire along the fuselage.' Now it was the force of Bob Hodges' character that kept up the morale of the squadron through these difficult weeks. 'He was the connecting link with the great Lysander pilots of the past. He was utterly unflappable.'[52]

The middle of February saw another much-needed new arrival for 'A' Flight – Bill Taylor from 51 OTU. He did not make an impression. The March moon period started with Anderson taking out William Jean Savy, a Paris barrister, and his wireless operator, Eileen Nearne known as *Didi*, for F Section's WIZARD *réseau* just outside Paris.[53] Anderson brought back Georges de Lovinfosse (a liaison officer with the Belgian Resistance), and the one-legged Maurice Durieux (who had lost a limb in a parachuting accident). The same night, 2 March, Dinger Bell took the racing driver Robert Benoist and his radio operator, Denise Bloch, to a field south-east of Chartres to set up a new circuit. They were soon on a train to Paris.[54]

The following night Whitaker and Anderson carried out an uneventful double (*Fantome*), which brought back, amongst others, Claude Bouchinet-Sereulles, who had worked under Moulin in the CNR, but had become a troublesome leader in Paris. Other passengers recalled by SIS for sanctuary in Britain included Svagrovsky and Jean-Louis Chancel (*Chavagnac*) whose DAVIS network in Nice had been betrayed.[55]

Bell was in action again in a double with Hysing-Dahl, for the Norwegian's first Lysander operation. Dinger embarked Count Elie de Dampierre (*Coco*), a 26-year-old small, fair aristocrat who had only come back from France (by boat) in January, and Robert Lorilleux, for SIS's ALLIANCE network, on Operation *Framboise*. He took off from Tangmere at 2140hrs, but soon after crossing the French coast his Mercury engine began to fail. He carried out all the emergency checks, which failed to restore the engine to life. The propeller continued to turn wistfully, without generating any power. Bell turned round and headed for England again, crossing the coast at Hermanville. 'I got to about six miles out to sea, but as I could not maintain height, I turned back and re-crossed the coast at about the same point I had left. I flew in at about six hundred feet, and found a stretch of flat treeless ground, where I made a crash landing.'[56] He had brought back the stick, and let the Lysander descend at as slow a forward speed as possible to flop into the field, just east of Plumetot, and barely inland from the heavily militarized coastal zone, and indeed only two miles from Sword Beach where the British were to land two months later.

A forced landing at night is not for the faint hearted, but Bell carried it off magnificently. The Lysander wings and tail had fallen off, but Bell only suffered a jarred backside and scratches on his face and leg, Lorilleux suffered heavy bruising, whilst de Dampierre was entirely unharmed. They were exceptionally lucky that the Lysander did not catch fire, and that their arrival in France had somehow gone unnoticed.[57] The trio walked two miles to the farm of Mme Lechavalier, who gave Bell some first aid, and the trio set off on foot for Caen, some seven miles south.

It was the early hours of the morning (and therefore well after the curfew) when they shambled into a hotel in the Normandy city to ask for two double rooms. It was difficult to look less like a Frenchman than Dinger at that hour – tall and wearing his RAF greatcoat (without a belt), under which was his RAF battledress and a dark blue polo sweater. The hotel was heaving with Wehrmacht so, speaking no French, Dinger was rightly petrified. But the following day the group made it to Paris by train, and a radio message was sent assuring London that they were safe. Whilst Hysing-Dahl had carried out his part of the mission without issue, Tangmere and Tempsford had assumed that Bell and his passengers were dead.

SIS had taken a monopoly on 161's Lysander operations for the March moon period, and clearly the highest priority now was to retrieve Bell and his two erstwhile passengers, if they were still alive. It would be unthinkable to allow him to fall into the hands of Bleicher, Bömelburg or Klaus Barbie (head of the Gestapo in Lyon). A double on 3 March (*Fantome*) brought back the ailing Jean Lacroix, burned in McDonald's fatal crash. On arrival back at Tangmere, he was transferred to McIndoe's Burns Unit at East Grinstead. Before he was manhandled into the ambulance, he gave Barbara Bertram a small envelope; it contained the French stamps her young son Robert had requested.

Anderson and Whitaker did another double on the 6th, bringing back six agents of the Deuxième Bureau. But the critical mission in this moon period was *Lautrec* on the 15th to retrieve F/O Bell and his colleagues. After they had been hidden in Paris for eight days, a female agent escorted them to Angers by train, as a field towards Tours had been selected. The group underwent security checks by German police at the Paris station, on the train, and again at Angers railway station. They survived each, and loitered for two days in the vicinity of the chosen field near Pont Joubert.

The weather for *Lautrec* was not propitious – Hysing-Dahl turned back from another mission that dark night, encountering light flak, then heavy cloud and thick haze. Anderson felt the pressure to collect his colleague: he turned onto his track for Angers over the French coast in the same mucky rain clouds, not having seen the ground since leaving Tangmere two hours earlier. Forty miles from the Loire 'suddenly I broke out into clear sky, filled with stars, and to the south peeped the yellow rim of the rising moon.'[58] He descended to 2,000 feet and located a town which indicated he was ten miles off track, and then noticed a wiggle of low-lying mist that could only indicate the winding Loire valley. A few minutes later he saw a weak light flashing at him through the mist, to which he responded, and the landing torches were illuminated. Anderson did a low-level circuit and observed that his slipstream blew away the film of miscible mist over the landing field, so put down on his second circuit. He landed on a 'good, firm surface' to be greeted by a relieved Dinger.

His fellow passengers for the return home included Micheline Grimprel (the secretary of the intelligence section of ALLIANCE) and Jean Sainteny, who carried in his mailbag one of the most important documents ever transported back to England by 161. Sainteny, who owned a farm near what was soon to become Omaha Beach, was head of ALLIANCE's Normandy network, specializing in the collection of intelligence about German docks and coastal defences. He had been tasked by SIS the previous autumn to start collecting what plans he could. His trusty chief for the Caen sub-sector, the extrovert and extravagant Robert Douin, got to work. Douin, the director of an art school, now had his life's masterwork to complete, and cycled from Dives in the east to the Cotentin in the west making sketches of what he saw. By early March, the 55-foot-long map was completed; he soon passed it to Sainteny who realized it must be transported to London as soon as possible, and hence he piggy-backed on Bell's rescue mission. Anderson brought Bell back to Tangmere at 0500hrs, and the party started: Bell told his survival tale until the sun came over the horizon. He was not to carry out any more missions for 161, but acted as a conducting officer shepherding agents down from London, not leaving the squadron until the end of April.

1944 AND THE DÉRICOURT DÉNOUEMENT

Marie-Madeleine Fourcade, still in the UK, was delighted with Sainteny's cargo, as were her chiefs at SIS – it was probably the single most important source of intelligence about German defences on and behind the landing beaches.[59]

The secrecy of 161's operations was now open to question. On 9 February, the *Daily Telegraph* ran a piece 'Allied Planes Secret Landings in France', in which the Special Correspondent in Berne stated:

> The Germans are now reported to have ordered any stretch of land which might serve Allied planes as a landing field in the 'suspected areas' to be ditched or covered with debris. Allied planes landing on French soil at night are said to be carrying not only French resistance chiefs and foreign agents to and from France, but to be laden with arms and materials for French Partisans. The parachuting of material for beleaguered French patriots is reported to have been discarded as too risky and wasteful.

Yet in March, *Aeroplane*, one of Britain's two aviation magazines of record, declared that 'Lysanders have now been taken off operational work'.[60]

The Hudson flight ended March in some gloom after F/O Robert Baughan and all his crew perished on a training flight on the 28th.

Preparations for D-Day were now reaching a high pitch across the UK, which meant that Tangmere was given a new role as a base for ground attack aircraft. So towards the end of March it was decided to relocate Lysander operations back to Tempsford. The curtains had been drawn on raucous nights at the Cottage.

17

The Boxer Era

Bob Hodges had led 161 with aplomb, and earned the affection of all who served under him. His tour ended on 10 March, and he was replaced by W/Cdr Alan Boxer.

Born in Hastings, New Zealand, in 1916, Alan Hunter Cachemaille Boxer's father died when he was only nine. This meant young Boxer had to take on a series of jobs to sustain the family's finances, and left Nelson College in 1935. Somehow he managed privately to take some flying lessons.

With war clouds gathering he travelled to England and enlisted in the RAF in January 1939. Already having 175 flying hours before starting initial flying training, on graduation he was soon posted to become a flying instructor. His first operational tour was on the Whitley before moving to 161 to fly Stirlings and Halifaxes. He moved to 138 as a flight commander and was awarded the DFC. His immediate posting prior to taking command of 161 was at the Air Ministry in AI2(c), taking over from Guy Lockhart; in Verity's view, he had made the department 'immensely efficient and smooth running'.[1]

By now 28, square-jawed, blue-eyed, handsome, smartly dressed and serious, Boxer was taller than his predecessor. The new boys at 161 had not known the delights of being commanded by Hodges. But for those who had, such as Murray Anderson, the change was stark – and for the worse. Boxer 'seemed cold, aloof, and superior, without an ounce of humour in him. I loathed him after exchanging less than a dozen words. My attitude was unfair. He was inferior to Hodges.'[2]

As part of the preparations for the invasion of Europe, Tempsford and its squadrons had been moved from the aegis of Bomber Command to 38 Group, which was essentially the air logistics support for D-Day. Its

AOC was AVM Hollinghurst. Robin Hooper had taken over Boxer's role at AI2(c), leaving the job of flight commander of 'A' Flight vacant. Hollinghurst appointed Bunny Rymills to the post, but was discomfited when Rymills returned from Tempsford having greeted Mouse Fielden on arrival, who told him that he had appointed Sqn Ldr Guy de Grave Sells to the job. Hollinghurst gave Fielden an earful on the telephone, but Sells remained in place.

From now on, the Hudson flight focused on dropping agents by parachute, its aircraft having been suitably modified, but the March and April missions were blighted by being unable to locate reception groups at the French locations – more missions failed than were successful. In 'A' Flight, Flt Lt Bill Taylor had arrived in mid-February from 51 OTU, a night-fighter training unit, and went into action for the first time on a double with fellow new boy George Turner on 5 April. The landing field was in a popular area just east of Tours. The outbound cargo included André Studler of F Section, and some luminous SOE agents – Philippe Liewer, Violette Szabo ('the best shot in SOE') and the wireless operator Lilian Rolfe.[3]

Szabo's mission was to check whether some circuits were blown. Taylor retrieved Jean and Julienne Besnard – their Parisian bar had been heavily used by local resisters but was now thought to be compromised. Turner brought back the diminutive radio operator P.A. Watt (known as 'demi-Watt').

Whitaker and Anderson did a double that night for SIS, which was thwarted by a lack of reception. But Hysing-Dahl carried out a successful solo trip retrieving Claude Arnould (*Colonel Olivier*), co-founder of the JADE-AMICOL circuit of SIS, and his secretary Marguerite Froger (*Mireille*). They were only in England a week before being returned by George Turner. Four nights later, the Whitaker/Anderson duo were sent out again, but Whitaker's engine cut during take-off from Tangmere, and, with no other Lysanders being available, Anderson had to fly on alone. On arrival at the field south of Bourges, Anderson was only expecting two passengers – an agent, and a 74-year-old politician, Louis Marin, who was loosely connected to the FFI, and was being chased by the Gestapo. But the heavily moustachioed Marin shoehorned his mistress, Mlle Hartman, into the Lysander as well, despite having been told there was no place for her.[4] On the same night, 9 April, Taylor took out two very experienced hands – Lise de Baissac and Philippe de Vomécourt, together with Capt Charles Corbin for SOE, on the quaintly named *Chauffeur*. Having broken her leg in parachute training, Lise could only be inserted by Lysander. Bill brought back Jean Savy with a briefcase full of V-1 secrets, SOE agent Maurice Southgate's wife Josette, and the exhausted radio operator Jacqueline Nearne. But this was only after Nearne had donated her England-bound seat to a political refugee on a previous pick-up. This time, Buckmaster had ordered that 'Jacqueline MUST come' be chalked on the side of Taylor's machine.[5]

The Cottage having been relinquished, 'A' Flight's life changed for the worse; Rymills, for example, hated Tempsford – 'cold, damp and miserable'.[6] It also meant that the Bertrams had to leave Bignor Manor, to be installed as SIS hosts at Wootton Hall, 'a lovely Queen Anne house' near Tempsford, which became the new staging post for their agents. An Algerian chef (and his wife) and six French soldiers as staff were employed, but the place lacked the intimacy of Bignor. Still in the UK, Marie-Madeleine Fourcade for one loathed it: 'The huge place felt like a haunted house.'[7] The benefit for the Bertrams was a lot more space – even their children had their own rooms for once.

The demand on 161's services was becoming intense – the number of SOE agents in France that it was supporting had risen from seven in 1941 to 200.[8] Not only were pilots at full stretch through the moon period, but the Lysanders were frequently taking three passengers each way. Expediency trumped discomfort. Indeed on the double when Turner returned the recovered Claude Arnould and Marguerite, Hysing-Dahl returned Jean Sainteny (an ALLIANCE operative who had been arrested and escaped, plucked to England by Anderson, and was now returning to Fourcade's fold) to a field south-east of Chartres, his mission being to restore radio communications for ALLIANCE between Paris and London. The Norwegian then picked up what he thought were three agents from the JADE-FITZROY circuit. On landing back at Tangmere, he was surprised to see four disembark. The Chiefs of Staff decided that where there were insufficient aircraft for the numbers of pick-up operations requested, SIS must take priority over SOE.[9] Air Marshal Tedder, Eisenhower's deputy in the *Overlord* hierarchy, was a chip off the Portal block. He too was loath to support the activities of the Special Duties squadrons, protesting even in April 1944 in a memo to (US) General Bull that the allocation of 25 extra Liberators to Maquis support operations was 'quite unjustified'.[10]

Although he had been awarded a DFC and then a DSO during two tours in Bomber Command, the latter in the Pathfinder Force, Guy de Grave Sells cannot have been a success as commander of the Lysander

Flight, and indeed never flew a Lysander mission. He was succeeded after only a month by Len Ratcliff, who moved over from command of the Hudson Flight. De Grave Sells was returned to RAF Feltwell, whence he had come. Boxer's squadron report for that month[11] gives no hint for the reason for his dismissal of de Grave Sells, which would surely have raised eyebrows at 3 Group, and reflected poorly on Mouse Fielden.

But more trouble was on the horizon. Boxer's management style had begun to irritate his Lysander pilots, none more so than Anderson. A week before the end of the April moon period, AI2(c) had asked for an operation to Burgundy, a popular area for the services of 161 but which was towards the limit of the Lysander's effective range. Anderson pointed out that the outbound flight would be done in darkness and only a feeble moon would rise in time for the landing; moreover, it would be dawn by the time the French coast was reached on the return. Nothing more was heard.

Two days later, Anderson, in his normal rather scruffy attire, was summoned to see Boxer in the Tempsford Operations Room, the CO as usual crisply dressed in his number ones. 'Right, Anderson. There is some good news at last. Mâcon flight is on for tonight. You will ferry a Lysander to Tangmere, pick up the Joes, and continue to Mâcon.' The blue touch paper had been lit – Anderson gasped for breath at this 'good' news, his immediate retort: 'Not by me, sir. We've been at Tempsford for two days, and there's no moon.' Anderson was correct in his stance – Verity's attempt at an operation on a moonless night 18 months earlier had been an abject failure, and as Lysander flight commander at the time, Verity had issued an edict that a moonless flight was not to be attempted again.

Boxer was astonished; Anderson explained his reasoning, concluding, 'Do it yourself!' It was Boxer's turn to be stunned. 'You refuse? You refuse an order?' Anderson underlined that this was so, pointing out it could have been carried out during the previous moon period, and suggesting that Boxer might have been on the receiving end of some criticism from AI2(c) for not organizing it then. By this time, the many WAAF staff in the Operations Room resembled marble statues as they listened rapt to this exceptional exchange. Boxer was incandescent. Anderson underlined his objections. 'I refuse to repair your blunder. Have you checked the met? Am I to fly one hour to Tangmere, then seven hours to Mâcon and back? You have no right to order anyone to do this, when the moon period is over.'

When later thinking back to this episode, Anderson recalled: 'My pathological aversion to W/Cdr Boxer only grew. I found it difficult to be precise about my reasons for disliking him. I may have been under nervous

THE BOXER ERA

strain which my outward cheerfulness and equanimity hid, but did not alleviate. I needed a father figure; Nebbie [Wheeler] and Hodges had these qualities, but Boxer did not.'[12]

Boxer told Anderson he would see Station Commander Fielden. Anderson realized he had perhaps overstepped the mark in his language, if not his stance. The following day, he was summoned to Fielden's office, whose initial response was to threaten sending Anderson to a RAF disciplinary unit. Anderson had a great sense of humour, but a direct manner, and it was the latter that had been to the fore. He pointed out that as an Army man he was only on secondment to the RAF, and suggested to the group captain that it might be best if he himself secured a posting to another (non-disciplinary) unit. Fielden agreed. Anderson was removed from 161's operations immediately – the squadron discarding an undoubtedly talented pilot whose skills were sorely needed. Anderson went to the 'A' Flight crew room and related the conversation to Bob Large, who suggested he go down to Fighter Command HQ at Stanmore, where one of Large's chums would secure a decent posting that would enable Anderson to remain on operations for D-Day.

That night, Large and Whitaker invited the morose Anderson to a party in the WAAF sergeants' mess. Here much ale was downed, and he encountered a small blonde WAAF who took a shine to him. Intimacy ensued. It was therefore a rather hung over Anderson who the following morning, even more bedraggled than normal, stumbled to the hallowed portals of RAF Bentley Priory. He was walking around the mansion's perimeter wondering whom he should ask for, when he bumped into the bulky figure of Gp Capt John Stratton, who had been RAF Benson's station commander when Anderson was based there. Stratton remembered him, and moreover was now in charge of postings. When Anderson expressed a desire to be moved to a fighter squadron, Stratton was optimistic. After four days dwelling on his miseries at home, Andy received a letter telling him to report to the Spitfire OTU at RAF Kirton-in-Lindsey. Painful memories of Boxer could be consigned to the bin.[13]

Educated at Daventry Grammar School, the tall, fair-haired and athletic John Perry Alcock joined the Coldstream Guards in 1932, and left to join the police in Cheshire in 1936 (whilst staying as an Army reservist). After the outbreak of the war, he transferred into the Military Police, but switched to the RAF in 1941, in the expectation of more action. Having acquired the name 'Cocky', he began pilot training at 4 EFTS at Brough. After advanced training in Canada and several locations in the US, he gained his wings on 5 August 1942, and returned to England on the *Queen Mary*. But his desire for action was thwarted for he was now despatched to the dullest backwater the RAF could find – No. 631 Army Co-Operation Squadron at Towyn in Wales, doing target towing and shot observation duties in superannuated Hurricanes and Hawker Henleys. He escaped this unit and joined 161 on 20 April 1944, by which time he was the grand old age of 31. He had married Dosie in London in 1942, and they had a daughter, Carolyn, a month before his move to Tempsford.

Boxer clearly did not consider that new boys needed much training, since Cocky's operational debut came only ten days later in a double with Bob Large, *Organist*. They took out three passengers including F Section's Denis Rake (the wireless operator for SOE's Nancy Wake), to a pasture south of Châteauroux.

The return passengers, Violette Szabo and Philippe Liewer, had had an eventful rail journey down from Paris to Orléans, with the Gestapo conducting a very thorough search and shots being fired at some other *résistants* on the run. But at Les Aubrais station the pair was picked up by someone from the STATIONER circuit in a *gazogène* van who took them to a farmhouse near the landing field. By the time the Tangmere pair arrived overhead, there was a ground mist on the field but they made safe landings, albeit that Large's engine cut on the landing run as the bumpy ground applied some momentary negative G to the carburettor.

Large embarked Szabo, Alcock took Liewer. The take-offs were hampered by the wet stubble that covered the chosen field, but they lifted into the damp air at 0140hrs. Retracing his route, Large suddenly found himself in cloud, and drifted off his track. The next thing Large noticed was some flak shells whizzing past the cockpit window – he had put the Lysander too close to the Luftwaffe base at Châteaudun, home of 180 night-fighters. Flak guns opened up. 'The lady in the back squeaked, so I switched off the intercom', Large later told Hugh Verity.[14]

The pair made it back to Tempsford by just after 0500hrs; as he touched down, Large's Lysander performed a ground loop and slewed sideways, the tyres shredded by flak, throwing Szabo against the side of the rear cockpit. A figure in blue/grey uniform wrenched open the canopy and she threatened him in vituperative French, brandishing an umbrella. 'My schoolboy

French only picked out the bad words – and there were plenty of them!' Large had forgotten to turn the intercom back on, and his passenger had thought they had crashed in France, and she was being arrested by a German![15]

It was a busy night on 3 May; the weather was kind with clear skies and good visibility. There was a rare Hudson pick-up carried out by Affleck (*Halberd*), with eight passengers each way. Hudson pilots were by now wary of the field surfaces – Affleck's destination was on the slightly rising ground east of the River Ain, north of Mâcon. He found soft patches and high grass, which combined to make the heavy Hudson difficult to taxi. The operator was again the very experienced Paul Rivière; he and Henry Thackthwaite were on the return trip, the latter to update Baker Street on conditions on the Vercors.

Hysing-Dahl did a solo (*Pipe*) for SIS, to a field at Ségry near Issoudun. He was not impressed by the operator Rogatien Gautier's choice of pasture: 'extremely bumpy, I consider it unsafe for pick-up operations' (it was his third landing there).[16] He took out two agents and brought back Guy Jaffelin and Marcel Grandmaire.

It was, and is, the custom in France on 1 May to give a spray of *muguets* (lily of the valley) to those one loves as a token of good luck. One of Hysing-Dahl's passengers gathered some *muguets* on the landing field, brought back the posy in the Lysander, and when back in England presented it to Mrs Bertram for her breakfast table.[17]

NEW BOYS FARE BADLY

The third mission for 161 on the night of 3 May was a solo by Leslie Whitaker. He left Tangmere without any passengers but loaded with parcels of francs headed for a field east of Chartres – a short, easy trip in prospect. But his intelligence briefing had omitted details of RAF bombing raids at Châteaudun, near his route. This caused a sudden deviation for Whitaker, and also stirred up German searchlights and night-fighters based at Étampes Montdésir. On this his seventh operation, the cheery Yorkshireman was shot down by flak (or possibly an Me 110 night-fighter), to be buried later at nearby Guillerval. None felt his loss more keenly than his old chum and comrade-in-arms, Murray Anderson.

F/O G.F.J. 'Alex' Alexander had joined the squadron on 20 March, and on 6 May carried out his first op – *Silène*, near to where Whitaker had met his maker three days earlier. It reflects the urgency of this pre-invasion period (or perhaps Boxer's poor management) that a *débutant* should be sent near to where a colleague had very recently encountered fatal trouble. He retrieved two SIS agents who drank wine and sang songs on the return journey. The third passenger was a USAF pilot, Bud Mahurin. Newly promoted to major, on 27 March he had had to bail out of his 63rd Fighter Squadron P-47 Thunderbolt when the rear gunner of the Do 217 bomber he was attacking shot him to bits. Rescued by the Resistance, he had been supposed to return to England in Whitaker's doomed Lysander.

Two days later, on the night of the full moon, another *débutant* took to the skies for SIS on *Utrillo II*. E.A.G.C. Bruce had had plenty of excitement in his RAF career to date. On 2 October 1941, P/O Bruce had been flying his Spitfire Vb on a No. 92 Squadron fighter sweep over the Pas de Calais, when his machine was badly damaged in a combat. He managed to limp back across the Channel before crashing in Kent. In July 1942, now a flying officer but still flying Spitfires, he was operating from Malta and was shot down over the Mediterranean. Bruce paddled his dinghy the 15 miles back to the island.

On 9 May, SIS mandated a most unusual operation – a Lysander treble. *Mineur* was to a popular area south of the small Loire town of Bléré. It was slickly organized on the ground by the fiercely Breton operator Félix Guilcher, of the ÉCARLATE network, which was just as well with the need to co-ordinate the movements of three Lysanders. Large, Hysing-Dahl and Ratcliff (this was one of Len Ratcliff's only two Lysander operations) met at the agreed rendezvous of Bléré within only three minutes of each other. Bob Large found the field but flew away to allow Len Ratcliff to land first, as had been agreed at Tempsford. Unfortunately, Large became a little disorientated, and the circling Hysing-Dahl demanded to know why he was late to the field. Sorry to have been so long, the irrepressible Large responded over the radio, 'I've been getting my hair cut.' 'What, on company time?' asked the cross Norwegian. 'Well it grew on company time' was the retort![18]

After Bob Large's landing, Guilcher handed him an inscribed bottle of Moet & Chandon Brut Imperial champagne. Six BCRA agents had been taken out; the return included one SOE agent (the burly Richard Heslop of F Section, who had headed MARKSMEN in the Ain and Haute-Savoie), Colonel Maurice Belleux, a pilot and BCRA intelligence officer who had been tracking Luftwaffe operations, but was returning to London to join the Free French Air Force, and two agents of the PHATRIE network. This was the last night Bignor Manor was used; the Bertrams then sub-let

Bignor to Elizabeth, the widow of Stephen Hankey, who shared it with the widow of another pilot.

The operation that Whitaker was attempting when he was shot down still needed to be carried out. It was given to another new arrival, F/O Lucky Newhouse, who attempted it on 10 May. In good weather, he had an uneventful flight until he was picked up by searchlights and light flak near Orléans on his way to Whitaker's destination south-east of Chartres. He made several runs to the field using the railway line just to the west as his lead-in guidance, but found no reception lights, and had to return home.

Alexander finally completed it in the June moon period. The harvest was of the highest quality: on the outbound leg he took out Joseph Camapana from the JADE-FITZROY network, who had been in England for six weeks, and now brought instructions from Biffy Dunderdale of SIS; for the return, he retrieved Cmdt Gustave Bertrand and his wife. Bertrand was one of France's foremost experts on the Germans' Enigma machine, running the French Cipher Bureau (Cadix), and liaising with his Polish counterparts. In January he had been arrested by the Germans, who thought that a substantial amount of francs would convince him to become a double agent. Instead he fled with his wife. After some delay, he heard the message '*Les lilas blancs sont fleuris*' ('The white lilas are in bloom'), and headed for his appointed field. The third passenger was Hogbin, a Jesuit priest who had been acting as a courier for the Polish Resistance. Once in London he was wined, dined and debriefed by Biffy and joined the BCRA.[19]

SOE had been squeezed out of 161's operations, at least for the moment – all but one of the Lysander flights in the month up to the invasion had been on behalf of SIS. This was because the *Overlord* planners had kept SOE in the dark, and only told Baker Street of the invasion a week beforehand.[20] During that week leading up to D-Day, the Hudson Flight carried out eight parachute-drop missions, losing one aircraft when the Canadian Flt Lt Warren 'Sugar' Hale's Hudson was shot down over Tilburg in Holland with the death of all four crew members. But the same weather systems that provoked the difficult decision to postpone D-Day by 24 hours, and then produced storms in the following days, also disrupted 161's flying programme. 'Only a minimum number of operations were laid on.' Bruce was posted out as he 'was found unsuitable for the work required' (of the Lysander Flight).[21] It is of note that de Gaulle, too, and much to his disgust, had been kept in the dark about the invasion until the last minute. Churchill summoned him back from Algiers and to be briefed on the Prime Minister's stationary train at Portsmouth on the eve of D-Day. Churchill's stance was coloured by the fact that a member of de Gaulle's team was said to have leaked Allied plans to assault Dakar in September 1940.[22]

On 5 July, (Acting) Flt Lt John Menzies was sent off on *Fives I*, with four agents to drop from his Hudson. Known as Ian, he became a victim of the RAF knowing less about night-fighter and flak defences over the Low Countries than over France. The Hudson was intercepted by Feldwebel Heinrich-Karl Lahmann who shot it down just south of Harlingen before Menzies had a chance to drop the men.[23]

The first Lysander flights after the invasion were on 7 July. With an almost full moon, Taylor did a mail pick-up, whilst Turner and Hysing-Dahl carried out a double for SIS to a field near Châteauroux. The weather was rather cloudy over England but had cleared by the time they reached the French coast. Mid-Channel, one of Turner's three passengers alerted him to a fighter closing in from behind, 450 yards away. Turner took immediate evasive action and shook him off. Hysing-Dahl was late at the agreed rendezvous at Bléré but proceeded to the field, with his three agents and a parcel containing 11 million Francs.[24] However, radio communications between the pair were poor. Turner landed and exchanged his three passengers for another three, returning home safely. The Norwegian thought he had found the target field and circled for five minutes without seeing any light signals from the ground. So he headed back to Bléré and then set course for Trouville on the coast (which was well to the east of the invasion beaches).

Hysing-Dahl's navigation was poor, and when he realized he was heading north over the invasion beaches, 'the coast was very near and as I had not been shot at, I proceeded. However the flak started to come up, which was very accurate.' Taylor, on his mail pick-up mission, heard his Norwegian colleague radioing Tangmere for a fix, but the Lysander was hit in the wings, engine, fuel tanks and propeller. The cockpit filled with oil from the punctured reservoir behind the pilot's head. With the engine continuing to run, Hysing-Dahl thought it best to carry on flying north out of the beachhead area. But shrapnel had given him a wound in the hand, and 20 miles from the coast his engine failed.

Luckily, a few months earlier he had attended an air/sea survival and rescue course. He carried out a text book ditching, letting his machine flop into the sea tail first at just under 70mph. With its large main undercarriage, the Lysander was always going to nose over rapidly, but he kicked himself out of the cockpit and rose to the surface. Although his damaged lifejacket would not inflate, the three passengers, who had sensibly opened their canopy before ditching, had been catapulted out and were swimming nearby; however, one disappeared from sight as Hysing-Dahl was sorting out his dinghy. The gas bottle refused to work, but despite his wound, Per managed to inflate it with his lungs.[25] Pushing it towards where he had heard voices shouting in the darkness, he helped the nearest passenger stay afloat by hanging on to mail bags and the dinghy, and pulled the other, more exhausted passenger on top of the dinghy. After one and a half hours the sodden trio sighted a corvette on the horizon, so Hysing-Dahl fired off four cartridges from his flare pistol, with no immediate response. It was another two and half hours before they were finally rescued by an American MTB, and were lifted from the Channel at 0710hrs, having been in the water for at least five hours. Two of his passengers, BCRA agents Bernard Gagnant and André Leseur, died; Paul Baudry survived. The genial Hysing-Dahl had carried out his last mission for 'A' Flight – at the end of the following month he was posted to 1 Ferry Squadron at Pershore to fly a variety of two- and four-engine types.[26] But in January 1945, Len Ratcliff secured Per's release and brought him back to Tempsford to fly Stirling and Halifax missions to Scandinavia.

148 SQUADRON JOINS THE FUN

Back in May, Lysanders were flying into France from another direction. 161 had spawned an offspring: No. 148 Squadron had been established at Bari in Italy to support Special Duties work in the campaign in that country. Churchill was worried that Italy might descend into civil war like Greece, so Gubbins initiated 40 SOE operations from its Force 399 HQ at Bari, described by a Kiwi military doctor as a 'bureaucratic merry-go-round, where stores were plenty, but apathy high'.[27] Bari was also usefully the base for SIMCOL, MI9's operations in Italy and beyond.

148's crest featured two crossed axes – perhaps a reference to the Fascist symbol in Italy; its motto was 'Trusty'. 148 had Halifaxes and Stirlings, but also six Lysanders on its charge. After 161, Peter Vaughan-Fowler had been plucked by Pickard into one of his Mosquito squadrons (No. 21); but this was only a brief sojourn as he was now posted with some urgency to 148 to bring his great Lysander Special Duties experience to bear on its operations in the Mediterranean theatre.

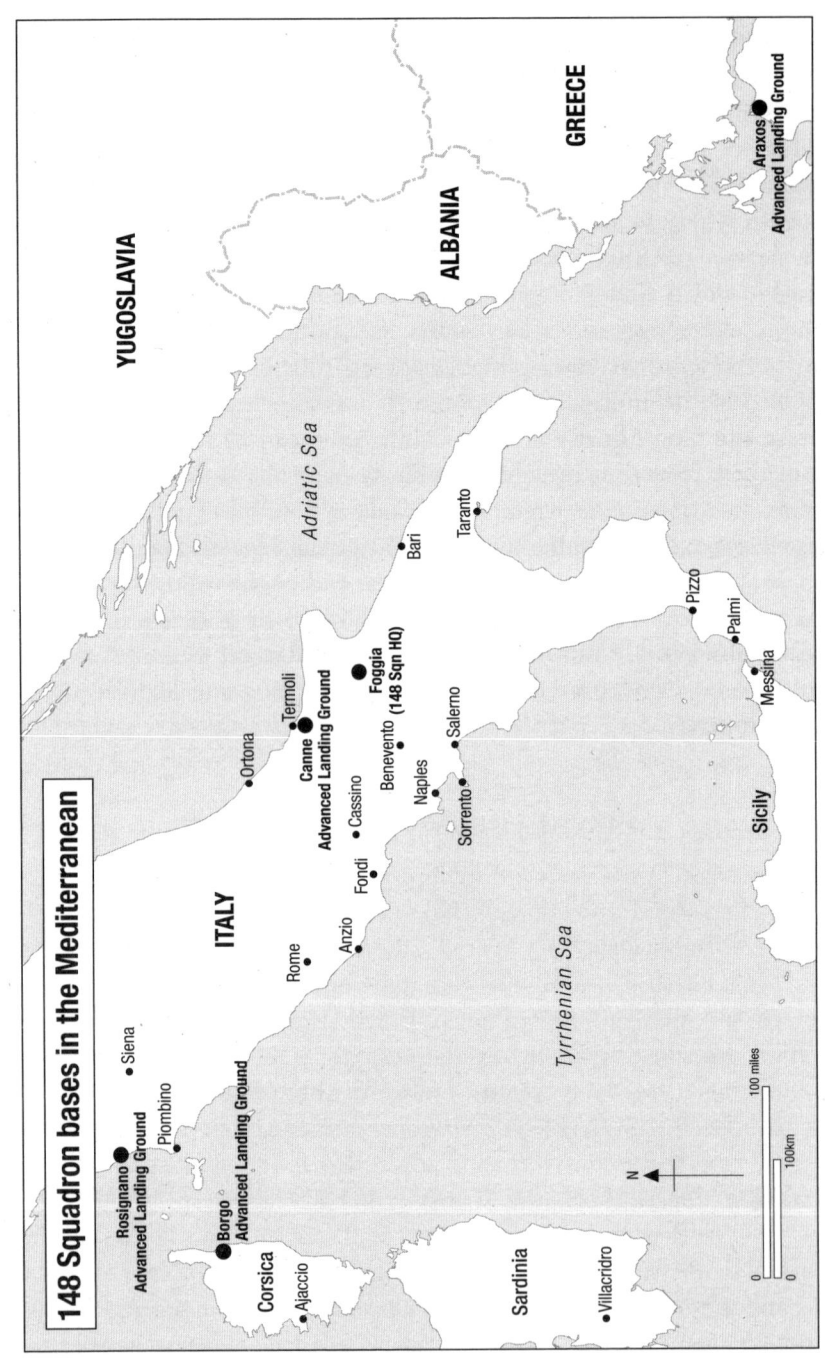

Marie-Madeleine Fourcade had been itching to return to France to re-join her colleagues in ALLIANCE for some weeks. This was despite having heard in London that Sainteny and many of his men had recently been arrested. In the event, BCRA only gave her two hours' notice of her departure on 5 July. She packed her suitcase hurriedly, including an identity card in the new name of Germaine Pezet, as she would be posing as the wife of fellow passenger 36-year-old Raymond Pezet (*Poisson Volant*, 'Flying Fish'). Affleck flew them and six others to a field south-east of Paris, which he found in perfect condition, although it was not the field he had been shown in the recce photograph. Fourcade leaped back onto home turf (but was arrested only 13 days later), and Affleck took on board another eight BCRA agents, including Christian Pineau's son.[28]

The shooting down of Hysing-Dahl prompted a rethink at Tempsford. Fielden and Boxer belatedly realized that it was probably not a good idea to send their Lysanders over to France on a route that would almost inevitably take them over invasion maritime traffic (and amongst aerial traffic). So Ratcliff arranged accommodation for 'A' Flight at RAF Winkleigh in the middle of Devon. Station Commander Gp Capt The Duke of Hamilton was most helpful. Agents would now be picked up early in the evening from Tempsford and flown down to Devon, where they could enjoy an hour or so of rest in a Nissen hut with 'simple cooking facilities available, and such stores as tea, bread, milk, etc'. Blaber, by now a flight sergeant, was to be sent down to supervise such luxury – the joys of the Cottage at Tangmere, and his rewarding role there, were fading into distant memory![29] Ratcliff had a room at the end of the hut; the boys slept in the main room. Blaber's spartan breakfast rations were supplemented with mushrooms picked from local meadows.

On 27 July, CO Alan Boxer carried out his first pick-up mission (*Tenerife*) in a Hudson. The difficult boss had heeded Anderson's ill-tempered words to carry out missions himself on moonless nights if he wanted them done, for the 27th was the first non-moon operation for the Hudson Flight. But it was to a disused aerodrome at Le Blanc near Châteauroux, so there should have been no worries of clipping trees on the field boundary. There was solid cloud up to 7,000–10,000 feet most of the way to his destination. Boxer saw the reception's lights shining through the lowest layers; he reported later that his landing was hampered by a hump on the airfield and a slight ridge across his path (which is strange for a pre-existing aerodrome, but the Germans had done some preventative ploughing only two days earlier). Boxer was forced to swallow his harsh words to

Anderson for he concluded his report with 'It is strongly recommended that further "dark period" pick-ups be laid on only under conditions of extreme emergency.'[30] He took out only two passengers – RF Section sabotage instructors – and some medical supplies. The return passengers were injured British warriors: the leader of the Jedburgh team ANDY, Major (Maj) Ronald Parkinson, who had suffered a double compound fracture of his left leg during his parachute landing into France. His colleague, also on the Hudson, Cmdt J. Vermeulen, had a severely injured foot.[31] Other passengers included Lt Carl H. Bundgaard, a P-51 pilot with the 505th Fighter Squadron at Fowlmere, who three weeks earlier had suffered engine failure north of Tours on his very first mission.

Peter Arkell was the eldest son of Sir Noel, who had been shot in the shoulder in World War I, but survived to take his place at the head of the family brewery in Wiltshire founded by his grandfather. The surname was apt for Peter as its Viking origins mean 'eagle helmet'.

Peter's brother joined the Gurkhas (and was later killed in action). Graduating from Oxford University in 1940, Peter joined the RAF, with the by now normal pattern of basic training in the UK followed by advanced flying training in Canada and then Falcon Field, Arizona, where he very much took to the American way of life. The journey across the Atlantic had been in appalling weather, which perhaps ensured the convoy's survival. His first solo was 12 days after Pearl Harbor in a PT-17 Stearman, after which he flew the BT-13A Valiant and the AT-6A Texan (better known in the UK as the Harvard). With a group of fellow cadets, he hitchhiked to Hollywood on a weekend's leave, and enjoyed the attention which his RAF uniform engendered.

Having returned across the Atlantic in the *Queen Elizabeth*, he was immediately commissioned. Posted to No. 26 Squadron, Arkell flew Mustangs on tactical reconnaissance and day intruder missions with some night operations over the Netherlands, shooting up invasion barges in the canals. But there were not enough operations for his taste: 'Didn't have much to do, enough ops, on that squadron'; when he saw a request for applications for Special Duties squadrons on the notice board, he followed it up. The 21-year-old Arkell was soon invited to Tempsford for an interview by Ratcliff and Boxer; the Mustang pilot was very impressed with the number of highly decorated pilots milling about. The pair gave him a 'harsh, stern' briefing on the Official Secrets Act, before making him sign it – 'You can't tell anybody', which he found troublesome, as he was 'bubbling over with excitement'. Peter's accent betrayed his position in Wiltshire's landed gentry.

No one else joined at the same time as Arkell and he did not find his 161 colleagues very hospitable at the outset. He had three months of intensive training in all weathers before his first operation with the squadron. Arkell found the weeks between the moon periods 'a bit boring', but the excitement of operations more than made up for it, and he felt frustrated he could not tell people outside the squadron's circle about it. He soon rather wished he had joined 161 earlier.[32]

The first operations from Winkleigh were carried out on 4 August, which was a very busy night for the squadron. Several Halifaxes departed on operations from Tempsford. As for Lysanders, Lamberton could not find his reception, but Alexander and Newhouse did a double to a field south-east of Le Mans (*Scimitar*). With thick spectacles, Newhouse did not have the air of a normal 161 pilot. Very inexperienced, he flew out with three passengers to pick up, amongst others, John Oliphint, a 20-year-old evading US pilot from Shreveport, Louisiana, who had had a very eventful couple of months.

The night of 4/5 August was to be Oliphint's return. With some of the family that had sheltered him, he made his way by bicycle to the landing field. Allied domination of the air meant that German troops now tended to move only by night, and the chosen pasture was surrounded by the noise of clanking Panzer tanks not far away. Lucky Newhouse landed in his Lysander at 0130hrs and disgorged three passengers together with several boxes. Oliphint leaped on the port wheel spat of the Lysander and shouted to Newhouse: 'I am a fighter pilot. Panzer unit on main road.' Newhouse gave him instructions on how to use the alert buttons in the rear cockpit if he saw night-fighters. The American pilot scrambled into the back alongside Paule-Denise Corre, 23, and another. Oliphint was pleased to be in an aircraft again, glad he was returning to liberty, but frustrated he had no guns with which to shoot down any German night-fighters that dared to disturb his journey. The Canadian pilot kept the Lysander at little more than 400 feet over the Sarthe countryside; Oliphint was impressed – 'He was a magnificent seat-of-the-pants night pilot.'

Alexander encountered some light flak over France, and overshot from his first approach. Second time around, on landing on stubble, he found some more significant obstacles – stooks of wheat. Oliphint had ordered that stooks were to be laid out at one end of the field which, when lit, would point to the landing area. This was of course in contravention of standard 161 practice.

As Alex noted the following day in a memo to Len Ratcliff, his flight commander: 'My first approach was bad and I went through the overshoot procedure. On my second attempt I touched down on stubble on coming up level with lamps B and C and ran into a narrow belt of standing crop. Coming out of this I ran into stubble again, but this seemed to have obstacles in the form of stooked corn or bundles of hay. On hitting one of these I damaged my tail oleo.'[33]

The unlit stook damaged Alex's elevator as well as the tail oleo; he embarked two JADE agents, one of whom was Anne-Marie Chatenay, a 16-year-old girl from a very active Angers Resistance family who had acted as a courier, but now had a broken hip.[34]

Alex sensibly used the emergency boost on his engine to control the aircraft on the ground, with its now errant tailwheel, and also during take-off to ensure he cleared all the obstacles ahead. He was unimpressed with the photo recce shots of the field he had been given beforehand.

His problems were not over – he found that the elevator damage meant that the only way he could make the Lysander climb or descend was through judicious use of the trim wheel; moreover, to compound his problems, the radio failed on his return flight. As if that was not bad enough, coming back to south-west England the weather deteriorated, but when he approached St Merryn on the north Cornish coast, he noticed that airfield was using its FIDO fog dispersal system. It was lucky they had the system operating, because Alex could not call them up to request it. He put down on the runway in the opposite direction to a squadron of Liberator bombers that had just taken off, and just before the FIDO system was turned off. As he could not control the Lysander on the tarmac he shut down the engine, and walked off to find help for his injured passenger. In the mist it took him an hour to find the control tower, and explain (in his scruffy civilian clothes) his predicament. On learning of the tribulations experienced by his men at Oliphint's field, Boxer was unimpressed: 'It is recommended that this agent be struck off the list as a pick-up operator, he is obviously a dangerous fool or quite clueless.' Robin Hooper at AI2(c) concurred. As the operator, Robert Bloc, had been brought back to Britain on this mission, it was not too difficult to enact Boxer's wishes. Fielden also agreed, but thought that Alexander was ill-advised to try to fly the machine (which had to be rebuilt afterwards) back to England in that state.[35]

There was another double that night, *Pirogue*. For Peter Arkell, it was his first Lysander sortie; for John Alcock, it was only his second – he had not been on operations since the end of April. *Pirogue* was an SIS mission to a field west of Issoudun, with Guilcher again in charge on the ground. Arkell found the operation smooth and well organized; he took out two BCRA agents, and retrieved another three females who 'weren't that chatty', one of whom was 'like one's grandmother'![36]

Alcock and his wife Dosie were in grief at the death two weeks earlier of Carolyn, their four-month-old daughter. He set off in V9758 from Winkleigh in tandem with Peter Arkell. In the back he carried another agent from ÉCARLATE, Lucien Germereau, who was in charge of its Châteauroux sector. As the Lysander crossed the Channel outbound, it was picked up by British radar, and the controllers scrambled a Mosquito night-fighter from RAF Colerne, Wiltshire, to intercept it. Flt Lt W.G. Dinsdale, with P/O J.E. Dunn alongside him, was vectored for the kill. The Royal Canadian Air Force pilot from No. 410 Squadron caught up with the Lysander over Brittany; he lowered his flaps to maintain station with the dark aircraft ahead, which he identified as a Henschel HS 126 – the German equivalent of a Lysander, with a single engine and a high wing (but without the Special Duties Lysander's under-slung long-range fuel tank). Dinsdale dropped back and descended for his attack, and fired two bursts from his four 20mm cannons into the target's belly. The fuel tank exploded, and Alcock and Germereau were killed instantly, the pilot becoming the oldest killed in action on 161's Lysander flight. A shocked Arkell witnessed the incident: 'Alcock, flying ahead of me, went down in a ball of flame. I didn't at the time realise it was him. When I landed [in France] I had to pick up his agents, so I was a bit overloaded.'[37] Perhaps if another RAF unit was so ignorant of the possibility of Special Duties Lysanders flying over France, it was testament that the secrecy surrounding 161's activities was still largely maintained.

In his report of the mission Dinsdale later said, 'I had great difficulty in identifying the aircraft I intercepted, as it had a long range fuel tank between the undercarriages [sic] but I could see no national markings.' The unanswered question is why he felt the need to shoot down an aircraft he had not positively identified, and which was not a threat to him or the British Air Defence region.[38]

In his monthly reports on operations, Boxer was not backward in patting himself on the back; in his verbose August report he noted of the Lysander Flight: 'three of the operations carried out were the final undertaken by F/O Lamberton, F/O Newhouse, and Flt Lt Arkell – operational cross-countries were also carried out by the remaining pilots under training and now are fully operational. Unfortunately for the moment the valuable work required of them seems to be out of commission and news is awaited as to the future plans.'[39] The speed of the Allied advance across France had surprised AI2(c), and rendered much of 161's capabilities superfluous. The problem of course was that neither SOE nor SIS had many resources on the ground in Germany, so the sort of missions that 161 had been carrying out in France and, to a lesser degree in Holland and Scandinavia, could not be extended towards the home of the Third Reich. Boxer could see his little empire withering through lack of use.

18

Last Flights

The only good part of war is its ending.

Abraham Lincoln[1]

B Squadron, 1 SAS had been parachuted into the Vienne in south-west France by 161 in the early hours of D-Day. This was one of the main Allied special forces interventions to hinder the 2nd SS Panzer (*Das Reich*) Division moving to Normandy from its base in Montauban in the Tarn et Garonne in order to counteract the Allied invasion. The SAS operation was christened *Bulbasket*, possibly because the nickname of its leader, the 23-year-old Capt John Tonkin, was 'Bullshit Basket'. The main tasks of these hardy warriors were to disrupt the north–south railway lines, destroy petrol stores usable by these SS tanks, and tie down German troops who would inevitably be sent to find them.

With 55 men at its greatest extent of the unit, 34 SAS men were captured when their camp in a wood outside Verrières was surrounded on 3 July. Sadly, this also included US Mustang pilot 2nd Lt Lincoln Delmar Bundy, who had joined the troopers after being shot down in combat and was *en route* to freedom via Spain. He had introduced himself to the B Squadron boss, 'Captain, I see no reason why the lack of an aircraft should stop me from fighting.'[2] He had been welcomed into the fold. After prolonged interrogation, the SAS captives, together with seven members of the Resistance, were executed four days later by the Germans.

Helped by a Jedburgh team in the area, Tonkin and the other survivors had already successfully called in 140 Wing Mosquitos (more accurate than their heavy bomber colleagues) to destroy German fuel dumps.[3] Tonkin had radioed his UK HQ the details of the deaths and the location of the units responsible. Basil Embry, AOC 2 Group, was delighted to send his Mosquito squadrons under Peter Wykeham-Barnes on several raids to exact retribution on the SS, but ground his teeth when he was prevented from flying the missions himself.

From RAF Thorney Island (only eight miles west-south-west of Tangmere), Wykeham-Barnes led a couple of two-and-a-half-hour missions to destroy barracks and châteaux housing the SS men. In the second raid, two German officers sheltered in a basement, but had not considered the effects of the pressure waves from a bomb blast. Their hidey-hole was covered in excrement from a ruptured sewer – *'Ach! In der Scheisse für Hitler!'* ('Oh, in the shit for Hitler!') was their reaction.[4]

After this revenge, an exhausted Capt Tonkin and his eight colleagues needed extraction. By now several evaders and a Phantom team had joined the party, which was so large that Tonkin signalled on 6 August that he needed three Hudsons to get them back to England. Within four hours, he was told there was no chance a third could be procured and he would have to prioritize his passenger list.[5]

David Surrey Dane was a lieutenant who had joined the Paras, but had recently been seconded to the SAS. Having been given some instructions on airstrip preparation, he was now parachuted to the *Bulbasket* survivors. Tonkin's group had lost three of the four jeeps that had been dropped to them, but in a requisitioned battered Citroen (rashly flying the flag of the Free French), Dane drove around the parched countryside looking for suitable fields. He discounted two on the shortlist he had been given, but liked one just south-east of Saint-Savin. Under his guidance, the airstrip, now codenamed *Bon-Bon*, was prepared.[6] He commandeered a harrow and other farm implements from the nearby farms of La Nocilière and Les Pageneaud. The harrow was towed behind the SAS men's surviving jeep, and the troopers set to with the tools. A hedge that ran west–east across the chosen two fields was removed. Along the hedgerow was a walnut tree which was dear to its farmer owner; initially he wanted recompense for its felling, but relented.[7] The SAS men completed their task in three sweltering days of hard toil.

This was a most unusual task for 161 – it had never extracted a military unit before. With too many passengers for a Lysander triple, it had to be a double Hudson mission. The field had now been extended to 900 yards in its longest direction – still a hundred yards shorter than ideal for a Hudson field. 161's CO Alan Boxer had shown no desire to convert to the Lysander; he most probably preferred the comfort blanket of a navigator and at least two engines. So he decided to take on this novel Hudson operation himself, with young F/O Harry Ibbott skippering the other machine. Ibbott had been flying Hudson parachute operations since April, but this would be his first pick-up.

Conditions on the night of 6 August were perfect – good weather and it was almost a full moon. The two machines lifted from Tempsford just after 2200hrs. Once past the Loire, Ibbott followed the River Gartempe down to Saint-Savin. Under orders from Surrey Dane, the troopers lit a small bonfire; the SAS men heard the rumble of Ibbott's Hudson just at the expected time. Having exchanged the correct light signals, Ibbott did a descending circuit to land (after a very big bounce) in a southerly direction at *Bon-Bon* at 0136hrs. When Boxer landed 15 minutes later, he found it 'soft and very dusty' – unsurprising given the work that had been put into it at the height of summer – and with many areas of stubble. There was one bad bump at the end of the landing run, and he nearly became stuck in the soft grass at the northern end. Boxer had taken out six fresh soldiers from 3 SAS, and embarked Capt Tonkin and nine of his dirty, weary troops.[8]

Ibbott brought back the two other troopers, three members of the Phantom unit (Capt Sidoine, and signallers Armitage and Plumb), three USAAF airmen (Norton, Bradley and Harper), and Capt René Amédée Louis Maingard de la Ville-ès-Offrans, the Mauritian leader of SOE's SHIPWRIGHT circuit. (It was as well passenger manifests were not written out on the landing ground.) Capt Raymond John McCulloch Sadoine was possibly a Belgian, whose real name was Octave Dupont, son of Baron Sadoine and the Englishwoman Esther McCulloch. He had commissioned in the Irish Guards, and joined the Phantom unit in February 1941, to be remembered later as 'a volatile and difficult officer'.[9]

For Ibbott, Sidoine was a high-risk passenger since some of Tonkin's men thought he had betrayed the location of the SAS camp to the Germans (no evidence was ever offered to support this, and it was later thought the camp's existence had been revealed by two SAS troopers who had been captured earlier and subjected to brutal interrogation by the SS, but only after holding out for the requisite 24 hours). Ibbott needed full throttle to budge the Hudson in the soft grass, and found there was 'not much spare room on the take-off, which was a bit shaky'.[10] A dust trail signalled their departure track as they headed back northwards.

On the return journey there was a contretemps on board Boxer's aircraft, with Tonkin disobeying the pilot's orders. The SAS leader 'contacted his

Headquarters. Thereupon the Dakota awaiting the party at Tempsford was ordered to proceed to Tangmere.' Both Boxer and Corby, the station commander at Tempsford, were most unhappy.[11] When SAS HQ heard of Boxer's moans, their telegram in retort was succinct and in character: 'Bulbaskets to you Boxer!'[12]

Hudson doubles were now considered a practical method of bringing back up to 20 people at a time. The *Bon-Bon* strip was used three nights later to bring back the nine remaining soldiers (including Surrey Dane and his radio transmitter) in a USAF Dakota of the Carpetbaggers squadron. Although it was skippered by a senior US pilot (the square-jawed Col. Clifford J. Heflin, the squadron commander), it nearly decapitated Surrey Dane and other members of the torch party on its landing run, due to Heflin not understanding the flarepath layout.[13] Perhaps not up to 161 standards then. The Americans had an unusual approach to supposedly clandestine operations: amongst Heflin's outbound passengers was a military photographer, who recorded the pick-up at *Bon-Bon* in the middle of the night in a series of flash photos. Back at Tempsford Boxer decided that *Bon-Bon* was not suitable for future Hudson ops, but 'remains acceptable for Lysanders'.[14]

The following night, Sqn Ldr Reginald Wilkinson, who had transferred from 138 in April 1944, took a Hudson down to a favourite pasture east of the River Ain, and had a trouble-free journey until he was diverted to Tangmere on the return, instead of Tempsford. Boxer, however, huffed that he was 'rash to return with thirteen [BCRA] bodies. The maximum reasonable load for a Hudson is ten people.' The Hudson Flight spent most of August dropping agents by parachute into Holland and Belgium, ahead of the advancing Allied armies.

At the end of August, another Hudson double (*Dauntsey*), was mounted. Whilst Ibbott took out three and brought back four agents, Wilkinson took out only two, and his return cargo was just one letter. Fielden described 'this operation, which involved both aircraft making a difficult landing in heavy rain, as an outrageous waste of effort'. Robin Hooper was in full agreement.[15] It turned out that Wilkinson's outbound cargo was supposed to include a load of machine guns, anti-tank weapons and ammunition, which all made it no further than Tempsford's bomb dump.

Mouse Fielden's last operation was *Failsworth* on 5 September, to a field in the foothills of the Pyrenees. This was a double with Sqn Ldr Wilkinson, which passed without incident – except that Fielden aborted it due to weather, yet his colleague Wilkinson carried it out with no fuss, describing the weather as being merely 'as briefed'. Perhaps it was time for Mouse to hang up his helmet.

That night, Boxer and F/O Ferris also did a double (*Dullingham*) to an airfield named Francazal,[16] just south-west of Toulouse – a long trip that was destined to be the last pick-up operation carried out by 161 in the war. It was also destined to be enveloped in tragedy.

Ferris reported: 'Direction of landing from East to West, ordered by instruction of ground controller. No lights flashed from the ground but a green fired at a/c from the ground.' Ferris had a flight time from Tempsford of four hours nine minutes and landed in France at 0028hrs. But he had landed in the opposite direction to that expected by the reception party.[17]

Boxer landed 42 minutes after his junior colleague. Yet Boxer encountered graver problems; he reported:

> Rather a regrettable trip… the reception was laid in the most confusing manner. It was down wind and incorrectly laid, as we had to land with the lights on our right. However, not before an attempt was made to land with the lights to the left was it realised that this was the case, with the result that I was suddenly aware as I flattened out, that about 15 or 20 men were in my direct path. I opened the throttles and eased the stick forward in an endeavour to bounce over them, as normal overshoot action would never have cleared them. They scattered, fell flat, crouched and waved and unfortunately I only managed to bounce about 4 ft. Two of these men were killed.[18]

Cmdt Maurice Parisot, who was the 45-year-old leader of the Armagnac Battalion of the Maquis in the Gers (and was in charge of security of the field that night) and Lt Pierre Austruit were the two men killed instantaneously by the wheels of Boxer's Hudson. The French affirmed that Boxer too had landed in the opposite sense to that expected, and moreover had not, as was normal practice, done a circuit of the field to assess the conditions. 'Regrettable' indeed! 161's squadron diary (written, or at least supervised, by Boxer) unforgivably dismissed Parisot and Austruit as 'sightseers'.

On 8 September came the last 161 night-time flight into a clandestine strip in France. Ancient at 31, Sqn Ldr Wilkinson carried out another *Failsworthy* to the same field north of Pau. Although he took out five agents, the trip's value was diminished because his intended return load of airmen were judged too badly wounded to be carried. The Hudson flight had now evolved into a much less secret mini-airline transporting in daylight hours agents, SIS folk and airmen needing repatriation from liberated aerodromes across France and the Benelux countries. A useful service, but just as the dangers for the aircrew were much diminished, so were the thrills.

In all the euphoria of a newly liberated France, the deeds of 161's pilots were in danger of being overlooked. The agent Robert Boiteux noted: 'What rankled with me was that in all the newspapers of that period of heady freedom, in all the speeches reported, in all the stories about the Resistance... there was no mention that a few Englishmen had stood at the side of the résistants, nor where those vital arms and supplies had come from.'[19]

Meanwhile, at 148, in 334 Wing operating as part of Force 139, Vaughan-Fowler's Lysander Flight remained busy.[20] The fleet had been supplemented by two Lysanders from the French Air Force, which continued to carry the Croix de Lorraine.[21] Mission planning was complicated by communications with the Air Ministry in London (which had to be by secure Top Secret telexes) routed via Rome.

With four machines and three other inexperienced pilots, his Lysander flight was detached to Borgo, south of Bastia in Corsica, to use as a base from which to mount operations to north-west Italy and ahead of the invasion of southern France (Operation *Anvil*). To Vaughan-Fowler's great delight, James McCairns had been liberated from his role in the Air Ministry in London, and offered the job of his training instructor. They stayed in a couple of 'liberated' villas, reliving their bachelor exploits of Tangmere days, and 'within a month we were busy churning out six Lysander operations a week.'[22]

On 4 June, Operation *Thicket* was mounted with a double from Borgo to the old Hudson landing ground of *Figue* near Saint-Vulbas on the Plaine de l'Ain.[23] Initiating operations from a Corsican launch point had the added advantage of avoiding a long flight over France at a time of year when the nights were at their shortest. But the French pilots were less than happy that they had a full load of three passengers each for the 270-mile return over the Alps. On 10 July, Lts Bernard Cordier and Georges Libert attempted a double to *Figue* but found no reception.

Now they set off from Borgo on *Thicket* on 11 July with some success; the pride of being the first French Special Duties pilots to return to their homeland on operations can only be imagined. Moreover it was to the same field south of Ambérieu from where they had escaped in Verity's Hudson on *Buckler* in July the previous year.

Three passengers were unloaded, including the Vercors leader Eugène Chavant equipped with 2.5 million francs. But Libert's engine stopped, and nothing could be done to persuade the Mercury to restart. Now, increasingly worried, he turned the propeller by hand and then tried his starter, but the battery soon became flat. He then signalled Cordier to land, and made another attempt to start using the starting handle. He told Cordier he would have another go once the engine had cooled, but Cordier saw the folly of this. The duo had to leave quickly to take advantage of the remaining minutes of darkness, and gave instructions to the operator how to torch the aircraft after their departure. The 34-year-old Libert hitched a lift back to Borgo with his colleague.

They landed at 0435hrs to tell the sorry tale to Vaughan-Fowler.[24] It is probable that the reason for the original stoppage of the engine was the Mercury's dislike of negative G, however momentary; Libert probably had insufficient experience on the type to carry out a hot restart in a calm fashion.

334 Wing demanded a full report on the reasons for the Lysander's intransigence. This explained that the field was 'rather rough', and 'his engine stopped even though he tried to prevent it by the use of the slow running cut out'. Libert had extensive pre-war experience with the Armée de l'Air (French air force) and airline Air Bleu, but in July 1940 had been made chief pilot of what was effectively the Vichy government's air taxi service. He used this as a cover for transmitting information to the Resistance. By July 1943, the BCRA feared he might be arrested by the Germans, so arranged for his transport to London by 161.[25]

In August 1944, Peter Vaughan-Fowler himself carried out four missions from Borgo, having reminded London that some chosen landing grounds were unsuitable.[26] He then had two frustrating attempts to carry out *Tyler* for the Office of Strategic Services (OSS, the US equivalent of SOE), finding no reception on two successive nights, before successfully depositing two agents south-west of Lyon on 6 August. On the 10th – and after the end of the moon period – he carried out his last 148 flight to the very same field to which he had flown on his first mission almost two years earlier! This marked the last Lysander pick-up into Occupied France: he retrieved a sole agent from this favourite field next to the Saône near Pont de Vaux. That month, Mac gleefully took part (as 'technical advisor') in an epic USAF Dakota rescue of 22 Frenchmen and evading US airmen from a very compromised strip in the south of France.

One of the regular passengers for 148's Lysanders at this time was Christopher Lee. As a cousin of Ian Fleming (then a staff officer in Naval Intelligence), it was no surprise that Lee had graduated to SOE in the Balkan theatre after distinguished action with the Long Range Desert Group.[27] At 6 feet 5 inches, the man destined to be a famed horror film actor must have found the back of a Lysander as comfortable as an undersized coffin.

Vaughan-Fowler had enjoyed the freedom of action and greater responsibility of his post out at Borgo and Calvi, but by the end of August tasking dried up, yet he was still itching for work. On 16 September, 334 Wing sent a message to Balkan Air Force HQ (under whom they operated): 'Request Lysander Flight of 148 Squadron be given immediate and continuous operational tasks or be disbanded this flight has only carried out one task since its return from Corsica STOP Pilots cannot be employed and their morale is suffering STOP Suggest they be returned to the UK or some theatre where their particular training may be of use.'[28] The OSS could not provide employment either. But a Maj E.P.M. de Haan of No. 1 Special Force rather wanted the Lysander Flight kept in theatre for him. It was not to happen.

In September, P/O Ferris attempted an operation in a Hudson into Germany to drop two agents, but on reaching the destination, one refused to jump, so a frustrated Ferris brought them both back to Tempsford. When Wilkinson tried the same mission three weeks later, he had to give up after encountering fog over the Rhine. The Lysander Flight was now reduced to ferry operations, mostly involving the transport of mid-ranking officers around the swathes of Western Europe now under Allied control. A very regular service was also inaugurated between RAF Benson in Oxfordshire and the headquarters of 21st Army Group in Brussels, ferrying the photos taken by Benson's PRU Spitfires to staff officers to judge German dispositions ahead of the Allied advance. On 29 September, the Cumbrian Flt Lt James Lamberton was given a routine Lysander mission to fly to Paris Le Bourget and bring back three officers for SIS. A fellow pilot found the weather so poor he decided to remain in Paris overnight (hardly a hardship for a young RAF pilot aged only 20). But Lamberton foolishly decided to set off for Tempsford: he carried Maj John Saunders of the Signals and two RAF officers – Flt Lt Charles Clark and Canadian Sqn Ldr Tony Compton. The latter had worked as an SIS conducting officer with 161 since 1942, and was a good friend of the Bertrams. No word was heard from Lamberton and his passengers again.[29] It is likely that, disorientated by the grey pall of sky merging into the Channel, he flew into the waves.

At the end of October, DDI 2 issued a memo to Bomber Command informing them that with only a very modest need to put agents into Germany, 161's Lysander resources were to be cut from 13 to three aircraft. Only Bob Large, Alex Alexander and W/O Pointer remained as aircrew.[30]

But Bomber Harris saw no reason to sheath his dagger: in November he noted in a letter, 'and even the nearly defunct SOE had raised its bloody head and produced what I hope is now its final death rattle'.[31] Peter Arkell, who had arrived so late to the party he only had time to do one pick-up operation in France, volunteered for Burma as 'I hate doing nothing'.[32] At the end of 1944, he joined George Turner's Lysander Flight at No. 357 (Special Duties) Squadron, whose CO was Bob Hodges. 357 was assisting Force 136 in Burma's liberation. But before starting his voyage to the Far East, Arkell had a weekend of leave, so he sent a telegram to his girlfriend in Yorkshire: 'Am arriving Leeds 4.15p.m. Can you meet me any time from this time onwards. LAST OPPORTUNITY.'[33] Presumably, he had more in mind than testing the quality of Yorkshire ale.

148's Lysanders carried out a handful of operations landing agents to support Yugoslavian partisans, but they too became more of a transport service. As Mac noted, 'we were inundated with requests for landings, mainly to take in officers of an age which rendered parachuting dangerous.'[34]

F/O John Rayns had volunteered for special operations and joined Vaughan-Fowler's flight in April 1944, aged 21. Educated at Loughborough Grammar School, and again trained in the US, he had so far done just two transport missions over Italy and Greece. On 5 October, he was taking off from an advanced landing ground in Greece when his engine started losing power; he put back on the airfield but ground looped the Lysander trying to avoid some workmen on the runway. Thankfully, damage was light.

With only a relatively modest 500 flying hours, on 22 November he set off in the same Lysander (T1456) on Operation *Templar* with an escort of P-51 Mustangs from a field near Ancona on Italy's east coast, to a strip in the foothills of the Dolomites. This was a somewhat blighted operation: at the first attempt, Rayns returned with his three passengers because he had failed to identify the landing ground; the second was thwarted by weather; this was his third try for the mission on behalf of IS9, the branch of MI9 responsible for the support and repatriation of escapers and evaders in the Mediterranean theatre. With 60 miles to go, a single USAF P-51 descended from the heavens and, in an astonishing error, shot Rayns' Lysander out of the sky. All on board were killed.[35] The USAF handled investigations into the tragedy.

Meanwhile, at 161 four days later, Reginald Wilkinson took off in a Hudson from Tempsford with three other crew members and a Polish agent, Paul Penczock, to drop him over Arnstadt in Thuringia, Germany. The drop proceeded to plan and the Hudson was heading back to Tempsford; it had just crossed the Luxembourg border into Belgium, the crew by now looking forward to their combat breakfast of bacon and eggs, when it was shot down over Brisy.[36] Luftwaffe night-fighter sorties were rare by this stage, and it is likely that Wilkinson too was attacked by a US fighter. It took some time for his death to be confirmed to Winifred, his widow in Essex, but he was buried in Brussels on 2 December.

Fielden's 1944 ended rather poorly – he was injured in a car accident and had to be replaced as station commander by Gp Capt E.J. Palmer, an Australian. Fielden's unrivalled period of service to 161 and Tempsford drew to a close. He had nurtured Special Duties operations from toddlerdom to ripe old age, using his unique contacts to defend predations from above. Promoted to air commodore, once recovered he was given charge of RAF Woodhall Spa, best known as the home of 617 Squadron.

F/O Raymond (Ray) Manning was born in Winchester and educated at Brighton College. After a peripatetic childhood he could speak German, Hungarian and Serbo-Croat by the time he joined the RAF. So he was ideally suited for 148's role in the Mediterranean theatre and the Balkans. Ray had been with 148 since April 1944 and had carried out eight missions. But in the meantime the 21-year-old had fallen in love with a very attractive FANY based on the station. Cadet Ensign Diana Mary Portman, known as 'Dipsy', was the daughter of a good Army family from Sussex, and the same age. She accepted his proposal, and Raymond obtained his CO's permission to marry her. It was not difficult to find a British chaplain in Florence, so with a few days' leave given, they hitched a ride on a flight down to the Tuscan capital, were betrothed, and enjoyed a fortnight's honeymoon. Due back at Capodichino airfield near Naples, on 4 February, the happy young couple secured a flight from Florence in a Hudson. But soon after take-off its port engine failed, the pilot could not contain the swing, and all on board perished.³⁷

Only 29 when given command of 161, W/Cdr George Watson DFM was of Lancashire working-class stock. His first Bomber Command tour had been three years earlier as a sergeant pilot. He was now transferring from 138. Despite the weakening of the Nazi war machine, the post was no sinecure. Boxer was transferred briefly to HQ Tempsford in charge of Operations, and finally to HQ Bomber Command. Flt Lt Large DFC (it is not clear if this was Bob Large, but it is likely) was subject to a court martial on 16 January and found guilty of being absent without leave, 'sentence not yet promulgated'.³⁸ Large was subsequently posted to No. 504 Squadron on the 19th, his punishment to fly possibly the best mark of Spitfire ever created – the MK IX!

The crew of a 161 Stirling were all killed on 14 February within sight of Tempsford. They were approaching the aerodrome's circuit after an exercise over England when a USAF Mustang made a dummy attack. Kiley, the American pilot, misjudged it, and slammed into the Stirling. A week later Watson decided to check up on his unit's flying operations, and accompanied Flt Lt Oliver in his Hudson on an SIS mission, Operation *Croc*. They left Tempsford just after 2100hrs. By now, the German flak guns were manned only by Hitler Youth or soldiers too old for front-line service, but nonetheless they found Hudson T9405, and it fell to earth south-east of Meppen, Lower Saxony, killing all on board.

Watson was replaced as CO of 161 Squadron by a local lad (local to Tempsford that is) – the 32-year-old Irishman Sqn Ldr Michael Brogan DFC from 138 Squadron, who was immediately promoted to wing commander. Although the weather improved, March was a dismal month. The Hudson fleet had ceased pick-up operations and of that period's 17 operations, most were dropping agents into Germany, and only seven were successful. Brogan was determined to lead from the front. On 4 March, he captained a seven-man crew in a Stirling on a supply drop to the Danish Resistance.

The 334 Wing Lysanders were given increasingly strange missions. *Piccadilly Jane* in February was one such. Newly commissioned Pilot Officer RC Dalziell was instructed to fly from Brindisi to Biferno to pick up a generator and 50lb of stores to take to the Piccadilly Jane strip, which he was assured measured 300 x 35 yards cleared of snow; his mission was also to collect a severely burned airman. When he landed at Biferno, he found that the stores were 500lb not 50lb so had to leave the generator behind. The strip was only 200 yards long and he only narrowly avoided running into a snow bank. To add to his anguish, the airman was found to have only minor burns and was treated at station sick quarters when brought back to Termoli, rather than taken to hospital. Vaughan-Fowler's little empire was finally disbanded on 15 May.

Len Ratcliff left a post at the Air Ministry to take over command of 161 Squadron – the third CO in as many months. After his Channel dunking, Hysing-Dahl had been transferred to a relative sinecure – Ferry Command. Here he teamed up with a fellow Norwegian, Trygve Kleve, as navigator, delivering new aircraft to Egypt. This included a forced landing in the Sahara, which meant spending three days at an oasis. One of Len Ratcliff's first acts was to pull him back to Tempsford to fly the Stirling.

161 had a poor night on 20 March: three Hudsons were shot down on their way to drop agents over Germany. One was piloted by Canadian Flt Lt Bob Ferris on Operation *Norvic* – all four crew died. Another Canadian 161 pilot perished that night: the fresh faced F/O George Ragan, aged only 21, was shot down at Rheine, Nordrhein-Westfalen, possibly by a US night-fighter.

The third Hudson to be lost that night was FK803. Its pilot, Flt Lt Terence Helfer (who had done many Hudson operations, but only a single pick-up), had an astonishing escape. His Hudson was intercepted and destroyed by a night-fighter over Luxembourg. He later recounted: 'the whole thing blew up in mid-air [and] I was blown out of the cockpit. We were only at about 600ft. I just pulled my 'chute, but it didn't open properly. The whole thing was on fire, my back was on fire, my uniform was on fire. I fell into a ploughed field. I jumped up straight away and ran because I thought I was in Germany.'[39] So despite the lack of a functioning chute, he had survived a 600-foot fall into a ploughed field. Burned and temporarily blinded, Helfer pleaded for help from the occupants of the first house he found, who turned out to be a priest and his housekeeper. Initially, they brusquely told him to disappear, until he shouted, '*Je suis Anglais!*' ('I am English!') They smothered his burns in flour and sheltered him before US soldiers collected him the following day.[40] He was soon repatriated to Horton Hospital at Epsom where he was given skin grafts on his badly burned face. Helfer was awarded the DFC in July, and later an AFC.

On 22 April, in the dying embers of the European war, 148 Squadron mounted a Lysander double from Rosignano in Livorno. They had been using this military field near Pisa to aid the Allies' attempts to break through the Germans' Gothic Line. Whilst at Rosignano the pilots would have been able to have a good squint at the Nazi machine that came nearest to matching their Lysanders – a Fieseler Fi 156 Storch. This had been captured from the Italian air force, and repainted in Allied colours for the use of 148. It could fly so slowly that a decent headwind would see it go backwards, and thus the leggy machine could land on the proverbial postage stamp. These attributes had been used the previous year in plucking the deposed Mussolini from a mountain top at Gran Sasso in Abruzzo; the famed Nazi test pilot Hanna Reitsch was also to use one in landing in front of Russian guns in Berlin in a failed attempt to rescue Hitler in the last days of the war.

F/O N.H. Attenborrow and P/O R.C. Dalzell were flying the double from Rosignano to Mereto di Tomba, amongst the vineyards of the Friulian plain near Udine. Attenborrow completed his pick-up smoothly; however Dalzell found his Lysander's compass was faulty so had to switch aircraft. He then crashed on landing at the destination; he later claimed that his starboard brake had seized on landing, causing a swing and the collapse of the Lysander's undercarriage. Fortunately, he and his three passengers were uninjured, but they had to await rescue until the Allies over-ran the area on 2 May.

On the evening of 8 May, about 1,500 personnel assembled in a hangar at Tempsford for its VE Day party. Len Ratcliff wandered over to Hysing-Dahl and his crew and told them to go easy on the beers as he had an operation for them the following day. This was not what the jovial Norwegian wanted to hear. He was pinged to depart at 0900hrs for Bergen, the city he had left in 1944 – barely more than 12 months previously, but it felt like a decade ago. His task was inoffensive – to drop leaflets on the German forces giving them Eisenhower's instructions on how to surrender. Fortunately, the German troops at their drop zone, Festung Herdla, did not fire their flak guns. As Per turned his Stirling homewards to fly over the city, he could not help but notice his countrymen rushing into the streets waving flags at his aircraft. 'A beautiful country in the warm flood of Spring and a liberated people spontaneously overwhelmed with joy', he observed. His navigator, Dick Sutton, chimed in on the intercom, 'You are not kidding Skipper, this is truly a beautiful country.' Per was choked with emotion, and swung the Stirling back towards England: 'The country where our friends live.'[41]

Per's war was not yet done. That day a Stirling had flown to Trondheim, but not returned. So the following day, Len Ratcliff took Per in a Hudson to see what had happened; they found it peacefully at rest on a rather short runway of an inland aerodrome. With some caution they landed the Hudson and taxied up to it, to be greeted by members of the Norwegian Resistance (*Milorg*). There was no sign of the Stirling's crew, who were fully occupied being feted by delirious locals.

Per's armed countrymen informed him that the local Luftwaffe headquarters was up the road, and Len deputed Per to go there to take their surrender. A staff car appeared and a dishevelled Per in his flying gear soon entered the office of Generalleutnant der Luftwaffe Mensching and his adjutant Captain Kunath, who rose and saluted him. Per repeated Eisenhower's instructions, demanded vehicles for transport into the city, accommodation at its main hotel, the Britannia (naturally), and a guarantee of security for the RAF aircraft. At each demand the 57-year-old Karl-Albrecht Mensching clicked his heels and said, '*Jawohl, Herr Hauptmann*' ('Yes, Captain'). Force of habit, if not to a Norwegian in RAF uniform.

After some dutifully modest celebrations with the Milorg men that night, they flew the Hudson back to England the following morning, radioing for a new engine to be put onto a Stirling by the time of their return. So it was that for the third successive day Per and his crew traversed the North Sea to Bergen, this time with a replacement Bristol Hercules engine strapped in the bomb bay of another Stirling. Having delivered it, Per tried to contact his fiancée, Dagny, only to find she had already left Bergen on her way to Trondheim. But two days later they were reunited on the destroyer HMS *Broadway* in Bergen harbour. When over dinner in the wardroom the captain asked if they were married, they coyly admitted to being merely engaged. As was his right, Lt Cdr Thomas Boyd offered to do the deed for them on the spot. Another two days later, the happy couple had a more formal ceremony in Trondheim Cathedral. Once the engine had been satisfactorily tested in the stranded Stirling, Per's stint in his homeland was over. He dearly wanted to bring his new wife back to England, but how? Another sailor came to the rescue: Captain Philip Ruck-Keene, Allied commander in the region, was all for the newlyweds to return together, and simply wrote a slip authorizing Dagny's trip on the RAF aircraft and her immigration into the UK. It worked.[42]

LAST FLIGHTS

The last flight in Per's RAF logbook was: 'May 25 1945. Stirling, Trondheim to Base'. It did not mention that the freshly minted Mrs Hysing-Dahl was a passenger.

On 27 May, the Chiefs of Staff Committee met to discuss the future of SOE. Lord Selborne had submitted an impassioned plea for its retention to the Prime Minister (and copied to the Committee). He catalogued its handicaps and successes and concluded that 'it is a defensive weapon for use in peace as well as an offensive weapon for use in war.'[43] He was ignored. By contrast, SIS had begun planning its post-war future at the end of 1943.[44] On 5 June, 364 days after D-Day, 161 Squadron was disbanded.

Meanwhile the RAF's commitment to the Far Eastern theatre was substantial; as Verity later noted, 'In the end in SE Asia, we had more four-engined bombers parachuting men and supplies than dropping bombs.'[45] Indeed special operations here lasted well beyond VJ Day – see Rymills' career described in the Epilogue. The Lysander carried on the war in Burma in the hands of 357 Squadron. A handful of airframes had been shipped out to Bombay via the Suez Canal, for the flight commanded by George Turner. Peter Arkell was one of the pilots and had a salutary lesson in March when he crashed in a heavy landing at Salawas in Jodhpur. Petter's fault had struck again – Arkell, by now with 650 hours, had set the tail trim fully nose down before landing (he later claimed the tail trim bolts had fallen out). This had caused him to approach too fast, and his problems had been compounded by a 45-degree cross-wind. George Turner had had another landing accident in May.

Although all the missions were in daylight, life was tough – rations were terrible, and water was always in short supply. Pilots were handicapped by their landing fields being chosen and laid out by operators who had not been through the rigorous training enacted by 161 earlier – and the terrain was very unforgiving. In Arkell's words: 'They used to pick out these tiny little valleys between the mountain clefts for us to land on and creep up the mountain passes underneath the cloud and go into cloud and then do the entire thing by the map in cloud, come out of the cloud and find one of these idyllic little landing strips about five or six thousand feet [up].'[46] The Lysander's engine did not like the conditions – altitude compounded by heat, humidity, and dust and sand in the air filters, sapped its power. Moreover operations had to carry on through the monsoon period.

Another 357 pilot, Flt Sgt 'Stubby' Stubbings, had two landing accidents in Burma that summer, the second whilst carrying out a pick-up from a strip behind the lines. Western Burma is notoriously short of emergency landing possibilities – the jungle-covered mountains slope steeply down to the sea. He had been sent to land on a narrow strip of beach to rescue the crew of a downed Dakota, which had managed to land there, but he crashed on the beach himself, fortunately without serious injury.[47]

Peter Arkell's war came to an abrupt halt on 24 August. Having completed an astonishing 34 operations in Burma, this time he crashed at his destination on a pick-up operation in the jungle. Although the Japanese Emperor had capitulated a few days earlier, the message had not reached all his troops and the war was grinding on. Arkell was tasked with taking an agent and some ammunition to an airstrip named *Hyena*. In very cloudy weather, he narrowly missed a mountainside, but despite pouring rain found his destination. However, he landed too fast on what was a very short strip; having set his trim correctly he would have been able to go around for another attempt – were it not for the side of a mountain now staring at him through the Lysander's cockpit. His only option was to slow the Lysander and pancake into the tree canopy. This worked – to a degree – but the Lysander inverted, a wing fell off, and whilst his passenger extricated himself successfully, Peter was left semi-conscious. A group of Gurkhas and local tribesmen hacked their way through the jungle and pulled him out, his left arm badly damaged. George Turner flew in the following day to retrieve him. In due course Arkell was patched up at the RAF hospital at Wroughton in his home county of Wiltshire.[48] It is ironic that one of the last Special Duties operations of the Lysander's war ended in such injury. 357's record was remarkably good, given the challenging conditions in which it operated.

Conclusions

In terms of skill and courage, the pick-up pilots of 161 (and 148) were at or near the top of the pyramid of RAF aircrew. Unlike Fighter Command men they ventured into enemy skies alone or essentially so. Unlike Bomber Command pilots, they flew without a navigator (unless in a Hudson) and had to determine their own courses across enemy territory (unlike Bomber Command navigators). They were unarmed: their only salvation from searchlights, flak or night-fighters was a rapid dive to ground level to flee amongst the weeds. Moreover, they knew that in the event of crashing and capture, they would be subject to the most brutal interrogations that the Gestapo could conjure – for the details of special operations represented a particular treasure.

Or, as an official post-war review put it:

> Perhaps the most peculiar feature of the work for the pilot was that, except on the Hudson operations, he was alone. Everything depended on him until he landed at the Landing Ground, and then he was almost entirely in the hands of an amateur who had had at best ten days training in recent times, at worst two or three days a considerable time before. He set off in a most vulnerable machine to find a field 'somewhere in France' and if he had not outstanding skill and cool persistence, in many cases he would never have found it.[1]

161's pilots found the role immensely fulfilling, if exhausting; Hugh Verity, for example, recalled, 'it gave one a great sense of achievement if you could pull it off successfully – but largely because of the contacts one had with the passengers who were amazingly interesting and stimulating people'.[2]

SUCCESS

Although the resources required to mount a Lysander mission were nugatory compared to those for a heavy bomber raid, they were nonetheless significant. From the teams at Baker Street and AI2(c) through to the ground crews at Tempsford and Tangmere, the pilot was but the tip of the sword. Moreover, the infrastructure in France to get the right 'bods' or 'Joes' to the right field at the right time should not be underestimated. If the 161 Lysander pilot failed in any way, he was letting down a lot of colleagues. It is to the credit of these special pilots that very few of them did, as can be seen by the success ratios noted in Appendix A. The handful of pilots who were less than excellent were weeded out quickly. The primary causes of mission failure were the weather or the absence of a reception committee. The latter was usually the result of a communications issue – hardly surprising given the difficulties involved. All this made the occasions when an operator was late to the field or entirely absent, sometimes due to being drunk, more inexcusable. But such cases were thankfully very rare.

THE LYSANDER

When the RAF came to choosing a machine for special pick-up operations, the Lysander was the only game in town. It had become the sole single-engined Army Co-operation type through a War Office procurement process where true competition was wanting: the Lysander's only rival had been easily dismissed with its low-wing design. The lack of a competitive threat thus emboldened Teddy Petter into ignoring his test pilot's qualms about its dangerous landing characteristics. Combined with a tailwheel that was insufficiently robust for rough field operations, mainwheels that disliked cross-winds, brakes prone to fading, and an engine prone to carb icing, the Lysander was a compromised tool for 161 Squadron (and its forebears).

LOSS RATES

Nevertheless, 161's Lysanders and Hudsons displayed astonishing mechanical reliability. There was only one Lysander loss in France on special operations due to mechanical problems – Dinger Bell's crash. This is a huge testament to the skill and diligence of the ground crews at Tempsford and Tangmere. As we have noted above, the failure rate of missions was low. The 161 pilots were so highly skilled that almost all worked around the Lysander's potentially deadly attributes in the landing and go-around phases of flight. The death of Bartrum on a training flight was almost certainly due to his inability to overcome these flaws. But the impact of its design weaknesses could be more subtle: Nesbitt-Dufort's aborted mission in January 1942 was certainly not helped by the Lysander's engine being prone to carburettor icing.

Verity later summarized:

> Thirteen Lysanders were lost, four were shot down over France, four crashed on landing in France for various reasons, three crashed in fog on returning to England and two were inextricably bogged in mud. Seven of these 13 pilots survived, and only six were killed on pick-up operations. On the other hand, the reception teams and the farmers and their wives who sheltered the agents and their passengers had heavy losses, and many of them died in concentration camps in Germany.[3]

In my count, 15 airframes were lost, with ten pilot fatalities, and nine passengers or crew members dead (see Appendix E). Verity was unaware of Coghlan's mission and death, and appears to be including losses of Lysander airframes in non-fatal training accidents.

Noreen Riols concluded, 'Of the 329 high risk landings and PU operations by plane organised by SOE, 105 failed... and in France alone landed 324 agents and picked up 593. There were in total 600 casualties amongst their air crews, whose effective strength was 200. So between 1943 and 1945 the effective force was literally wiped out three times.'[4] She is, of course, including the Stirling and Halifax missions.

The Whitley/Stirling/Halifax Flight of 161 did indeed suffer very high losses, broadly in line with that of Bomber Command. This was due to their flying missions that involved deep penetration into enemy territory in easily noticed aircraft (the Germans had no four-engined bombers so Allied machines were easily identified as belonging to the enemy). In addition, the missions involved parachute dropping at night from little more than 1,000 feet above ground level, often in mountainous terrain; this was not a recipe for collecting a pension. By contrast, as we have seen, the Lysander and Hudson flights suffered remarkably low casualty rates.

Riols adds that (including SIS) 446 passengers were landed in France by air, and 655 brought back to the UK.[5] This compares to equivalent maritime insertions and extractions by the Royal Navy of 211 and 470, respectively. These numbers broadly equate to those given by Verity[6] where he adds that there were a total of 324 sorties of which 67 per cent were successful. The success rate of the 44 Hudson missions within that total was significantly better than the average at 82 per cent.

Verity reckoned that piloting a Lysander 'was quite easy if carefully planned before taking off. If the selected route was clear of flak defended zones, and went from coastline to a river, and there was no cloud, it was fairly easy. Hudson landings a little more difficult as it came in a little bit faster.'[7]

PILOTS

Forty-three pilots carried out pick-up operations, be it in Lysander, Hudson or Anson. Details are shown in Appendix A. However, only 11 carried out operations in double figures. Several who tried to attain the high standards of 161 were washed out during their training, or were banished after failing at the first or second mission they were given.

As noted above, Hudson operations tended to have a higher success rate, contributory factors being the carriage of a navigator, and greater attention paid to ensuring that the operator was at the right place at the right time.

In terms of the number of missions, there is a select bunch who shouldered a heavy workload: Vaughan-Fowler (26 operations), Mac (35) and Verity (36). It is no coincidence that they all served in the period from autumn 1942 to the close of 1943, when the operational requirement was at its peak, when the squadron was well commanded, and before the catastrophes of December that year. More than three-quarters of their missions were successful – altogether a performance worthy of the highest praise. One should also note that Pick Pickard carried out seven missions in seven months despite also leading the squadron at the time.

The special demands put on these men by pick-up operations carried a real risk of burn out, and we have seen that Lockhart and Verity in particular were exhausted by the end of their tour. One senses that Lockhart might have been retained by the squadron for longer had he not been stranded in France (and extracted).

The quality of its pilots, and the dangers they faced, was recognized in that 161 Squadron gained 142 gallantry medals during the conflict, albeit that the true reasons for their awards could not be revealed at the time.[8]

In the key period of 1942–43, 161 Squadron was very cohesive, its morale high. The unit had two great COs in succession, notably Bob Hodges, who was dearly loved by most of his men. Morale diminished in 1944 for two reasons. Firstly, there was an influx of new talent after the death of two modestly experienced pilots (which itself understandably depressed the mood), at the same time as the exodus of old hands, with insufficient overlap. Secondly, the management style of Boxer differed vastly from his predecessor, did not lead to the same *esprit de corps*, and indeed directly led to the departure of at least one skilled pilot.

RESOURCES

The assets devoted to pick-up operations grew from two Lysanders (plus two in reserve) with 419 Flight in August 1940, to 12 (plus one) Lysanders and five (plus one) Hudsons for 161 by May 1944.[9]

The arrival of the Hudson on Special Duties operations was a mixed blessing: of course, it allowed the carriage of ten passengers who could offload and embark much more quickly than if they had been transported in three Lysanders. But the Hudson was designed to operate from aerodromes, with tarmac or grass runways. Fully loaded, it weighed almost 8 tons. The Lysander was designed as an Army Co-operation machine to operate from almost wherever the Army was – including meadows. It weighed less than half the amount of the Hudson (3.3 tons was its absolute maximum), and had disproportionately large wheels and tyres. So it is unsurprising that most of the critical moments when a machine was bogged down in a French pasture involved Hudsons. It was only luck (and the toil of the population of more than one village) that meant that no Hudsons were lost in this way.

Portal and Harris were nothing if not constant in their disregard for special operations and the requirement for air assets that they posed. Whilst they decried the output of SOE and SIS before even assessing their potential (at least of the former), operational research even during the war showed that the heavy bomber campaign was a very blunt tool with regard to the enormous resources it consumed.

However, the Special Duties squadrons should not have felt that they had been singled out for special disregard – Harris was assiduous in defending his resources from predations from all directions. The Navy, RAF's Coastal Command and the Middle Eastern theatre in general were all often frequently the butt of similar treatment to that accorded the Special Duties squadrons. But perhaps another issue was at the back of Harris' mind: he was acutely conscious of the need for the public's support for his enterprise, and the need for publicity as oxygen for that. The main driver here was to uphold the morale of his bomber crews.[10] If he were to devote assets to clandestine operations, he knew that they would not be sustained by that oxygen of publicity. But then, the morale of the men of 161 was undimmed, and they were more than content in their obscurity. Their hard-earned medal ribbons enabled them to hold their heads high in Chichester's pubs.

For pick-up operations, the creation of a standalone Lysander squadron by say the beginning of 1943 would not have placed much of an additional burden on Bomber Command. Existing Lysanders were being employed only in Army Co-Operation tasks or secondary duties, and Westland could have converted more to Mk III SCW specification. Similarly, would it have been impossible to procure more Hudsons from Lockheed to create a standalone Hudson squadron? One doubts this would have inhibited the procurement of other light bombers or coastal command reconnaissance machines.

Recruitment of suitable Lysander pilots was at times difficult even at the scale that was achieved. But had the Flight been upgraded to squadron status, the recruitment criteria (which had focused on high hours, 250 hours of night flying, and ideally a French speaker) could have been relaxed a touch, to be offset by the creation of a longer, more structured induction and training regime.

The attitude of the Chief of the Air Staff was only sustainable regarding any potential enlargement of the numbers of bombers at 138 and 161 Squadrons used to drop agents and supplies. Here it is clear that Portal managed to sway the War Cabinet and Chiefs of Staff Committee to his advantage. It is worth pondering a counterfactual: if SOE had been under direct military control, would Portal's antipathy (and indeed SOE's friction with SIS) have been any less?

Mouse Fielden was both a very competent and useful man to head the Special Duties flying operations. There is little doubt that Churchill knew Fielden had the ear of the King, but one senses that Fielden was too much of a diplomat (and courtier) to bend the monarch's ear about Portal's stance.

Bob Hodges (clearly wearing his Halifax pilot hat) did not think that Bomber Command's not releasing resources 'was a major problem'. He considered the balance was about right for the number of agents and stores coming through. 'Losses were quite high due to the dangers of the type of flying we had to do – low level parachute drops. It was quite dangerous flying in mountainous areas.'[11]

SOE

ACM Sir Philip Joubert de la Ferté was in charge of Coastal Command for much of World War II, and his last service post was as Inspector General of the RAF; he knew whereof he spoke. After he retired from the service, he wrote several volumes; the last, *Fun and Games*, was published the year before he died. It therefore carries the trenchant opinions of a man of advanced years. He had 'the greatest admiration' for the output of the Intelligence Service. But he had much more nuanced praise for what he termed the 'resistance movement': 'For example, when a German officer was shot in the back in the Paris Metro extensive police precautions were at once taken by the occupying forces, which made it impossible for the Intelligence Service network to function until excitement died down. This happened not once but again and again.'[12] He saw that the more dubious members of French society were happy to hitch their wagon to that of the Germans initially, or to the Resistance later, when the tide of war had changed.

He went on: 'There must always be a division of opinion between those who believe that the encouragement of resistance movements in an occupied country is a worthwhile operation of war and those who are convinced that until these movements can be immediately supported by military success they are merely a waste of blood and treasure.'[13]

Dodds-Parker summarized SOE's legacy (which arguably was squandered with its peremptory demise): 'SOE was not very welcome, and still isn't in certain circles (in Whitehall more than Westminster), but it left behind it a most extraordinary liaison all over the world.'[14] Malcolm

Muggeridge, who had arrived at SIS via the Intelligence Corps, once remarked that 'MI6 and General de Gaulle's joint hatred of SOE was stronger than their hatred of the Abwehr'.[15]

Buckmaster as head of F Section was a divisive figure. Looking back, Gubbins reckoned Buckmaster had got the job 'because there was nobody else'.[16] His pre-war experience in the motor trade had left him with a good knowledge of French commercial life, but not the cynicism and ability to judge human nature that was essential to his wartime role. In de Vomécourt's view he had little understanding of the daily perils of working in the field, and did not fight his section's corner with sufficient aggression. Perhaps most critically, his defence of Déricourt – to the end – resulted in the deaths of many agents, and imperilled 161's pilots.

Gubbins on the other hand received plaudits from all quarters: Robin Brook for example could not 'imagine another soldier in the British Army who could have done as well'.[17] General Bedell Smith and his aide, Lt Gen Sir Frederick Morgan, wrote in a joint report to the Chiefs of Staff 'without the organisation, communications, material, training and leadership which SOE provided, "resistance" would have been of no military value'.[18]

In 1946, Buckmaster set de Gaulle in context:

> Men like Felix Gouin, Pierre Bloch, Jules Moch, Cusin and André Malraux were, I think, the real architects of French resistance, but who, because they were working with the British, are minimised by the de Gaulle clique (notoriously payers of lip service to de Gaulle because of the comfort of Carlton Gardens cum Duke St. life). The real resisters in France recognised de Gaulle as the symbol & the flag, but they resented his detached superiority, and his assumption that any resister who was not in his recognised (and between ourselves relatively inefficient) groups was 'working in the interests of a foreign power'... The groups with British officers at their heads (there were over 200 such groups with picked men numbering tens of thousands) were ignored by de Gaulle, although they in fact accounted for more than 2/3rds of the sabotage effected and 4/5 of the effective work at and after D-day. On no less than 3 occasions the entire French de Gaulle underground organisation was 'blown'... What I am trying to say is that by and large the French underground movement was undisciplined and ineffective, except when it worked under the guidance of a trained British (or a British-trained French) officer. De Gaulle

was extremely intolerant of our methods and refused to recognise our work, although constantly receiving proof that the British were 100% honest in their work on behalf of France. He ended up by ordering 2 of their best British officers ignominiously out of France. On the other hand, the French in France loved, admired even worshipped the British officers who shared their dangers – not as de Gaulle's staff did, give advice from a 'safe'? capital [sic]. Whilst I have every regard for a man like Médéric, who died nobly, or for Mme Aubrac, whom I knew well, I can't help feeling that the best of the French resisters were those who were recruited by our British officers & whose professed ambition was to have contact with Britain.[19]

If SOE was of worth, its success was down to: the introduction of STO (the forced recruitment into slave labour of young Frenchmen) in June 1942; its militarization in 1943 – the introduction of uniformed teams and greater professionalism; and the increasing utility of the air transport with which it was provided by 138 and 161 Squadrons. If much of the stores parachuted by the RAF ostensibly into Resistance hands went missing, SOE and its circuits were extremely economical in their use of munitions. Foot asserts that their industrial sabotage exploits in total required only c.3,000lb of explosives – only three-quarters of the bombload of a single de Havilland Mosquito![20] As for the human cost, Bomber Command's nightly losses could exceed those of F Section for the entire war.

Although, having fought a rear-guard action, SOE itself was despatched unceremoniously after the cessation of hostilities, its effects were long lasting. After the war Gubbins averred to Lord Selborne that SOE's wartime efforts led to many Western European countries joining the shelter of NATO, when they could otherwise have been lost.[21]

SIS

161's Lysanders and Hudsons became the only route by which the elderly, immobile, unhealthy or weak could speedily travel back to Britain. These categories encompassed many senior figures after the collapse of France. They would otherwise have remained in the Vichy/German orbit. But more importantly, Churchill's secret airline provided the only route by which Moulin and his lieutenants could travel to and from England with any despatch, to meet with de Gaulle and senior British figures. It is difficult to envisage how the young French general could have woven the almost incompatible strands of French politics together to create a unified resistance and, equally importantly, a governmental structure for post-war France. Without 161's travel service, de Gaulle would have been a hollowed-out leader with little democratic mandate. In that sense 161 helped to create the French nation we now know.

Remember the young men of 161, their skills and their sacrifices, the next time you sip a glass of French wine!

Epilogue

When once you have tasted flight, you will forever walk the earth with your eyes turned skyward. For there you have been, and there you will always long to return.

Leonardo da Vinci

THE LYSANDER

Its final role was most fitting: after earning its keep in Europe by bringing hope to those in occupied countries, its last operations (after Japan's surrender on 15 August) were to fly to Japanese PoW camps with medical personnel and supplies to bring aid to the Allied prisoners who had been treated so abominably by their Japanese guards.

After the end of the war, Philip Schneidau and Duff Cooper (British Ambassador to France at the time) arranged for a Lysander to be gifted to the French Air Ministry, in recognition of its wartime role. The handover ceremony took place on 27 January 1946 at Les Invalides in Paris. Many 161 pilots and agents were present, so it is little surprise that celebrations carried on until three the following morning. The aircraft was destined for the Musée de l'Air at Le Bourget, but was towed on its wheels (without its wings) to a store at Berne. This rendered the undercarriage unusable, and the airframe was scrapped unceremoniously in 1949.[1] A rather sad end to the Lysander's connection with France.

As Leonardo da Vinci noted above, pilots find it very difficult to relinquish the skies. It will be seen below that those pilots from 161 who remained in the RAF rose to senior rank. Many that left the service after VE Day moved into commercial aviation.

PILOTS

John Affleck
John moved to Farnham, and became a senior training captain in BEA post-war.

Murray Anderson
After being dismissed by Boxer from 161, Murray flew P-51 Mustangs for 65 Squadron carrying out 70 interdiction and ground attack sorties over northern France. He was then sent to the Far East to fly the DC3 in Transport Command. Post-war, he moved into airline flying on the HS748 with Dan–Air, where with his great personality and sense of humour he was revered by fellow crew members. He moved to Skyways Air Freight for a few years and retired from that role at the age of 60 with more than 22,000 flying hours! His brother Lindsay found fame as a film director. Anderson died in 2016 aged 96.

Peter Arkell
After recovering his health, Peter was sent by his father to the Tadcaster Tower Brewery in Yorkshire for some work experience before he joined the family brewery in Wiltshire in 1954, becoming Chairman in 1971. Under his command (and later), Arkell's Brewery went on to make several brews alluding to his service, including Moonlight and Mustang ales, the former for his 80th birthday. He retained an aviation link by becoming Chairman of the Anglo-American Relations Committee at RAF Fairford (an important US base in Gloucestershire in the 1960s and 1970s). He died in August 2010.

Douglas Bell
Dinger stayed in the RAF after the war, and went to the Central Flying School (CFS) at Little Rissington in 1951 to train as an instructor, where he won the CFS Trophy for best all-round student. He was awarded the AFC in 1954. He featured in several contemporary aerobatic teams, even into the Jet Provost (JP) era. His displays in the JP were legendary. Later, he flew Victor and Vulcan bombers, and commanded No. 139 Squadron.

It is thought he ended his flying days with the Missionary Aviation Fellowship in Africa.

Alan Boxer
The Kiwi was another to remain in the service after the war. After the RAF Staff College at Bracknell and the Army College at Haifa, he flew B-29s over Korea when on secondment to the USAF. In his capacity as OC 7 Squadron flying the Valiant, Alan was involved in Britain's nuclear test programme.

His last appointments were as Senior Air Staff Officer at HQ 1 Group, and then Defence Services Secretary (a new role involving liaison with Buckingham Palace) before retiring as AVM Sir Alan Boxer in 1970. Bob (by then Sir Lewis) Hodges read the oration at his funeral in 1998.

John Bridger
After Tempsford, he went to 4 Group to fly Halifaxes from Rufforth and Lissett. He was shot down by flak on 10 July 1943, and was incarcerated in the famous Stalag Luft III (he was not a participant in The Great Escape). After the war, he became a transport pilot flying for Air Charter Limited. On 23 April 1959, he was flying an Avro Tudor IV (G-AGRH) to Australia, with 12 engineers and some rather secret cargo for the UK's rocket testing range at Woomera, when he crashed into Mount Ararat in Turkey. Everyone on board perished. Despite the inaccessible terrain, British authorities acted quickly to destroy the remnants of the secret equipment.[2] Bridger had found his more exciting role.

Bernard Cordier
Immediately after the war he worked as a pilot for Air France, but in 1950 became a Trappist monk. In later life he was known as Prêtre Baudoin.

Edward Fielden
Immediately after VE Day, Fielden joined HQ Transport Command as Senior Air Staff Officer: he took over the organization of the routes at a time when reinforcements were being sent to the East, and men brought home for demobilization. 'Mouse proved a great organiser who left nothing to chance.'[3] In January 1947, he was appointed CO of the reformed King's Flight, and managed the procurement and use of helicopters. After retirement from the RAF in 1962, he was made Senior Air Equerry to

HM Queen Elizabeth II. Whilst in this role, he accompanied the young Prince Charles and Princess Anne on their first aircraft flight (from Aberdeen to Heathrow). In 1963, he was badly affected by the death of his only son, Mark, in a racing car accident at Silverstone. Mouse was knighted in the Royal Victorian Order, and died in Edinburgh in 1976 at the age of 72.

Andrew Geddes
Continuing his switches between khaki and Russian blue, Andrew Geddes returned to the Army and was made major in 1943. He had a tour in North Africa (Operation *Crusader*) in which he studied and consulted on Army/RAF co-operation. It was a case of round peg in a round hole as by now he had a unique experience of both Army and RAF ways, and understood the differing modus operandi. Returning to the UK on leave in January 1942, he piloted a Pan Am DC3 over West Africa to Nigeria. Back in England, he made recommendations on air attack of ground troops and armour which resulted in the re-equipping of Hurricanes with powerful cannon (the 'Tankbuster'). He drafted Army Training Instruction Number 6, which governed Army Co-Operation Command, and the Air Support Bible. This led him to a role in planning the aviation component of Operation *Overlord*, the invasion of northern Europe.

More formally he was head of Operations and Plans at HQ 2 TAF (the medium bomber and ground attack part of the RAF). At 0930hrs on D-Day he took off from RAF Gatwick in a P-51 Mustang. Half an hour later, he arrived over the British and Canadian sectors of the invasion beaches at an altitude of no more than 1,000 feet. Conscious that in the event he was shot down, such a high ranking officer with *Bigot* knowledge (an insider on D-Day plans) would be subject to extreme interrogation, he carried neither rank badges nor dog tags but had secreted a cyanide pill retained from his days with 1419 Flight. Gunner Geddes was the first pilot to bring photos back to England.[4]

At Eisenhower's invitation in spring 1945, Air Cdr Geddes was placed in charge of the air aspect of Operation *Manna*, the effort to drop food supplies to a starving Dutch nation. He negotiated face-to-face with the Germans to obtain secure drop zones, and subsequently became a friend of Prince Bernhard of the Netherlands. Post-war, he was charged with reducing the head count of officers in the RAF's rationalization programme, and

EPILOGUE

after a course at Staff College went to Africa to command a major RAF Flying Training School. He retired from the RAF in 1954. In 1976, at the age of 70, he took up hang gliding on the South Downs near where he lived, and died in 1988.

Bob Hodges

After Tempsford he was awarded a DSO, and went to the RAF Staff College. He then had a rest tour at Bomber Command HQ, but missed operations so much he dropped a rank to become CO of 357 Squadron, the Special Duties unit in South-east Asia (based in Jessore), flying Liberators and Dakotas as well as Lysanders; his arrival there was welcomed as a breath of fresh air. Like its counterparts in Europe, 357 Squadron acted in conjunction with SOE and SIS. 'Unlike Europe the territory over which we flew was dense jungle, with many more Japanese troops in evidence on the ground', he later recalled.[5]

He remained in the RAF after VJ Day, and stayed within the bomber orbit, later commanding elements of the V-Force. He commanded (and flew in) the RAF team of three Canberras in the 1953 London to Christchurch (New Zealand) air race. His final service post was as Air ADC to Her Majesty the Queen, and Deputy Commander-in-Chief Allied Forces Central Europe at Supreme Headquarters Allied Powers Europe (SHAPE) from 1973 to 1976. After retirement that year, as ACM Sir Lewis Hodges, KCB, with 2,361 flying hours, he became heavily involved in charity work; in the military sphere, he chaired the RAF Club, the RAF Association, and the RAF Escaping Society. He was diligent in keeping up with the friends he had made in the French Resistance.

Bob Hodges died in 2007 at the age of 88. At his funeral, which was attended by the senior echelons of military aviation (not to mention Peter Arkell), his son David read from the works of poet, codemaker and codebreaker Leo Marks.

Robin Hooper

Having been appointed British Ambassador to Tunisia in 1966, Hooper was knighted in the 1968 Queen's Birthday Honours; he served as British Ambassador to the Greek government from 1971 to 1974, after which he retired from the Diplomatic Service. Hooper attended a few RAF Museum and Special Forces events but, ever the diplomat, generally kept a low profile. He died in 1989 at the age of 74.

Per Hysing-Dahl

Decorated in Norway, France and Great Britain, Hysing-Dahl started an air taxi service in Norway. In 1969, he was elected to the Storting, the Norwegian Parliament, in due course becoming its Speaker. He had an emotional return to the Loire valley in 1984, and thereafter visited his Resistance friends frequently. In 1985, he visited Washington in his political guise, and had a meeting with Vice President George H.W. Bush. Per was astonished when Bush presented him with a trophy recording his rescue by US Navy Patrol vessel P567 from the Channel. He died in April 1989 after a long battle with cancer.[6]

Bob Large

After 161, Bob manoeuvred himself onto a squadron flying the new jet fighter, the Meteor. Bob Large remained in the RAF after the war, leaving regular service in 1947, and joined British European Airways (BEA), whilst remaining in the Royal Auxiliary Air Force, but had not become more responsible with age. His zest for life was undiminished: his dog, Patrick, entered the Guinness Book of Records as the first dog to fly in a jet aircraft – his 601 Squadron Meteor. By this time, he was a commercial pilot, remaining in the RAFVR, where he was 'always jocular, and one of the squadron's best raconteurs.'[7] Latterly, he flew cross-Channel flights (in aircraft somewhat bigger than a Lysander) for Silver City Airways.

He was also an accomplished sailor and completed a transatlantic crossing at an age when most men would be playing carpet bowls. Bob Large died in the last days of 2015 at the ripe age of 94.

Philippe Livry-Level

The Frenchman was posted out to 21 Squadron at the end of 1943 to rejoin Pickard. After the war, he retired with his wife Nicole to his château at Audrieu in Normandy, becoming *maire* there and then *député* for Calvados. He died in 1960.

Guy Lockhart

Guy was posted to the Air Ministry to work in AI2(c)'s Operations Room, a move designed to ease his shattered nerves. In November 1943, he moved to 627 Squadron as a flight commander in this Pathfinder unit flying Mosquitoes. At the dawn of 1944, he was given command of his own Mosquito squadron, No. 692, a Pathfinder light night-fighting unit.

But in March he became CO of 7 Squadron, flying Lancasters, and was killed on 27 April 1944 in an operation to Friedrichshafen. He is buried in the Durnbach War Cemetery.

James McCairns
After his advisory role with 148 Squadron in the Mediterranean theatre, he flew the Hawker Tempest fighter/bomber with 3 and 56 Squadrons until VE Day. The lure of the air remained strong and Mac joined the Royal Auxiliary Air Force with No. 616 Squadron in Yorkshire along with some wartime chums. He was killed on 13 June 1948 in a needless accident near RAF Finningley whilst flying one of their Mosquitos (his port engine failed at low level). Mac is buried at Retford – his epitaph is fittingly 'Better one crowded hour of glorious life, than an age without a name'. His son Chris joined the RAF and flew Jaguars, and had Peter Vaughan-Fowler's wife as godmother.

John Mott
Leaving the RAF in 1959, John Mott opted for a quieter life, becoming a tax inspector. Having twice been an evader, he retained close links with those Resistance members who had aided him. Awarded an MBE in 1944, he died in 2002. His son Dick flew Lightnings and Phantoms in the RAF (and was killed in one of the latter in 1980).

Alan Murphy
After a ground tour, Sticky did a conversion course onto Mosquitoes, and progressed to No. 23 Squadron in Malta initially as flight commander then as CO, when he created a joyous atmosphere in his team. The squadron returned to the UK in May 1944 and operated Mosquito night-fighters on Serrate missions (for radar counter-measures) in support of Bomber Command. W/Cdr Alan Murphy (Croix de Guerre avec Palme) lost his life on 2 December 1944 whilst hunting German night-fighters over the Ruhr. His Mosquito PZ456 was hit by flak and plunged to the ground near Oldebroek in the Netherlands, where Sticky now lies.

John Nesbitt-Dufort
See Appendix D for his very unusual posting after 138 and 161. He resigned his commission when he was offered a job in Yugoslavia in 1944. This came to nothing so he was reinstated. He was appointed station commander at

Gardemoen (Oslo airport) in 1945. Perks of this job included flying a Fiesler Storch (one of the Nazi's near-Lysander types) and a Messerschmitt Me 108 (with a German NCO in the back). Whippy left the RAF after VE Day.

He was OC Troops on HMS *Andes*, and later crossed the Atlantic in a solo yacht voyage. Whippy joined Trans Mediterranean Airways flying Avro Yorks (derived from the Lancaster) – flying vegetables from Beirut to the Gulf, and also Hajj passenger flights. Engine failures on such flights were 'very common'. His wife Beryl became a librarian at MI5.

Having been housebound for two years with arthritis and not having been granted a medical pension, Whippy died in 1964 of a heart attack. He was at the time writing another memoir on his life covering the period after *Black Lysander*.[8]

Percy Pickard
Pickard's Old English sheepdog Ming went with his widow to Rhodesia post-war and is said to have died making the same crying noise as when his master was killed in the Amiens raid aged only 28.

Len Ratcliff
After leaving the RAF in December 1945, he became a grain merchant in his home county of Essex, eventually becoming a director of Spillers. Like many 161 pilots, he was made Chevalier of the Légion d'Honneur; closer to home he became High Sheriff of Essex. He died on 1 April 2016, aged 96.

Frank Rymills
After 161 he ended up at 38 Group, and towed gliders to Normandy on D-Day. Henry, Bunny's cocker spaniel, was stolen just before the end of the war when he was being taken for a walk in Regent's Park, London.

Rymills disappeared from view in April 1945 before reappearing in July 1947, having been uncontactable even by his wife. His family believe he was carrying out clandestine missions of some sort in the Far East, most probably for SIS. His *Times* obituary mentions his participation in Operation *Termite* to flush communist guerrillas from the Malaysian jungle. Later moving to West Suffolk, he began pig farming, but then set up a business making scientific instruments in Cambridge. He never lost his love for the countryside. Bunny died in 1997.

EPILOGUE

Gordon Scotter
Gordon became a service test pilot during the war, serving at RAF Boscombe Down with the feted Battle of Britain pilot Paddy Barthropp, and was awarded the DFC and a King's Commendation for Valuable Services in the Air in 1946. Scotter progressed to becoming a test pilot for Rolls Royce, and later flew at Air Service Training Limited at Hamble, Southampton. He died in Cairo in 1969 at the age of only 49.

George Turner
George went on to lead the pick-up flight of 357 Squadron in Burma commanded by Bob Hodges. He flew the airborne Lysander scenes in the film *Now It Can Be Told*, which dramatized 161's wartime exploits (Bob Large did the landing sequences). After the war, Turner rejoined the Metropolitan Police, and died whilst gardening in 1976.

Peter Vaughan-Fowler
At Pickard's invitation, Peter had a short period with 21 Squadron flying night-fighter Mosquitoes, where Livry-Level joined him as navigator. As noted in Chapter 18, he then commanded 148 Squadron's Lysander Flight in Italy and Corsica. After D-Day, he commanded a Mustang ground attack squadron, and was awarded the DSO. Immediately post-war, he carried out intelligence staff work, and then became CO of No. 247 Squadron flying Vampires, after which he was posted to the Central Fighter Establishment. Peter was awarded the AFC in the 1954 New Year's Honours. He became Wing Commander (Flying) at RAF Wildenrath as the Cold War heated up, and then a more sedate appointment followed as Deputy Captain of the Queen's Flight in 1963 (which resulted in a CVO (Commander of the Royal Victorian Order) in 1967). His last service role was in public relations at the Ministry of Defence with the rank of group captain, retiring in 1975. He met his wife Hilary through Stephen Hankey's wife, and they went on to have an astonishing four sons and four daughters. Peter Vaughan-Fowler died on 24 April 1994 in Oxford.

Hugh Verity
After SOE and AI2(c), Hugh supervised Special Duties flying in Southeast Asia, where he continued to bump into Hodges and Vaughan-Fowler. After VJ Day, he contracted polio in India but was repatriated to the UK and recovered. He had posts in command of a Meteor night-fighter squadron,

OC Flying at Hahn in Germany, and Wing Commander Operations at 2 TAF. Towards the end of his service career, he was posted to Central Treaty Organization (CENTO) HQ in Turkey and then became station commander at Akrotiri in Cyprus. He left the RAF in 1965 and served in management positions at various industry bodies.

A keen founder member of the Special Forces Club, he took on the mantle of keeping the flame of the Lysander pilots alive, and was a key figure in post-war reunions with Resistance colleagues in France. Hugh died in November 2001, aged 83.

CHARLES DE GAULLE

On the steps of the Hotel de Ville in Paris, 25 August 1944, Charles de Gaulle proclaimed: 'Paris liberated! Liberated by its own efforts, liberated by its people with the help of the armies of France, with the help of all of France, that is France in combat. The one France, true France, eternal France.'[9]

His programme to disown his comrades in arms and rewrite history had begun. De Gaulle's attitude to those who had been helped by 161 was atrocious. In the weeks after parts of his homeland had been liberated, he crushed the euphoria of FFI officers who had co-ordinated behind-the-lines resistance, ordering them to remove decorations such as the Croix de la Libération.[10] Gildea argues that de Gaulle created a myth of a France unifying to liberate itself – that myth was military, national and male.[11] In December 1964, ahead of his upcoming re-election, de Gaulle had the remains of Jean Moulin (who had of course been de Gaulle's emissary to attempt to unite the Resistance factions in 1942) reinterred in the Panthéon.

He was bitter that France was not a participant at the Yalta Conference drawn up by the Allies to discuss a new world order, but France was given command of a slice of Germany, and was granted a seat on the Security Council of the newly formed United Nations. His immediate post-war task was to commute many of the death sentences the French law courts handed down to collaborators. After years in the political wilderness he was appointed president in 1958 and became a driving force in the creation of the European Economic Community (EEC). Surviving several assassination attempts (*Day of the Jackal*, etc.) he resigned in 1969, and died in November the following year.

EPILOGUE

AGENTS

There were 20,000 Resistance members killed in action or shot shortly after capture, and 200,000 French were killed in the Nazis' concentration camps. Only 24 London-trained F Section agents and six from RF survived captivity.[12] Of 470 F Section agents sent into the field (by 138/161 or by other means), 118 failed to return, a casualty rate therefore of 25 per cent (the rate for female agents was 33 per cent).[13] Of the 50 female agents sent to France by SOE, 15 were captured, of whom only three survived.[14]

Pierre Brosselette
In February 1944, he was returning to England by boat, but it sank off the shore of Brittany, and he was arrested by the Gestapo. It took a while for the Germans to realize the value of their prize, after which the torture started in earnest. After three days, he realized he was in danger of breaking, and in an act of ultimate bravery, threw himself from a fifth-floor window of the Gestapo's Paris HQ. His ashes now lie in the Panthéon.

Mathilde Carré
Having been interrogated in England, Mathilde was sent back to France after the Liberation, tried for treason, and sentenced to death. Soon commuted to life imprisonment, she was released in 1954, and wrote a self-exculpating autobiography. She died in Paris in 2007.

Peter Churchill
After imprisonment in Fresnes, Peter spent more than ten months in solitary confinement at Sachsenhausen. In April 1945, he was moved to Dachau via Flossenburg, and was shepherded to Austria ahead of the advancing Americans. He was liberated at the end of the month. He and Odette Sansom married in 1947, and in the film of their exploits (*Odette*), he was played by Trevor Howard. They divorced in 1956, and he remarried, living in France until his death in 1972.

Roman Czerniawski
He played a key role in Allied deception plans (*Fortitude*) ahead of D-Day. The Pole offered to work for MI6 after the war, but was regarded as too much of a handful. He ended up as Minister of Information of the Polish government-in-exile in London and died there in 1985.

Jacques Vaillant De Guélis

He died in hospital in Lichfield on 7 August 1945, of injuries sustained in a car crash near Flossenburg concentration camp whilst travelling for his post-war duties.

Henri Déricourt

After D-Day, Henri did some flying for the Free French, but had a bad crash near Châteauroux in September 1944.

Francis Cammaerts later summed up Déricourt as 'a completely heartless deceiver who enjoyed the kicks involved; that was the way he was going to get the best out of the war'.[15] After the war his supporters, namely Buckmaster and Bodington, continued to protest his innocence. But amongst 161 pilots, even his cheerleaders such as Verity now recognized he was a wrong 'un. Tried by the French, 'he chose a Court-Martial because the sentence of a Court-Martial is final, the decision of a CM cannot be challenged afterwards and at that CM he was acquitted, and it was since then really that evidence has come to light to show that he was definitely guilty.'[16]

Astonishingly, Buckmaster never mentioned Déricourt, or indeed Paul Frager, in his autobiography *They Fought Alone*. Likewise Gubbins never mentioned him in his own autobiography.

In May 1946, Déricourt was arrested in the UK, after being described as 'an active and cunning smuggler', in this case of gold and platinum. After a few days in Brixton prison, he was deported to France. His wartime conduct was outed in December 1946, when the *Sunday Empire News* carried an article entitled 'Gestapo Papers Name Trick Spy', after papers at the Gestapo HQ in Paris had been found by the French Securité.[17] At this time he was flying for Air France on the London–Paris route. He was arrested by the French on charges of treason.

He supposedly died in Laos on 21 November 1962 while piloting a small aircraft. It was said he was smuggling gold bars and heroin at the time.[18]

Pierre de Vomécourt

Pierre was arrested in autumn 1943, and incarcerated for the rest of the war in Colditz, where he was a colleague of David Stirling (founder of the SAS) on the Escape Committee. He died in 1986.

EPILOGUE

Marie-Madeleine Fourcade
Marie-Madeleine was commissioned as a full colonel, and went back to France after the war to search for her missing agents. She continued working for SIS for some years, becoming Mme Fourcade on her remarriage in 1947, and had three more children. She hitched her colours firmly to de Gaulle's political mast, and was a member of the European Parliament for a time, living in Mougins in Provence. This outstanding agent published her memoirs (*L'Arche de Noé*) in 1968 and died in Paris in 1989. Her honours included the OBE, Croix de Guerre, and Commander of the Légion d'Honneur.

Pierre Hentic
Hentic endured interrogation and torture in Paris, and was transported to Dachau in June 1944. He survived to rejoin the French Army after VE Day. He had an illustrious military career, serving in French Indo-China and Algeria, received many decorations and died in 2004.

Claude Lamirault
Hentic's colleague died in strange circumstances in a car accident only days after being liberated from Dachau in May 1945. His network, JADE-FITZROY, had suffered substantial casualties.

Jean Moulin
The traitor who led to the Caluire arrests was never identified. Tortured barbarically by Klaus Barbie in Lyon, Moulin gave little away. The Berlin Gestapo summoned him, but he died on the train to Germany. His ashes are in the Panthéon; his place at the summit of Resistance leaders is secure.

Christian Pineau
After his capture during the attempted extraction with Guy Lockhart, he escaped, but was arrested again in 1943, interrogated by Barbie in Lyon, and ended up in Buchenwald where he survived to be liberated by the Americans. He was a minister in de Gaulle's post-war government, and in fact was France's signatory to the Treaty of Rome. He died in 1995.

Philip Schneidau
He remained with SIS in Paris until retirement in 1947, after which he resumed his career as a chartered accountant, and died in 1984.

OTHERS

Many of the central staff of SOE rose to senior positions in politics (on both sides of the floor).

Kenneth Cohen
From 1945 to 1947, KC was Director of Production for SIS, being awarded the CMG (Order of St Michael and St George) in 1946. He was then promoted to Chief Controller of Europe, until retiring with a CB (Companion of the Order of the Bath) in 1953, later working in the steel industry and Euratom. As a good SIS man, his memoirs remained private. He died in 1984.

Douglas Dodds-Parker
Post-war, Douglas became a Tory MP for Banbury for five years and rose to Under Secretary of State in the Foreign Office. He was a founder member of the Special Forces Club in London. He wrote two volumes of memoirs, and died in 2006.

Colin Gubbins
The SOE was officially disbanded in January 1946, leaving Gubbins jobless – 'SOE's brilliant, bloody-minded CD [Gubbins] had been dismissed like a redundant doorman.'[19] He became director of a textile company where his man management skills were put to good use. Along with Dodds-Parker, he became a founder member of the Special Forces Club. Becoming involved in the cause of European unification, he remarried in 1950 – to a Norwegian with strong wartime Resistance connections. They moved to the Highlands in 1970, and six years later, shortly before he died, Gubbins was appointed Deputy Lieutenant of the Islands Area, Western Isles. At his memorial service in St Martin's in the Fields in 1976, more than a thousand people from many nations attended.

Harald Penrose
He carried on the life-threatening role of being Westland's chief test pilot, with the Wyvern aircraft giving him particular challenges. In due course, he ceased test flying and became a sales manager for Westland, Bristol and Saunders-Roe, all companies which progressed to manufacturing helicopters. Having amassed 5,000 flying hours, Harald became an assiduous and gifted writer, producing five autobiographical tomes, and chronicled

EPILOGUE

British aviation history in a well-received five volume series. He died in 1996, aged 92.

Teddy Petter
Teddy moved to English Electric after World War II, where he worked on the P1 (which became the Lightning). Considering British fighters were becoming too complex, he moved to Folland to design smaller combat aircraft (including the successful Gnat). He left to join a Swiss religious commune, and died young in 1968.

Lord Selborne
Judgement on his wartime performance at the head of MEW included that he 'brought just the right qualities to the department of delegation within, and firmness without, which one would expect of a long political apprenticeship.' He chaired the National Provincial Bank for three years, and died in 1971.[20]

THE REMNANTS

The UK
The barn at Gibraltar Farm, the epicentre of Tempsford's special operations (it was where agents were kitted out immediately before embarkation) survives, but is on private land. It is used for an annual commemoration service. However, in 2024, Tempsford was designated as a potential site for housebuilding. The very qualities that caused Harris to bequeath it for special operations – that it is boggy – may yet save it, since it is on a flood plain.

RAF Tangmere closed in 1970, but in the north-west corner of the old airfield is the Tangmere Aviation Museum. It is densely packed with exhibits, but the legacy of the 161 receives just attention. Just beyond the museum's entrance lies the Cottage, once more a desirable residence, its World War II excitement just a blip in its long history. Likewise, Bignor Manor remains in its aloof position to the north-east, giving little hint of the characters that passed its doors in wartime.

Two Lysanders remain in flying condition in the UK, one at the excellent Shuttleworth Collection in Bedfordshire, the other at John Romain's (very skilled) Aircraft Restoration Company at Duxford. Both are to be seen on the airshow circuit.

France

There are several regional museums devoted to keeping alive the memory of the Resistance. To varying degrees they credit 161 for nourishing the Maquis, but understandably devote greater attention to the operators who organized the Lysander and Hudson sites. Of more national importance is the museum in Lyon, since that became the default capital of Resistance activities. There Jean Moulin is granted almost saint-like status. In Lyon, a visit to the Montluc prison is recommended, albeit chilling, for there stayed many of 161's passengers after their capture, and before or during their torture by Klaus Barbie.

There is a national memorial at Valençay, which lists the names of all SOE agents who died in action. Again there is an annual service of remembrance. Some of the Lysander and Hudson landing sites are marked by small monuments (which the French call a *stèle*) showing the names of the personnel involved. The handful of 161's pilots who fell to earth in France lie of course in Commonwealth War Graves Commission cemeteries, all beautifully tended. Duty done, may they rest in peace.

Appendices

APPENDIX A: PICK-UP PILOT AND SQUADRON STATISTICS

Number of sorties

Pilot	Lysander	Hudson	Anson	Total	Dates	Success rate (%)
Coghlan	1	0	0	1	Aug 1940	0
Geddes	1	0	0	1	Sept 1940	100
Farley	1	0	0	1	Oct 1940	100
Pickard	7	5	0	12	Oct 1942–Apr 1943	67
Scotter	4	0	0	4	Apr–May 1941	100
Nesbitt-Dufort	6	0	0	6	Sept 1941–Jan 1942	67
Murphy	5	0	1	6	Sept 1941–May 1942	83
Huntley	2	0	0	2	Aug–Sept 1942	0
Lockhart	11	0	0	11	Mar–Dec 1942	55
Mott	1	0	0	1	May 1942	0
Vaughan-Fowler	26	0	0	26	Sept 1942–Sept 1943	81
McIndoe	3	0	0	3	Oct 1942	0
Bridger	13	0	0	13	Sept 1942–May 1943	77
McCairns	35	0	0	35	Nov 1942–Nov 1943	83

MOONLIGHT CRUSADERS

Pilot	Lysander	Hudson	Anson	Total	Dates	Success rate (%)
Verity	30	6	0	36	Dec 1942–Nov 1943	83
Rymills	13	0	0	13	Jan–Jul 1943	85
Fielden	0	4	0	4	May–Jul 1943	50
Hooper	12	0	0	12	Aug–Nov 1943	42
Hankey	13	0	0	13	Sept–Dec 1943	38
Bathgate	11	0	0	11	Sept–Dec 1943	82
Hodges	4	8	0	12	Jul 1943–Feb 1944	67
Affleck	0	9	0	9	Oct 1943–Aug 1944	67
Ratcliff	4	1	0	5	Mar–Aug 1944	80
Ferris	0	1	0	1	Apr–Sept 1944	100
Milstead	1	0	0	1	Feb 1944	0
Ibbott	0	2	0	2	Apr–Aug 1944	100
McBride	6	0	0	6	Oct–Dec 1943	50
Whitaker	7	0	0	7	Feb–May 1944	57
Bell	3	0	0	3	Feb–Mar 1944	33
Anderson	9	0	0	9	Feb–Apr 1944	89
McDonald	3	0	0	3	Feb 1944	67
Hysing-Dahl	8	0	0	8	Mar–Jul 1944	75
Taylor	5	0	0	5	Apr–Jul 1944	60
Turner	5	0	0	5	Apr–Aug 1944	100
Large	3	0	0	3	Apr–Aug 1944	100
Alcock	2	0	0	2	Apr–Aug 1944	50
Alexander	3	0	0	3	May–Aug 1944	100
Bruce	1	0	0	1	Apr–May 1944	100
Lamberton	1	0	0	1	Aug 1944	0
Newhouse	2	0	0	2	May–Aug 1944	50
Arkell	1	0	0	1	Aug 1944	100
Wilkinson	0	4	0	4	May–Sept 1944	100
Boxer	0	5	0	5	May–Sept 1944	80
Total	**263**	**45**	**1**	**309**		

Notes:
1. Excludes 148 and 347 Squadrons operations (as documentation is less thorough).
2. Excludes Hudson agent dropping by parachute and Lysander mail only pick-up operations.
3. Bolded pilot names lost their lives on missions.

Total 161 and 138 Squadron operations

Aircraft	Sorties	Operations	Success	Aircraft losses	Success rate (%)
Lysander	266	263	187	13	70
Hudson PU	39	38	33	0	85
Hudson	140	143	72	10	51
Whitley	139	147	105	6	76
Halifax	786	1162	667	17	85
Stirling	273	307	190	6	70

Source: TNA, AIR 277/1068/40, 161 ORB April 1945
Note: Excludes 'Ascension' operations.

APPENDIX B: LYSANDER ACCIDENT STATISTICS, 1937–45

Categorization of aircraft accidents is necessarily a little subjective. I have analysed all Lysander accidents in the RAF records in the period above. Discarding those not down to any flying mishap – for example, a Lysander written off as a result of the collapse of a hangar roof – there are 839 reported accidents.

What is striking is firstly how few (less than 2 per cent) are due to the airframe, such as bits falling off during flight or malfunctioning. Secondly, as this is a machine that was used for training and by pilots with few flying hours, there is unsurprisingly a reasonable number (52, or 6 per cent) caused by the stupidity of low flying or Controlled Flight into Terrain (CFIT) – in one instance, a pilot flew into a ship in the Irish Sea. In fairness to those pilots, the Lysander's role of Army Co-operation flying would have required much low-level work.

Forced landings are caused by many factors, not the least engine issues, another being poor weather. A quarter of accidents were occasioned by a forced landing going wrong. The 'Miscellaneous' category contains a few accidents where the pilot flew his Lysander into a barrage balloon cable, a natural hazard in World War II.

However, the design flaws noted in Chapter 1 make themselves evident in these statistics. Adding together the categories of overshoot, stall on landing and landing accounts for 333, or 40 per cent, of all accidents. These are categories where Petter's tailplane trim flaw is likely to have contributed to the total.

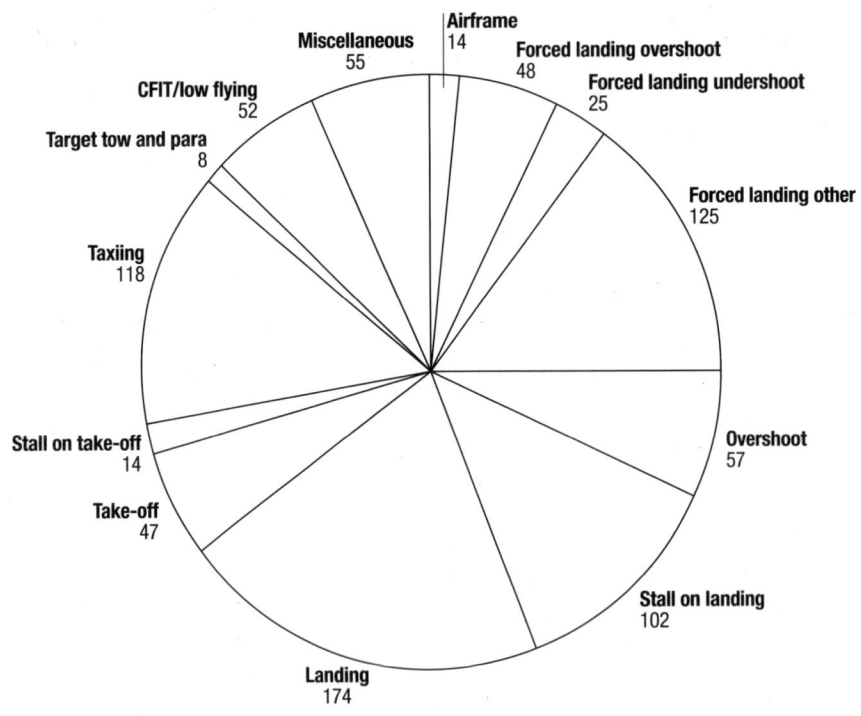

APPENDICES

APPENDIX C: MEMO FROM GP CAPT BRADBURY (DDI 2) TO AVM SIR CHARLES MEDHURST (ACAS (I)), 25 AUGUST 1941

Most Secret
Night Emplaning of Lysander Aircraft

1. I would like to draw your attention to the recent developments which have been made in perfecting the technique of these operations. I think that it is quite possible that the possibilities of this type of operation may not have been fully appreciated, and I submit the following notes and suggestions in the hope that you will pass them on to ISRB and SIS with any comments and amplifications that you may care to add.
2. The Lysander used has an operational range of 1200 miles and is capable of delivering one man, or 100 lbs freight, and of carrying away two men and equivalent weight. Its take-off run is now 100 yards, and landing run 250 yards.
3. It has already been proved that the operation is perfectly feasible. Recently there have been technical improvements in homing, in take-off, and in defensive armour. Co-operation with Fighter Command has led to valuable improvements in safety precautions. The weak point of comparative defencelessness over the enemy fighter area has been fairly well covered. The apparent weak point of the landing has been completely covered. Intensive training in night landings has given the two pilots [Scotter and Nesbitt-Dufort] a mathematical certainty in the accuracy of touch-down and the length of run has now been arrived at. With the new flare path technique, the complete embarkation from touch-down to take-off, including disposal of flare-path, is completed in 60 seconds [this is an over-claim in practice]. The special course given to the agent guarantees a sensible selection of landing ground and a correct flare-path layout.
4. I am now confident that the operation may be regarded as no more hazardous than a bombing trip to a well-defined area; it is

probably less so, because although the aircraft is defenceless to the rear, it lends itself excellently to evasive tactics at night.

5 The probability of success at present depends on the weather. In good weather the chances of success are 95% and in bad weather they are nil. Installation of a blind-approach apparatus has improved the safety of the return journey. The date of operation, which in the past had perforce to be rigidly fixed, can now have a degree of flexibility, due to improved communications.

6 We now have a method of transport which for this type of work, in wartime, is reasonably efficient. Its possibilities are far-reaching, and in my opinion the organisations for which we cater have not yet realised its full potentialities.

   a) (i) With its operational range of 1200 miles (1620 absolute) the Lysander can pick up in Denmark, Western Germany, Belgium, Holland, and the whole of France. Of course, however, there are many factors, topographical and strategic, which eliminate the use of large areas of these countries.

   (ii) It can fly non-stop to Gibraltar, and thence to Malta. From Malta it could operate in Crete, Greece, Sicily, and the major part of Italy. In case these ranges should appear to be beyond the bounds of feasibility, I would mention

   (1) That the VHF homing we use, contacts the aircraft over 100 miles from base.
   (2) Food extracts and benzadrine derivatives are available to keep the pilot fresh and fit. A recent 6 hour flight over France proved the efficacy of these aids.
   (3) The pilots are night-flying specialists with 3,000 hours flying.

   b) At present an agent is earmarked for pick-up. He is given a week's course; possible landing sites are given him from our records; signalling details are settled; and when communications have confirmed the arrangements on the chosen date, the pilot goes off and brings him back.

   This arrangement is satisfactory, but it is suggested that it may shortly be supplemented on the following lines.

Into each enemy-occupied country there will be placed an agent with previous flying experience who has been given a special course by 1419 Flight in the selection of sites and flare-path technique. His function will be two-fold:
- (1) To select in his country as many sites as possible which would be ideal from every point of view, to survey them and to communicate their fullest details to this country. We will arrange for air photographs and agree to his selections.
- (2) To be present, when required, at the site of a proposed pick-up and to supervise the flare-path layout and embarkation procedure.

7 The far-reaching implications of this proposed development should at once be obvious. The Lysander will bring back two men or equivalent weight. The two men embarked need have no knowledge of aircraft. They need not be agents; they may be political refugees, or highly placed sympathisers, or even important escaped prisoners-of-war. When two-way communications can be relied upon up to two hours before a flight is scheduled to begin, kidnapping operations should be feasible. The sudden arrival in this country of one or two highly placed enemy-sympathisers would have tremendous propaganda value.

Source: TNA, 138 Squadron Policy, AIR 20/8242

APPENDIX D: JOHN NESBITT-DUFORT'S NEXT POST

From John Nesbitt-Dufort's unpublished memoir, via Dick Nesbitt-Dufort

After about three months, during which I had scared the living daylights out of myself more than once in various highly unsuitable tug and glider combinations, the vexed problem of positioning the glider behind the tug while on tow on a dark night arose. I suppose at the time I was the most experienced Lysander pilot in the unit, so it was natural that I should be detailed for the first night tug trial of the type. The glider for the test was a Hotspur, an eight-seater, with the famous Robert Kronfeld at the controls. The problem was that, at night, glider pilots found it extremely difficult to maintain the correct tow position relative to the tug. To overcome this, the boffins had stumbled on the bright idea of mounting an Angle-Of-Approach-Indicator on outriggers immediately behind the rudder of the Lysander, without, it transpired, much thought as to the aerodynamic consequences of the arrangement. This now antique piece of apparatus was a heavy metal rectangular box standing about 3 foot six inches high containing a bright light which shone through three strips of amber, green and red glass. The apparatus used to be carefully levelled on the ground to the left of the runway threshold, and when it was switched on, all the tired pilot had to do when returning from a mission on a dark night was to adjust his approach angle so that the light showed green all the time; if he got too high, it showed amber, and if too low, red. An excellent system for the ground, but would it work in the air?

On 11th June 1942, which was an extremely dark moonless night, with 8/8ths overcast at about 2,000 feet so not even a glimmer of a star showed, I viewed with a torch and a considerable amount of misgiving the untidy arrangement at the back of the Lysander. The boffins had assured me that this heavy lump of metal would not put the centre of gravity out of the aft limit, or otherwise seriously affect the handling characteristics of the aircraft, and I, poor fool, believed them! At 23.30 hours that evening, Lysander 9276 lined up on the main runway with Robert in his Hotspur hooked up behind. He called over the intercom, routed along a cable attached to the towrope, that he was ready, so I took up the slack, and, obtaining clearance from the tower, opened up using the automatic boost control cut-out to obtain full power.

At first, everything seemed to be OK; naturally Robert was airborne fairly early, but I then seemed to be stuck at about 48 mph, with my madly shimmying tailwheel still firmly on the ground and half the runway gone already. 'High tow, now!' I yelled. Robert, at the same time, had instinctively spotted my trouble; up he went slightly above the high tow position, up came my tail, and our speed slowly started to build again. With the stick hard forward and full nose down trim I saw the red boundary lights getting nearer and nearer. We had been committed to take-off as soon as the glider got airborne. Now at only 55 mph, I had to do something about it fast. 'Down a shade, Robert, for Christ's sake!' Again he had almost anticipated my trouble, as just before I eased a fraction of forward pressure off the stick, I got a slight acceleration, the tailwheel banged back on the ground, its oleo bottoming, and at only 57 mph, with the good old

Mercury screaming defiantly, we were airborne and the red lights flickered by a few feet below.

The boffins must have been joking about that centre of gravity, as it was certainly a hell of a way aft of limits. Robert, in fact, did that take-off, his superb skill being responsible for us getting airborne at all, as with a less experienced glider pilot, we would have been ploughing a deep furrow in the adjacent field. He permitted himself a mild 'Phew!' over the intercom, and I mentally agreed, but was too busy to answer, as although our speed had now built up to 59 mph, our rate of climb, which was showing as only 50 feet per minute, seemed infinitesimal and the cylinder head temperatures were well over their limits already. Normally the stalling speed of a Lysander was well below this, but it should be remembered that I had the additional weight of the heavy nylon towrope, not to mention the massive steel box on the outriggers behind me.

Anyone who has flown over England during the blackout on a really dark night knows that it is absolutely essential to stick on instruments, but I must admit that the temptation to look ahead for the inevitable obstacles which must have been tearing by a few feet below my undercarriage was nearly unbearable. At just over 60 feet, Robert called cheerfully that he was having no difficulty staying in the green, but how about a little more height? Sweating profusely I was too busy to answer, but after an age we seemed to have wallowed up to a hundred feet with the ASI stuck at a steady 65 mph, so I called Robert and told him that I would have to level out for a minute or so to try to build up enough speed to cool my engine, as the cylinder head temperatures were now off the clock. Reluctantly, he agreed, as a seized engine at that altitude would have meant curtains for both of us. In view of the fact that I had very limited forward movement of the stick to play with, I had some difficulty in getting the position of the little aeroplane a fraction lower on the artificial horizon, but eventually the speed started to creep up without any perceptible loss of height. At 74 mph and just over 110 feet, the engine temperature was back on the clock but still dangerously high.

Wonderful! I'll see if she'd hold that speed in a shallow climb. I was about to ease off a shade of the forward pressure on the stick again when I noticed a slightly sloppy feeling about the rudder pedals. Before I could investigate, there started such a violent juddering of the tail that the instruments blurred in front of my eyes, and suddenly the rudder pedal snapped over to the full left position and the Lizzie slewed off course. There was a loud yell from Robert of 'Take it easy, John!' as I applied brute force to the right pedal and tried to centralise the rudder, but with a loud bang, it flipped over to the full right position, a savage correction and over it went again. For what seemed an age I fought those madly kicking rudder pedals, as, whilst still on instruments, I careered all over the inky black landscape with Robert grimly hanging on behind. A snap glance at the engine instruments showed me that it would be suicidal to slow up again, and soon the cylinder head temperatures had gone off the clock again, but in addition the oil temperature was now also way above limits and the oil pressure about half what it should be. The unfortunate Mercury was still screaming away at full boost and revs in fine pitch with the cooling gills wide open. To bale out at that altitude was impossible, so I must at all costs save my engine, and this meant maintaining my present speed or better. Eventually, by half standing up and bracing myself against my straps with my legs rigid I was able to keep that rogue rudder centralised, but it was a bitter struggle and before long both my legs were aching abominably. There had been silence from Robert since his call on my first frantic swerve, but this was understandable. It must have been complete hell trying to keep line astern formation in the dark on an unpredictable and wildly weaving tug. Afterwards, he told me that he realised at about the same time as I did what was happening, which was that that damn angle of glide indicator, being immediately behind the rudder, had exactly the same effect as if it had been immediately in front of it. It blanketed the rudder off completely, actually creating back pressure over the rudder and fin, and rendering them worse than useless.

I now reassured Robert, and myself, that things were more or less under control, and, subject to the engine not having an epileptic fit with a rate of climb of very nearly 20 feet per minute, we might even gain sufficient altitude over base for a safe cast off and landing. At peak revs we were galloping through the gravy, and as our weight slowly came down, our speed crept up, but with only an infinitely small improvement in engine temperatures. At about 78 mph, a further complication set in, and for me it was very nearly the last straw. With a gentle thud, the leading edge slots closed, also automatically raising the flaps, necessitating forward trim, which was something I had run out of from the start. Up came the nose out of control, down came the speed, the slots opened, down went the flaps again, and so on, with the rudder still trying to break free every few seconds. This was altogether too much for me. To hell with it! If the engine cooks, it cooks! After expelling every oath I knew, the next time the flaps came down, I caught her and kept the ASI at about 75 mph or below.

APPENDICES

I longed to be rid of my towed burden, but there's an unwritten understanding between tug and glider pilots that the tug pilot never releases, that is always the glider pilot's responsibility, and quite rightly so, unless there is an extreme emergency, such as a fire, in the tug aircraft. On eventually reaching 500 feet, I called for a back bearing and was lucky at that height to get a very faint Class C. Somehow I managed to get the aircraft round onto its reciprocal and we headed for home. Fifty five minutes after take-off we were back over base at just under 1000 feet, and Robert gave me a brief 'Cheerio' and cast off. The Lizzie leaped forward and I immediately felt the effect of the whole weight of the towrope as the aircraft reared up like a frightened horse. Without the slightest compunction, I immediately dropped the rope and was myself on the ground four minutes after the Hotspur had touched down further up the runway. (The towrope was retrieved from someone's back garden a couple of days later.)

I drew a large exclamation mark on the otherwise blank test report on my kneepad, unstrapped it and handed it in. Silently, Robert and I made our way over to the mess, woke up the barman and dragged him out of bed. After four double scotches, Robert was normally pretty abstemious, we looked at each other and started giggling. The tension was over but we were still both sweating. For this and many other equally exciting exploits, Squadron Leader Robert Kronfeld became the first Austrian to be awarded the AFC, a common enough award for test pilots at Farnborough and Boscombe Down, but strangely very rare amongst the test pilots at Ringway. Tragically, not long afterwards, he was killed testing a tail-less glider.

APPENDIX E: LYSANDER LOSSES ON PICK-UP FLIGHTS BY 419/1419 FLIGHTS, 138 AND 161 SQUADRONS

Dates	Names	Locations	Pilot fatalities	Passenger fatalities	Comments
Crashed on operations in France					
18 Aug 1940	Coghlan	Channel	1	1	
28 Jan 1942	Nesbitt-Dufort	Near Issoudun			Weather
28 May 1942	Mott	Issoudun			Bogged in
31 Aug 1942	Lockhart	Macon			Bogged in
16 Nov 1943	Hooper	Châtellerault			Bogged in
10 Feb 1944	McDonald	Near Bourges	1		Poor landing technique
29 Sept 1944	Lamberton	Channel	1	2	Weather (not traditional PU)
Crashed on operations in the UK					
16 Dec 1943	Hankey	Near Tangmere	1	2	Fog
16 Dec 1943	McBride	Near Tangmere	1		Fog
Shot down					
10 Dec 1943	Bathgate	Near Vervins	1	1	
3 May 1944	Whitaker	Étampes	1		
7 Jul 1944	Hysing-Dahl	Normandy		2	Friendly fire
4 Aug 1944	Alcock	Vallon, south of Loire	1		Friendly fire
Crashed in training in the UK					
28 Nov 1941	Laurent	Farnham	1	1	CFIT in weather
16 May 1943	Bartrum	Tempsford	1		Poor landing technique
Total Losses			**10**	**9**	**15 aircraft**

Note: 148 Squadron, for which records are not as robust, indicate one fatality due to being shot down by friendly fire (Rayn) and one non-fatal crash in enemy-held territory.

APPENDICES

APPENDIX F: LAYOUT OF LYSANDER LANDING STRIP FOR PICK-UP OPERATIONS

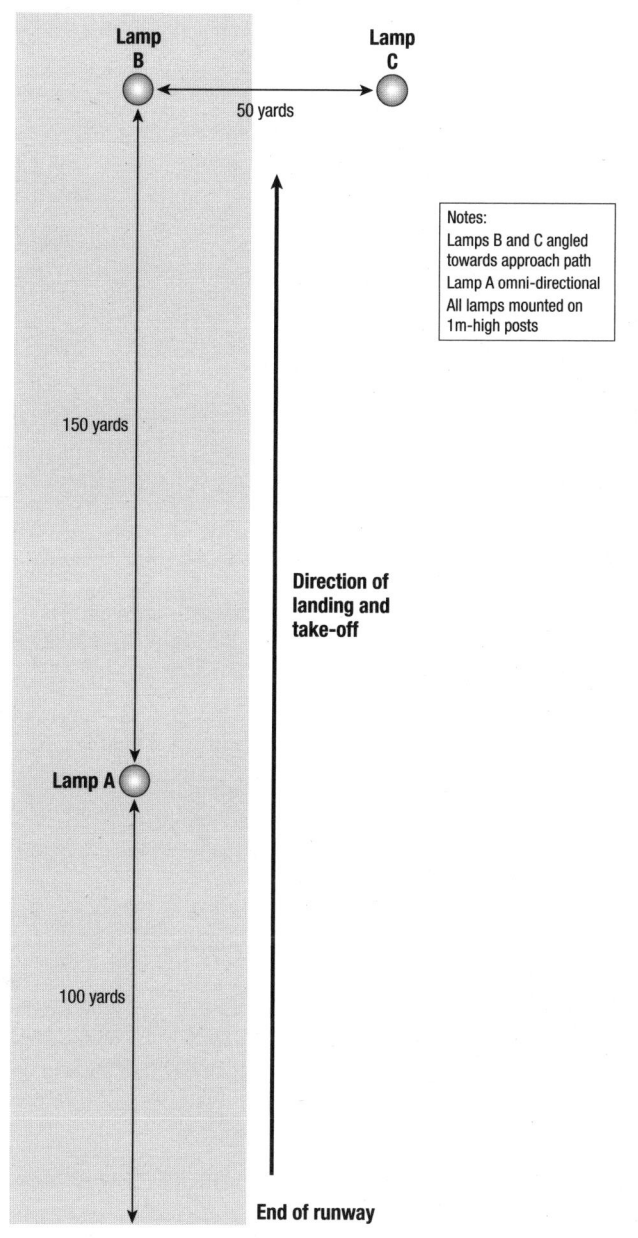

Glossary

ACAS Assistant Chief of the Air Staff

ACM Air Chief Marshal

ADC Aide de Camp

AFC Air Force Cross

AOC Air Officer Commanding

Armée Secrète Lit. 'Secret Army', de Gaulle's Resistance army in the Unoccupied Zone

AVM Air Vice Marshal

BCRA Bureau Central de Renseignements et d'Action (de Gaulle's intelligence organization)

CAS Chief of the Air Staff

CEO Chief Executive Officer

CFIT Controlled Flight Into Terrain

CMDT Commandant

CND Confrérie Notre-Dame (one of the first BCRA networks)

CNR Conseil National de la Résistance (National Council of Resistance)

CO Commanding Officer

DCAS Deputy Chief of the Air Staff

DDI Deputy Director of Intelligence

Deuxième Bureau The French equivalent of MI6

GLOSSARY

DFC Distinguished Flying Cross

DSO Distinguished Service Order

EFTS Elementary Flying Training School

ETA Estimated Time of Arrival

FANY First Aid Nursing Yeomanry

FFI Forces Françaises de l'Intérieur (the conglomeration of French Resistance networks that coalesced after D-Day)

Flt Lt Flight Lieutenant

Flt Sgt Flight Sergeant

F/O Flying Officer

F Section Section of SOE dealing with France

FTS Flying Training School

Gp Capt Group Captain

ISRB Inter-Service Research Bureau (a cover name for SOE)

LAC Leading Aircraftsman

Maquis The French Resistance, so named after the scrubland in which they spent much time

MC Military Cross

MEW Ministry of Economic Warfare (SOE)

MI5 The arm of the British Security Services tasked with domestic security

MI6 The arm of the British Security Services tasked with overseas intelligence gathering

MI9 The British secret service organization tasked with helping escapers and evaders

MM Military Medal

MVO Member of the Victorian Order

NCO Non-Commissioned Officer

OC Officer Commanding

ORB Operations Record Book

OTU Operational Training Unit

P/O Pilot Officer

PoW Prisoner of War

PM Prime Minister

PR Photo Reconnaissance

RAeS Royal Aeronautical Society

RAF Royal Air Force

RAFVR Royal Air Force Volunteer Reserve

RF Section Section of SOE dealing with de Gaulle's agents

RFC Royal Flying Corps

SAS Special Air Service

SD Sicherheitsdienst (the counter-intelligence branch of the Gestapo)

SIS Secret Intelligence Service

SOE Special Operations Executive

Sqn Ldr Squadron Leader

STO Service du Travail Obligatoire (Germany's system of forcibly recruiting young Frenchmen as slave labour)

STOL Short Take-Off and Landing

TMAM Tangmere Military Aviation Museum

UAS University Air Squadron

USAF United States Air Force

VCAS Vice Chief of the Air Staff

WAAF Women's Auxiliary Air Force

W/Cdr Wing Commander

Bibliography

Anderson, Murray, *Saint Praftu*, Grosvenor House Publishing (2009)
Arthur, Max, *Lost Voices of the RAF*, Hodder & Stoughton (2005)
Ashdown, Paddy, *Game of Spies*, Collins (2016)
Ashdown, Paddy, *The Cruel Victory*, Collins (2015)
Bailey, Roderick, *Forgotten Voices of the Secret War*, Penguin (2009)
Basu, Shrabani, *Spy Princess: The Life of Noor Inayat Khan*, The History Press (2008)
Bauduin, Philippe, *Philippe Livry-Level, Squadron Leader*, Apiéton éditions (2005)
Beevor, J.G., *SOE, Reflections & Recollections 1940–1945*, Bodley Head (1981)
Bertram, Barbara, *French Resistance in Sussex*, Barnworks Publishing (1995)
Bertram, Anthony and Barbara, *The Secret of Bignor Manor*, Lulu (2014)
Bishop, Edward, *Daily Telegraph Airmen's Obituaries*, Grub Street (2002)
Bishop, Patrick, *Air Force Blue*, Wm Collins (2017)
Body, Robert, *Runways to Freedom*, Lulu (2016)
Bowman, Martin W. and Tom Cushing, *Confounding the Reich: The RAF's Secret War of Electronic Countermeasures in WWII*, Casemate (2005)
Buckmaster, Maurice, *They Fought Alone*, Biteback (2014)
Burns, Michael (ed.), *The Queen's Flight*, Blandford Press (1986)
Byron, Reginald and David Coxon, *Tangmere: A famous RAF Fighter Station*, Grub Street & TMAM (2013)
Churchill, Peter, *Duel of Wits*, Hodder & Stoughton (1963)
Clutton-Brock, Oliver, *RAF Evaders*, Grub Street (2009)
Cobb, Matthew, *The Resistance*, Simon & Schuster (2009)
Coley, Peter James, *Sticky Murphy, Lover of Life*, Fighting High (2018)
Colville, John, *Winston Churchill and his Inner Circle*, Wyndham New York (1981)
Cookridge, E.H., *Inside SOE*, Arthur Barker (1966)
Cooper, Alan, *Free to Fight Again: RAF Escapes & Evasions 1940–45*, Wm Kimber (1988)
Cowburn, Benjamin, *No Cloak, No Dagger*, Folio (2009)

Coxon, David and Reginald Byron, *Tangmere's Own – Pilots who Served King & Country from a Sussex Airfield 1918–1958*, Tangmere Military Aviation Museum (2017)
Crowdy, Terry, *SOE Agent: Churchill's Secret Warriors*, Osprey (2008)
Dalton, Hugh, *The Fateful Years: Memoirs 1931–1945*, Frederick Muller (1957)
Dodds-Parker, Douglas, *Setting Europe Ablaze*, Springwood Books (1983)
Doré-Rivé, Isabelle, *War in a City, Lyon 1939–1945*, Centre d'Histoire de la Résistance et de la Déportation
Doyle, Paul A., *Where the Lysanders Were: The Story of Sawbridgeworth's Airfields*, Forward Airfield Research Publishing (1995)
Embry, Sir Basil, *Mission Completed*, Methuen (1957)
Foot, M.R.D., *Six Faces of Courage*, Leo Cooper (2003)
Foot, M.R.D., *SOE: The Special Operations Executive 1940–1946*, BBC (1984)
Foot, M.R.D., *SOE in France*, HMSO (1966)
Foot, M.R.D. and J.M. Langley, *MI9 – Escape & Evasion 1939–1945*, Book Club Associates (1979)
Furse, Anthony, *Wilfrid Freeman: The Genius behind Allied Survival and Air Supremacy*, Spellmount (1999)
Gildea, Robert, *Fighters in the Shadows: A New History of French Resistance*, Faber & Faber (2015)
Gildea, Robert, *Marianne in Chains*, Macmillan (2002)
Grehan, John and Martin Mace, *Unearthing Churchill's Secret Army*, Pen & Sword (2012)
Griffiths, Frank, *Winged Hours*, Wm Kimber (1981)
Hamilton, Alexander, *Wings of Night*, Wm Kimber (1977)
Hamlin, John F., *The Royal Air Force at Newmarket* (2nd edn), privately published (1989)
Helm, Sarah, *A Life in Secrets: The Story of Vera Atkins and the Lost Agents of SOE*, Little Brown (2005)
Hentic, Pierre, *Agent de L'Ombre*, Éditions de La Martinière (2012)
Hillary, Richard, *The Last Enemy*, Pan (1980)
Hore, Peter, *Lindell's List: Saving British and American Women at Ravensbrück*, The History Press (2016)
Howarth, Patrick, *Undercover*, Routledge Keegan & Paul (1980)
Hue, André and Ewen Southby-Tailyour, *The Next Moon*, Penguin (2004)
Iliff, Jay, *Daily Telegraph Airmen's Obituaries*, Book Two, Grub Street (2007)
Jackson, Robert, *The Secret Squadrons*, Robson Books (1983)
James, Derek N., *Westland Aircraft since 1915*, Putnam (1995)
Jeffery, Keith, *MI6, The History of the SIS 1909–1949*, Bloomsbury (2010)
Jenkins, Ray, *A Pacifist at War: The Life of Francis Cammaerts*, Hutchison (2009)
Johns, Philip, *Within Two Cloaks*, Wm Kimber (1979)
Joubert de la Ferté, Sir Philip, *Fun and Games*, Hutchinson (1964)
Kersaudy, François, *Churchill and De Gaulle*, Atheneum (1982)

BIBLIOGRAPHY

Kightly, James, *Westland Lysander*, Stratus (2006)
Kinsey, Gordon, *Martlesham Heath*, Terence Dalton (1975)
Kramer, Rita, *Flames in the Field*, Michael Joseph (1995)
Le Chêne, Evelyn, *Watch for Me by Moonlight*, Corgi (1974)
Legrand, Jean-Michel, *Lysander… "L'Avion qui Venait de Londres"*, Editions Vario (2000)
Lucas, Laddie (ed.), *Voices in the Air 1939–1945*, Arrow (2003)
Macintyre, Ben, *SAS: Rogue Heroes*, Penguin (2016)
Marnham, Patrick, *War in the Shadows*, Oneworld (2020)
Marshall, Bruce, *The White Rabbit*, Pan (1955)
Mason, Tim, *The Secret Years: Flight Testing at Boscombe Down 1939–1945*, Hikoki (1999)
McCairns, James Atterby, *Lysander Pilot*, Tangmere Military Aviation Museum (2016)
McCall, Gibb, *Flight Most Secret*, Wm Kimber (1981)
McCue, Paul, *SAS Operation Bulbasket*, Leo Cooper (1996)
Merrick, K.A., *Flights of the Forgotten: Special Duties Operations in WW2*, Arms & Armour (1989)
Millar, George, *Road to Resistance*, Little Brown (1979)
Milton, Giles, *The Ministry of Ungentlemanly Warfare*, John Murray (2016)
Mulley, Clare, *The Spy Who Loved*, Macmillan (2012)
Neave, Airey, *Saturday at MI9*, Coronet (1973)
Neil, Tom, *The Silver Spitfire*, Weidenfeld & Nicolson (2014)
Nesbitt-Dufort, John, *Scramble*, Speed & Sports Publications (1970)
Nesbitt-Dufort, John, *Black Lysander*, Jarrolds (1973)
Oliphint, John H., *Mad Rebel – A Youth at War*, Oliphint (1998)
Oliver, David, *Airborne Espionage*, Sutton Publishing (2005)
Olson, Lynne, *Madame Fourcade's Secret War*, Scribe (2023)
Olson, Lynne, *Last Hope Island*, Scribe (2018)
Onderwater, Hans, *A Winged Gunner: The Life & Times of Andrew Geddes*, Nedvision (2020)
Pattinson, Juliette, *Behind Enemy Lines: Gender, Passing and the SOE in the Second World War*, Manchester UP (2007)
Penrose, Harald, *Adventures with Fate*, Airlife (1984)
Penrose, Harald, *British Aviation: The Ominous Skies*, HMSO (1980)
Penrose, Harald, *No Echo in the Sky*, Cassell (1958)
Pineau, Christian, *La Simple Vérité*, Juillard (1960)
Pitchfork, Graham, *Daily Telegraph Airmen's Obituaries*, Book Three, Grub Street (2020)
Probert, Henry, *Bomber Harris: His Life and Times*, Greenhill Books (2001)
Ratcliff, Leonard and Fitch Ratcliff, *Memoirs*, 2004 (privately published)
Rayment, Sean, *Tales from the Special Forces Club*, Harper Collins (2013)
Richard, Christian, *1944 Special Air Service dans la Vienne*, La Geste (2018)

Riols, Noreen, *The Secret Ministry of Ag & Fish*, Pan (2014)
Robertson, Bruce, *Lysander Special*, Ian Allan (1977)
Robertson, K.G. (ed.), *War, Resistance & Intelligence*, Leo Cooper (1999)
Rymills, Bunny, 'Henri Déricourt – Double or Triple Agent', Lulu.com (undated)
Saward, Joe, *The Grand Prix Saboteurs*, Morienval (2006)
Seaman, Mark, *Saboteur*, John Brown (2018)
Spicer, Tim, *A Suspicion of Spies*, Barbreck (2024)
Stafford, David, *Secret Agent*, BBC (2000)
Stafford, David, *Britain and European Resistance, 1940–1945*, Macmillan (1983)
Stroud, Rick, *Lonely Courage*, Simon & Schuster (2017)
Suttill, Francis J., *Shadows in the Fog*, The History Press (2014)
Szabo, Tania, *Violette: The Missions of Violette Szabo*, The History Press (2018)
Tickell, Jerrard, *Odette*, Pan (1955)
Tillotson, Michael (ed.), *SOE & the Resistance, as told in The Times Obituaries*, Continuum (2011)
Verity, Hugh, *We Landed by Moonlight*, Ian Allan (1978)
Wake-Walker, Edward, *Westland Lysander 1936–46 (all marks) Owners' Workshop Manual*, Haynes (2014)
Wake-Walker, Edward, *A House for Spies: SIS Operations into Occupied France from a Sussex Farmhouse*, Robert Hale (2011)
Ward, Chris with Piotr Hodyra, *138 Squadron, RAF Bomber Command Squadron Profiles*, Mention the War (2017)
Ward, Chris and Steve Smith, *3 Group Bomber Command*, Pen & Sword (2008)
West, Nigel, *MI6*, Frontline (2019)
White, Rowland, *Mosquito*, Bantam (2023)
Wilkinson, Peter and Joan Bright Astley, *Gubbins & SOE*, Leo Cooper (1997)
Winfield, Dr Roland, *The Sky Belongs to Them*, Wm Kimber (1976)

MAGAZINES

Ellis, Ken, 'Very Special Duty', *Flypast* magazine, June 2005
Marsh, Elliot, 'Lysander Cockpit Report', *Pilot* magazine, June 2020
RAF Historical Society Journal, editions 5 and 54, available at https://rafhistoricalsociety.org.uk/journals

INTERVIEWS

Keith Dennison, July 2021; Dick Nesbitt-Dufort, 2019; Simon Rymills, July 2022; William Murrell, September 2022; Dave Hadfield, July 2024; Anne Alexandre, October 2024.

BIBLIOGRAPHY

LECTURES, SEMINARS AND FILMS

Soldiers of Oxfordshire Museum lecture by Ingram Murray – *Saboteurs, Assassins, & Subversives, an Everyday Story of SOE*, 1 March 2022

Timeline documentary: *The Secret WWII Spies Who Flew by the Light of the Moon*, 23 August, 2020

Tempsford Museum Seminar, 2 July 2023

Secret WW2 Network Conference, October 2024

ARCHIVES

Imperial War Museum, Kennington
The National Archives, Kew
RAF Museum, Hendon

Notes: After a (convenient) post-war fire at its headquarters, only an estimated 13 per cent of SOE's original documentation survives. Moreover, of a payroll at its peak of 10,000 in The UK, and some 5,000 agents in the field, only 1,654 personnel files survive in The National Archives. Whilst SIS files have not been subject to a convenient fire, the modest proportion that has been made available has clearly been subject to some extensive post-war weeding and redaction. The situation with SIS files is even more parlous, and government coyness extends to this day.

Notes

ABBREVIATIONS

AM: Air Ministry
IWM: Imperial War Museum
RAFHS: RAF Historical Society
RAFM: Royal Air Force Museum
TMAM: Tangmere Aviation Museum
TNA: The National Archives

INTRODUCTION

1. Quoted in Bailey, *Forgotten Voices*, p.355
2. Quoted in Coley, *Sticky Murphy*, p.36

CHAPTER 1 – THE GESTATION OF THE LYSANDER

1. Penrose, *No Echo in the Sky* (*NEitS*), p.96
2. Penrose, *British Aviation* (*BA*), pp.81–82
3. James, *Westland Aircraft since 1915*, p.232; Robertson, *Lysander Special*, p.4
4. James, op. cit., p.232
5. Penrose, *Adventures with Fate* (*AWF*), p.158
6. Neil, *The Silver Spitfire*, p.40
7. Penrose, *BA*, p.82
8. Penrose, *AWF*, p.162
9. Penrose, *NEitS*, p.93
10. TNA, AIR 10/2502
11. TNA, AVIA 18/637; Penrose, *AWF*, p.180
12. Penrose, *BA*, p.110; Keith Dennison in Wake-Walker, *Lysander Owner's Workshop Manual*, p.140
13. Penrose, *AWF*, p.163

NOTES

14 *RAFHS Journal* 54, p.50
15 Ibid., p.55
16 Penrose, *BA*, p.11
17 Ibid., p.236
18 Ibid., p.236
19 Legrand, *Lysander... L'avion*, p.21
20 Penrose, *BA*, p.228
21 Robertson, *Lysander Special*, p.8
22 Snarey later went on to the Supermarine Aviation Company to test its Spitfire prototypes. Penrose, *BA*, p.92
23 RAFM Accident Records, AM Form 78. Malcolm survived and went on to win a posthumous Victoria Cross (VC) in North Africa in 1943, by then a wing commander
24 Neil, op. cit., p.40
25 Mason, Tim, *The Secret Years*

CHAPTER 2 – THE CUSTOMERS: THE SPECIAL OPERATIONS EXECUTIVE AND THE SECRET INTELLIGENCE SERVICE

1 Stafford, David, *Churchill and the Secret Service*, The Overlook Press (1998), p.343
2 Stafford, 'Churchill & Intelligence: His Early Life', in Robertson, *Lysander Special*, p.166
3 Foot, *SOE in France*, p.2
4 TNA, CAB-85-94, author's translation
5 Letter from Douglas Dodds-Parker to Patrick Maclure, 9 December 2001, Winchester College Archives
6 Dodds-Parker, *Setting Europe Ablaze*, p.42
7 Wake-Walker, *House for Spies*, p.38
8 Colville, *Winston Churchill and his Inner Circle*, p.9
9 TNA, CAB 121/305
10 Foot, *SOE 1940–46*, p.29
11 Ibid., op. cit., p.29
12 Howarth, *Undercover*, p.17
13 IWM sound archive #9482, J.G. Beevor interview
14 Stafford, *Secret Agent*, pp.12ff
15 Dalton, *The Fateful Years*, p.379
16 Ibid., p.366
17 Jenkins, *Pacifist at War*, p.50
18 For an extended discourse see Gildea, *Marianne in Chains*
19 *RAFHS Journal* 5 (February 1989), p.43
20 Stafford, *Secret Agent*, p.15; see Johns, *Within Two Cloaks*, p.141
21 IWM sound archive #10057, Sue Ryder interview
22 Wilkinson and Astley, *Gubbins & SOE*, p.102

23 Dunderdale deeply impressed his friend Ian Fleming, and some of his characteristics are said to have been incorporated in James Bond
24 Gildea, *Fighters in the Shadows*, p.28
25 Passy, Colonel, *Souvenirs: 2e Bureau Londres*, Solar (1947)
26 Beevor, *SOE*, p.147
27 See for example, Cowburn, *No Cloak, No Dagger*, p.17
28 Vera Atkins, SOE & Air Communications Conference, IWM, 27 October 1998
29 Johns, *Within Two Cloaks*, pp.11 and 136
30 Ibid., pp.113–14
31 Foot, *SOE in France*, p.79
32 Ibid., p.28

CHAPTER 3 – THE LYSANDER GOES TO WAR: BLOODIED AND BOWED

1 Philip Saxon in *RAFHS Journal* 5 (February 1989), p.41; https://www.europeansineastafrica.co.uk/_site/custom/database/default.asp?a=viewIndividual&pid=2&person=18754
2 West, *MI6*, p.9
3 Caption at the museum at Stow Maries airfield, where he served after his return to the UK
4 Oliver, *Airborne Espionage*, pp.2ff
5 *RAFHS Journal* 5 (February 1989), p.4
6 Hillary, *The Last Enemy*, p.54
7 Ibid., p.51
8 Onderwater, *A Winged Gunner*, p.16
9 Ibid., p.28
10 Ibid., p.32
11 Geddes also obtained a civilian licence – at the RAE Farnborough Flying Club – in November 1931
12 Onderwater, op. cit., p.36
13 Ibid., p.69
14 RAFM Accident Records, AM Form 78
15 Onderwater, op. cit., p.112
16 Wake-Walker, *Westland Lysander Owner's Manual*, pp.31ff; Onderwater, op. cit., pp.112ff
17 Bishop, *Air Force Blue*, p.131
18 Foxley-Norris went on to have a very distinguished career in the RAF, not without some scrapes, and retired in 1974 as an Air Vice-Marshal
19 Foxley-Norris, *A Lighter Shade of Blue*, Ian Allan (1978) p.16, quoted in Bishop, op. cit., p.131
20 Wake-Walker, op. cit., pp.33ff
21 Onderwater, op. cit., p.133
22 Doyle, *Where the Lysanders Were*, pp.11ff

NOTES

23 Riols, *The Secret Ministry*, p.199
24 Howarth, *Undercover*, p.162
25 Jeffery, *MI6*, p.390; Ward and Hodyra, *138 Squadron*, p.11; and https://www.bbc.co.uk/history/ww2peopleswar/stories/32/a2304532.shtml
26 Riols, op. cit., p.201
27 Kersaudy, François, *Churchill and De Gaulle*, p.138
28 Jeffery, op. cit., p.388; http://www.cieldegloire.fr/002_raf_coghlan_j_h.php; https://beforetempsford.org.uk/category/all/operations/; note – this operation does not feature in most official records of SIS/SOE, including Foot's volumes on the latter. After the war, Hugh Verity became the guardian of the flame for the Lysander Special Duties operations. He did extensive research into operations of 419/1419/138/161 before his time on 161, and had absorbed all the folklore of those units before his time. He was unaware of Coghlan's mission. I therefore conclude that it was done outwith 419 Flight. The attribution of the airframe to 419 Flight (in the accident report card) may have been an administrative expedient. Coghlan is buried in the Boulogne East Cemetery
29 Trevor-Roper, Hugh, *The Secret World*, IB Tauris (2014), p.206, quoted in Marnham, *War in the Shadows*, p.227
30 Jeffery, op. cit., p.392

CHAPTER 4 – FINDING THEIR FEET

1 Author's analysis of RAF accident reports in the RAFM archives (AM Form 78), see Appendix B
2 https://aviation-safety.net/wikibase/131519
3 AM Form 78; these serial mistakes cannot have harmed his career, since by the following summer he was flying Blenheims as a squadron leader
4 Doyle, *Where the Lysanders Were*, p.25; Onderwater, *A Winged Gunner*, p.149
5 Merrick, *Flights of the Forgotten*, p.19
6 In the Battle of Britain, the Lysander performed a valuable search and rescue role, in which it could drop dinghies to pilots in the Channel, from its wing stubs
7 Army parachute instructor to Sir Roger Keith, quoted in lecture 'SOE & Air Communications' by Clive Richards, IWM, 27/10/1998
8 Its last bombing mission was in April 1942
9 TNA, AIR 40/2659 Pick-Up book
10 Dalton, *The Fateful Years*, p.374
11 IWM sound archive #9697
12 Webster and Frankland quoted in McCall, *Flight Most Secret*, p.29
13 Merrick, op. cit., p.19
14 http://www.bbm.org.uk/airmen/Farley.html
15 Merrick, op. cit., p.20; Ward and Smith, *3 Group*, p.17
16 Oliver, *Airborne Espionage*, p.38 and p.44
17 See diagram at Appendix F

18 History of Bomber Cmd Support to SOE & SIS, TNA AIR 20/8450
19 *RAFHS Journal* 5 (February 1989), p.9
20 https://www.key.aero/article/determined-dutchmen; Kinsey, Gordon, *Aviation – Flight over the Eastern Counties*, Terence Dalton (1976), p.140
21 Merrick, op. cit., p.18, and https://beforetempsford.org.uk/1940/10/
22 P/O Crittall (21/10/40); F/Sgt Steele (1/11/40); Sgt Andrzejewski (5/11/40)
23 Ward and Smith, op. cit., p.24; Merrick, op. cit., p.21; TNA, AIR 40/2659, Pick-Up Book
24 *RAFHS Journal* 5 (February 1989), p.14
25 Quoted in Merrick, op. cit., p.22
26 Doyle, op. cit., p.25
27 Verity, *We Landed by Moonlight*, pp.37ff
28 Nesbitt-Dufort, *Black Lysander*, p.23
29 Interview with Dick Nesbitt-Dufort, 2019. After the flying career of Nesbitt-Dufort Sr had ended, he discovered he had had three hairline fractures in his vertebrae from his various crashes. An alternative story, featured widely (including Ward and Smith, op. cit., p.32), has it that Whippy's nickname came about as a result of a forced landing within the confines of Whipsnade Zoo
30 Nesbitt-Dufort, op. cit., p.93
31 Dick Nesbitt-Dufort interview, op. cit.
32 Nesbitt-Dufort was subsequently proved right, and Leigh-Mallory had to send his group navigation officer down to Ford to resolve the issue. Nesbitt-Dufort, op. cit., pp.94ff
33 Ibid., p.95
34 Ibid., p.96

CHAPTER 5 – RACING AHEAD: NEWMARKET TAKES ON MILITARY GARB

1 Note to Sporborg, TNA, widely quoted e.g. by Hué & Southby-Tailyour, *The Next Moon*, p.xxii (and unreferenced)
2 TNA, CAB 79-8-80; Foot, *SOE 1940–46*, p.20
3 *RAFHS Journal* 5 (February 1989), p.94
4 Note by Sporborg, 9 November 1945
5 *RAFHS Journal* 5, op. cit., p.11
6 See Colville, *Winston Churchill and his Inner Circle*, p.81
7 IWM sound archive #9482, Beevor interview, 1986
8 TNA, AIR 20/2901
9 TNA, AIR 20/2901, letter from Jebb to Harris, 6 March 1941
10 TNA, AIR 20/2901, memo 29 March 1941
11 Stafford, *Britain and European Resistance*, p.68
12 Said to Colville on his leaving Churchill's private office to join the RAF as a pilot in 1943, Colville, op. cit., p.184
13 Letter to Beaverbrook, quoted in Colville, op. cit., p.185

NOTES

14 TNA, AIR 40/2659
15 RAFM Accident Records, AM Form 78
16 TNA, AIR 20/2901, 'Air Facilities for SO2', 19 February 1941
17 TNA, AIR 20/2901, letter from Jebb to Maj-Gen Sir H.L. Ismay, 22 February 1941
18 Quoted in Roberts, Andrew, *Masters and Commanders*, Allen Lane (2008), p.111
19 Colville, op. cit., p.165
20 Doyle, *Where the Lysanders Were*, p.21; Kenning stayed with II Squadron for quite some time, as he was awarded the DFC in June 1943, when still serving on the unit
21 Ibid., p.26; Jackson, *Secret Squadrons*, p.30
22 Dodds-Parker, *Setting Europe Ablaze*, p.74
23 Its haunting was vouched for by the singer Suzi Quatro, who lived there in the 1980s; see https://www.sbwhistory.com/wp-content/uploads/2018/11/hyde-hall.pdf
24 Doyle, op. cit., p.26. This is not corroborated by Alanbrooke's *War Diaries* (Phoenix, 2002), which state that on that day he was on the Dungeness front, where he had lunch with Monty Stopford in the Dymchurch redoubt, and had dinner at home. The following day, 22 May, he could have stopped by Sawbridgeworth as he wrote that he went to St Neots for a 'bridging demonstration', and 'after lunch motored back [home]'. However, in these diaries, Alanbrooke has a habit of overlooking his contacts with the secret services. The name of neither Gubbins nor Menzies appears in them, yet he saw them often
25 Winfield, *The Sky Belongs to Them*, pp.95ff
26 Nesbitt-Dufort, *Scramble*, p.52
27 Interview with Dick Nesbitt-Dufort, 2019
28 Nesbitt-Dufort, op. cit., p.56
29 Coley, *Sticky Murphy*, p.12
30 Ward and Hodyra, *138 Squadron*, p.49; Coley, op. cit., p.13
31 Coley, op. cit., p.21
32 Ibid., p.22
33 Ward and Hodyra, op. cit., p.49
34 Dodds-Parker, op. cit., p.81
35 Lecture by Clive Richards, IWM, 27 October 1998; latter comment by an Army parachute instructor to Sir Roger Keith
36 Bowman and Cushing, *Confounding the Reich*, ch. 5; Ward and Hoydra, op. cit., p.32. Even by summer 1943, only 10 per cent of aircraft bombed within half a mile of their target and only 50 per cent were within 1.8 miles (W/Cdr John Stubbington, RAeS, lecture on 24 November 2011)
37 Ward and Hodyra, op. cit., p.32
38 TNA, AIR 20/8242
39 Dalton, *The Fateful Years*, p.372
40 TNA, AIR 20/8242
41 TNA, AIR 20/8242

CHAPTER 6 – SCALING UP: THE FORMATION OF NO. 138 SQUADRON

1. Riols, *The Secret Ministry*, p.80
2. TNA, AIR 20/8242
3. TNA, JP (41) 649 in CAB 121/305
4. TNA, AIR 20/8242, memo from Bradbury to ACAS (I), 25 August 1941
5. Nesbitt-Dufort, *Black Lysander*, p.98
6. John Nesbitt-Dufort appears to have made a mistake in his autobiography, *Black Lysander*, in which he attributes this flight to 6 August. On that date, he appears to have been sent on a training sortie in his Lysander to give him experience of solo night-time navigation over France. The operation described in the text here appears in the 138 Sqn ORB on 4 September. This is the date for the operation ascribed by Foot, Jackson and Verity. Morel accomplished his mission and traversed the Pyrenees before arriving at Lisbon, from where he was brought back to London
7. Foot, *SOE in France*, p.171; Ward and Hodyra, *138 Squadron*, suggest (p.23) that de Guélis was asked for his papers outside the hotel, and was taken to the police station for a more thorough examination of his papers there
8. Brooks Richards at the IWM Special Ops Conference, 1998, who claimed that De Guélis was the first entirely bilingual person with an Oxford education to come out of France
9. Nesbitt-Dufort, op. cit., pp.101–02
10. TNA, AIR 20/2842, memo from Portal to General Sikorski, 4 September 1941
11. TNA, AIR 20/2842, memo from Portal to General Sikorski, 9 September 1941
12. Nesbitt-Dufort kept in touch with Garby, when he lived in London after the war
13. Gildea, *Fighters in the Shadows*, p.217; Tremain, David, *Double Agent Victoire*, The History Press (2018). INTERALLIÉ is said to have been named after the international aviation magazine *Interavia*
14. Robertson, *Lysander Special*, p.171; TNA, KV 3/75; his case and others of this era set the tone for the procedures of treatment of escapees by MI9 subsequently
15. Nesbitt-Dufort, op. cit., p.110; West, *MI6*, relates (p.152) that *Armand* was picked up by Schneidau on 11 October and flown back to Tempsford by him. This would appear to be incorrect on several grounds, not the least that Tempsford was not open by then!
16. Milton, *The Ministry of Ungentlemanly Warfare*, p.26
17. Dodds-Parker, *Setting Europe Ablaze*, pp.9–10
18. Jeffery, *MI6*, p.192; Farm Hall was regarded by Pevsner as the finest house in Godmanchester. After VE Day, it was used to accommodate ten German scientists (under the codename Operation *Epsilon*) who were thought possibly

NOTES

to have been working on Germany's nuclear weapons programme. Their conversations were, of course, bugged

19 Jeffery, op. cit., pp.392–93
20 Hentic, *Agent de l'Ombre*, p.133
21 The date of Laurent's arrival at 138 is unusually not noted in the squadron's ORB. His career details are sourced from http://ecole.nav.traditions.free.fr/officiers_laurent_antoine.htm
22 TNA, WO8/2604, his interrogation report on arriving in the UK
23 RAFM Accident Records, AM Form 78. Despite his obvious culpability in his own demise, Laurent was posthumously awarded the Légion d'Honneur and Croix de Guerre
24 Coley, *Sticky Murphy*, p.27
25 TNA, KV 3/75; O'Connor, *Agent Fifi*, Amberley (2015), p.20
26 Coley, op. cit., pp.148ff
27 TNA, KV 3/75
28 TNA, AIR 27/956, 138 Sqn ORB; Verity (and others) have a slightly different version
29 Verity, talk to the Church Fellowship on 'Cloak and Dagger Activities', 19 September 1956, IWM 17254
30 Coley, op. cit., p.30
31 TNA, AIR 40/2659, Pick-Up Book
32 TNA, AIR 20/2842, memo from OC 138 Sqn to DDI (Easton), 10 January 1942
33 Beevor, *SOE*, p.62; Stafford, *Britain and European Resistance*, p.76; Dalton, *The Fateful Years*, p.384
34 TNA, AIR 20/2842, letter on 2 January 1942

CHAPTER 7 – 1942: THE FORMATION OF NO. 161 SQUADRON

1 Wake-Walker, *House for Spies*, p.43
2 Ibid., p.65
3 Many years later, an x-ray revealed he had suffered a triple whiplash fracture
4 For Vichy's misinterpretation of the sequence of events, see TNA, AIR 40/2659
5 TNA, AIR 27/1068 1-1; Nesbitt-Dufort, *Black Lysander*, pp.114ff; Verity, *We Landed by Moonlight*, p.28
6 TNA, AIR 81/11824
7 Stafford, *Secret Agent*, p.124
8 Lecture by Sqn Ldr Graham Laurie, MVO, on the History of Royal Flying, to the Honourable Company of Air Pilots, 31 January 2023; when Edward VIII abdicated, he took the Dragon Rapide (G-ACZE) with him to Paris. The Flight acquired an Airspeed Envoy in its stead, but when war was declared, it was realized that an aircraft with armament was needed, so in turn this was replaced by a Lockheed Hudson. However, this was of dubious worth since the

tail gun position was occupied by a footman from the Royal Household, as no RAF man was allowed through the royal cabin!
9. Untitled press cutting in the Fielden papers, RAFM X006-0298
10. TNA, AIR 20/8242, memo to AVM Baldwin, 19 January 1942
11. TNA, AIR 20/8242, memo 20 January 1942
12. The King's Flight's Airspeed Envoy, another twin-engined aircraft, but one used for shorter journeys, was not sent over to 161
13. TNA, AIR 27/1068 1-1
14. Wake-Walker, op. cit., p.103; TNA, AIR 40/2659. Perhaps the best result from the CND network was the intelligence about the German radar installation, which led to the Bruneval Raid being mounted in the first place
15. Verity, *We Landed by Moonlight*, p.11
16. TNA, WO 208 3307/75. McCairns, *Lysander Pilot*, p.15, suggests that Lockhart's parachute had not opened properly and he suffered both broken ribs and legs when he landed
17. TNA, HS 9/932/8
18. TNA, HS9/932/8
19. Ward and Smith, *3 Group*, p.50; Coley, *Sticky Murphy*, p.136
20. Bertram, *The Secret of Bignor Manor*, p.274; West, *MI6*, p.150; Coley, op. cit., p.33, mentions that the last-minute addition to the return passenger list was a General J. Kleeberg ('head of Polish Secret Forces in France'). This is not substantiated by e.g. https://adb.anu.edu.au/biography/kleeberg-juliusz-edward-10756
21. Coley, op. cit., p.169
22. TNA, AIR 27/1068 1-1
23. Bertram, op. cit., p.273
24. IWM sound archive #16367, Barbara Bertram interview
25. TNA, AIR 40/2649
26. Hamilton, *Wings of Night*, p.80
27. TNA, AIR 20/8242, memo 1 January 1942
28. TNA, AIR 20/8242, memo to Sinclair, 17 January 1942
29. TNA, AIR 20/8242, memo 23 March 1941
30. Merrick, *Flights of the Forgotten*, pp.49ff; Dodds-Parker, *Setting Europe Ablaze*, p.95
31. Wilkinson and Astley, *Gubbins & SOE*, p.100
32. TNA, FO 1093-155, letter from Selborne to Eden, 31 March 1942
33. TNA, FO 1093-155, memo 27 March 1942
34. TNA, FO 1093-155; for a good description of the reasons for underlying tensions between SOE and SIS, see Beevor, *SOE*, pp.75ff
35. TNA, FO 1093-155, 12 May 1942
36. TNA, HS 8/897/7, report dated 10 April 1942
37. TNA, HS 8/897/7

NOTES

CHAPTER 8 – A HOME IS FOUND: TEMPSFORD

1. Ward and Smith, *3 Group*, p.53
2. TNA, AIR 20/8242
3. TNA, AIR 20/8343
4. Letter from Harris to CAS, 28 March 1942, TNA, AIR 20/2901
5. Harris initially took a similarly parochial stance when Barnes Wallis first mooted his Bouncing Bomb, obstructing the creation of a special squadron (No. 617) and diversion of his precious Lancasters to it. He sanctioned the creation of 617 on 15 March, and relished the mission's success
6. Probert, *Bomber Harris*, pp.137 and 260
7. TNA, AIR 20/8160
8. Wake-Walker, *House for Spies*, p.13
9. Cobb, *Resistance*, p.103; Pineau, *La Simple Vérité*, pp.130ff (author's translation); Pineau was founder of the Resistance network LIBÉ-NORD, and Faure was an assistant of Rémy
10. Cobb, op. cit., pp.105ff; Pineau, op. cit., pp.140ff (author's translation)
11. Robertson, *War, Resistance & Intelligence*, p.174, and http://www.plan-sussex-1944.net/anglais/pdf/infiltrations_into_france.pdf; TNA, AIR 20/8455
12. Pineau, op. cit., p.155 (author's translation)
13. Gildea, *Fighters in the Shadows*, p.118
14. Pineau, op. cit., p.159 (author's translation)
15. Cookridge, *Inside SOE*, p.206; https://www.thetimes.com/article/the-dirty-war-on-our-doorstep-5f859p6t67l
16. Vera Atkins, talk at the Special Operations Conference, 1998, IWM #18592
17. TNA, AIR 27/1068, 161 Sqn ORB
18. TNA AIR 20/8455; Combat Report A606, RAFM
19. *Daily Telegraph* obituary, 31 May 2002; Cooper, *Free to Fight Again*, pp.122ff
20. TNA, AIR 20/8455
21. TNA, AIR 20/8455
22. *Daily Telegraph* obituary, 31 May 2002
23. http://www.conscript-heroes.com/Art48-Lockhart-960.html
24. TNA, AIR 20/8455
25. IWM sound archive #18783
26. Bertram, *The Secret of Bignor Manor*, p.133; after the war, Popeye married the daughter of the Mercier champagne dynasty
27. Passy, Colonel, *Souvenirs II*, Monte Carlo (1947), p.66; Gildea, op. cit., p.273
28. According to the ORB; however, according to Nesbitt-Dufort's *Black Lysander*, he was transferred to the Airborne Forces Experimental Establishment at Ringway 'for an operational rest'
29. Dodds-Parker, *Setting Europe Ablaze*, p.95. He asserts they were shot down over Mannheim
30. TNA, AIR 40/2659, Pick-Up Book

31 Ian Titman avers that the cause of Mott's demise was that the far end of the field had been ploughed just that morning. Some accounts have the French truck driver stalling his lorry on a level crossing, and the same result was achieved – a passing train destroyed most of the evidence. Others have the machine ending up intact in a German museum. See also https://www.conscript-heroes.com/Art07-Alex-Nitelet-960.html
32 TNA, AIR 27/1068/1-1
33 TNA, AIR 27/1068/1-1
34 Coley, *Sticky Murphy*, p.39
35 Griffiths, *Winged Hours*, p.23; Foot, *SOE in France*, p.171
36 Allan, Stuart, *Commando Country*, NMS (2007), p.211; Milton, *Ministry of Ungentlemanly Warfare*, p.255
37 Dodds-Parker, op.cit., p.91
38 TNA, AIR 20/4659, Pick-Up Book
39 TNA, AIR 20/4659
40 Spicer, *Suspicion of Spies*, p.160

CHAPTER 9 – THE 1942 PAUSE AND KNOWLES LURCHES TO HIS MAKER

1 Foot, *SOE in France*, p.194
2 Alanbrooke, *War Diaries*, p.278
3 Marnham, *War in the Shadows*, p.99
4 TNA, AIR 81/17155
5 http://www.bbm.org.uk/airmen/beaumontsg.htm
6 TNA, AIR 81/17155
7 TNA, AIR 81/17155
8 V9353 on 22 July, when a wingtip hit the ground after a swing in strong wind
9 Jean Boutron quoted in Olson, *Madame Fourcade's Secret War*, p.39
10 http://www.nbk-histoire.fr/Marie-Madeleine-Fourcade-cheffe-du-reseau-Alliance.j.htm; see Lucas (ed.), *Voices in the Air 1939–1945*, p.118, about an entertaining saga when a Blenheim and several Hurricanes landed at Ussel as a safe haven in bad weather
11 McCairns, *Lysander Pilot*, p.22
12 Gildea, *Fighters in the Shadows*, pp.42 and 320. Pineau, *La Simple Vérité*, p.101. Cavaillès was to be arrested in August 1943, and shot in the fortress of Arras on 17 February 1944
13 Pineau, op. cit., p.233 (author's translation)
14 TNA, AIR 40/2659; Pineau, op. cit., p.235, claims that he and Lockhart and Tarn walked off together, and there was no one-hour delay in Lockhart destroying his machine. Pineau also omits to mention that Tarn was drunk
15 TNA, AIR 20/8455
16 Pineau, op. cit., p.237 (author's translation)
17 McCairns, op. cit., p.22; Jackson, *Secret Squadrons*, p.48; Robertson, *War, Resistance & Intelligence*, p.175; Verity, *We Landed by Moonlight*, p.52; TNA,

NOTES

AIR 40/2659; Pineau, op. cit., pp.235ff (author's translation). Some accounts say the battle was with Germans, Pineau and others with French coast guards/border police. Pineau had an interesting time: he had foolishly given away his real papers identifying him (correctly) as a Minister of Supply in the Vichy government to someone on the beach. He was compromised by false papers when he and Cavaillès were stopped walking away in the early hours

18 McCairns' own account of his being shot down is told very well in the Tangmere Aviation Museum (TMAM) Logbook, https://tangmere-museum.org.uk/wp-content/uploads/2016/11/Tangmere-Logbook-Autumn-2014-rev-2-Web.pdf; see TNA, WO 208/5582 for Mac's incarceration and escape
19 McCairns, op. cit., pp.8ff
20 TNA, WO 208/5582
21 McCairns, op. cit., p.14
22 Ibid., p.15
23 Ibid., p.17. As well as a genuine desire to test Mac's commitment, Lockhart's comments probably also reflect his own battle fatigue by this stage in his career
24 Ibid., p.20
25 Ibid., p.19
26 IWM, Fielden file, press cutting
27 Len Ratcliff interview, in Rayment, *Tales from the Special Forces Club*, p.180

CHAPTER 10 – THE DREAM TEAM FORMS

1 Draft obituary by Hugh Verity, Verity papers, IWM #160622
2 Robertson, *War, Resistance & Intelligence*, p.180
3 TNA, AIR 27/1068
4 TNA, AIR 40/2659; Boutron succeeded in leaving by submarine 8 November 1942
5 TNA, AIR 40/2659
6 Neave, Airey, *Saturday at MI9*, Hodder & Stoughton (1969), p.195; *Women of Courage*, Yorkshire TV, Peter Morley, 1976, quoted in Hore, *Lindell's List*, p.77
7 Verity, *We Landed by Moonlight*, p.54; Hore, op. cit., p.79
8 Verity, op. cit., p.54
9 *The Times*, 31 July 2018
10 See also *Talking Tangmere*, Spring 2023, Tangmere Military Aviation Museum, p.16
11 Foot, *SOE in France*, p.229
12 Le Chêne, *Watch for Me by Moonlight*, pp.811ff; TNA, AIR 20/8455
13 Cowburn, *No Cloak, No Dagger*, p.131
14 TNA, AIR 40/2659; Verity, op. cit., p.61
15 TNA, AIR 40/2659, pp.76ff; Verity, op. cit., p.62
16 Interview with William Murrell, 2022, whose father Neil was three years Pickard's junior at Framlingham College

17 Hamilton, *Wings of Night*, p.20
18 John Maynard, 'Pickard, Hero of Amiens', *Aeroplane Monthly*, March 1994
19 Hamilton, op. cit., p.28
20 Framlingham College Old Boys records
21 Coxon and Byron, *Tangmere's Own*, p.89
22 Maynard, op. cit.
23 Hamilton, op. cit., pp.41ff
24 Verity, op. cit., p.12
25 Caption to a painting of the Amiens Raid held in Framlingham College
26 Hamilton, op. cit., p.52; https://www.albowlly.club/biography.html
27 Foot, op. cit., p.86; Dodds-Parker, *Setting Europe Ablaze*, p.98, relates a Cold War tale: 'Many years later, at a government reception in Warsaw, a man came up, clicked his heels, bowed and said "My Rebecca is still working well. When will you send me some more arms to help drive out the enemy?"'
28 McCairns, *Lysander Pilot*, p.37
29 Interview with Simon Rymills, 2022
30 Letter to *The Times*, 19 February 1997
31 Merrick, *Flights of the Forgotten*, p.46; the taxiing incident does not feature in Rymills' log book, which records that he left 19 OTU with a 'High Average' grading
32 https://www.courlaoux.fr/page/histoire-du-terrain-daviation (author's translation)
33 Bourdet, Claude, *L'Aventure Incertaine*, Stock: Paris (1975), p.33
34 Aubrac, Raymond, *Ou La Mémoire S'Attarde*, Odile Jacob (1996), p.60
35 Cobb, *Resistance*, p.60; Gildea, *Fighters in the Shadows*, p.5
36 Funk, Arthur L., 'Churchill, Eisenhower & the French Resistance', *Military Affairs* 45:29–34, quoted in Cobb, op. cit., pp.237–38
37 Frenay, Henri, *La Nuit Finira*, R. Laffont (1973), p.103; for more on the animosity between this pair see Cobb, op. cit., pp.96ff
38 Verity, op. cit., p.55
39 Howarth, *Undercover*, p.134
40 Pickard did not include McCairns' name in his operational report or the ORB
41 TNA, AIR 27/1068 and Verity, op. cit., p.58
42 TNA, AIR 40/2659
43 Verity, op. cit., p.63; Jackson, *Secret Squadrons*, p.53
44 TNA, AIR 20/8296
45 McCairns, op. cit., p.23

CHAPTER 11 – 1943

1 Probert, *Bomber Harris*, p.220
2 Dodds-Parker, *Setting Europe Ablaze*, p.100
3 Tickell, *Odette*, pp.143–44

NOTES

4 TNA, AIR 27/1068; Churchill, *Duel of Wits*, pp.190ff; Churchill claims the operation was repeated on 27 December, but that it failed because the team left the field after four hours, with the Hudson arriving half an hour after they had left, due to Churchill's forgetting the time difference between GMT and France. However, this flight does not appear in the 161 Squadron ORB
5 Penrose, *Adventures With Fate*, p.198
6 Verity, *We Landed by Moonlight*, pp.24–26; in order to preserve the secrecy of 161's operations, the accident was described in RAF accident reports as having happened at Tangmere; TNA, AIR 27/1068/1
7 Testimony of Daphne Maynard at https://www.iwm.org.uk/collections/item/object/80028369
8 TNA, AIR 40/2659
9 Verity's operational report at TNA, AIR 20/8474; Legrand, *Lysander... L'avion*, p.65
10 Wake-Walker, *House for Spies*, pp.218ff
11 He did this most successfully. After arrest and incarceration by the Germans in late 1943, he escaped again, but on his return to the UK was imprisoned for several months on suspicion of now being a double agent. For details of his work, see Clutton-Brock, *RAF Evaders*, pp.161–66
12 Letter to his mother, IWM 160622
13 Letter to his mother, later annotated in August 1939, IWM 160622; he goes on to discuss the moral issues of the time in quite a surprising and in-depth fashion for a letter to one's parents
14 Diary, IWM 160622
15 Letter from Verity to parents from Internment Camp B, Curragh, Eire, dated 24 May 1941, Hugh Verity, Verity Papers, IWM #160622
16 Letter to his parents 24 May 1941, IWM 160622
17 Letter to his parents 14 November 1942, IWM 160622
18 Verity, op. cit., p.9
19 Letter to his parents 14 November 1942, IWM 160622
20 Interview with Simon Rymills, 2022
21 161 Sqn Line Book
22 Timeline documentary: *The Secret WWII Spies Who Flew By The Light of the Moon*, 2020; https://www.legasee.org.uk/veteran/hugh-verity/
23 161 Sqn Line Book
24 Hamilton, *Wings of Night*, p.90
25 This mission does not feature in the squadron's ORB
26 Bailey, *Forgotten Voices*, p.41; IWM sound archive #9331, Selwyn Jepson interview, 1986
27 Churchill and Odette separately had a narrow escape after fleeing several miles across the icy River L'Isle, pursued by soldiers and dogs; see Churchill's *Duel of Wits*
28 Verity, op. cit., p.32

29 IWM sound archive #9939, Hugh Beresford Verity interview
30 TNA, AIR 20/8474
31 In November 1944, Massigli wrote a touching letter to *The Times* praising the courage and skill of Pickard on this operation and his fatal Amiens one. Massigli was later to become Foreign Minister in the French government in Algiers, and after the war, French Ambassador in London
32 Merrick, *Flights of the Forgotten*, pp.75ff
33 Cobb, *Resistance*, pp.154 and 269; Manhès was arrested in Paris only two weeks later and ended the war in Neuengamme concentration camp
34 161 Sqn Line Book. Verity includes about a third of the comments in the Line Book in Appendix D of his tome. With his customary propriety about 161's legacy, he excluded any that reflected less well on himself and his colleagues. Unsurprisingly, this particular extract was not included in that appendix
35 TNA, AIR 40/2659 and AIR 27/1068; Verity, op. cit., p.85; Jackson, *Secret Squadrons*, p.72; McCairns, *Lysander Pilot*, p.44; Churchill, op. cit., pp.241ff
36 Verity, op. cit., pp.73ff
37 Ibid., p.59
38 161 Sqn Line Book
39 Bauduin, *Philippe Livry-Level*, pp.4ff; Verity, op. cit., pp.79ff
40 McCairns, op. cit., p.50; RAFM Accident Records, AM Form 78
41 Verity, op. cit., p 75; Wake-Walker, op. cit., p.221. It is of note that the post-war Pick-Up report (TNA, AIR 40/2659) does not deem this critical operation worthy of mention
42 Pineau, *La Simple Vérité*, p.19 (author's translation)
43 Said by Daniel Cordier (*Jean Moulin: La République des Catacombs*, Gallimard, 1999) to be from TNA, per Cobb, op. cit., p.97
44 Gorodetsky, Gabriel (ed.), *The Maisky Diaries*, Yale University Press (2016), p.483
45 TNA, AIR 20/8474
46 Verity, op. cit., pp.76ff; Mulley, *The Spy Who Loved*, pp.183ff; Jenkins, *Pacifist at War*, pp.3ff
47 TNA, HS 9/258/5
48 Churchill in *Duel of Wits* (p.291) claims that Verity ran into a 'sea of fog' over the Channel, which also engulfed Tangmere, and that he landed via search-lights in similar fashion to his previous foggy flight (but without crashing). This must be fantasy as it is not mentioned the ORB's record of the flight
49 161 Sqn Line Book

CHAPTER 12 – TANGMERE LIFE

1 Quoted in Michael Palin, *Great-Uncle Harry*, Hutchinson Heinemann (2023), p.151

NOTES

2 ACM Sir Frederick Rosier (last Commander-in-Chief Fighter Command) with David Rosier, *Be Bold*, Grub Street (2011), p.25; and Fred Rosier's private papers
3 Townsend, Peter, *Time and Chance: An Autobiography*, Collins (1978), p.78
4 Ibid., p.103
5 McCairns, *Lysander Pilot*, p.25; yet Verity, *We Landed by Moonlight*, p.21, states that the pilots sometimes wandered over to the Mess when they 'had no secret visitors'
6 TNA, AIR 40/2659
7 Verity, *We Landed by Moonlight*, p.21
8 TNA, AIR 40/2659
9 Verity, op. cit., p.20
10 Verity, talk to RAFA Hemel Hmpstead, op. cit.
11 161 Sqn Line Book
12 McCairns, op. cit., p.25
13 Dodds-Parker, *Setting Europe Ablaze*, p.90; Bertram, *The Secret of Bignor Manor*, p.221
14 161 Sqn Line Book
15 McCairns, op. cit., p.50; he was in due course to marry Moira
16 Timeline documentary, see https://alanmalcher.com/2020/08/11/raf-161-special-duty-squadron-lysanders-occupied-france/
17 161 Sqn Line Book
18 TNA, KV 2/1132/2, p.23, interrogations of Roger Bardet
19 Bertram, *French Resistance in Sussex*, p.19
20 TNA, AIR 20/8298; Verity, op. cit., p.68
21 Quoted in Howarth, *Undercover*, p.26
22 Robertson, *War, Resistance & Intelligence*, p.178 (this section by Verity); talk by Verity to RAFA Hemel Hempstead, op. cit.
23 TNA, AIR 27/1068
24 Verity, op. cit., p.66
25 161 Sqn Line Book
26 Bertram, *The Secret of Bignor Manor*, p.309
27 TNA, AIR 40/2659
28 Colville, *Winston Churchill and His Inner Circle*, p.219
29 Bertram, *The Secret of Bignor Manor*, p.309; Verity, op. cit., p.206
30 TNA, AIR 40/2659
31 161 Sqn Line Book
32 161 Sqn Line Book
33 *The Times* obituary, 8 January 2007
34 TNA, WO 298/3304, MI9 records, 16 June 1942
35 McCairns, op. cit., p.51
36 Interview with Len Ratcliff, www.legasee.org.uk/veteran/leonard.ratcliff
37 Quoted in Stafford, *Secret Agent*, p.136
38 Kramer, *Flames in the Field*, p.66; TNA, AIR 40/2659

39 Suttill, *Shadows in the Fog*, p.90. That reason suits Suttill's (the author) narrative. Yet Buckmaster, in *They Fought Alone*, states (p.227) that the main reason he recalled Suttill was to brief him on 'the changeover from economic warfare to planning for D-Day'
40 TNA, AIR 40/2659; Bertram, *The Secret of Bignor Manor*, p.310
41 RAFM Accident Records, AM Form 78
42 *Isle of Wight Mercury*, 21 May 1943, via http://www.isle-of-wight-memorials.org.uk/churches/stlawrence_bartrum_je.htm
43 Kramer, op. cit., p.66; TNA, AIR 40/2659
44 TNA, AIR 20/8474
45 IWM sound archive #9331, Selwyn Jepson interview, 1986
46 Basu, *Spy Princess*, p.29
47 TNA, AIR 40/2659
48 Verity, op. cit., p.97; McCairns, op. cit., p.51; Bridger was posted to 4 Group at Rufforth in Yorkshire to fly Halifaxes
49 161 Sqn Line Book
50 Cordier, Daniel, *Jean Moulin: La République des Catacombs*, Gallimard (1999), p.322, quoted in Cobb, op. cit., p.161

CHAPTER 13 – TREACHERY

1 Basu, *Spy Princess*, p.122
2 TNA, HS 9/836/5, report dated 21 May
3 Millar, *Road to Resistance*, p.317
4 Jenkins, *Pacifist at War*, p.94
5 Interview with Simon Rymills, July 2022
6 Interview with Simon Rymills, July 2022
7 Marnham, *War in the Shadows*, p.63
8 TNA, AIR 27/1068
9 TNA, AIR 40/2659, Pick-Up Book; the first part of the report on this mission has been removed from this file
10 Verity, talk to RAFA at Hemel Hempstead, p.15, IWM GB62
11 Churchill, Peter, *Spirit in the Cage*, Mirror Books (2019), p.93, quoted by Larry Loftis in *Code Name: Lise*, Mirror Books (2020), pp.160ff, yet seemingly contradicted by note 16 in the previous chapter
12 TNA, KV 2/1131
13 Memo from Capt Vaudreuil to Major Younger, 7 December 1942, (author's translation), TNA, KV/2/1131
14 TNA, KV 2/1131/3, memo November 1943
15 Verdict by Dr Josef Goetz, one of his staff, noted in Rymills, *Henri Déricourt*, p.27
16 Helm, *A Life in Secrets*, p.339
17 Vera Atkins' interrogation of Kieffer, quoted in Helm, op. cit., p.340
18 Rymills, op. cit., p.38

NOTES

19 161 Sqn Line Book
20 The squadron's ORB does not mention any passengers at all on the flight that Suttill took
21 Suttill, *Shadows in the Fog*, p.90
22 TNA, KV 2/1131/3, memo November 1943
23 TNA, KV 2/1131/3, memo 10 June 1943
24 Verity, *We Landed by Moonlight*, p.100 says 'I decided "Never again"'. But Verity's draft report in the squadron's ORB displays a more gung-ho attitude – 'I am satisfied that, in cases of emergency, similar operations can be carried out by experienced Lysander pilots in the future. The great snag is that we are all so busy during the dark period, and such operations would have a bad effect on the training of agents.' The last phrase has been crossed out (presumably by Fielden) and does not appear in the typed up record
25 Clutton-Brock, *RAF Evaders*, p.225
26 Timeline documentary: *The Secret WWII Spies Who Flew By The Light Of The Moon*, 2020
27 Collection Michel Lemesle, Angers, Renaud de Razilly, 'La Résistance dans la Maine-et-Loire', MS
28 Suttill, op. cit., p.204
29 Démocrates-Chrétiens, Féderation Républicain, Alliance Démocratique, Parti Communiste, Parti Radical, SFIO, CFTC, CGT, Combat, Libération Sud, Ceux de la Libération, Libération Nord, Franc Tireur, Organisation Civile et Militaire, and Front National. The author does not claim that this list is exhaustive
30 Pineau, *La Simple Vérité*, p.121 (author's translation)
31 TNA, HS 8/250
32 Marnham, op. cit., pp.251 and 259
33 Jackson, *Secret Squadrons*, p.78
34 TNA, KV 2/1131/3, memo November 1943
35 See Keith Ellison, www.academia.edu/65957703/Special_Counter_Intelligence_in_WW2_Euro.pdf
36 Wake-Walker, *House for Spies.*, pp.134ff
37 Olson, *Madame Fourcade's Secret War*, p.101
38 Wake-Walker, op. cit., p.144, although other sources suggest it was Pierre Hentic, 'a very courageous agent', who pulled the trigger. Cobb points out (*Resistance*, p.369) that *Bla*'s German handler, Robert Alesch, alleged that *Bla* had not been killed, but was given money to leave the country, and fled to Tunisia
39 Verity, op. cit., Appendix B, and www.plan-sussex-1944.net, and Bertram, *The Secret of Bignor Manor*, p.318, disagree on their identities
40 The third agent returning to the UK was probably André Liess, but Verity has him on the outbound flight; West, *MI6*, p.162, Olson, op. cit., pp.230 and 244, and Foot, *Six Faces of Courage*, p.46

41 Bertram, op. cit., p.322; Olson, op. cit., p.240
42 Cordier, Daniel, *Jean Moulin: La République des Catacombs*, Gallimard (1999), p.495, quoted in Cobb, op. cit., p.235
43 Interview with Lise de Baissac, quoted in Pattinson, *Behind Enemy Lines*, p.97
44 TNA AIR 20/2901, memo to Director of Policy, 16 July 1943
45 Foot, op. cit., p.325
46 Saward, *The Grand Prix Saboteurs*, p.200
47 Quoted in Foot, op. cit., p.85
48 Verity, talk to RAFA Hemel Hempstead, op. cit., p.14
49 Saward, op. cit., p.202
50 Verity, op. cit., pp.112ff
51 IWM sound archive #9851; Le Chêne, *Watch for Me by Moonlight*, pp.124ff; see https://grahamthomasauthor.wordpress.com/2022/01/30/the-le-chene-family-and-the-special-operations-executive/ for the remarkable Le Chêne clan
52 Verity, op. cit., p.114
53 161 Sqn Line Book
54 Hankey's father-in-law, Pelham Papillon, lived in barely less impressive surroundings – Crowhurst Park, which he was to sell in 1942 as he had no heirs
55 Verity, op. cit., pp.101ff
56 Anderson, *Saint Praftu*, p.102; Verity, op. cit., p.101
57 Verity, op. cit., pp.101ff
58 161 Sqn Line Book
59 TNA AIR 20/8474
60 Verity, op. cit., p 117; www.aucklandmuseum.com/war-memorial/online-cenotaph/record/C31765
61 Timeline interview with Verity and Gardiner at https://alanmalcher.com/2020/08/11/raf-161-special-duty-squadron-lysanders-occupied-france/
62 TNA, AIR 40/2659
63 Timeline documentary: *The Secret WWII Spies Who Flew By The Light Of The Moon*
64 Bailey, *Forgotten Voices*, p.118
65 Foot and Langley, *MI9*, p.214; this source only mentions summer 1943, but there are no other 161 flights in the summer of 1943 that fit this story
66 TNA, AIR 40/2659
67 TNA, AIR 20/8474
68 Churchill, *Duel of Wits*, p.173
69 Verity, talk to RAFA Hemel Hempstead, op. cit., p.15
70 TNA, AIR 21/1068
71 Verity, op. cit., p.132; Jackson, op. cit., p.84
72 Foot, *SOE in France*, p.295
73 Merrick, op. cit., p.87
74 TNA, AIR 40/2659

NOTES

CHAPTER 14 – A MISSION

1. M.R.D. Foot quoting Sir Robin Brook, *RAFHS Journal* 5 (February 1989)
2. TNA, COS (43) 404, in CAB 80/72
3. TNA, AIR 20/8160; Foot, *SOE in France*, p.235
4. TNA, AIR 8/2385, Chiefs of Staff Directive to Bomber Command, 25 August 1943
5. TNA, AIR 8/2385, letter from Payne to Portal, 10 January 1944
6. TNA, AIR 8/2385, letter undated from Selborne to Archibald Sinclair
7. TNA, CAB 121/305
8. TNA HS 8-897-81, memo to the PM from unnamed author, 9 November 1943
9. Beevor, *SOE*, p.59
10. TNA AIR 20/2842, memo 3 January 1942, re 138 Sqn operations December 1941–January 1942
11. CD 1134, 'The Second World War – Meteorology', AM Air Historical Branch, 1954. As this was published in 1954 before the activities of SOE (and the Special Duties squadrons) were acknowledged, there is no specific mention of them in this tome
12. https://www.rmets.org/sites/default/files/hist03.pdf
13. McCairns, *Lysander Pilot*, p.26
14. Roger Malengreau, *Clandestine Courage*, Brussels (1982), quoted in Lucas (ed.), *Voices in the Air*
15. McCairns, op. cit., p.25
16. TNA, AIR 20/8242, Function of AI2(c)
17. Stafford, *Secret Agent*, p.133
18. In his memoirs Mac mentions swerving to avoid 'violent' thunderstorms and flashes of lightning, one such illuminating Cabourg; his official operational report makes no mention of thunderstorms
19. Possibly including Senator Azais. Three is cited in the operational report (and other sources), but in his memoirs, Mac only records (a more sensible) one
20. McCairns, op. cit., p.56
21. TNA, AIR 20/2659

CHAPTER 15 – TANGMERE DEATH

1. Verity, *We Landed by Moonlight*, p.131; Anderson, *Saint Praftu*, p.102
2. McCairns, *Lysander Pilot*, p.58
3. Clutton-Brock, *RAF Evaders*, pp.175ff; TNA, AIR 20/8474; Bertram, *The Secret of Bignor Manor*, pp.340–41
4. Verity, op. cit., p.166; John (Jean) Manesson was an Anglo-Frenchman who had taught at the Lycée Français in London before the war, and had already done one tour as an SOE agent in France with the SPRUCE circuit. Foot, *SOE in France*, p.303, avers four agents were tailed and arrested

5 TNA, KV 2/1132/2, p.55; Verity, op. cit. pp.141 and 166; Oliver, *Airborne Espionage*, pp.120–21; Rymills, *Henri Déricourt*, p.94. Verity relates how he was told by Jean Overton-Fuller that Déricourt was paid four million francs by the Germans for this betrayal, which more than paid for his purchase of a chicken farm in Provence
6 Foot, *SOE in France*, pp.246ff; McCairns, op. cit., pp.59ff; Marshall, *White Rabbit*, pp.86ff
7 D'Oultrement was a descendant of England's King George I
8 TNA, AIR 40/2659
9 McCairns, op. cit., p.23; Bertram, op. cit., p.97
10 Timeline documentary, see https://alanmalcher.com/2020/08/11/raf-161-special-duty-squadron-lysanders-occupied-france/
11 Verity, op. cit., p.162
12 *The Times* obituary, 27 May 2016; Verity, op. cit., p.162
13 TNA, AIR 20/8304, letter from 4 November 1943
14 The Pick-Up Book quotes Hooper's later report of this mission in full. In it, Hooper starts, 'On the night of 17th/18th November 1943 I took off from Tangmere. The weather was very much better than it had been the night before…' Yet the squadron's ORB (TNA 27/1068/6) clearly states the mission from which Hooper failed to return started on the night of the 16th. That date is also shown in Hooper's account in the TMAM Logbook (Autumn 2007 edition)
15 Presumably this exercise had not featured in the stress calculations of Petter's team during the design of the Lysander
16 Articles by Sir Robin Hooper, Tangmere Aviation Museum (TMAM) Logbook, Autumn 2007 (p15ff) and Summer 2008 editions; Hooper's report is quoted verbatim in the Pick-Up Book, but strangely this mentions different turning points and landmarks from these articles
17 McCairns, op. cit., p.62
18 161 Sqn Line Book
19 161 Sqn Line Book
20 TMAM Logbook, op. cit., Autumn 2007
21 161 Sqn Line Book
22 TNA, AIR 20/8160; Merrick, *Flights of the Forgotten*, p.96
23 West, *MI6*, p.252
24 Verity, op. cit., p.152; TNA, HS 7/251, SOE War Diary vol. 30
25 Report by Agent 'Gramme', SOE War Diary vol. 30, op. cit.
26 The ORB (TNA, AIR 27/1068/8) says Bathgate was buried in the World War I cemetery of Juvi Court (sic), presumably Juvincourt et Damary; but he now lies at La Ville-Aux-Bois, 15 miles south-south-west of his destination that night. Cossoneau is buried alongside Bathgate in this Commonwealth War Graves Commission cemetery – a great rarity for someone who was not a member of British Forces
27 Anderson, *Saint Praftu*, p.102

NOTES

28. Verity, op. cit., p.154; Hooper's account in TMAM Logbook, op. cit.; TNA, AIR 40/2659
29. McCairns, op. cit., p.64
30. 161 Sqn Line Book
31. McCairns, op. cit., p.64
32. Timings differ in Mac's account; Verity had come down to Tangmere in his new role as Air Liaison Officer for SOE, but was blissfully asleep in the Cottage's overflow accommodation. See Verity, op. cit., p.160
33. Byron and Coxon, *Tangmere*, p.118; Verity, op. cit., p.156
34. https://www.aerosociety.com/news/audio-the-harald-penrose-interview-part-1/
35. By some accounts, he was already at the tower. See Anderson, *Saint Praftu*, pp.104ff. Anderson's record of timings differs from that in the Operational Reports – I have used the latter
36. Hooper says it was him and Sofiano; this is not mentioned by Anderson
37. Hooper's account in TMAM Logbook, op. cit.
38. Hankey had 1,055 flying hours at the time of his death, McBride 1,213; many accounts report that Hankey flew into high ground, but his crash site is only 30 feet above sea level
39. Tempsford lecture, 2 July 2023
40. TNA, AIR 40/2659; Bertram, op. cit., p.349
41. 161 Sqn Line Book, entry dated 7 September 1943
42. Oliver, *Airborne Espionage*, p.122; TNA, AIR 20/8461, squadron diary
43. Ward and Smith, *3 Group*, p.107
44. Letter in Fielden file, IWM
45. There were no Hudson operations during the month and only four Lysander operations

CHAPTER 16 – 1944 AND THE DÉRICOURT DÉNOUEMENT

1. TNA, AIR 40/2659
2. Marshall, *White Rabbit*, p.94
3. Ibid., p.94
4. TNA, AIR 20/8496; AIR 40/2659
5. Interview at www.legasee.org.uk/vetearn/leonard-ratcliff
6. Ratcliff, Leonard and Fitch Ratcliff, *Memoirs*, 2004 (privately published)
7. Verity, *We Landed by Moonlight*, p.163
8. Rayment, *Tales from the Special Forces Club*, p.174
9. TNA AIR 27/1068/40, ORB
10. Interview at https://www.legasee.org.uk/veteran/leonard-ratcliff/; Ratcliff, op. cit., *Memoirs*; Rayment, op. cit., pp.168ff
11. TNA, AIR 20/2901, letter from VCAS, 29 February 1944
12. Quoted in Lucas (ed.), *Voices in the Air 1939–45*
13. https://www.wwiinorge.com/our-stories/the-tempsford-taxis/
14. Ratcliff, op. cit.

15 Per Hysing-Dahl private papers, IWM #3200, Box 95/18/1
16 Verity, op. cit., p.162
17 Anderson, *Saint Praftu*, p.109
18 Ibid., p.109
19 Ibid., p.110
20 TNA, AIR 20/8355, undated memo
21 Names from Bertram, op. cit., p.351, but 'Milson' probably refers to Eric Milstead
22 Interview at www.legasee.org.uk/veteran/leonard-ratcliff
23 Jackson, *Secret Squadrons*, p.102; Body, *Runways to Freedom*, p.163; Merrick, *Flights of the Forgotten*, p.112
24 Aubrac was originally Raymond Samuel, but he had changed his name to hide his Jewish origins; he was initially implicated as the traitor who had betrayed the meeting of Resistance leaders where Jean Moulin was arrested. The argument was that he might have been turned by the Gestapo after having been arrested in March 1943. 'The accusation was shown to be completely unfounded.' Gildea, *Fighters in the Shadows*, p.286; TNA AIR 27/1068/12; Oliver, *Airborne Espionage*, p.129
25 TNA, AIR 40/2352, letter from Affleck to OC 161 Squadron, 2 March 1944
26 TNA, AIR 27/1068/12
27 TNA HS 7/252, SOE War Diary vol. 31
28 TNA, AIR 20/8355
29 TNA HS 7/252, SOE War Diary vol. 32
30 Johns, *Within Two Cloaks*, pp.169ff
31 Verity, op. cit., p.175
32 161 Sqn Line Book
33 Verity, op. cit., p.175
34 Rymills, *Henri Déricourt*, p.93
35 Material has been removed from his file in TNA, KV/2/1131/1, from 6 February 1942 to 3 March 1944
36 Mockler-Ferryman had indeed been lobbying for some recognition for the double agent on account of his 'great ability and complete disregard of danger'; Foot, *SOE in France*, p.299
37 Rymills, op. cit., p.98
38 Maloubier and Ratcliff met at the annual reunion dinner at Valençay 67 years later, and fell into each other's arms, Riols, *The Secret Ministry*, p.271
39 Verity, transcript of IWM interview in his IWM file, p.16
40 Draft memoir of Audrey Verity in Verity files, IWM; Verity, op. cit., p.165
41 IWM file, op. cit.
42 IWM sound archive #10444
43 TNA, HS9/421, from which many potentially useful documents have clearly been removed
44 TNA, KV-2-1131.1, Minute 44
45 Boyd, Douglas, *Voices from the Dark Years*, Sutton Publishing (2007), p.192

NOTES

46 Rymills, op. cit., pp.105ff, and interviews with Simon Rymills
47 Helm, *A Life in Secrets*, p.292; Saward, *The Grand Prix Saboteurs*, p.231, contends (without sourcing, as is his wont) that in summer 1944, Déricourt was flying General Koenig around for the Free French, and 'by September 1944 had switched to reconnaissance work'. This seems implausible
48 TNA, AIR 20/8475
49 TNA, AIR 20/8475
50 TNA, AIR 40/2352, memo to Ops 1(s) from AI1(c), 15 February 1944
51 Bertram, *The Secret of Bignor Manor*, p.354; McDonald is buried in the local cemetery at Farges-en-Septaine, a few miles to the north of the crash site
52 Anderson, op. cit., p.114
53 Nearne was later arrested and survived both Ravensbruck and Buchenwald
54 Strangely, this SIS operation does not feature in 161's ORB. Benoist was murdered in Buchenwald, Bloch in Ravensbruck
55 Jeffery, *MI6*, p.526
56 TNA, WO 208/3319/1841, Bell escape file; Dampierre had previously been interned in Drancy, and escaped from Germany
57 Anderson, op. cit., p.115
58 Ibid., p.116
59 Olson, *Last Hope Island*, pp.298ff; Anderson in *Saint Praftu* reports he brought back four passengers, but all other sources only mention the three I have noted; Count Elie de Dampierre must have returned to England around this time, for he was sent back to France on *Rubens* on 9 April
60 *Aeroplane*, 3 March 1944 in 161 Sqn Line Book

CHAPTER 17 – THE BOXER ERA

1 Verity, *We Landed by Moonlight*, p.171
2 Anderson, *Saint Praftu*, p.114
3 http://www.plan-sussex-1944.net/anglais/infiltrations_into_france.pdf, a thorough and normally reliable source, suggests Szabo and Rolfe were in the Lysanders; most other sources (e.g. Foot, Szabo, Helm) suggest they were dropped by parachute
4 Bertram, *French Resistance*, p.365
5 Cookridge, *Inside SOE*, p.372
6 Interview with Simon Rymills, July 2022
7 Bertram, op. cit., pp.370 and 371
8 Buckmaster, *They Fought Alone*, p.56
9 TNA, AIR 20/8355, letter from HQ Bomber Command to OC Tempsford, 8 April 1944
10 Beevor, *SOE*, p.62
11 TNA, AIR 27/1068/15
12 Anderson, op. cit., p.117
13 Ibid., pp.118ff

14 Verity, op. cit., p.176
15 The operational report makes no mention of landing at Tempsford rather than Tangmere, but Verity reports the former, and the return flight time of almost three and a half hours was easily enough to make the more northerly aerodrome; Szabo's account, op. cit., pp.318ff, also mentions Tempsford; she also alleges that Alcock's propeller was damaged by flak – it would appear improbable that a holed prop would not shake an engine to bits over the course of more than three hours! Interview with Large in EAA *Warbirds* magazine, March/April 2025
16 TNA, AIR 20/8475
17 IWM sound archive #18783, reel 4, Barbara Bertram interview; TNA, AIR 40/2659. She gave the posy to Tangmere Museum
18 Verity, op. cit., p.178
19 https://journals.openedition.org/rfcb/8545; Spicer, *Suspicion of Spies*, p.191
20 Foot, *SOE 1940–1946*, p.225
21 TNA, AIR 27/1068
22 Beevor, op. cit., p.148
23 Menzies was listed just as 'Missing' for years until the Hudson was recovered in 1997; his remains were found in the cockpit and formally identified. He now lies in Wonseradeel Cemetery; https://aircrewremembered.com/menzies-john-watherston.html
24 TNA 40/2659, Pick-Up Book, commenting on this mission says this was because Hysing-Dahl's take-off from Tempsford was delayed by mechanical issues – this is not borne out by the pilot's own report of the operation
25 https://www.wwiinorge.com/our-stories/the-tempsford-taxis/
26 TNA, AIR 20/8475; Verity, op. cit., p.181; Per Hysing-Dahl private papers, IWM #3200; Hysing-Dahl had been shot down by a US cruiser on which George H.W. Bush was serving – the two had an interesting reunion many years later when the former was Chairman of the Political Committee of NATO, and the latter President of the US
27 Churches, Neil, *The Greatest Escape*, Pan (2023), p.205
28 TNA, AIR 20/8475; Bertram, op. cit., p.372; Olson, op. cit., p.308
29 TNA, AIR 14/669, letter from W/Cdr John Corby (OC Ops, Tempsford) to Ops 1(s), Bomber Command, 23 July 1944,
30 TNA, AIR 20/8475
31 https://www.ampltd.co.uk/digital_guides/special_operations_executive_series_1_parts_1_to_5/Extracts-from-Documents-Part-1.aspx
32 Interview with Arkell, IWM, doc 24829
33 TNA, AIR 27/1068
34 https://www.angers.fr/fileadmin/plugin/tx_dcddownloads/web_770x3000_totem_1_maj12mai.pdf
35 TNA, AIR 20/8475; Verity, op. cit., pp.185ff

NOTES

36 His testimony about his passenger load in his IWM interview does not tally with other sources about his passenger load
37 IWM interview, op. cit.; BBC documentary *Set Europe Ablaze*, doc 8670
38 www.stevenageatwar.com; Verity, op. cit., p.184 note. Alcock and passenger are buried at Messac
39 TNA, AIR 27/1068/23

CHAPTER 18 – LAST FLIGHTS

1 Quoted in Riols, *The Secret Ministry*, p.217
2 MacIntyre, *SAS: Rogue Heroes*, p.221 (unsourced)
3 White, *Mosquito*, p.223
4 Ibid., p.230 (unsourced)
5 Richard, *1944 SAS dans la Vienne*, p.298
6 McCue, *SAS Operation Bulbasket*, pp.110ff
7 Conversation with local historian Christian Richard, July 2024, who indicated that the farmer did not demand cash but accepted its demise 'for the glory of France'; McCue indicates he was paid the equivalent of £40 by Surrey Dane
8 Per Plan-Sussex: Lt H. Morris, Lt P. Weaver, Sgt J. Holmes, Cpl G. Rideout, Troopers A. Brown, T. Cummings, J. Fielding, L. Keeble, A. McNair, R. Smith, S. Smith, and W. Smith
9 Randall, John and M.J. Trow, *The Last Gentleman of the SAS*, Mainstream (2016), p.67
10 TNA, AIR 20/8475
11 TNA, AIR 20/8355, memo from Corby to Gp Capt G.F. Wood, HQ Bomber Command, 8 August 1944 (the file contains no record of Wood's reply, if any)
12 McCue, op. cit., p.130
13 Ibid., pp.127ff. The Carpetbaggers Squadron had carried out its first Dakota mission into Occupied France only a month earlier carrying six politicians and three SOE operatives
14 TNA, AIR 20/8355, memo from Robin Hooper to the ISRB, 9 August 1944
15 TNA, AIR 20/8355, memo from Hooper to Gp Capt Wood, Bomber Command
16 Now the factory airfield for Airbus
17 See https://fr.wikipedia.org/wiki/Maurice_Parisot
18 TNA, AIR 20/8475
19 Quoted in McCall, *Flight Most Secret*, p.195
20 See also *No. 1 Special Force and Italian Resistance*, vol. II, FIAP Special Forces Club, Editrice Club Bologna
21 McCairns, *Lysander Pilot*, p.69
22 Ibid., p.68
23 https://www.anciens-aerodromes.com/?p=31539
24 TNA, AIR 20/8424; strangely, this incident does not appear in the RAF's accident records; Ashdown, *Cruel Victory*, p.164

25 https://www.laguerretombeeduciel.fr/Georges-Libert.VB.htm, which mistakenly attributes his stranding to becoming stuck in the mud
26 TNA, AIR 20/8424
27 Oliver, *Airborne Espionage*, p.150; https://www.forces.net/services/army/sas-gurkhas-story-sir-christopher-lee
28 TNA, AIR 20/8424
29 Body, *Runways to Freedom*, p.202
30 Merrick, *Flights of the Forgotten*, p.131
31 McCall, op. cit., p.30
32 IWM interview #24829
33 161 Sqn Line Book
34 McCairns, op. cit., p.69
35 https://camp59survivors.com/2014/02/16/i-s-9-history-air-operations/
36 Other sources put the crash at near Aachen; https://www.tempsfordmuseum.co.uk/raf-tempsford
37 https://www.brightoncollegeremembers.com/roll-of-honour/raymond-julius-guy-manning. The Hudson had a full complement of passengers; it is likely the rest of them came from No. 40 Squadron
38 TNA, AIR 27/1068/33
39 https://www.dailymail.co.uk/news/article-10586137/World-War-Two-heros-medals-sale-Pilot-survived-600ft-fall-plane-no-parachute.html
40 https://www.keymilitary.com/article/astonishing-raf-survivors-medals-soar
41 https://www.wwiinorge.com/our-stories/the-tempsford-taxis/
42 https://www.wwiinorge.com/our-stories/the-tempsford-taxis/
43 TNA, COS (45) 360 (O), CAB 121/305
44 Spicer, *Suspicion of Spies*, p.300
45 Verity, talk to the Church Fellowship on 'Cloak and Dagger Activities', 19 September 1956, IWM 17254
46 IWM sound archive #8670, Peter Arkell interview
47 https://www.awm.gov.au/collection/C304850
48 Interview with Arkell, *FlyPast* magazine, June 2005

CONCLUSIONS

1 TNA, AIR 40/2659
2 Bailey, *Forgotten Voices*, p.95
3 *RAFHS Journal* 5 (February 1989), p.25
4 Riols, *The Secret Ministry*, p.63
5 Ibid., p.206
6 Verity, *We Landed by Moonlight*, p.191
7 IWM 18593, panel discussion, Special Ops Conference, 1998
8 Foot, *SOE in France*, p.45
9 Ibid., p.76
10 Probert, *Bomber Harris*, p.314

NOTES

11 IWM 18593, op. cit.
12 Joubert, *Fun and Games*, p.145
13 Ibid., p.213
14 *RAFHS Journal* 5 (February 1989), p.41
15 Riols, op. cit., p.198
16 Helm, *A Life in Secrets*, p.432
17 IWM sound archive #9697
18 Howarth, *Undercover*, p.160
19 Letter from Buckmaster to Sir John Pollock, 12 May 1946
20 Foot, op. cit., p.436
21 Stafford, *Britain and European Resistance*, p.208

EPILOGUE

1 Wake-Walker, *Lysander Owners' Workshop Manual*, p.108
2 https://mayday365.wordpress.com/2015/04/23/1959-air-charter-turkey-crash/
3 Tribute in IWM Fielden file, press cuttings
4 https://www.gov.uk/government/news/raf-tornado-jets-recce-d-day-beaches; Onderwater, *A Winged Gunner*, p.246; his photos now reside with *Shiny Two* at RAF Lossiemouth
5 Oliver, *Airborne Espionage*, p.214
6 For more see https://www.wwiinorge.com/our-stories/the-tempsford-taxis/
7 Moulson, Tom, *The Millionaires' Squadron*, Pen & Sword (2014)
8 Interview with Dick Nesbitt-Dufort, 2019
9 Gildea, *Fighters in the Shadows*, p.3
10 Ibid., p.411
11 Ibid., p.452
12 Foot, *SOE in France*, p.424
13 Foot, *SOE 1940–46*, p.59
14 Foot, *SOE in France*, p.428
15 Jenkins, *Pacifist at War*, p.102
16 Hugh Verity, Verity papers, IWM #160622, interview p.17
17 TNA, KV 2/1132/1, Déricourt file
18 Helm, *A Life in Secrets*, p.371
19 Marks, Leo, *Between Silk and Cyanide*, Simon & Schuster (2000), p.593
20 Obituary in the *Wykehamist*, 27 October 1971

Index

Note: page numbers in **bold** refer to illustrations and tables.

Aboulker, Dr José 222, 225–226
Affleck, John 212–213, 220, 253–255, 273, 279, 312, **328**
Agazarian, Francine 165, 190, 199
Air France 80, 193, 203, 313, 322
Air Intelligence Directorate 58
  AI2(c) 58–59, 85, 217–218, 220–221, 233, 240, 252–253, 255, 267–268, 270, 282, 284, 302, 316, 319
Air Ministry (British) 16, 18–19, 21, 54, 62, 71, 90, 92, 95–96, 100, 102, 114, 119–120, 137, 148, 172–173, 194, 226, 231, 233–234, 237, 240, 248, 250, 267, 290, 296, 316
aircraft:
  Armstrong: Whitworth Whitley 13, 47–50, 52–53, 55, 58–60, 62–69, 72–73, 75–77, 79, 81, 85, 87, 91, 97–98, 100, 102, 104, 109, 114, 118–119, 124, 128, 141–142, 144–145, 149, 207, 218, 222, 251, 267, 303, **329**
  Avro 21: 504: 36, 131; Anson 65, 96–97, 154, 249, 251, 304, **327**, **328**; Lynx 36; Tudor IV (G-AGRH) 313; Yorks 318
  De Havilland 17, 40, 49: Dragon Rapide 18, 41, 92; Gipsy Moth 91–92; Mosquito 197, 227, 252, 257, 277, 283, 285–286, 309, 316–317, 319
  Handley Page 92: Halifax 13, 68, 73, 76, 83, 85, 91, 93, 100, 102, 104, 112, 114, 143, 149, 164–165, 168, 180, 183, 187, 194–195, 201, 207, 222, 227, 245, 249–251, 254, 267, 277, 281, 303, 307, 313, **329**
  Hawker 21: Audax 16, 139, 153; Fury 54; Hart 16, 139; Hector 21, 38; Henley 272; Hurricane 19, 24, 39–40, 42, 48, 52, 54, 64, 80, 272, 314; Tempest 317
  Junkers: Stuka 39, 170
  Lockheed 306: Electra 49; Hudson 13, 73, 93, 96, 145, 149–150, 159–162, 164–165, 174, 177, 180–181, 191–192, 196, 199, 203–205, 209, 211–212, 217, 220, 229, 232, 248, 250–255, 258, 261, 265, 268, 270, 273, 275–276, 279–280, 286–290, 292, 294–296, 298, 301–302, 304–306, 309, 326, **327**, **328**, **329**
  Messerschmitt 126: Bf 109: 46, 52, 59, 126; Me 108: 318
  North American: P-51: 280, 293–294, 312, 314
  Short: Stirling 13, 142, 222, 267, 277, 295–299, 303, **329**
  Supermarine: Spitfire 19, 24, 35, 59, 94, 126, 128–129, 158, 221, 226, 233–234, 251, 256, 271, 274, 292, 295
  Vickers: Wellesley 23, 181; Wellington 62, 65, 138, 140, 207
  Westland Aircraft 15–18, 20–23, 40, 47, 62, 64, 117, 306, 324: Lysander 12–13, 15–16, 18–19, 21–24, 34–35, 38–43, 45–55, 58–65, 67–69, 72–76, 78–85, 87–91, 93, 95, 97–100, 102, 104–106, 108, 110, 112–114, 121–123, 125, 128–129, 131–132, 134–137, 142–143, 146–152, 155–159, 163, 165, 167–168, 171–178, 180–185, 187, 190, 192, 197, 202, 205–206, 209–210, 215, 218–221, 223, 225–228, 231–234, 236–237, 239–243, 245–248, 250–252, 255–257, 259, 261–263, 265, 268–270, 272–277, 279, 281–284, 286, 288, 290–295, 297, 299–300, 302–306, 309, 311, 315–316, 318–320, 325–326, **327**, **328**, **329**, **330**, 331–335, **338**, **339**; V9353: 166, 178; V9822: 176, 198, 223, 261; Wallace 139; Wapiti 15, 92; Widgeon 15
airfields/bases:
  Andreas 118–119
  Benson 233–234, 260, 271, 292
  Béthune 39–40
  Boscombe Down 17, 319, 337
  Brough 249, 272

INDEX

Carpiquet 157, 175, 186
Farnborough 36, 337
Feltwell 252, 270
Gatwick 63, 314
Hatfield 17–18, 40
Hawkinge 23, 37–38, 54, 59
Hendon 18, 48, 52, 92, 127
Lissett 181, 313
Manston 43, 54
Martlesham Heath 18–20, 55
Newmarket Heath 46, 48, 57, 62–63, 73, 76, 78–80, 83, 91, 96, 119, 140, 218
North Weald 42, 47–48, 50, 52
Northolt 19, 92
Old Sarum 16, 21, 34–35, 37, 233
Ringway 23, 42, 63, 81, 99–100, 111, 118, 337
Sawbridgeworth 46, 55, 60–62
Somersham 115–116, 128, 208, 221–222, 234, 260
Stapleford Tawney 47–48, 50
Stradishall 48, 50, 52, 55, 60–61, 81, 83, 100, 145, 207
Tangmere 49, 51, 61, 73–74, 77, 82–83, 87, 93–94, 96–98, 105, 107–108, 110, 121, 125–126, 128, 131–138, 147, 151–152, 155–158, 162–163, 165, 167, 169–171, 174, 176–180, 186, 190–191, 195–196, 202, 204–207, 209, 212, 218–219, 221, 223–224, 226–228, 231, 233–235, 237–240, 242–243, 250, 252, 256–257, 259, 262–265, 268–270, 272–273, 276, 286, 288, 290, 302–303, 325, **338**
Tempsford 92–93, 99, 103, 105, 114–115, 124, 128–129, 131, 136, 138, 141, 143, 147, 155–156, 158, 165, 172, 174, 179–181, 183–185, 191, 194, 201, 208, 212–213, 218–220, 222, 226–227, 238, 241, 245, 248–251, 253–254, 257, 260–261, 263, 265, 267–270, 272, 274, 277, 279–281, 287–289, 292, 294–297, 302–303, 313, 315, 325, **338**
Uxbridge 53, 155
Winkleigh 279, 281, 283
Wittering 19, 139, 141, 170
airframes 24, 45, 88, 299, 303, 311, 329
Aisner, Julienne (Mme Besnard) 177, 183, 185, 195, 268
Alcock, John Perry 271–272, 283, **328**, **338**
Alexander, F/O G.F.J. ('Alex') 248, 273, 275, 281–282, 293, **328**
Algiers 133, 192, 196, 211, 217, 250, 275
ALLIANCE 121, 124–125, 132, 136, 178, 200–202, 238, 262, 264, 269, 279
Anderson, Flt Lt Murray 233–234, 240, 242–243, 252, 256, 258, 260, 262–264, 267–271, 273, 279–280, 312, **328**
Angers 190, 196, 204, 213, 220, 229, 258, 264, 282
Angoulême 210, 220, 231
Antelme, France 165, 198, 202
Arkell, Peter 280–281, 283–284, 293, 299–300, 312, 315, **328**

Armée Secrète ('Secret Army') 146, 159, 198, 258, 340
Armistice, 1940: 42, 80, 111, 122, 194
Army Co-operation 16–17, 20–21, 34, 36–38, 45, 47, 68–69, 272, 302, 305–306, 314, 329
Atkins, Vera 149, 189–190
Aubrac, Lucie 254, 309
Aubrac, Raymond 145, 254

de Baissac, Claude 165, 202
de Baissac, Lise 202, 268–269
Baker Street 31, 66, 95–96, 117, 136, 151, 172, 176, 183, 186, 195, 199, 205, 213, 221, 233, 237–238, 258, 273, 275, 302
Baldwin, Air Marshal Sir John (Jack/Jackie) 93, 139
Barbie, Klaus 263, 323, 326
Bartrum, Flt Lt Jack Edward 184–185, 303, **338**
Bathgate, James Robertson Grant 207, 209–211, 220, 223, 228, 231, 238–239, **328**, **338**
Battle of Britain 35, 40, 42, 45, 47–48, 65, 120, 155, 319
Battle of France 25, 35, 39–41, 43, 48, 59, 98, 146, 191, 206
Beevor, John 28, 31, 58
Belgium 26, 38, 43, 46, 51, 53, 81, 122, 127–128, 163, 206, 208, 219, 232, 288, 294, 332
Bell, F/O Douglas Stuartson ('Dinger') 41, 187, 248, 251–252, 261–264, 303, 312, **328**
Benoist, Robert 204, 212–213, 258, 262
Berlin 78, 82, 189, 245, 297, 323
Bertram, Barbara 98–99, 107, 110–111, 151, 174, 177, 201–202, 222, 240, 244–245, 263, 269, 273–274, 292
Bertram, Maj Anthony 98–99, 107, 110, 115, 152, 174, 177, 202, 222, 233, 241, 244–245, 252, 269, 274, 292
Bignor Manor 98–99, 111, 174, 201–202, 222, 226, 240, 244, 252, 269, 274–275, 325
Bleicher, Hugo ('Colonel Henri/Heinrich') 117, 192–193, 195, 199, 259, 263
Bodington, Maj Nicholas 195, 260, 322
Bomber Command 58, 65–66, 90, 93, 96, 100, 104–105, 126, 129, 141–142, 149, 155, 181, 208, 212, 218–220, 240, 245–246, 261, 267, 269, 293, 295, 301, 303, 306–307, 309, 317
  3 Group 50, 60, 114, 124, 218, 238, 245, 270
  11 Group 47–48, 54
  HQ 238, 252, 295, 315
bombers 13, 19, 23, 32, 39, 47–48, 58–59, 66, 68, 76, 83, 91–92, 104, 115, 118, 121, 129, 138–140, 143, 149, 150, 155, 165, 170, 186, 207, 246, 249, 251, 274, 277, 282, 285, 299, 302, 303, 306, 312, 314–315, 317
Bömelburg, Karl 195, 257–258, 260, 263
Bottomley, AVM Norman 67–69, 76, 99, 104, 216, 238
Boulogne 59, 144
Bourges 150, 206–207, 261–262, 268, **338**
Boutron, Jean 124, 132

Boxer, W/Cdr Alan 194, 267–268, 270–272, 274, 279–280, 282, 284, 286–289, 295, 305, 312–313, **328**
Bradbury, Gp Capt John 59, 67–68, 72–73, 331
Bridger, John Cameron 121, 125, 132–135, 143, 145–147, 149, 151, 165–166, 174, 176–178, 180, 186, 313, **327**
British Army 24, 34–37, 75, 100, 116, 137, 139, 144, 187, 194, 205, 233, 248, 271, 294, 305, 308, 314
British Broadcasting Corporation 41, 96, 135, 145, 156, 160, 190, 221, 238
Brittany 41, 58, 68, 109, 122, 153, 181–183, 232, 283, 321
Brook, Sir Robin 48, 189, 215, 308
Brooke, Gen Sir Alan (Lord Alanbrooke) 62, 75, 84, 91, 116–117, 166
Brooks, Tony 29, 34, 203–204
Brosselette, Pierre ('Pierre Le Gris') 106, 111, 158, 177, 210, 229, 239, 247, 321
Bruce, P/O Tony 248, 251, 274–275, **328**
Bruneval Raid 93, 141–142
Brussels 46, 82, 127–128, 292, 294
Bryant, Sqn Ldr Walter ('Whippy') 54–55, 64, 73–76, 78–79, 81, 83, 87–90, 95–97, 99, 318
Buckmaster, Maurice 14, 31, 107, 117, 183, 189–190, 193, 196, 199, 204, 258–260, 269, 308, 322
Bulbasket, Operation 285–286, 288
Bureau Central de Renseignements et d'Action (BCRA) 31, 84, 93, 107, 111, 122, 146, 158, 176, 179, 194, 196, 211, 222, 239, 242–244, 250, 253, 274–275, 277, 279, 283, 288, 291, 340

Cabourg 125, 143, 178, 224, 235
Cammaerts, Francis (*Roger*) 167–168, 199, 229, 322
Canada 94, 185, 207, 251, 272, 280
Carré, Mathilde (*La Chatte*) 77, 93, 117, 321
Cavaillès, Jean 122–123, 176
Chartres 220, 262, 269, 273, 275
Châteauroux 61, 74, 98, 109, 147, 162, 272, 276, 279, 283, 322
Chêne, Evelyn Le 135–136
Chêne, Marie-Thérèse le (*Adèle*) 203–204
Chiefs of Staff 32, 57–58, 73, 77, 91, 116, 217, 269, 308
Chiefs of Staff Committee 60, 71, 215, 299, 306
Churchill, Peter 150, 156–157, 159–162, 167–168, 175, 192, 321
Churchill, Winston 25, 27–28, 39, 41–42, 48, 58–60, 73, 75, 85, 93, 100–102, 104, 112, 133, 146, 172–173, 179, 189, 191–192, 198, 215–218, 231, 247, 250, 275–277, 299, 307, 309
Clech, Marcel (*Bastien*) 175, 183, 185, 196
Clément, Remy 194, 196, 210, 229
Coastal Command (RAF) 149, 154–155, 164–165, 203, 252, 306–307

Coghlan, John Hunter 42–43, 47, 50, 303, **327, 338**
Cohen, Commander Kenneth ('KC') 30–31, 98, 324
communication 26, 50, 52, 93, 97, 101, 109–111, 137, 139, 142, 146, 197, 215, 218, 233, 253, 257, 269, 276, 290, 302, 308, 332–333
compass 13, 51, 54, 89, 94, 99, 127, 140, 158, 204, 240, 297
Compiègne 29, 77, 79, 186, 189, 208, 232, 238
concentration camps 109, 182, 303, 321–322
Confrérie Notre-Dame (CND) 93, 111, 137, 158–159, 340
Conseil National de la Résistance (CNR, National Council of Resistance) 159, 166, 210, 262, 340
Cordier, Lt Bernard 290–291, 313
courier 79, 87, 106, 151, 168, 195, 201–202, 223, 225–226, 244, 255
Cowburn, Benjamin (*Benoit* or *Valérien*) 134–136, 209
crashes 23, 39, 46, 50, 52, 54, 60, 94, 100, 108, 112, 119–120, 154, 163, 181, 206–208, 243–245, 251–252, 254, 263, 273–274, 297, 299–301, 303, 313, 322, 329, **338**
cross-wind 212, 225, 299, 302

D-Day 217, 219, 257, 265, 267, 271, 275–276, 285, 299, 308, 314, 318–319, 321–322, 341
Dallas, Pierre 125, 132, 134, 178, 200–201, 208
Dalton, Hugh 27–29, 31, 48, 58–59, 67, 84, 91, 93, 101
Dansey, Claude 30, 43, 197
de Gaulle, Charles 30–31, 41–42, 75, 77, 80, 106–107, 110–111, 114, 117, 122, 135, 146, 152, 159–160, 164, 166–167, 187, 191–192, 197–198, 202, 211, 217, 231, 247, 250, 258, 275–276, 308–310, 320, 323, 340, 342
debriefing 13, 54, 66, 94, 105, 111, 128, 142, 147, 152, 189, 228–229, 231, 245, 275
Delahayes, Pierre 225–226
Delestraint, Gen Charles 146, 159–160, 166, 192, 198
Denmark 68, 217–218, 332
Depraetere, Jean ('Georges') 236–239, 241
Déricourt, Henri 165, 175–176, 185, 190, 193–199, 202–204, 209–210, 212–213, 229, 257–261, 308, 322
Deshayes, Pierre 229–230, 239
Deuxième Bureau 41, 96, 145, 191, 263, 340
Dewavrin, Col André (*Passy*) 30–31, 41, 84, 87, 93–94, 107, 111, 152, 159, 176–177, 179, 211, 222
Dodds-Parker, Capt Douglas 26, 61, 66, 75, 78, 100, 112, 115, 149, 307, 324
DONKEYMAN circuit 190, 195, 229
Dubourdin, Georges (*Alain*) 134–136, 167
Duclos, Maurice 84, 87–90, 96
Dunderdale, Commander Wilfred ('Biffy') 30, 79, 275
Dunkirk 40, 74, 219

INDEX

Eden, Anthony 100–101, 164, 172, 205–206
Eisenhower, Dwight D. 133, 219, 269, 297–298, 314
Elementary Flying Training Schools (EFTS) 144, 249, 272, 341
elevator (longitudinal) control 17, 19, 126
elevator trim 20, 52, 119, 126, 136, 150, 282
Embry, Air Vice-Marshal Basil 257, 286
engines 15, 19, 22, 24, 43, 53, 82, 88, 105, 108–110, 118, 149, 161, 204, 225–226, 243, 253, 282, 287, 298–299, 336
  Bristol Mercury 17, 40, 62, 74, 88, 134–135, 223, 225, 228, 262, 291, 335–336
  failure and problems 34, 43, 46, 53–54, 108–110, 124, 126, 140, 154, 175, 177, 179, 190, 195, 203, 250, 262, 268, 272, 276, 280, 291, 293, 295, 299, 302–303, 317–318, 329, 335
  four-engined aircraft 13, 76, 83, 149, 277, 299, 303
  single-engined aircraft 64, 73, 251, 283, 302
  twin-engined aircraft 13, 23, 47, 68, 143, 161, 165, 249, 251
  Twin Wasp 161, 204
  two-engined aircraft 13, 277
England 25, 31, 41–42, 61, 73, 75, 81–82, 84, 95, 105–107, 111, 113, 122, 125, 132, 138, 146, 150–152, 154–155, 157–158, 162, 164, 171–172, 175, 178, 184, 192–193, 199, 203, 219, 227–229, 234, 240–241, 247, 252, 258, 260, 262, 264, 267–269, 272–276, 282–283, 286, 295, 298, 303, 309, 314, 321, 335
English Channel 15, 29, 38–42, 59, 61, 73, 87, 93, 105, 121, 125, 224, 125, 133–134, 136–137, 151, 155–156, 162, 176–177, 198, 223, 224, 226, 231–232, 240, 247, 256, 274, 276, 277, 283, 293, 296, 316, **338**
Europe 26, 28–32, 41, 59, 63–64, 66, 68, 76, 104, 111, 138, 155, 159, 201, 217–219, 246, 267, 297, 311, 315, 324
  northern 38, 59, 133, 228, 314
  Occupied 26, 42, 66, 73, 155
  Western 13, 27, 31, 101, 135, 189, 215, 233, 246, 251, 292, 309

Farley, Walter Flt Lt ('Wally') 47–55, 59, 77, 80–81, 84–86, 112, 115, **327**
Faure, François (*Paco*) 105–106, 110
Faye, Maj Léon (*Eagle*) 121, 125, 132–133, 136, 151, 167, 202, 208
Ferris, F/O Bob 289, 292, 296, **328**
FIDO (fog dispersal system) 242, 245, 282
Fielden, W/Cdr Edward Hedley ('Mouse') 18–19, 91–93, 95, 98, 100, 103, 107, 110, 114–115, 128–129, 131, 149–150, 158, 174, 180, 185, 191–192, 203, 213, 220, 227, 246, 250, 252, 268, 270–271, 279, 282, 288–289, 294, 307, 313–314, **328**
Fighter Command 39, 45, 54, 126–127, 155, 219, 257, 271, 301, 331
fighters 24, 48, 55, 158, 162, 170–171, 257, 316, 331
  aircraft 19, 22–23, 36, 39, 54, 91, 154, 227, 253, 272–273, 276, 283, 294, 317, 319, 325
  airfields, bases and stations 47, 171, 201, 224, 272–273, 283
  night-fighters 13, 54, 61, 74, 83, 108, 151, 155, 167, 177, 201, 227, 239, 268, 272–273, 276, 281, 283, 294, 296, 301, 317, 319
  pilots 13, 35, 77, 80, 112, 170–171, 210, 249, 257, 281
  squadrons 35, 42, 48, 91, 155, 171, 257, 271, 274, 280, 319
First Aid Nursing Yeomanry (FANY) 114–115, 222, 234, 294, 341
flak 53, 76, 107, 125, 136, 140, 159, 162, 172, 175, 186, 220, 224, 228, 264, 272–273, 275–276, 281, 301, 304, 313, 317
  battery 13, 43, 126, 179, 224, 232
  guns 147, 157, 272, 295, 297
Flying Training Schools (FTS) 19, 34, 36, 37, 54, 315, 341
fog 50, 74, 76, 80, 112, 150, 153, 157, 159, 161–162, 165, 204–205, 219, 228, 236, 240–243, 245, 247, 282, 292, 303, **338**
Forces Aériennes des France Libres (FAFL, or Free French Air Forces) 164, 274
Forces Françaises de l'Intérieur (FFI) 197, 211, 268, 320, 341
Foreign Office 25, 28–29, 102, 154, 201, 217, 324
Fourcade, Marie-Madeleine (Méric, *Hérisson*) 121, 136, 200, 202, 208, 265, 269, 279, 323
Frager, Henri (*Louba*) 167–168, 175, 199, 258–260
Frager, Paul 212–213, 322
France 12–13, 16, 21–22, 25–26, 28–30, 32–34, 36, 38, 41–43, 49, 51, 53, 68, 72–79, 89–90, 95–98, 104–105, 107–110, 112–113, 115, 117–118, 126, 128, 132–133, 136–137, 139, 147–153, 162, 164–168, 171–172, 175–177, 183, 186–187, 190–191, 193–199, 202–203, 208–209, 211–212, 216–217, 222, 226, 228, 231–233, 236–238, 242, 246–247, 250, 254, 257, 259–260, 262–263, 265, 268–269, 273, 275–277, 279–281, 283–284, 289–290, 293, 301–305, 308–311, 316, 320–323, 326, 332, **338**, 341
  central 13, 87, 132, 196, 219, 242
  coast 74, 81, 83, 88, 107–108, 126, 143, 157–158, 162, 179, 201, 203, 220, 224, 231–232, 262, 264, 270, 276
  north-east 197
  north-west 93, 201
  northern 30, 49, 55, 65, 73, 94, 111, 126, 133, 146, 191, 210, 229, 232, 240, 312
  Occupied 99, 152, 291
  rural 106, 134, 200, 208

south-east 121, 166
south-west 29, 74, 285
southern 27, 96, 149, 290–291
Free French (Fighting French, La France Combattante) 30, 41, 58, 80, 93, 98, 102, 117, 147, 191, 286, 322
Freeman, ACM Sir Wilfred 58, 61, 100, 103
Frénay, Henri 106, 145–146, 192
French Air Force 22, 121, 150, 235, 290–291
French Army 41, 55, 60, 196, 323
French Navy 80, 134, 145, 228
fuel tanks 23, 53, 61, 82, 96, 158, 176, 179, 276, 283

Garby-Czerniawski, W/Cdr Roman 77–79, 321
Geddes, W/Cdr Andrew James Wray 35–41, 46, 50, 53, 55, 59, 61, 67, 206, 314, **327**
gendarmes 75, 123, 182, 237–238
George VI, King 93
Germany 40, 49, 51, 72, 83, 89–90, 100, 118, 129, 137, 154, 173, 182, 215, 249, 284, 292–296, 303, 320, 323, 332, 342
Gestapo 87–88, 90, 95, 109, 124, 136, 152, 166, 184, 192, 195–199, 202–204, 210, 230, 237, 254, 263, 268, 272, 301, 321–323, 342
Gibraltar 72, 80, 95, 107, 109, 124, 127–128, 153, 182, 193, 207, 250, 332
de Grave Sells, Flt Lt Guy 252, 268–270
Greece 277, 293, 315, 332
Gubbins, Brigadier Colin McVean 29, 60, 67–68, 72, 75, 78, 83–84, 99–100, 115–117, 250, 260, 277, 308–309, 322, 324
de Guélis, Jacques Theodore Paul Marie Vaillant 74–75, 322

Hankey, Elizabeth 242, 245, 275, 319
Hankey, Flt Lt Stephen 187, 205–208, 220–224, 226, 228, 232–233, 237–238, 240, 242–245, 275, 319, **328**, **338**
Harris, AVM Arthur 48, 58–59, 66, 68, 100, 103–104, 114, 116, 121, 139, 149, 216, 246, 250, 293, 305–306, 325
Helfer, Flt Lt Terence 296–297
Hentic, Pierre 79, 112, 161–162, 201–202, 208, 228, 323
Heslop, Richard 197, 274
Hitler, Adolf 59, 78, 111, 140, 154, 286, 297
Hockey, F/O Ron 52–53, 63, 66, 75–76, 83, 85, 100, 112, 114, 141
Hodges, ACM Sir Lewis Macdonald ('Bob') 164, 181–183, 187, 199, 204–205, 209–210, 212, 220, 228–230, 232–235, 239–243, 245–246, 249–251, 255, 261–262, 267, 271, 293, 305, 307, 313, 315, 319, **328**
Holland 34, 48, 218, 275, 284, 288, 332
Hollinghurst, ACM Leslie 216, 256–257, 268

Hooper, Robin 201–202, 206–210, 220, 223, 228, 233–235, 237–241, 243–245, 249, 252, 261, 268, 282, 288, 315, **328**, **338**
Housman, Flt Lt A.E. 53, 59–60
Hunt, Flt Lt John 173, 240, 244
Huntley, Flt Lt 121, 124, 131, **327**
Hysing-Dahl, Flt Lt Per 248, 250–251, 262–264, 268–269, 273–274, 276–277, 279, 296–299, 316, **328**, **338**

Ibbott, F/O Harry 287–288, **328**
India 35, 37, 129, 131, 186, 234, 319
intelligence 25–26, 30, 38, 41, 48, 60, 64, 71, 77, 111, 124, 176, 197, 221, 229, 255, 264–265, 273, 340–341
  counter-intelligence 195, 199, 342
  gathering 60, 124, 149, 164
  Naval Intelligence 91, 292
  networks 26–27, 79, 93, 122, 124
  officers and staff 85, 95, 145, 164, 173, 183, 233, 274, 319
INTERALLIÉ 77, 93, 117, 159, 238
Inter-Service Research Bureau (ISRB) 85–86, 331, 341
INVENTOR network 183, 185
Ireland 28, 51, 155, 220, 222
Irish Sea 118, 154, 159, 253, 329
Issoudun 87–90, 96, 112, 240, 273, 283, **338**
Italy 68, 113, 207, 277, **278**, 290, 293, 319, 332

Jackson, Sqn Ldr A.D. 59, 73, 249
JADE-AMICOL circuit 238, 268, 282
JADE-FITZROY network 79, 161, 208, 269, 275, 282, 323
Jebb, Gladwyn 28–29, 31, 57–58, 60–61, 67–68, 71, 73, 101

Keast, Flt Lt Francis 48, 52–53
Kent 23, 36, 40, 43, 94, 274
Kieffer, Sturmbahnführer Josef 229, 257–258
Kohan, Albert 242, 244–245

Lacroix, Jean (*Jean Lestanges*) 261, 263
Lamberton, Flt Lt James 281, 284, 292, **328**, **338**
Lamirault, Claude (*Fitzroy*) 79, 108, 112–113, 160–162, 323
Large, Flt Lt Ronald Geoffrey ('Bob') 248, 256–257, 271–274, 293, 295, 316, 319, **328**
Leigh, Vera 183, 185
Leigh-Mallory, AVM Trafford 54–55
Lejeune, Pierre 166, 190
LIBÉRATION 146, 211
liberation 152, 293, 321
Libert, Georges 290–291
Liewer, Philippe 75, 175, 258, 268, 272
Livry-Level, Philippe 164–165, 211, 227, 249, 316, 319

INDEX

Lockhart, W/Cdr William Guy 81, 94–95, 98, 105–106, 109–110, 112, 114, 121–125, 128–129, 136, 142–143, 147, 150–152, 155, 158–159, 162, 177, 267, 304, 316, 323, **327**, **338**

Loire 75, 97–98, 105–106, 124–125, 142–143, 147, 153, 165–166, 175, 178, 191, 196–197, 207, 209, 224, 228, 235, 240–241, 264, 274, 287, 316, **338**

London 13, 27, 31, 49, 51, 61, 73–75, 77–78, 81, 83–85, 87, 89, 92–96, 98, 100, 103, 106–107, 109–111, 121–123, 133–134, 138–139, 141, 146–147, 152, 160, 164, 166–168, 171, 176, 178, 183, 187, 190–196, 198, 200–203, 206, 211–213, 218, 222, 226, 228–232, 237–240, 244–245, 248, 254–256, 258–260, 263–264, 269, 272, 274–275, 279, 290–291, 315, 318, 321–322, 324

Low Countries 68, 216, 276

Luftwaffe 18, 26, 47, 52, 58, 81, 272, 274, 294, 298

Luxembourg 81, 294, 296

Lyon 106, 123, 134–135, 151, 166, 198, 203, 263, 291, 323, 326

machine guns 21, 39, 43, 50, 154, 209, 255, 288

Mâcon 123, 125, 132, 157, 192, 270, 273, **338**

Madrid 33, 109, 124, 127

Malta 154, 207, 274, 317, 332

Marseille 95, 113, 125, 139, 145, 182, 193–194, 200, 209

McBride, F/O James McAllister 227, 231, 238, 240, 242, 244–245, 247, 252, **328**, **338**

McCairns, P/O James Atterby ('Mac') 121, 126–129, 136–137, 142–143, 147–148, 152–153, 156–159, 163, 165, 171, 174–176, 178–180, 183–186, 190, 195, 198, 202, 206, 209–210, 213, 219–233, 237–238, 240–243, 245, 252, 290–291, 293, 304, 317, **327**

McDonald, F/O John Walter 248, 252, 260–263, **328**, **338**

McIndoe, F/O R.G. 123, 133, 143, 263, **327**

Medhurst, Charles 58, 67–68, 72, 99, 104, 216, 331

Mediterranean 67, 72, 274, 277, 294, 317

Menzies, Stewart ('C') 30, 58, 68, 116, 197

MI5 27, 30, 194, 199, 259, 318, 341

MI6 27, 145, 308, 321, 340–341

MI9 95, 112, 124, 128, 133, 153, 204, 208, 228, 232, 277, 294, 341

Middle East 27, 187, 206, 239, 306

Milstead, F/O Eric 234, 248, **328**

Ministry of Economic Warfare (MEW) 28, 104, 325, 341

Mitchell, Lt Roger (*Brick*) 77, 79, 84, 87, 89–90, 96

Mitterand, François ('Captain Moreland') 212, 229

Mockler-Ferryman, Col Eric ('The Moke') 189, 246

monoplanes 17, 19, 33–34, 66, 92, 158, 195

Morse code 35, 123, 208, 221

Mott, Flt Sgt Arnold John 108–109, 112–113, 317, **327**, **338**

Moulin, Jean 111, 146, 159–160, 162–163, 166–167, 192, 197–198, 210, 247, 262, 309, 320, 323, 326

Murphy, W/Cdr Alan 'Sticky' 64–65, 73, 81–83, 91, 93–94, 96–98, 107, 110–111, 113–114, 141, 155, 171, 225, 317, **327**

Nazis 13, 27, 59, 79, 83, 172, 176, 195, 198, 200, 219, 250, 297, 321

Nearne, Eileen 212, 262

Nesbitt-Dufort, Beryl 78, 90, 318

Nesbitt-Dufort, P/O John 12–13, 53–55, 66, 73–74, 77–83, 87, 89–90, 96–99, 111, 113, 163, 303, 317, **327**, 331, 333, **338**

Newhouse, F/O Lucky 275, 281, 284, **328**

Normandy 87, 110, 121, 147, 164, 197, 200, 238, 263–264, 285, 316, 318, **338**

North Africa 133, 164, 191, 207, 222, 255, 314

North Sea 76, 140, 154, 250, 298

Northern Ireland 118, 154

Norway 68, 216, 250, 316

Oettle, Flt Lt Jack 48–49, 79

Operational Training Units (OTU) 35, 64, 65, 69, 96, 144, 145, 184, 234, 249, 251, 252, 253, 262, 268, 271, 341

Operations Record Book (ORB) 46, 91, 110, 158, 233, 235, 252, 329, 341

Operations Room (Ops Room) 63, 140, 151, 172, 174, 234, 240, 242, 270, 316

d'Oultremont, Georges 232, 236–237

Overlord, Operation 269, 275, 314

Oxford 26, 75, 78, 101, 153, 184, 201, 280, 319

Palmer, Roundell (Lord Selborne) 84–85, 100–102, 104–105, 116–117, 198, 215–216, 218, 299, 309, 325

parachuting 32, 63, 66, 81–82, 155, 251, 262, 265, 293, 299

Paris 13, 22, 26, 30–31, 33, 41, 75, 79, 87, 90, 93–94, 96, 106, 108, 111, 123, 127, 133, 153, 159, 164, 167–168, 176, 186, 190, 192, 194–195, 197–203, 206, 210, 222, 224, 228–230, 232, 258–259, 262–264, 268–269, 272, 279, 292, 311, 320–323

Penrose, Harald 15–23, 64, 92, 150, 243, 324

Pétain, Marshal 29, 113, 238, 257

Petter, William Edward Willoughby ('Teddy') 15–18, 20–23, 34–35, 45, 52, 64, 92, 148, 158, 184, 225, 299, 302, 325, 329

PHALANX network 122, 159, 166

photo reconnaissance (PR) 26, 233, 342

photo reconnaissance units (PRUs) 220, 221, 226, 233–234, 292
Pickard, W/Cdr Percy Charles ('Pick') 129, 138–143, 147–148, 151–152, 156, 158–162, 165, 167, 173–174, 177–182, 186, 213, 257, 277, 304, 316, 318–319, **327**
Pineau, Christian 105–107, 110, 122–124, 151–152, 159, 166, 198, 279, 323
Poitiers 165, 228, 235, 241
Portal, ACM Sir Charles 57–59, 61, 76–77, 104, 110, 116, 149, 215–216, 246, 269, 305–307
prisoners of war (PoW) 53, 127, 153, 163, 170, 186, 311, 342
propellers 17–18, 20, 34, 39, 62, 74, 158, 163, 176, 178, 223, 262, 276, 291
PROSPER network 183, 190, 197, 199, 202, 209
Pyrenees 75, 95–96, 109, 112, 182, 193, 211, 288

radar 13, 93, 113, 140, 154–155, 176, 220, 223–224, 228, 241, 283, 317
Ratcliff, Acting Sqn Ldr Leonard Fitch 183, 187, 248–252, 258, 270, 274, 277, 279–280, 282, 296–298, 318, **328**
Rayns, F/O John 293–294
Resistance 13, 25, 29, 31, 49, 79, 84, 88, 90, 95, 98–99, 104, 106–107, 109–111, 114, 122, 124, 128, 142, 145–146, 149, 160, 164, 166, 168, 173, 183, 187, 197–199, 203, 208, 210, 215, 219, 221–222, 225, 230–231, 233–234, 247–248, 254–255, 257–258, 274, 282, 285, 290–291, 307–310, 316–317, 320–321, 323–324, 326, 340
  French Resistance 14, 24, 61, 107, 111, 117, 159–160, 198, 217, 255, 265, 308–309, 315, 341
  Maquis (French Resistance) 187, 197, 219, 269, 289, 326, 341
  Polish Resistance 67, 77, 275
Reynaud, Paul 26, 42
Rheims 194, 208, 222
Rivière, Paul (*Galvani*) 157, 192, 205, 211–212, 253, 255, 273
Robert, Jacques ('Popeye') 111, 198
Rodriguez, Ferdinand 133–134, 202
Rouen 93, 137, 175, 210
Royal Air Force (RAF) 12, 14, 19, 22, 32, 34, 36, 38–39, 41–43, 45–49, 52–53, 57–59, 62–63, 66–68, 72, 77, 80, 89–92, 94–95, 97, 100, 103, 113, 115–116, 120, 125, 127, 131–132, 137, 139–141, 144, 152–155, 158, 163–165, 169–173, 176, 180–182, 184–185, 193, 197–198, 201, 205, 216, 218, 223, 227–228, 232–234, 236, 239, 247–251, 256–261, 263, 267, 271–274, 276, 279–280, 283, 286, 292, 294, 298–302, 307, 309, 312–319, 320, 329, 342
  1 Squadron 42, 59, 80
  II Squadron 37–39, 46, 53, 55, 59, 61, 206
  II (AC) Squadron 37, 54
  13 Squadron 23, 38, 40

56 Squadron 42, 64, 317
138 Squadron 59, 71, 73, 76, 80–81, 91, 93–95, 100, 102–104, 112–113, 116, 118, 124, 139, 141–143, 145, 149, 180, 187, 201, 215, 218, 220, 245, 247, 254, 267, 288, 295, 306, 309, 317, 321, **329**, 333, **338**
148 Squadron 277, **278**, 290–294, 297, 301, 317, 319, **328**, **338**; 334 Wing 290–292, 295
161 Squadron **11**, 13, 72, 87, 90–93, 95, 98–100, 102–108, 110, 113–117, 121, 124–126, 128–129, 131, 133–138, 141–145, 148–151, 153, 155–156, 158, 163–165, 171–172, 174–175, 180–184, 186–187, 192–195, 203, 205–207, 209–211, 215, 217–223, 226, 228, 232–234, 237–240, 243–251, 253–255, 257, 260, 263–265, 267, 269–273, 275, 277, 281–286, 288–296, 299, 301–306, 308–312, 316–322, 325–326, **329**, **338**
296 Squadron 80, 118
616 Squadron 126, 256, 317
617 (Dambusters) Squadron 245, 294
'A' Flight 42, 73, 134, 143, 165, 172, 174–175, 180, 183, 186, 194, 201, 206–207, 210, 222, 232–233, 237, 239–240, 242, 247, 252, 261–262, 268–269, 271, 277, 279
Royal Air Force Volunteer Reserve (RAFVR) 119, 129, 144, 195, 248, 316, 342
Royal Flying Corps (RFC) 33–34, 36, 138, 342
Royal Navy 124, 142, 304
Russia 30, 37, 76, 112, 133, 152, 205, 242, 244, 297, 314
Rymills, P/O Frank Ernest ('Bunny') 143–145, 156–157, 164–165, 168, 174–175, 185–186, 191, 194, 206, 260, 268–269, 299, 318, **328**

Sainteny, Jean 264–265, 269, 279
Sandeyron, Marcel 243–244, 252
Savy, William Jean 198, 262, 269
Schneidau, Philip 47, 49–52, 59, 61, 77, 108, 311, 323
Schock, André 222, 225–226
Scotland 52, 65, 67, 69, 76, 139, 197
Scotter, Flt Lt Gordon 53, 59, 61–62, 108, 319, **327**, 331
searchlights 13, 50, 76, 125, 162, 177, 273, 275, 301
Secret Intelligence Service (SIS) 26–27, 30–32, 34, 41, 43, 46, 48–53, 58, 60–61, 68, 71–72, 76–79, 84–85, 87, 91, 96, 98–99, 101–102, 107–109, 111, 113, 115–116, 121–122, 133, 135–137, 149, 151–152, 158, 161–162, 166, 171, 173, 176–178, 180, 184, 186–187, 191, 197–200, 202, 206–208, 216, 218, 220–221, 226, 235, 238, 243–245, 252, 260–265, 268–269, 273–276, 283–284, 290, 292, 295, 299, 304–306, 308–309, 315, 318, 323–324, 331, 342
Z Organisation 30, 43

INDEX

Seine, River 87–88, 97, 107–108, 137, 153, 224
Simon, André 75, 112–113, 198
Sinclair, Sir Archibald 100, 120, 179–180
Skate, Operation 125, 143, 147
Southampton 42, 53, 319
Spain 95–96, 105, 181–182, 259, 285
Special Air Service (SAS) 285–288, 322, 342
Special Duties 58, 65, 67, 104–105, 131, 174, 221, 277, 319
  Lysanders 46, 80, 128, 283
  operations 43, 48, 66, 103, 294, 300, 305, 307
  pilots 12, 61–62, 90, 219, 227, 232, 238, 290
  squadrons 104, 205, 216, 218, 269, 280, 293, 306
  units 47, 51, 55, 59, 66, 68, 121, 315: 419 Flight 42–43, 47–50, 52–53, 59–60, 66, 80, 305, **338**; 1419 Flight 60–64, 66–69, 72–73, 76, 314, 333, **338**
Special Operations Executive (SOE) 14, 26–32, 34, 48, 52, 57–60, 67–69, 71–74, 76, 78, 83–85, 91, 95, 99–102, 105, 107, 109, 113–117, 123, 134–135, 141–142, 147, 149–151, 156–157, 161, 163, 165, 167–168, 172–173, 176, 182–183, 185–187, 189, 193–199, 203, 205, 208, 210, 215–222, 231, 233, 238, 246–247, 256, 259–260, 268–269, 272, 274–275, 277, 284, 287, 291–293, 299, 303, 305–309, 315, 319, 321, 324, 326, 341–342
  Belgian Section 31, 256
  D Section 25–26, 28, 41
  F Section 14, 30–32, 75, 107, 117, 134, 165–166, 172, 189, 193, 196, 198, 258–260, 262, 268, 272, 274, 308–309, 321, 341
  Intelligence Corps 31, 228, 308
  RF Section 30–31, 146, 176, 229, 231, 253, 280, 342
Squid, Operation 125, 142–143, 147
Stalin, Joseph 100, 112, 218
Suffolk 18, 48, 50, 63, 94, 138, 140, 142, 242, 318
Surrey Dane, David 286–288
Suttill, Maj Francis (*Prosper*) 183, 185, 190, 196
Svagrovsky, Felix 159, 261–262
Szabo, Violette 268, 272

tailplane 18, 20–21, 117, 150, 176, 329
tailwheel 45–46, 90, 110, 126, 137, 150, 161, 177, 190, 212, 282, 302, 334
Tangmere Cottage 105, 110, 126, 136, 147, 160, 168, 171–174, 176, 180, 185, 187, 190–191, 205–206, 220–222, 225–226, 228, 231, 233–234, 240–244, 265, 269, 279, 325
Tangre, Jean-Louis (*Tarn*) 122–123
Tayar, Jacques (*Cazenave*) 244–245
Taylor, Flt Lt Bill 262, 268–269, 276, **328**
test pilots 15, 22, 297, 302, 319, 324, 337
Tonkin, Capt John ('Bullshit Basket') 285–287
Toulouse 109, 182, 194, 289

Turkey 158, 313, 320
Turner, F/O George 248, 252, 268–269, 276, 293, 299–300, 319, **328**

undercarriage 17–18, 22, 38–39, 45, 54, 66, 75, 122, 161–163, 176–177, 236, 276, 283, 297, 311, 335
United Kingdom 14, 24, 27, 32, 37, 39–40, 42, 50, 65–67, 74, 76, 78–79, 84, 109, 111, 129, 133, 136, 146–147, 155, 176, 191, 196, 198, 207, 217, 219, 233, 240, 250–251, 253, 265, 269, 280, 285, 292, 298, 304, 313–314, 317, 319, 322, 325, **338**
United States Air Force (USAF) 171, 274, 288, 291, 294–295, 313, 342
University Air Squadron (UAS) 26, 153, 184–185, 201, 342
Unoccupied Zone (ZNO) 29, 88, 94, 98, 109, 113, 146, 193, 340

Vaughan-Fowler, Peter Erskine 117, 125, 131, 133, 135–138, 143, 147, 149, 151, 159–160, 165–166, 168, 174–176, 178–180, 185–187, 189, 195, 198, 200–202, 206, 208–210, 251, 277, 290–293, 296, 304, 317, 319, **327**
Verity, Audrey ('Mog') 154, 170, 174, 259
Verity, Sqn Ldr Hugh Beresford 141, 151–157, 159–160, 162–163, 165, 167–168, 174, 176–179, 183–186, 190, 192, 194–199, 201–203, 205–211, 213, 220–221, 223, 225–228, 232–233, 237, 240–241, 243, 248, 250, 253, 255, 257, 259–260, 267, 270, 272, 290, 299, 301, 303–304, 319–320, 322, **328**
Vichy 29–30, 80, 89–90, 111, 113, 124, 145, 166, 187, 191, 211, 257, 291, 309
de la Vigerie, Baron Emmanuel d'Astier 106, 145–146, 187, 203, 211–212, 250
de Vomécourt, Pierre de Crevoisier 146, 175, 308, 322

Wake, Nancy 182, 272
War Cabinet 27, 29, 57, 60, 71, 73, 102, 306
War Office 25, 28, 33, 37, 62, 74, 95, 115, 302
wheel spat 19, 21, 105, 132, 281
Whitaker, Flt Lt Leslie 233–234, 242–243, 252, 258–260, 262–263, 268, 271, 273–275, **328**, **338**
Whitehall 25, 28–29, 41, 53, 59, 66, 136, 169, 307
Wilkinson, Sqn Ldr Reginald 288–289, 292, 294, **328**
Wiltshire 16–17, 35, 280–281, 283, 300, 312
Women's Auxiliary Air Force (WAAF) 47, 65, 114, 118, 160, 162, 174, 190, 205, 221, 226, 234, 242, 252, 270–271, 342
World War I 22, 29–30, 33–34, 36, 38–39, 41, 55, 61, 90, 92, 98, 133, 138, 144–146, 164, 170, 179, 208, 244, 248, 280

Yeo-Thomas, Sqn Ldr Forest ('Tommy'/*White Rabbit*) 176–177, 210, 229–231, 247
Yeovil 16, 19, 22, 38, 40, 64, 117

BY THE SAME AUTHOR

Quicklook at Flying (Quicklook Books, 2012)
A Passion for Speed: The Daring Life of Mildred, The Honourable Mrs Victor Bruce (The History Press, 2017)